# THE [R]
# ACTIVE
# CITIZENSHIP
# TOOLKIT

## ■ GCSE CITIZENSHIP STUDIES
### SKILLS AND PROCESSES

KELSEY-FRY&DHILLON

New Internationalist

**THE RAX ACTIVE CITIZENSHIP TOOLKIT**
Published in the UK in 2010 by:
New Internationalist™ Publications Ltd
55 Rectory Road
Oxford, OX4 1BW, UK

Original illustrations and design (including cover): Anita Dhillon

Edited for New Internationalist by Chris Brazier

**AUTHORS' ACKNOWLEDGEMENTS**
We could not have written the Toolkit without: Dr David Davies, Jamie Lowe, Emily McDowell, Dan Raymond-Barker and everyone at New Internationalist. We would like to give a very special thanks to our editor, Chris Brazier, for his insight and superhuman patience!

Thank you to all the following who have helped make the Toolkit a reality:
Nigel Askew, Harriet Bell (www.1010global.org/uk), Mary Bolinbroke and Andy, Gareth Bowden (www.acpo.police.uk), Lesley Anne Bowles, John Brown and Fiona (www.thepopularsociety.co.uk), Adrian Bullock, Amy and Jamie Carol, Hector Christie, Deborah Curtis (www.houseoffairytales.org), Christoph Damian, The Dhillon family (Sascha, Vikram, Jo, Max, Izzy, Eva), Dom and Andy at Surfers Against Sewage (www.sas.org.uk), Noel Douglas, Jon Elek, Demo Epaminondas, Beth Evans and Archie, Lol Ford, David Francolini, Angela Glienicke and Marge Glynne (www.greenpeace.org.uk), Amelia Gregory, Bic Hayes and Jo, Mikel Hecken, Kate Jones (www.actionaid.org.uk), Sarah Jones, Chris Kasrils, Rosh Keegan, John Kelsey-Fry QC, Louise Kleboe, Yasmine Lunn, Robert Kraitt, Joel Malnick, Suzanne Martin and the Torriano crew, Mark McCarthy, Paul Mcloone and Jackie, Steve Merrick, Mo Morris and Adiana Kamaril Sapto, Orna Neumann, Rachel Newsome, Victoria Parks-Murphy at Euro Apple, Lucy Paul (www.itchfilm.com), Joanna Peacock (www.joannapeacock.com), Christylle Phillips, Ki Price, Amy Scaife, Millicent Scott (www.teachingcitizenship.org.uk), Guy Shrubsole (www.pirc.info), Georgia Slowe, Nick Stanton (www.unhcr.org), Jason Starkey, Alfie Thomas and Uccella (www.societyofimaginaryfriends.com), Guy Taylor, Robert Taylor, Jyoti Vaja, Carly Wise.

Our thanks also go to all the interviewees, who gave up their time to provide such inspiring material.

Printed in Italy by Graphicom

British Library Cataloguing-in-Publication Data.
A catalogue record for this book is available from the British Library.

Library of Congress Cataloguing-in-Publication Data.
A catalogue record for this book is available from the Library of Congress.

ISBN 978-1-906523-45-9

# CONTENTS

THE TOOLKIT CONTAINS ALL THE TOOLS YOU NEED TO TAKE INFORMED AND RESPONSIBLE ACTION TO BRING ABOUT CHANGE WITHIN YOUR COMMUNITY – LOCALLY, NATIONALLY AND GLOBALLY.

WELCOME .................................................................................... 7

### 1 HOW TO USE THE RAX ACTIVE CITIZENSHIP TOOLKIT .......... 10

What it means to be an active citizen ...................................... 8

Star System, How to Get Top Grades, The Record Book ...................... 10
The Rax Citizenship Website ....................................................... 10
The Classroom, Three Campaigns, Cross-curricular, Interviews, Links .... 12
The Toolkit Games Room, Newspaper Game ...................................... 14
Art Action, 3.9.27, Fight Your Corner ........................................... 16
Be The Bard, P.O.V .................................................................. 18
Alien's Eyes, The Mystery Game ................................................... 20
Heads Together ...................................................................... 22

LEARN HOW CHANGE HAS HAPPENED THROUGH HISTORY.

### 2 A SHORT HISTORY OF BIG CHANGE *thus far* ...................... 24

Why is this chapter important? ................................................... 24
Did we always have the rights and freedoms that we have today? ........... 24
How did we win the rights and freedoms that we have today? ............... 26
What are the prominent struggles of today? .................................. 26
How do struggles for rights and freedoms start? ........................... 28
How have ideas and struggles for new rights and freedoms developed
through history? (Timeline: Short History of Big Change) ................. 28
I'm only a teenager, what can I do? ........................................... 50
Interview with Craig Kielburger ............................................... 50

RECORD, EVALUATE AND REFLECT ON EVERYTHING YOU DO.

### 3 THE MIRROR ............................................................ 54

Why is this chapter important? ................................................. 54
What is self-directed learning? ................................................. 54
What is the Record Book? ....................................................... 56
How do I keep a record of my campaign? ...................................... 58
How do I tame the CAT? (Controlled Assessment Task) ...................... 60

THINK ABOUT WHICH ISSUES MATTER TO YOU, RESEARCH AN ISSUE AND UNDERSTAND IT FROM ALL PERSPECTIVES.

**4** THE PROCESSING PLANT ................................................. 62

Why is this chapter important? ................................................. 62
How do I find an issue that I feel connected to? ................... 62
What is critical thinking? ................................................... 64
How do I research an issue? ................................................. 70
How do I get to speak to an expert? ................................... 92
Why is it important to understand different points of view? ........ 96
Interview with Laurie Pycroft ............................................. 100
Interview with James Stevens ............................................. 101
Interview with Media Lens ................................................. 102
Interview with David Babbs ............................................... 103
Interview with UKYCC ..................................................... 104
Interview with Patrick Mercer MP ....................................... 105

REPRESENT AND SPEAK UP FOR AN ISSUE.

**5** THE GIFT OF THE GAB ........................................ 106

Why is this chapter important? ............................................ 106
What is advocacy and representation? ................................... 106
How have advocacy and representation contributed to change? ..... 108
How can I make a convincing argument? ............................... 110
What makes a great letter? ................................................ 124
How can I use manifestos, slogans and songs? ....................... 128
Interview with Nelu Miah ................................................. 134
Interview with Ms Dynamite .............................................. 135
Interview with Isla Brown ................................................. 136
Interview with Simon Hughes MP ....................................... 137
Interview with Sophie Bardy .............................................. 138
Interview with Jon Snow .................................................. 139

FIRST CAMPAIGN, LOCAL ACTION ................................. 140

What is the first campaign? What kinds of actions should you take?
What kinds of issues should you address? What's the process? ...... 142

UNDERSTAND AND USE ALL THE MEDIA TOOLS YOU CAN TO MAKE YOURSELF HEARD.

**6** THE PROJECTOR ROOM ................................................ 144

Why is this chapter important? ............................................ 144
In what ways can digital technology help a campaign? .............. 144
How do I make a good campaign film? ................................. 152
How does the medium affect the message? ............................. 154

## 6 THE PROJECTOR ROOM *continued*

How can you win media coverage? ......................................... 154
Interview with Franny Armstrong.......................................... 158
Interview with Robbie Gillett ............................................... 159
Interview with Peter Tatchell .............................................. 160
Interview with Emily Thornberry MP ..................................... 161
Interview with Undercurrents .............................................. 162
Interview with Jon Harris ................................................... 164
Interview with Thom Yorke ................................................. 165
Interview with Denzil Armour-Brown...................................... 166
Interview with Bob Crow .................................................... 168
Interview with Sir Hugh Orde .............................................. 168
Interview with Lord Phillips, President of the Supreme Court of the UK 169

## SECOND CAMPAIGN, NATIONAL ACTION ...................... 170

What is the second campaign? What kind of actions should you take?
What kinds of issues should you address? ............................. 171
CONSIDER CREATIVE WAYS OF CAMPAIGNING.

## 7 TOOLS FOR CHANGE ......................................... 172

Why is this chapter important?
How does active citizenship tie in with my other school subjects?
What kinds of creative campaign techniques are there? ............ 174
How can you use the underground music scene to help your campaign?..... 182
Interview with Ben Stewart.................................................. 191
Interview with the Space Hijackers ....................................... 192
Interview with Scott Forbes ................................................ 195
Interview with Jonathan Mazower ......................................... 196
Interview with Caroline Lucas MP.......................................... 197
Interview with Surfers Against Sewage ................................... 198
Interview with Jess Worth .................................................. 200
Interview with Tamsin Omond .............................................. 201
Interview with Des Kay ...................................................... 202

## THIRD CAMPAIGN, GLOBAL ACTION.......................... 203

What is the third campaign? What kinds of actions should you take?
What kinds of issues should you address? What's the process?

## GLOSSARY SPECIALIST LANGUAGE FOR ACTIVE CITIZENSHIP.................... 204

## INDEX.................................................................. 206

**Rax** 1. To stretch or extend. 2. To reach out. 3. To pass or give something to a person with the outstretched hand. *Old English.*

# Welcome to THE RAX ACTIVE CITIZENSHIP TOOLKIT

## THIS BOOK HAS EVERYTHING YOU NEED TO KNOW

if you are to become involved in the way your world is run. You will learn all the skills necessary to become an active member of your community, to be able to stand up for what you believe to be right and to do something about what you believe to be wrong.

The best way to learn things is by experiencing them. So this book is a doing book. It's much more about learning skills than about remembering information. For that reason you will find there are many games and activities for you to take part in, either as a group, in a pair or on your own.

## THE THREE CORE SKILLS CONTAINED IN THE TOOLKIT:

### CRITICAL THINKING

**1** HOW TO WEIGH UP INFORMATION, IDEAS AND OPINIONS SO AS TO ARRIVE AT YOUR OWN POINT OF VIEW.

### ADVOCACY AND REPRESENTATION

**2** HOW TO SPEAK UP FOR WHAT YOU BELIEVE IN OR ON BEHALF OF SOMEONE ELSE.

### TAKING INFORMED AND RESPONSIBLE ACTION

**3** HOW TO ORGANIZE A CAMPAIGN AND MAKE YOUR IDEAS FOR CHANGE BECOME A REALITY.

IN MY OPINION

IN OUR OPINION

**1** **2** **3**

## "WE ALL HAVE ABILITY. THE DIFFERENCE IS HOW YOU USE IT." STEVIE WONDER

**EVERYONE HAS THEIR OWN SPECIAL STRENGTHS.** THIS BOOK HELPS YOU FIND YOURS AND THEN PLAY TO THEM. EVERYONE HAS A CHANCE TO **EXCEL** BY USING THE TOOLKIT.

# BY THE END OF THIS BOOK, YOU WILL KNOW **WHAT IT MEANS** TO BE AN ACTIVE CITIZEN...

# ACTIVE CITIZENS:

★ FORM THEIR OWN OPINIONS AND THINK FOR THEMSELVES

★ CAN SEE THINGS FROM OTHER POINTS OF VIEW

★ CHALLENGE INJUSTICE, INEQUALITY AND DISCRIMINATION EFFECTIVELY

★ WIN ARGUMENTS USING FACTS RATHER THAN JUST OPINIONS

★ ARE ABLE TO RESOLVE CONFLICTS FAIRLY AND SUCCESSFULLY

★ CAN TALK KNOWLEDGEABLY ABOUT ISSUES THAT MATTER TO THEM

★ TAKE PART IN THEIR COMMUNITY, LOCAL AND GLOBAL

★ STATE THEIR OPINIONS CLEARLY AND HAVE THEM HEARD

★ DEVELOP THEIR OWN IDEAS FOR CHANGE AND ACT UPON THEM

★ MAKE A POSITIVE CONTRIBUTION TO SOCIETY

★ MAKE A DIFFERENCE TO THEIR WORLD

...YOU WILL ALSO KNOW **WHAT IT MEANS NOT** TO BE AN ACTIVE CITIZEN!

DON'T HAVE YOUR OWN OPINION

DON'T LISTEN TO THE OPINION OF OTHERS

*17 HOURS STRAIGHT ON GAMES CONSOLE*

ACTIVE CITIZEN... BUT ONLY ACTIVE IN A WORLD POPULATED BY ZOMBIE RAIDERS & BOMB-CARRYING ELVES GOVERNED BY ALIENS WITH ACID FOR BLOOD.

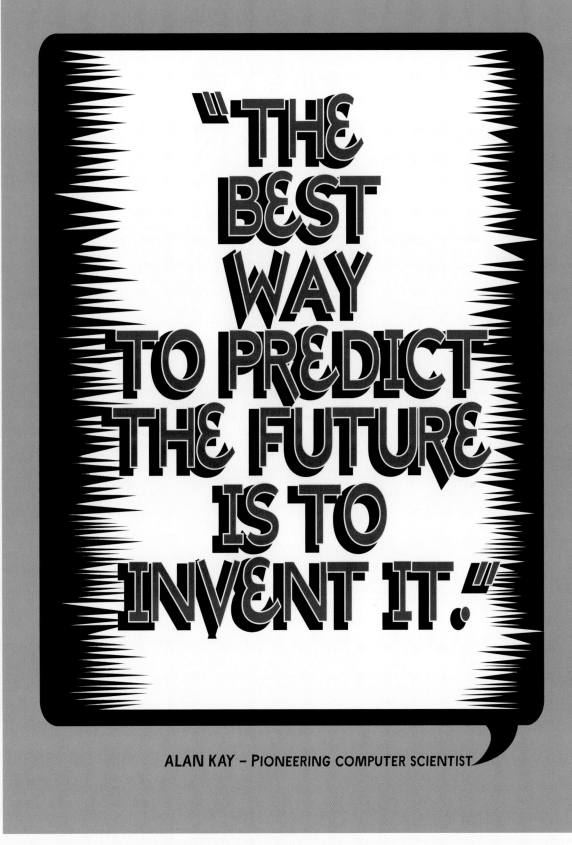

"THE BEST WAY TO PREDICT THE FUTURE IS TO INVENT IT."

ALAN KAY – PIONEERING COMPUTER SCIENTIST

POLICE ARRESTED TWO KIDS YESTERDAY, ONE WAS DRINKING BATTERY ACID, THE OTHER WAS EATING FIREWORKS. THEY CHARGED ONE AND LET THE OTHER ONE OFF!
– TOMMY COOPER, COMEDIAN & CONJUROR

# CHAPTER 1 HOW to USE the RAX ACTIVE CITIZENSHIP Toolkit.

## The Toolkit STAR SYSTEM

*In* most sections of the Toolkit, the left-hand pages contain the vital information that you need to learn. In amongst that information you will spot some stars with letters in them.

These stars connect to interesting and illuminating quotations, facts and ideas on the corresponding right-hand page. You make the link by looking for the same letter inside a star.

## How to GET TOP GRADES

*If* you are taking a GCSE, achieving a top grade is important for you. The good news is that, whether you are top or bottom of the class in your other subjects, it makes no difference to your chances here. The main qualities required for successful active citizenship are creativity, courage and passion. The Toolkit has been designed to meet the demands of all examination boards, whether you are doing the long or the short course. It covers the part of your Citizenship Studies GCSE called 'skills and processes', which is how you can become an Active Citizen. This part of the course is worth between 40% and 60% of your final grade, depending on the examination board your school is using. It is all coursework but you will have to sit and write a report on your citizenship activities in exam conditions. This is called the Controlled Assessment Task (CAT). There may be several of these but, don't worry, they are not exams and you will learn how to tame the CAT in the chapter called *The Mirror.* For GCSE candidates, the most important thing is to keep asking yourself: "How does this tie in with the content part of my course?" Always make the links between the work you are doing in the Toolkit and the work in the other part of your course. That is, wherever possible, tie everything into Rights and Responsibilities, Identity and Diversity, and Democracy and Justice.

## The Record BOOK

*An* important part of this course is how you keep a record of everything that you do. The Record Book is something you'll get used to and you'll find that it really helps to be able to look back at what you have done. The chapter called *The Mirror* tells you everything that you need to know about how to create the most effective record possible.

## The Rax CITIZENSHIP WEBSITE

*There* is a website dedicated to users of the Toolkit. If you go to the site, you will be able to read all the interviews featured in this book in their entirety – as well as read any new ones that are added. You will also find links to hundreds of campaigns, resource sites and other material to support you.

### THE WEBSITE ADDRESS IS: WWW.RAXCITIZENSHIP.ORG

The Rax Toolkit recognizes that 21st-century technology has made a huge difference to how students go about learning, in and out of their schools. It is, of course, vital that you stay within the rules and regulations that your school has relating to use of these technologies. However, we assume that most of you have access to computers, the internet and other technologies such as mobile phones that can shoot short films, take pictures and make recordings. We approve of and fully encourage the use of 21st-century technologies for self-directed learning as part of this course and as an extension to what you do within the classroom and the school. The chapter called *The Projector Room* is full of ideas about how new technologies can be used for campaigning.

# THE TOOLKIT STAR SYSTEM

**THE** TOOLKIT LEFT HAND/RIGHT HAND STAR SYSTEM IS INSPIRED BY EARLY RESEARCH INTO THE WAY THE HUMAN BRAIN FUNCTIONS. ALTHOUGH RECENT RESEARCH SHOWS THAT THINGS AREN'T QUITE AS SIMPLE AS SCIENTISTS FIRST THOUGHT, IT DOES LOOK LIKE YOUR BRAIN IS GENERALLY DIVIDED BY THE WAY IT DEALS WITH DIFFERENT TYPES OF THINKING.

*a*

## CROSS SECTION OF THE HUMAN BRAIN

THE **LEFT** SIDE EMPHASIZES

Language
Numbers
Logic
Words
Sequence
Mathematics

CORPUS CALLOSUM

**LEFT** HEMISPHERE

**RIGHT** HEMISPHERE

THE **RIGHT** SIDE EMPHASIZES

Imagination
Rhythm
Pictures
Rhyme
Music
Patterns

THE CORPUS CALLOSUM LINKS BOTH

TWO NEURONS CONNECTING

A NEURON IS A SPECIALIZED CELL CONDUCTING ELECTROCHEMICAL NERVE IMPULSES. NEURONS ARE CORE COMPONENTS OF THE BRAIN AND NERVOUS SYSTEM.

*b*

MOST STARS ARE BETWEEN ONE BILLION AND TEN BILLION YEARS OLD

## L. O., is anyone out there?

*h*

**THE** FIRST ELECTRONIC MESSAGE EVER SENT BETWEEN TWO COMPUTERS WAS "LO..." AT 10.30 ON 29 OCTOBER 1969, AMERICAN COMPUTER ENGINEERS, ONE IN LOS ANGELES AND ONE IN STANFORD, HAD INTENDED TO START THEIR MESSAGE BY TYPING "LOG IN" BUT THE COMPUTERS CRASHED AFTER THE FIRST TWO LETTERS! LATER, THE ENGINEERS SAID THAT THESE TWO LETTERS REMINDED THEM OF THE WORD "'HELLO" OR THE PHRASE "LO AND BEHOLD".

## School Report

Catherine Hurley (ed), *Could Do Better*, Simon & Schuster, 2004.

*e*

"*Russell is more able than he would have us think.*"
RUSSELL BRAND, COMEDIAN, ACTOR AND AUTHOR.

"*Very talkative. Unfortunately, what he has to say is not always relevant.*"
HARRY ENFIELD, COMEDIAN AND ACTOR.

"*Is a constant trouble to everybody and is always in some scrape or other.*"
SIR WINSTON CHURCHILL, FORMER PRIME MINISTER.

## http://www

*f*

**SIR TIM BERNERS-LEE,** THE INVENTOR OF THE WORLD WIDE WEB, HAS BEEN HAILED BY *TIME* MAGAZINE AS ONE OF THE 100 GREATEST MINDS OF THE CENTURY. HE VIEWS THE WEB AS A POWERFUL FORCE FOR SOCIAL CHANGE AND INDIVIDUAL CREATIVITY AND HAS NEVER PROFITED FROM HIS INVENTION. HIS DEVELOPMENT OF THE ELECTRONIC LANGUAGE, 'HYPERTEXT' OR 'HTTP', IS CONSIDERED BY SOME TO BE THE GREATEST DEVELOPMENT IN HUMAN COMMUNICATION OF ALL TIME. SIR TIM THINKS THE WEB IS STILL IN ITS VERY EARLY STAGES AND THAT THERE IS MUCH MORE THAT THE INVENTION CAN DO TO HELP HUMANITY DEVELOP.

**LEARN MORE/GET INVOLVED:**
www.ted.com www.w3.org/people/berners-lee

*THE MOST VALUABLE THING YOU CAN MAKE IS A MISTAKE. YOU CAN'T LEARN FROM BEING PERFECT.*

ADAM OSBORNE (1939-2003)
AUTHOR, PUBLISHER AND COMPUTER DESIGNER

*THE GREATEST MISTAKE YOU CAN MAKE IN LIFE IS TO BE CONTINUALLY FEARING YOU WILL MAKE ONE.*

*d*

ELBERT HUBBARD (1856-1915)
WRITER, PUBLISHER AND PHILOSOPHER.

HE0107-5240 IS 13.2 BILLION YEARS OLD!

## NATIVE OR IMMIGRANT?

**IF YOU** WERE BORN IN THE LATE 1990S OR AFTER, YOU ARE A **DIGITAL NATIVE** THIS IS SOMEONE WHO HAS GROWN UP WITH 21ST-CENTURY TECHNOLOGIES LIKE MOBILE PHONES, MP3 PLAYERS, COMPUTERS, THE WORLD WIDE WEB AND ONLINE GAMING. **DIGITAL IMMIGRANTS** ARE PEOPLE BORN BEFORE THEN. ALTHOUGH THEY MAY BE ACCOMPLISHED USERS OF NEW TECHNOLOGIES, THEY DO NOT HAVE A NATURAL APTITUDE FOR THEM. DIGITAL NATIVES ARE THE FIRST PEOPLE BORN WITH THIS TECHNOLOGY.

*g*

## EVALUATE & REFLECT

"**STUDENTS** SHOULD BE ABLE TO REFLECT ON THE PROGRESS THEY HAVE MADE, EVALUATING WHAT THEY HAVE LEARNT FROM THE INTENDED AND UNINTENDED CONSEQUENCES OF ACTION AND THE CONTRIBUTION OF OTHERS AS WELL AS THEMSELVES."
QUALIFICATIONS AND CURRICULUM AUTHORITY.

MIRROR, MIRROR ON THE WALL, DID I GET AWAY WITH DOING NO WORK AT ALL?

*c*

ZZZ

NO CHANCE!

# How To USE THE CLASSROOM

*Because* the Toolkit encourages self-directed learning, it's important that you as well as your teacher take responsibility for your classes. You will need to read ahead and see what may be needed for the next lessons – it may be necessary to book IT rooms, for example, to have a good selection of newspapers for the Newspaper Game, or to bring in some of your own research.

It is also important that you see these lessons as being open in the sense that your interests can guide how the lesson goes. For example, all the games and activities in the Toolkit finish with feedback sessions. These sessions are a great opportunity to develop discussion and debate. If a feedback session leads into a really useful discussion, don't feel that it has to be kept short to fit into the lesson, as you will find that a great discussion – which involves everybody – is an excellent way to develop your ideas about citizenship.

Remember, the classroom is not the only place where you will be learning. All your projects will involve work outside the classroom and the Toolkit encourages you to carry on outside school with the learning that interests you most.

# The THREE CAMPAIGNS

*Whether* you are taking a GCSE or not, you will be required to organize and run your own campaigns. The Toolkit provides you with three standard types of campaigns – local, national and global – but there should be some freedom in how many campaigns you run and what kinds of campaigns they are. If you are taking a GCSE, follow your teacher's guidance on this. The chapter called *The Mirror* gives you practical advice about your campaigns and you will find that, whatever examination board you are using, the Toolkit has it covered.

# Going CROSS-CURRICULAR

*Schools* are encouraged to make Citizenship Studies part of the other subjects they teach. As you go through the Toolkit, it will quickly become obvious how easy this is. Some schools have already taken to having whole-year or whole-school active citizenship projects in which everyone works on the same project, no matter what lesson they are in. This is easy to do, great fun and makes it more likely that your campaigns will be successful. The skills you develop through the Toolkit will help you in all of your other subjects.

# The Rax INTERVIEWS

*At* the end of most of the chapters in the Toolkit, there are exclusive interviews: from pop stars to politicians, from experienced activists to young campaigners doing it for themselves. They are there for you to sample many different points of view on young people's campaigning. No one point of view is more or less correct than any of the others – they are simply different points of view – and the Toolkit aims to present you with as wide a variety as possible. They are resources that will help you build up your own ideas and conclusions as you absorb and evaluate other people's ideas about change.

# Web LINKS

*Throughout* the Toolkit there are hundreds of web links, usually beside the words: **LEARN MORE/GET INVOLVED:**

The Toolkit has tried to use only the most reliable sites but there is no guarantee that these won't change and there is every chance that you will be able to find much better sites yourselves. There will also be lists of sites on the Rax Citizenship website for you to use.

"WE CAN USE OUR EXPERIENCES AND UNDERSTANDING OF HOW THE WORLD WORKS TO CREATE NEW AND INNOVATIVE IDEAS, AND WE CAN USE OUR YOUTH AND ENERGY TO THEN PUT THOSE IDEAS IN PLACE... THAT'S WHAT WE ARE DOING, AND WE CAN HONESTLY SAY THAT, AS CORNY AS IT SOUNDS, THE FEELING YOU GET FROM TAKING THAT CONTROL IS AMAZING."

UKYCC (SEE RAX INTERVIEW ON PAGE 104).

"GET INVOLVED IN A LOCAL CAMPAIGN THAT YOU SUPPORT OR BE BRAVE AND SET UP YOUR OWN CAMPAIGN IF THERE IS SOMETHING YOU'RE FED UP ABOUT. BY DOING THIS YOU'LL BE CONTRIBUTING TO A BETTER AND MORE POSITIVE FUTURE. WE CAN AND WE WILL BE THE GENERATION TO PROVIDE SOLUTIONS BUT WE MUST WORK AS ONE!"

SCOTT FORBES (SEE RAX INTERVIEW ON PAGE 195).

"DO IT NOW WHILE YOU'RE YOUNG, WHILE IT IS CLEAR IN YOUR MIND, WHILE THE ENERGY IS THERE READY TO BE USED... BEFORE YOU BECOME ENMESHED IN THE WEB OF RESPONSIBILITIES AND THE COMPLICATIONS OF LIFE THAT CREEP UP ON YOU UNAWARES."

THOM YORKE (SEE RAX INTERVIEW ON PAGE 165).

"I WOULD QUOTE MARGARET MEAD:

'NEVER UNDERESTIMATE THE POWER OF A SMALL BUT COMMITTED GROUP OF PEOPLE TO CHANGE THE WORLD. INDEED, IT IS THE ONLY THING THAT EVER HAS.'

HISTORICALLY WE HUMANS HAVE BEEN PRETTY GOOD AT GETTING OURSELVES OUT OF SCRAPES, BUT IT'S ALWAYS REQUIRED PEOPLE TO GET OFF THEIR BEHINDS AND MAKE IT HAPPEN. AND THERE ARE A FAIR FEW PEOPLE LIKE THAT. MAYBE YOU'RE ONE OF THEM."

BEN STEWART (SEE RAX INTERVIEW ON PAGE 191).

# The Toolkit GAMES ROOM.

**GAMES ACTIVITIES**

*Throughout* the Toolkit, you will find plenty of games and activities. You will recognize them by their icons, which are shown over the following pages. Because Active Citizenship is all about **DOING**, then you must get yourself **FULLY INVOLVED** in these games and activities in order to **SUCCEED**.

## THE BEST WAY OF LEARNING ACTIVE CITIZENSHIP IS BY DOING ACTIVE CITIZENSHIP.

These games and activities can be for individual work, pair work, group work or whole class work. Because of this, it is important that you decide on basic **GROUND RULES** for how everyone in the class expects to be treated when working with each other.

---

## ACTIVITY

### GET INTO GROUPS

*Decide* what the best **GROUND RULES** are for how to work together.

**EACH GROUP NEEDS SIX RULES. PUT THEM INTO AN ORDER OF PRIORITY.**
**TAKE CARE DOING THIS, AS THESE RULES ARE THE ONES YOU WILL HAVE TO STICK BY.**

To get you started, here are some ideas for your ground rules:

1) Decisions should be made democratically.
2) Everyone should be putting in the same amount of effort.

Feed back your group's ideas to the class and to your teacher. The whole class should then vote to decide on the final top six rules.

Make a note of these top six ground rules and turn them into a poster.
This poster should be on the classroom wall every time you have this lesson from now on.
That's it. For good. You chose them. You have to stick to them.

---

## The Toolkit GAMES AND ACTIVITIES

---

### NEWSPAPER GAME

*This* game should be done in pairs or groups and has a maximum time limit of 10 minutes. Because this game is one we use often, you will need to get into the habit of bringing a newspaper into every lesson from now on. It's important that there is a variety of newspapers available so it may be useful to get your teacher or school librarian to help supply the class too.

You will have up to 10 minutes to sift through the papers for particular kinds of articles: for example, stories about the environment, war or local transport services. When you have found an article that fits the description, you have to note the heading/title, the page number and the name of the newspaper.

The winning team is the one that has found the most articles on that subject in the given time. However, other groups or your teacher must check whether your articles definitely fit the description.

## STREET LAW ⭐c

IN BRAZIL, COMMUNITIES HAVE BEEN COMING TOGETHER AND EXPERIMENTING WITH MAKING NEW LAWS BY USING STREET THEATRE. *THE THEATRE OF THE OPPRESSED* WORK IN SUCH A WAY THAT LOCAL PEOPLE COME TOGETHER AND USE DRAMA SKILLS TO ACT OUT THE CONSEQUENCES OF NEW LAWS THAT THEY WOULD LIKE TO SEE OR ACTING OUT CURRENT LAWS WHICH THEY THINK ARE FAILING. IT HAS BEEN SO SUCCESSFUL THAT THE GOVERNMENT HAS TAKEN SERIOUSLY MANY OF THE IDEAS THAT HAVE COME FROM THESE STREET THEATRE PRODUCTIONS.

LEARN MORE/ GET INVOLVED:

www.theatreoftheoppressed.org

ONE OF THE OLDEST SURVIVING UK NEWSPAPERS WAS FIRST PRINTED IN 1665 AND WAS ORIGINALLY CALLED *THE CAMBRIDGE GAZETTE* BEFORE IT BECAME *THE LONDON GAZETTE*. THIS WAS BECAUSE, AT THE TIME, KING CHARLES II HAD MOVED THE ROYAL COURT TO CAMBRIDGE TO ESCAPE THE GREAT PLAGUE OF LONDON. PEOPLE WERE FRIGHTENED TO TOUCH NEWSPAPERS FROM LONDON IN CASE THEY CAUGHT THE PLAGUE.

*THE LONDON GAZETTE* IS NOT LIKE OUR NORMAL NEWSPAPERS AS YOU WON'T FIND GOSSIP ABOUT CELEBRITIES OR SPORTS PAGES. IT IS CONSIDERED TO BE THE AUTHORITY ON THE GOVERNMENT'S NEW OFFICIAL RULES OR REGULATIONS. THIS IS VERY USEFUL FOR AN ACTIVE CITIZEN BUT NOT FOR ONE WANTING TO KNOW WHO WON *X FACTOR*! ⭐e

LEARN MORE/GET INVOLVED: www.london-gazette.co.uk

## THE PEOPLE MAKE THE LAWS

YOUR SIX GROUND RULES ARE A FORM OF LAW-MAKING. THEY MAY BIND ONLY THE STUDENTS IN YOUR CLASSROOM BUT THEY HAVE BEEN ARRIVED AT DEMOCRATICALLY AFTER BEING DEBATED BY THE MEMBERS OF YOUR GROUPS. THAT'S NOT TOO DIFFERENT FROM HOW REAL LAWS ARE MADE IN THE UK. ⭐d

21ST-CENTURY TECHNOLOGIES ARE ALLOWING A TRANSFORMATION IN OUR WAYS OF COLLABORATION, CO-OPERATION AND COMMUNITY WHERE PEOPLE CAN NETWORK THROUGH MEDIA SITES AND CREATE THEIR OWN MOVEMENTS FOR NEW LAWS. ONE INTERNET-BASED 'PEOPLE POWER' CAMPAIGNING ORGANIZATION, CALLED 38 DEGREES, IS ALREADY HAVING SUCCESS IN INFLUENCING DECISIONS MADE BY THE GOVERNMENT.

LEARN MORE/GET INVOLVED: www.38degrees.org.uk

🌲 X24 = 1 TON 📰

THE AVERAGE PERSON IN THE UK GETS THROUGH 38KG OF NEWSPAPERS PER YEAR. IT TAKES 24 TREES TO MAKE 1 TONNE (WHICH IS 1,000 KG) OF NEWSPAPER. ⭐f

*YOU CAN LEARN MORE ABOUT A PERSON IN AN HOUR OF PLAY THAN IN A YEAR OF CONVERSATION.*

PLATO (420-348 BCE)
GREEK PHILOSOPHER ⭐a

PUT YOUR FEET ON THE PEDALS, SPIN YOUR LEGS ROUND, HOLD ON TO THE HANDLEBARS, KEEP BALANCE, TURN BY ROTATING THE HANDLEBARS BUT NOT TOO FAR... BLAH... BLAH... BLAH...

"WE LEARN 10% OF WHAT WE READ...

...15% OF WHAT WE HEAR...

...BUT 80% OF WHAT WE EXPERIENCE." ⭐b

WOMAN TRAUMATIZED AS TEENS CHARGE PAST HER ON THEIR EVIL BICYCLES!

TEEN TERROR OUTRAGE SHO...

SHOCK! HORROR! TEENAGERS MEET ON CORNER AND TALK! *Evening News*

The MOON CRAZED TEEN LOOKED AT ME FUNNY ⭐g

RESEARCH SHOWS THAT YOUNG PEOPLE ARE NOT BIG READERS OF NEWSPAPERS UNLESS THEY ARE FREE OR VERY CHEAP. TEENAGERS GENERALLY PREFER TO GET THEIR NEWS FROM THE INTERNET. ONE REASON THAT SOME YOUNG PEOPLE GIVE FOR NOT BEING INTERESTED IN NEWSPAPERS IS THAT THEY FEEL THEY ARE STEREOTYPED BY REGULAR NEWS STORIES THAT SEEM TO PORTRAY ALL TEENAGERS AS BEING DANGEROUS, VIOLENT AND FRIGHTENING.

A FEAR AND HATRED OF TEENAGERS IS CALLED **Ephebiphobia.**

## ART ACTION

*This* is an activity that can be performed individually, as a pair or in a group. You can do it quickly, in five minutes, or take longer if you are going to create a number of different pieces.

You will be given a situation and will need to create an appropriate piece of artwork. You can use your art skills to create any or all of the following:

A badge design, comic strip, logo, poster, pamphlet or fanzine, storyboard for a short film, information cards where you present illustrated bite-sized nuggets of information, T-shirt designs, adverts that make a point about the situation you have been given, (it's very effective if you use a famous advert and subvert it). You could even paint a painting, make a sculpture or a model to communicate your idea if you have time outside the lesson. You may be able to continue your citizenship work in an art lesson.

## 3.9.27

*This* game can be played individually or in pairs and takes between 5 and 10 minutes. 3.9.27 is based on the experience of campaigners using the media. They discovered that if you are being interviewed on a television or radio station, you need to be short and sharp to make your point about your campaign otherwise they may not use your soundbite. Even worse, you may come across as being confused, weak and unclear. This could damage your campaign.

The solution that campaigners came up with was to work out what to say in advance and keep to the rules of making...

## 3 POINTS IN 9 SECONDS USING 27 WORDS.

It's a difficult skill to learn but can make all the difference to how the media perceive and present your campaign. You will also find that this kind of skill will benefit other aspects of your life too!

You will be given a situation or opinion for which you will have to write a 3.9.27 soundbite. You should try to keep it to 27 words but can go over that limit if you are stuck. The class can vote on the 3.9.27 that they think is the most effective.

## FIGHT YOUR CORNER

*This* game is for groups or for the whole class and can be played in 15 minutes or can take the whole lesson, depending on how many speakers are used. An important part of Citizenship Studies is the idea of democracy – people voting for the idea or opinion

CONTINUED

I'M CRAZY ABOUT YOU BECAUSE YOU'RE SO FUNNY AND UM... KIND AND UM... YOU'RE REALLY COOL AND RELAXED AND ALWAYS SAY WHAT YOU THINK AND... WHAT YOU FEEL AND STUFF... UM... AND YOU NEVER ACT AND YOU'RE FUNNY... AND UM... YOUR EYES ARE LIKE MOONS TWINKLING... NO, LIKE STARS SHINING... AND UM... EVERYBODY THINKS YOU'RE THE COOLEST BECAUSE YOU'RE ALWAYS RELAXED AND UM... YOU LOOK AFTER PEOPLE AND CARE ABOUT THEM AND STUFF AND YOU'RE REALLY SHARP AND... QUICK AND STUFF AND UM... YOU'RE REALLY FUNNY AND UM... YOU'RE LIKE YOUR OWN PERSON AND STUFF... YOU KNOW?

★e I'M CRAZY ABOUT YOU BECAUSE YOU ARE A COMPLETELY GENUINE AND CARING PERSON, YOU'RE TRULY FUNNY, WITTY AND ENTERTAINING AND HAVE THE MOST STUNNINGLY BEAUTIFUL, RADIANT EYES!

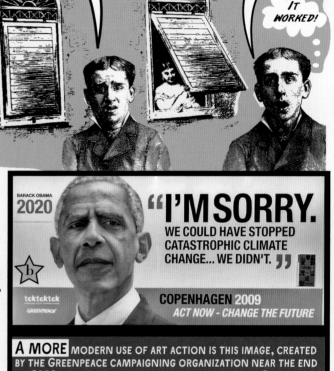

NOT A 3.9.27!

IT WORKED!

★d THE SURGEON GENERAL WARNS THAT SMOKING IS A FREQUENT CAUSE OF WASTED POTENTIAL AND FATAL REGRET.

**SUBVERTING** ADVERTISING IMAGES IS SOMETIMES CALLED CULTURE JAMMING. THIS POSTER USES THE FAMOUS IMAGE ASSOCIATED WITH A WELL-KNOWN BRAND OF CIGARETTES TO MAKE AN ANTI-SMOKING STATEMENT.

★c **MANY** OF THE MOST SUCCESSFUL ACTIVE CITIZENSHIP CAMPAIGNS HAVE RELIED HEAVILY ON THE USE OF ART ACTION. RATHER THAN READ A BOOK LAYING OUT AN ARGUMENT, PEOPLE FIND IT EASIER TO LOOK AT AN IMAGE THAT SUMS IT ALL UP. ONE OF THE FIRST EXAMPLES OF THIS WAS IN THE CAMPAIGN TO ABOLISH THE SLAVE TRADE IN THE LATE 18TH CENTURY.
AM I NOT A MAN AND A BROTHER?

★b BARACK OBAMA 2020 **"I'M SORRY.** WE COULD HAVE STOPPED CATASTROPHIC CLIMATE CHANGE... WE DIDN'T."
tcktcktck
GREENPEACE
COPENHAGEN 2009
*ACT NOW - CHANGE THE FUTURE*

**A MORE** MODERN USE OF ART ACTION IS THIS IMAGE, CREATED BY THE GREENPEACE CAMPAIGNING ORGANIZATION NEAR THE END OF 2009 AND POSTED THROUGHOUT THE AIRPORT IN COPENHAGEN TO GREET THE WORLD LEADERS AS THEY ARRIVED TO ATTEND A CONFERENCE TO DEAL WITH THE PROBLEMS OF GLOBAL WARMING.

# WHAT MAKES A SYMBOL

**THIS SYMBOL** IS ONE OF THE MOST FAMOUS CAMPAIGNING SYMBOLS WORLDWIDE. IT HAS BEEN USED ON POSTERS, BADGES AND T-SHIRTS SINCE THE 1950S TO SYMBOLIZE PEACE, THE END OF WAR AND NUCLEAR DISARMAMENT. IT WAS ORIGINALLY DESIGNED IN 1958 BY GERALD HOLTOM, A BRITISH DESIGNER AND ARTIST, FOR THE DIRECT ACTION COMMITTEE AGAINST NUCLEAR WAR (DAC). HE HAD ORIGINALLY CREATED A PICTURE OF A MAN WITH HIS ARMS HELD UP IN THE AIR IN DESPAIR BUT THEN THOUGHT THAT A PEACE MOVEMENT SHOULD BE MORE POSITIVE AND REVERSED THE SYMBOL SO THAT THE ARMS WERE POINTING DOWN. HE THEN LOOKED AT THE SEMAPHORE SYMBOLS FOR THE LETTERS 'N' AND 'D', SO THAT HE COULD REPRESENT THE WORDS 'NUCLEAR' AND 'DISARMAMENT'. BY COMBINING THESE TWO IMAGES, THE FAMOUS SYMBOL FOR PEACE WAS INVENTED. IT WAS ADOPTED BY THE CAMPAIGN FOR NUCLEAR DISARMAMENT (CND) AND WAS ALSO TAKEN ON BY THE MASS ANTI-WAR MOVEMENTS IN THE US.

SEMAPHORE FOR THE LETTER N

SEMAPHORE FOR THE LETTER D

★a THE SYMBOL FOR THE CND

## FIGHT YOUR CORNER

that they most agree with. An ideal way for you to use this system is in debating, where people get to hear arguments for and against a motion (the subject of the debate). You will be given a motion – for example, "This house believes that firefighters and paramedics should be paid the same as footballers and bank managers." ⓐ

Everyone in the group or class is randomly given a card that reads either FOR THE MOTION or AGAINST THE MOTION. Depending on which card you are given, you have to prepare a debating speech arguing that case. Your teacher then chooses people at random and they have to give their speech.

After the speeches (there can be up to six speakers for and against), the group or class votes on which side has made the better case. ⓑ

### TIPS 'n' HINTS

FIGHT YOUR CORNER RELIES ON YOUR SKILLS OF PERSUASION. YOU WILL LEARN A GREAT DEAL ABOUT THIS IN THE CHAPTER CALLED *THE GIFT OF THE GAB*. REMEMBER, WHETHER THE OPINION YOU HAVE TO ARGUE FOR IS A POPULAR ONE OR NOT WILL HAVE NO BEARING ON THE OUTCOME. IT WILL BE YOUR SKILLS OF PERSUASION THAT MAKE ALL THE DIFFERENCE.

## BE THE BARD

*This* activity is for individuals, pairs or groups and can take from 10 minutes ⓒ to a whole lesson – even longer if you discover that you are the new Tupac/Dizzee Rascal/Bob Dylan/Lily Allen.

ⓕ You will be given an idea, situation or campaign and will be asked to write the lyrics of a song about it. This can be a rap or a traditional song. If you are taking GCSE music or create your own music at home then go ahead and turn it into a proper recording. If you wish, post your song up on your own social networking sites, blogs and sites ⓖ like You Tube. You can also use your songs as part of your campaigns. ⓔ

### TIPS 'n' HINTS

GREAT CAMPAIGNING LYRICS GIVE A VOICE TO THE WAY MOST PEOPLE ARE FEELING.

## P.O.V

*This* is a group activity that should take at least 20 minutes and involves ⓓ your ability to get inside the skin of another person. This activity can take longer if your class and your teacher decide it is worth spending more time. You may even want to use a homework session or part of a lesson researching the situation being discussed.

You will be given six numbered 'character cards' for each group and a situation that needs a solution. Each person in the group rolls a die and has to take the character with that number. If there are fewer than six people in your group, then still take the character that your die roll gives you.

Once you have read the notes on your character and fully understood the situation then your group begins the discussion in role. It doesn't matter at all if you completely disagree

CONTINUED

# THE WHOLE PICTURE

*THE GUARDIAN* NATIONAL NEWSPAPER RAN A TV ADVERTISING CAMPAIGN IN 1986 THAT DEMONSTRATED HOW IMPORTANT IT IS TO SEE THINGS FROM MANY POINTS OF VIEW. THE MOST FAMOUS FILM CLIP STARTED BY SHOWING A YOUNG MAN WITH A SKINHEAD HAIRCUT RUNNING TOWARDS A MAN IN A SUIT WHO LOOKS LIKE A BUSINESS EXECUTIVE. OF COURSE, FROM THIS POINT OF VIEW, IT'S EASY TO MAKE THE ASSUMPTION THAT THE SKINHEAD IS ABOUT TO MUG THE MAN.

IN THE NEXT SECTION OF THE ADVERT, THE CAMERA PULLS BACK TO REVEAL THE WHOLE PICTURE. ONLY THEN DOES THE VIEWER REALIZE THAT A PALLET OF BRICKS IS ABOUT TO FALL ON THE MAN FROM ABOVE AND THE SKINHEAD IS IN FACT SAVING HIS LIFE.

THIS SHOWS WHY IT IS SO IMPORTANT TO SEE AN ISSUE FROM MANY POINTS OF VIEW BEFORE YOU DRAW YOUR OWN CONCLUSIONS.

**BARD** IS AN OLD ENGLISH WORD FOR A LYRICAL POET. WILLIAM SHAKESPEARE (1564-1616), CONSIDERED TO BE ONE OF THE GREATEST WRITERS OF ALL TIME, IS OFTEN CALLED SIMPLY 'THE BARD'. ONE OF HIS GREATEST TRAGEDIES, *MACBETH*, IS THOUGHT TO BE THE MOST PRODUCED PLAY OF ALL TIME, WITH A PERFORMANCE BEGINNING SOMEWHERE IN THE WORLD EVERY FOUR HOURS!

## DIY MUSIC MAESTRO

**BECAUSE** OF 21ST-CENTURY TECHNOLOGY, YOUNG PEOPLE ARE MORE AND MORE ABLE TO CREATE THEIR OWN MUSIC AND POST IT UP ON THE WEB WITHOUT HAVING TO GO THROUGH THE PROCESS OF BEING SIGNED TO A MUSIC COMPANY. THIS MEANS THAT, FOR THE FIRST TIME, YOU ARE FREE TO CREATE WHATEVER MUSIC YOU WANT WITHOUT BEING CONTROLLED BY ANY BUSINESS INTERESTS.

*WHO IS SHE? A FILM STAR? POP SINGER?*

*NO, SHE'S ONE OF THOSE FIREFIGHTER'S WIVES.*

**VIP AREA**

*YOUNG PEOPLE ARE VERY, VERY INTERESTED IN THE WAY THE WORLD IS RUN – EVERYTHING FROM EDUCATION TO THE NHS – BUT THERE IS NO-ONE IN THE CABINET THAT CAN RELATE TO ME OR THAT I CAN RELATE TO.*

MS DYNAMITE (SEE RAX INTERVIEW ON PAGE 135)

## LOVE MUSIC HATE RACISM

**THE** USE OF MUSIC AS A TOOL FOR CHANGE HAS EXISTED THROUGHOUT HISTORY. ONE SIGNIFICANT MUSICAL MOVEMENT IN RECENT TIMES STARTED IN 1976 WHEN PUNK ROCK BANDS CAME TOGETHER WITH REGGAE BANDS TO SPREAD AN ANTI-RACIST MESSAGE. THIS WAS CALLED 'ROCK AGAINST RACISM'. THE COLLECTION OF BANDS HELD MANY MAJOR CONCERTS AND BECAME THE FOCAL POINT FOR A LARGE ANTI-RACISM MOVEMENT. IN 2002, THE ROCK AGAINST RACISM CAMPAIGN WAS RENAMED AS LOVE MUSIC HATE RACISM WHEN BANDS FROM THE PUNK ROCK DAYS PLAYED WITH MORE MODERN ACTS, INCLUDING BABYSHAMBLES AND TINCHY STRYDER, TO CONTINUE TO SPREAD THEIR ANTI-RACIST MESSAGE. OVER 500 MUSICAL EVENTS HAVE SINCE TAKEN PLACE WHERE ACTS FROM ALL GENRES OF MUSIC, FROM HIP HOP, DRUM AND BASS AND GRIME TO PUNK, ROCK AND JAZZ HAVE PERFORMED TOGETHER, UNITED IN THEIR FIGHT TO END RACISM.

*TO BE PHOTOCOPIED BY YOUR TEACHER.*

LEARN MORE/GET INVOLVED: www.lovemusichaterracism.com

with your character – it's not your viewpoint you're representing, it's theirs. All characters have to be allowed to voice their opinions and must be heard clearly and fairly.

The aim of the activity is for your characters to argue for their solutions to the situation. At the end of your discussion, which would usually be after 15 minutes, you come out of role and vote AS YOURSELVES on what you think the solution should be.

P.O.V is a vital Active Citizenship activity, as you have to be able to understand issues from other people's points of view. For example, you may find yourself as a young Muslim having to be a member of the BNP or as a devoted peace campaigner having to be an MP arguing for war.

**TIPS 'n' HINTS** REMEMBER, TAKE YOUR ROLES EXTREMELY SERIOUSLY. ALWAYS STAY IN ROLE. IF YOU DO, YOU WILL BE AMAZED AT WHAT YOU TAKE AWAY FROM THIS ACTIVITY. ACTIVE CITIZENSHIP IS ALL ABOUT UNDERSTANDING THE MANY DIFFERENT WAYS THAT PEOPLE VIEW THE SAME WORLD.

# ALIEN'S EYES

*This* activity can be for individual, pair or group work. It is a quick activity and should take no longer than five minutes.

Have you ever thought about what the world would look like from the point of view of a being from another planet? Whether there are aliens out there or not, it's a useful perspective to use.

Try to imagine that you have just arrived in an invisible spacecraft above the earth and you have the ability to look down on this planet. Your job is to observe and transmit weekly reports back to your planet revealing what you have learnt about humans, their culture, their relationships with each other and with their planet.

What would you think kissing is?
How would you describe our relationship with televisions?
What would you say about the ways different human societies treat their elders?

You will be given a situation and you simply have to imagine what that situation would look like to an alien and work out how you would report back about this to your planet.

**TIPS 'n' HINTS** IT'S A SHORT, SHARP ACTIVITY THAT WILL PRODUCE MIND-BENDING RESULTS IF YOU ARE WILLING TO THROW YOURSELF INTO THIS MOST UNUSUAL OF ROLES! REALLY STEP BACK AND LOOK AT THE WORLD AS IF YOU HAVE JUST ARRIVED HERE AND KNOW NOTHING ABOUT IT.

# THE MYSTERY GAME

*This* activity can be for individual, pair or group work. It could take five minutes or you may even keep learning from it for the rest of your life.

CONTINUED

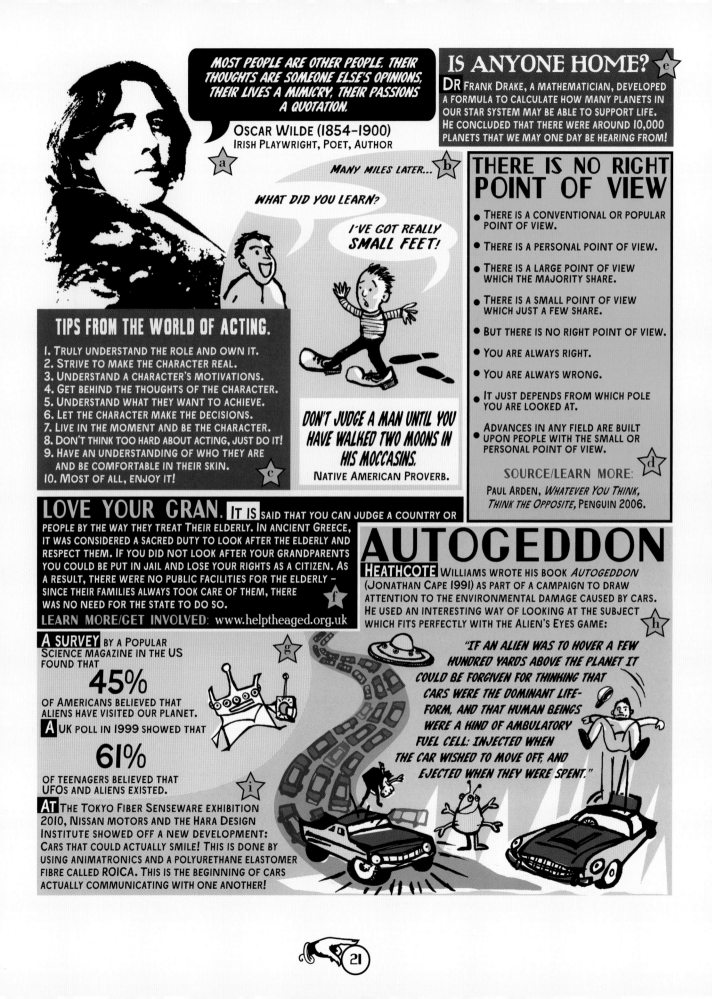

> MOST PEOPLE ARE OTHER PEOPLE. THEIR THOUGHTS ARE SOMEONE ELSE'S OPINIONS, THEIR LIVES A MIMICRY, THEIR PASSIONS A QUOTATION.

OSCAR WILDE (1854-1900)
IRISH PLAYWRIGHT, POET, AUTHOR

*a*

MANY MILES LATER... *b*

WHAT DID YOU LEARN?

I'VE GOT REALLY SMALL FEET!

## IS ANYONE HOME? *e*

DR FRANK DRAKE, A MATHEMATICIAN, DEVELOPED A FORMULA TO CALCULATE HOW MANY PLANETS IN OUR STAR SYSTEM MAY BE ABLE TO SUPPORT LIFE. HE CONCLUDED THAT THERE WERE AROUND 10,000 PLANETS THAT WE MAY ONE DAY BE HEARING FROM!

## THERE IS NO RIGHT POINT OF VIEW

- THERE IS A CONVENTIONAL OR POPULAR POINT OF VIEW.
- THERE IS A PERSONAL POINT OF VIEW.
- THERE IS A LARGE POINT OF VIEW WHICH THE MAJORITY SHARE.
- THERE IS A SMALL POINT OF VIEW WHICH JUST A FEW SHARE.
- BUT THERE IS NO RIGHT POINT OF VIEW.
- YOU ARE ALWAYS RIGHT.
- YOU ARE ALWAYS WRONG.
- IT JUST DEPENDS FROM WHICH POLE YOU ARE LOOKED AT.
- ADVANCES IN ANY FIELD ARE BUILT UPON PEOPLE WITH THE SMALL OR PERSONAL POINT OF VIEW.

*d*

SOURCE/LEARN MORE:

PAUL ARDEN, *WHATEVER YOU THINK, THINK THE OPPOSITE*, PENGUIN 2006.

## TIPS FROM THE WORLD OF ACTING.

1. TRULY UNDERSTAND THE ROLE AND OWN IT.
2. STRIVE TO MAKE THE CHARACTER REAL.
3. UNDERSTAND A CHARACTER'S MOTIVATIONS.
4. GET BEHIND THE THOUGHTS OF THE CHARACTER.
5. UNDERSTAND WHAT THEY WANT TO ACHIEVE.
6. LET THE CHARACTER MAKE THE DECISIONS.
7. LIVE IN THE MOMENT AND BE THE CHARACTER.
8. DON'T THINK TOO HARD ABOUT ACTING, JUST DO IT!
9. HAVE AN UNDERSTANDING OF WHO THEY ARE AND BE COMFORTABLE IN THEIR SKIN.
10. MOST OF ALL, ENJOY IT!

*c*

> DON'T JUDGE A MAN UNTIL YOU HAVE WALKED TWO MOONS IN HIS MOCCASINS.
>
> NATIVE AMERICAN PROVERB.

## LOVE YOUR GRAN. IT IS SAID THAT YOU CAN JUDGE A COUNTRY OR

PEOPLE BY THE WAY THEY TREAT THEIR ELDERLY. IN ANCIENT GREECE, IT WAS CONSIDERED A SACRED DUTY TO LOOK AFTER THE ELDERLY AND RESPECT THEM. IF YOU DID NOT LOOK AFTER YOUR GRANDPARENTS YOU COULD BE PUT IN JAIL AND LOSE YOUR RIGHTS AS A CITIZEN. AS A RESULT, THERE WERE NO PUBLIC FACILITIES FOR THE ELDERLY – SINCE THEIR FAMILIES ALWAYS TOOK CARE OF THEM, THERE WAS NO NEED FOR THE STATE TO DO SO. *f*

LEARN MORE/GET INVOLVED: www.helptheaged.org.uk

## AUTOGEDDON

HEATHCOTE WILLIAMS WROTE HIS BOOK *AUTOGEDDON* (JONATHAN CAPE 1991) AS PART OF A CAMPAIGN TO DRAW ATTENTION TO THE ENVIRONMENTAL DAMAGE CAUSED BY CARS. HE USED AN INTERESTING WAY OF LOOKING AT THE SUBJECT WHICH FITS PERFECTLY WITH THE ALIEN'S EYES GAME: *h*

A SURVEY BY A POPULAR SCIENCE MAGAZINE IN THE US FOUND THAT *g*

### 45%

OF AMERICANS BELIEVED THAT ALIENS HAVE VISITED OUR PLANET.

A UK POLL IN 1999 SHOWED THAT

### 61%

OF TEENAGERS BELIEVED THAT UFOS AND ALIENS EXISTED.

AT THE TOKYO FIBER SENSEWARE EXHIBITION 2010, NISSAN MOTORS AND THE HARA DESIGN INSTITUTE SHOWED OFF A NEW DEVELOPMENT: CARS THAT COULD ACTUALLY SMILE! THIS IS DONE BY USING ANIMATRONICS AND A POLYURETHANE ELASTOMER FIBRE CALLED ROICA. THIS IS THE BEGINNING OF CARS ACTUALLY COMMUNICATING WITH ONE ANOTHER! *i*

> "IF AN ALIEN WAS TO HOVER A FEW HUNDRED YARDS ABOVE THE PLANET IT COULD BE FORGIVEN FOR THINKING THAT CARS WERE THE DOMINANT LIFE-FORM, AND THAT HUMAN BEINGS WERE A KIND OF AMBULATORY FUEL CELL: INJECTED WHEN THE CAR WISHED TO MOVE OFF, AND EJECTED WHEN THEY WERE SPENT."

## THE MYSTERY GAME

Occasionally, we will spring a Mystery Activity on you. It will generally be pretty strange to do but will also teach you more subtle skills than are normally required in school. Here is an example:

Get a partner whom you can trust to look after you. Tie a blindfold around your eyes tightly and spend an hour going about your life as a blind person.

What problems do you come across?
What obstacles do you find that people should be aware of?
What does the world of the blind teach you?
What does this exercise teach you about the person you chose to look after you?

# HEADS TOGETHER

*This* activity is for groups or pairs and usually takes 5 to 10 minutes.

You will be given an idea or some facts. Then you have to put your heads together and come up with a list of responses to that idea. One of you will need to be the scribe, the person who writes down the group's ideas, and another of you will need to be the presenter, the person who feeds back the group's ideas to the class.

Here is an example of a Heads Together task:

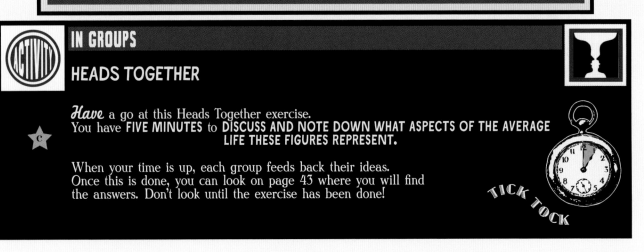

**WHICH ACTIVITIES TAKE UP THE FOLLOWING AMOUNT OF TIME IN THE AVERAGE HUMAN LIFE?**

30 YEARS
15 YEARS
4 YEARS
3 YEARS
2 YEARS (FOR WOMEN), 1 YEAR (FOR MEN),
6 MONTHS (FOR WOMEN), 3 YEARS (FOR MEN),
6 MONTHS (FOR WOMEN AND MEN).

## IN GROUPS

### HEADS TOGETHER

*Have* a go at this Heads Together exercise.
You have **FIVE MINUTES** to **DISCUSS AND NOTE DOWN WHAT ASPECTS OF THE AVERAGE LIFE THESE FIGURES REPRESENT.**

When your time is up, each group feeds back their ideas.
Once this is done, you can look on page 43 where you will find the answers. Don't look until the exercise has been done!

*TICK TOCK*

# BLIND AND VISUALLY IMPAIRED PEOPLE SAY...

OH WHAT A LOVELY DAY!

BUY LOTS OF STUFF NOW!

LEARN MORE/GET INVOLVED: www.rnib.org.uk

- YOUR OTHER SENSES ARE ENHANCED.
- YOU DON'T JUDGE PEOPLE BY THE WAY THEY LOOK.
- YOU ARE ABLE TO CONCENTRATE ON CONVERSATIONS WITHOUT VISUAL DISTRACTIONS.
- YOUR SENSE OF TOUCH MAKES HUMAN CONTACT FAR MORE MEANINGFUL.
- YOU DON'T HAVE TO SEE HOW 'UGLY' THE WORLD CAN BE!

**IN** THE FIFTIES WE USED TO SPEND 18 MINUTES LAUGHING A DAY ON AVERAGE. TODAY, IN THE UK, WE NOW LAUGH FOR 6 MINUTES A DAY ON AVERAGE! WHY DO YOU THINK THIS IS? DO YOU THINK THIS IS TRUE FOR YOU? DO YOUR FAMILY OR CARERS SPEND MUCH TIME LAUGHING? WHAT MAKES YOU LAUGH? PEOPLE HERE AT RAX SPEND AROUND 20 MINUTES A DAY LAUGHING – BUT THEN YOU HAVEN'T SEEN OUR FACES!

HA HA HA HA HA SNORT HA

**AN EXTREMELY IMPORTANT** PART OF ACTIVE CITIZENSHIP IS CRITICAL THINKING. THE CHAPTER IN THE TOOLKIT CALLED *THE PROCESSING PLANT* IS DEDICATED TO YOUR LEARNING THIS INCREDIBLY USEFUL SKILL. HOWEVER, THE MYSTERY GAME PROMOTES ANOTHER EQUALLY USEFUL WAY OF USING YOUR BRAIN AND IT'S ALMOST THE OPPOSITE OF CRITICAL THINKING.

THIS IS CALLED **LATERAL THINKING** AND IS ALL ABOUT LOOKING AT A PROBLEM AND USING ONLY YOUR CREATIVE SKILLS TO COME UP WITH AN ANSWER. WHEREAS CRITICAL THINKING IS ALL ABOUT EVALUATING EVIDENCE UNTIL YOU COME UP WITH A CONCLUSION, LATERAL THINKING IS LESS TO DO WITH EVALUATING THAN WITH OPENING YOUR MIND CREATIVELY SO THAT IDEAS JUST POP INTO YOUR HEAD.

UNTIL YOU HAVE ACTUALLY EXPERIENCED WHAT IT FEELS LIKE TO BE BLIND OR VISUALLY IMPAIRED, YOU WILL NEVER COME CLOSE TO UNDERSTANDING THE REALITY OF BLINDNESS. YOU WILL NEVER KNOW WHAT YOU CAN LEARN FROM THE EXPERIENCE AND WHAT UNEXPECTED INSIGHTS YOU WILL GAIN.

SOME OF THE BEST SOLUTIONS TO PROBLEMS IN THE WORLD, LARGE AND SMALL, HAVE COME FROM LATERAL THINKING.

**ONE** FAMOUS EXAMPLE OF LATERAL THINKING OCCURRED WHEN THE BRITISH SCIENTIST ISAAC NEWTON WAS SITTING UNDER A TREE AND AN APPLE FELL ON HIS HEAD. HE ASKED HIMSELF AN EXTREMELY UNUSUAL QUESTION:

"WHY DIDN'T THAT APPLE FALL UP INSTEAD OF FALLING DOWN?"

DONK

THAT'S LATERAL THINKING, ASKING UNUSUAL QUESTIONS. INSTEAD OF THINKING IN THE EXPECTED WAY, LATERAL THINKING ENCOURAGES YOU TO THINK IN UNUSUAL WAYS TO FIND A SOLUTION. BECAUSE NEWTON ASKED THAT UNUSUAL QUESTION, HE ENDED UP CREATING THE THEORY OF GRAVITY, WHICH IS ONE OF THE MOST IMPORTANT SCIENTIFIC THEORIES IN HUMAN HISTORY. LATERAL THINKING IS SOMETIMES CALLED:

**"THINKING OUTSIDE THE BOX."**

## LATERAL THINKING IS A WAY OF LOOKING AT HOW WE ACTUALLY USE OUR MINDS. THE TERM WAS ORIGINATED BY

**EDWARD DE BONO** PHYSICIAN, AUTHOR AND INVENTOR

DE BONO'S MAIN AIM IS TO SHOW THAT BY USING OUR MINDS CREATIVELY, IN AN INDIRECT RATHER THAN A DIRECT WAY, WE CAN COME UP WITH IDEAS THAT ARE EXCEPTIONALLY POWERFUL.

YOU WILL BE ENCOURAGED TO USE LATERAL THINKING THROUGHOUT YOUR USE OF THIS TOOLKIT – IN ADDITION TO MANY OTHER NOVEL WAYS OF THINKING. JUST REMEMBER, SOME OF THE GREATEST SOLUTIONS TO PROBLEMS HAVE COME FROM LATERAL THINKING!

LEARN MORE/GET INVOLVED: www.edwdebono.com

# START THINKING LATERALLY

**HERE** ARE A FEW BASIC QUESTIONS TO KICK START YOUR LATERAL THINKING (THE ANSWERS ARE ON PAGE 51)

A MAN MARRIED 20 WOMEN BUT ISN'T CHARGED WITH POLYGAMY (MARRYING MORE THAN ONE PERSON AT A TIME). HOW CAN THAT BE?

A WOMAN DRIVES A TRUCK INTO A TUNNEL BUT THE TRUCK IS TOO TALL AND IT GETS WEDGED AGAINST THE ROOF OF THE TUNNEL. SHE CAN'T DRIVE THE TRUCK BACKWARDS OR FORWARDS.
HOW CAN THE DRIVER GET THE TRUCK OUT OF THE TUNNEL WITHOUT DAMAGING THE TRUCK OR THE TUNNEL?

I'M GOING OUTSIDE AND I MAY BE SOME TIME....

# CHAPTER 2 A SHORT HISTORY of BIG CHANGE thus far . . . . . .

## 1 Why is this chapter important?

THE FREEDOMS AND RIGHTS WE ENJOY TODAY IN THE UK HAVE BEEN BROUGHT ABOUT BY ACTIVE CITIZENS CAMPAIGNING THROUGH HISTORY. THIS CHAPTER LOOKS AT WHAT THOSE BEFORE US HAVE ACHIEVED AND HOW THEY ACHIEVED IT.

Some of the campaigning skills you will be learning in the rest of the Toolkit rely on 21st-century technology, but the key tools of change have been developed over thousands of years of campaigning.

This chapter looks at that history so that you can identify those tools and skills and go on to create the most effective campaigns possible for yourselves.

a
b

## 2 Did we always have the rights and freedoms that we have today?

### IF YOU WERE AN ORDINARY PERSON LIVING 500 YEARS AGO,
# YOU'D HAVE NO REAL RIGHTS OR FREEDOMS.

IF you bought a potion from a travelling salesperson who had promised it would stop you going deaf but you ended up losing your hair as well as your hearing, there would be nothing you could do.

c

IF you were working as a coal miner and the conditions down the pit were so dangerous that lethal accidents happened on a regular basis, there would be nothing that you could do.

e

IF you thought that the way your community was being bullied by the local lord was wrong and you started to give speeches saying so in the town square, the lord could have you locked up and tortured and there would be nothing you could do.

TODAY, the Trade Descriptions Act (1968) would save you from this type of injustice. The Act says that it is illegal to mislead or lie to consumers. The salesperson would be breaking the law with his false claims and you would get your money back (but not your hair!).

d

TODAY, the Health and Safety Act (1974) would protect you. This Act states that employers have to take care of the safety of all those who work for them. The owner of the mine would be breaking the law and could be prosecuted, fined or even imprisoned.

TODAY, The Universal Declaration of Human Rights (UDHR) would protect you. Article 19 states: "Everyone has the right to freedom of opinion and expression." This means that anybody trying to stop you speaking your mind is breaking the law.

f

LEARN MORE/GET INVOLVED: www.protectthehuman/udhr.com

---

**ACTIVITY**

**IN PAIRS**

**ART ACTION**
Choose one of the situations from above and imagine you are campaigning for change 500 years ago. Use any of the Art Action activities to create work to support your campaign. You have 10 MINUTES.
Feed back your ideas to the class.

TICK TOCK

# SNAKE OIL

# WHY DO WE SAY HISTORY AND NOT HERSTORY?

MANY ACADEMICS TODAY ARE LOOKING AT HOW HISTORY HAS FOCUSED ON THE ROLE OF MEN THROUGH TIME AND EXCLUDED THE ROLE OF WOMEN. HISTORY HAS TENDED TO BE CONCERNED MORE WITH MONARCHS, SOLDIERS AND POLITICAL LEADERS (ALMOST ALL OF WHOM WERE MEN) AND TO IGNORE WOMEN'S CONTRIBUTION TO THE DEVELOPMENT OF ANY HUMAN SOCIETY.

AT EVERY STAGE OF YOUR ACTIVE CITIZENSHIP WORK IT'S IMPORTANT NOT TO EXCLUDE ANYONE BECAUSE OF GENDER, RELIGION, RACE, SEXUALITY OR ABILITY.

FOR EXAMPLE: YOUR CAMPAIGN MAY INVOLVE HOLDING AN EVENT FOR MEMBERS OF THE LOCAL COMMUNITY TO ATTEND. IF YOU DO NOT PROVIDE CRÈCHE FACILITIES THEN YOU HAVE JUST EXCLUDED ALL SINGLE MOTHERS FROM BEING ABLE TO COME. IF YOU SERVE BACON SANDWICHES AT THE EVENT, YOU WILL EXCLUDE JEWISH, HINDU, MUSLIM AND VEGETARIAN MEMBERS OF THE COMMUNITY FROM EATING. IN THE SAME WAY, SOMEBODY IN A WHEELCHAIR MAY HAVE THE BEST IDEAS TO CONTRIBUTE TO YOUR EVENT BUT, WITHOUT WHEELCHAIR ACCESS, YOU'LL NEVER HEAR THEM!

ACTIVE CITIZENSHIP IS ALL ABOUT INCLUSION.

> THOSE WHO CANNOT REMEMBER THE PAST ARE CONDEMNED TO REPEAT IT.
>
> GEORGE SANTAYANA (1863-1952)
> PHILOSOPHER, POET AND NOVELIST.

# CANARY IN A COAL MINE

IN THE EARLY DAYS OF COAL MINING AND RIGHT UP UNTIL THE MID-20TH CENTURY, MINERS USED CANARY BIRDS IN CAGES TO WARN THEM IF POISONOUS GASES SUCH AS METHANE HAD BEEN RELEASED INTO THE MINE. BECAUSE CANARIES ARE MORE SENSITIVE THAN HUMANS TO GASES, THEY WERE AN EARLY WARNING SYSTEM. IF THE CANARY STOPPED SINGING, THE MINERS WOULD RUN!

# FAKING BEAUTY

THE USE OF DIGITAL AIRBRUSHING IN THE BEAUTY INDUSTRY TESTS THE BOUNDARIES OF THE LAW. MANY PEOPLE ARGUE THAT THIS MISREPRESENTS THE PRODUCTS, IN ADDITION TO PUTTING UNFAIR PRESSURE ON ORDINARY PEOPLE, MAKING THEM FEEL INADEQUATE ABOUT THEIR LOOKS. A RECENT WEB-BASED CAMPAIGN FOCUSED ON AN ADVERT FOR SKIN CREAM THAT USED AN AIRBRUSHED PICTURE OF AN ELDERLY MODEL. SOME 700 PEOPLE CONTACTED THE ADVERTISING STANDARDS AUTHORITY, WHICH RULED AGAINST THE ADVERT.

SPOT THE DIFFERENCE

LEARN MORE/GET INVOLVED:
www.realwomen.org.uk
Advertising Standards Authority:
www.asa.org.uk

# FREEDOM OF SPEECH

SPEAKERS' CORNER IN LONDON'S HYDE PARK IS FAMOUS FOR BEING A PLACE WHERE PEOPLE CAN GO AND SPEAK THEIR MIND. THE TRADITION OF FREE SPEECH AT SPEAKERS' CORNER MAY DERIVE FROM THE FACT THAT BETWEEN THE 16TH AND 18TH CENTURIES THE TYBURN GALLOWS STOOD ON THIS SITE, WHERE LONDON CRIMINALS WERE HANGED. CONDEMNED PEOPLE WERE ALLOWED TO GIVE A LAST SPEECH BEFORE 'DANCING THE TYBURN JIG'.

FAMOUS THINKERS WHO HAVE SPOKEN THEIR MINDS AT SPEAKERS' CORNER HAVE INCLUDED GEORGE ORWELL, KARL MARX, VLADIMIR LENIN & WILLIAM MORRIS.

## 3 How did we win the rights and freedoms that we have today?

There are **TWO MAIN WAYS** that change can happen;

# WITHIN THE PROCESS OF GOVERNMENT AND
# OUTSIDE THE PROCESS OF GOVERNMENT.

## WITHIN THE PROCESS OF GOVERNMENT:

1. In Parliament through your democratically elected MPs. ⭐a

2. Through the work of pressure groups putting pressure on MPs.

3. Through the work of individual parliamentary campaigners.

4. Through a referendum, where the whole population can vote on a single issue. (The UK voted on whether the country should join the European Common Market in 1975.)

5. Through the law courts.

6. Through your local councils.

7. Through your school council.

## OUTSIDE THE PROCESS OF GOVERNMENT:

1. Through grassroots movements which often use demonstrations, mass petitions, protests and rallies. ⭐b ⭐c

2. Through movements led by the working class.

3. Through different sorts of campaigns.

4. Through great and powerful speeches.

5. Even books, films, television programmes, poems, a powerful picture or a moving song can bring about change. ⭐d ⭐e

6. Today, modern information and communication technology is opening up new and powerful ways to bring about change. ⭐f

OFTEN NEW RIGHTS AND FREEDOMS HAVE BEEN WON BY A MIXTURE OF THE ABOVE. FOR EXAMPLE, A CAMPAIGN FOR CHANGE CAN START AS A GRASSROOTS MOVEMENT AND THEN BECOME A PROCESS WITHIN GOVERNMENT.

## 4 What are the prominent struggles of today?

### THERE ARE MANY STRUGGLES FOR RIGHTS & FREEDOMS THAT STILL EXIST TODAY.

The Toolkit covers a wide range of issues and helps you to identify and connect to what you feel most strongly about.

### THE ISSUES CAN BE DIVIDED IN THE FOLLOWING WAY:

**SCHOOL**
e.g. access to 21st-century technology, bullying, how disruptive students are handled.

**LOCAL**
e.g. standard of housing, protecting a youth club from closure, anti-social behaviour.

**NATIONAL**
e.g. unemployment, the energy crisis, poverty, racial disharmony. ⭐g

**GLOBAL**
e.g. war, misuse of natural resources, abuse of human rights, global warming. ⭐h

### GROUP ACTIVITY
### NEWSPAPER GAME

You have **FIVE MINUTES** for your group to go through newspapers and find as many stories as possible that fit under each of these headings:

**SCHOOL ISSUES;**
**LOCAL ISSUES;**
**NATIONAL ISSUES;**
**GLOBAL ISSUES.** *TICK TOCK*

Feed back your answers to the class.

## HELP THEM WORK FOR YOU

**YOUR** DEMOCRATICALLY ELECTED REPRESENTATIVES WORK FOR YOU BUT IT'S IMPOSSIBLE FOR THEM TO DO ANYTHING ABOUT YOUR IDEAS FOR CHANGE IF YOU DON'T EVER TELL THEM WHAT THEY ARE. TO FIND OUT WHO REPRESENTS YOU, TYPE YOUR POSTAL CODE INTO THE SITES BELOW. AN ANGRY LETTER SIMPLY SAYING "DON'T CLOSE OUR LOCAL SWIMMING POOL" ISN'T GOING TO GET YOU VERY FAR. ON THE OTHER HAND, A CLEAR, POLITE AND DETAILED LETTER, WHICH CITES STATISTICS AS PART OF A BALANCED ARGUMENT, CAN HAVE A REAL IMPACT.

*(a)*

LEARN MORE/GET INVOLVED:
www.writetothem.com
http://findyourmp.parliament.uk

## THE WORLD'S LONGEST PETITION

**THE** WORLD'S LONGEST PETITION RECEIVED OVER 62 MILLION SIGNATURES FROM 11/07/08 TO 14/08/08. STARTED IN PAKISTAN, THE YEH HUM NAHEEN FOUNDATION ASKED PEOPLE TO SIGN IF THEY AGREED WITH THE STATEMENT: SAY NO TO TERRORISM.

*(b)*

**THE** SONG *STRANGE FRUIT* BY BILLIE HOLLIDAY HAD A GREAT INFLUENCE ON THE CIVIL RIGHTS MOVEMENT IN AMERICA. WHAT KIND OF FRUIT IS SHE TALKING ABOUT?

*(d)*

**IN 1791,** AN ENGLISH POLITICAL PHILOSOPHER CALLED THOMAS PAINE WROTE A 79-PAGE PAMPHLET CALLED *THE RIGHTS OF MAN*. ITS IDEAS OF REPUBLICANISM AND LIBERALISM WERE SO POWERFUL THAT THE POOR OF ENGLAND POOLED TOGETHER THEIR PENNIES TO BUY COPIES. SOON, IT WAS A CAPITAL OFFENCE TO BE FOUND IN POSSESSION OF THE PAMPHLET. THIS DIDN'T STOP *THE RIGHTS OF MAN* GOING ON TO CHANGE HISTORY, HAVING A CENTRAL INFLUENCE ON THE FRENCH AND AMERICAN REVOLUTIONS.

*(e)*

# CHEW ON THIS!

*(g)*

**THE** UK SPENDS AROUND £150 MILLION A YEAR (ENOUGH TO BUILD THREE HOSPITALS) ON CLEANING CHEWING GUM FROM OUR STREETS. IF THEY WEREN'T CLEANED YOU WOULDN'T BE GOING ANYWHERE FAST!

THIS IS JUST ONE OF THE 'STICKY' ISSUES IN YOUR NEIGHBOURHOOD THAT COULD INSPIRE YOU TO LAUNCH A CAMPAIGN.

LEARN MORE/GET INVOLVED:
www.chewinggumactiongroup.org.uk

May the force be with you....

...and also with you...

**A VIRAL** E-MAIL LED TO 390,000 PEOPLE STATING THEIR RELIGION AS JEDI ON THE 2001 ENGLAND AND WALES CENSUS FORM. EVEN THOUGH THIS DID NOT MAKE THE *STAR WARS* CREATION AN OFFICIAL RELIGION, THE CENSUS BOARD HAD TO CREATE A SPECIAL CODE TO DEAL WITH THE VOLUME OF PEOPLE WHO DECIDED THEY RATHER LIKED THE IDEA OF YODA BEING THEIR SPIRITUAL LEADER!

*(f)*

**ONE** OF THE MOST DRAMATIC SERIES OF DEMONSTRATIONS AND RALLIES TO HAVE HAPPENED IN THE 21ST CENTURY SO FAR TOOK PLACE IN ARGENTINA BETWEEN 2001 AND 2002. AN ECONOMIC CRISIS HAD CRIPPLED THE COUNTRY, THE BANKS LITERALLY HAD NO MONEY, SO PEOPLE BARTERED TO GET BY. ALL TYPES OF PEOPLE FILLED THE STREETS, BANGING POTS AND PANS IN NON-VIOLENT PROTEST. THEY HAD A SLOGAN ABOUT THE COUNTRY'S LEADERS: *¡QUE SE VAYAN TODOS!* ("ALL OF THEM MUST GO!") THE PRESIDENT RESIGNED AND THE PARLIAMENT REPLACED HIM BUT THE PEOPLE WERE STILL NOT HAPPY AND STAYED IN THE STREETS. THE PARLIAMENT TRIED PUTTING IN THREE PRESIDENTS WITHOUT SUCCESS. EVENTUALLY A GENERAL ELECTION WAS HELD AND THE PEOPLE STOPPED DEMONSTRATING ONCE THERE WAS SOMEONE IN POWER IN WHOM THEY HAD FAITH. NOW THAT'S PEOPLE POWER!

"ALL OF THEM MUST GO!"

¡QUE SE VAYAN TODOS!

¡QUE SE VAYAN TODOS!

CLANG!

BANG!

*(c)*

**IN** JANUARY 2010, TWO YEAR 10 STUDENTS WON AN AWARD AS YOUNG GLOBAL EDUCATION CAMPAIGNERS OF THE YEAR. THEIR CAMPAIGNING FILM, CONTRASTING BRITISH CHILDREN'S EXPERIENCE OF SCHOOL WITH THAT OF CHILDREN IN GHANA, WILL BE SHOWN ON LARGE SCREENS DURING THE LONDON OLYMPICS OF 2012.

LEARN MORE/GET INVOLVED:
www.sendmyfriend.org
www.joinlgoal.org

EXAMPLES OF LARGE CAMPAIGNING ORGANIZATIONS OR RESOURCES THAT COVER MANY DIFFERENT GLOBAL ISSUES:

www.peopleandplanet.org
www.actionaid.org.uk
www.newint.org
www.amnesty.org.uk
www.oxfam.org

*(h)*

# A SHORT HISTORY of BIG CHANGE *thus far . . . . .*

## 5 How do struggles for rights and freedoms start?

STRUGGLES FOR RIGHTS AND FREEDOMS ALWAYS **START WITH A SENSE OF INJUSTICE.** SOMEWHERE, SOMEONE DECIDES THAT PEOPLE ARE BEING MISTREATED AND FEELS PASSIONATE ABOUT IT.

HE OR SHE HAS AN **IDEA** ABOUT WHAT TO DO

**TO END THAT INJUSTICE.**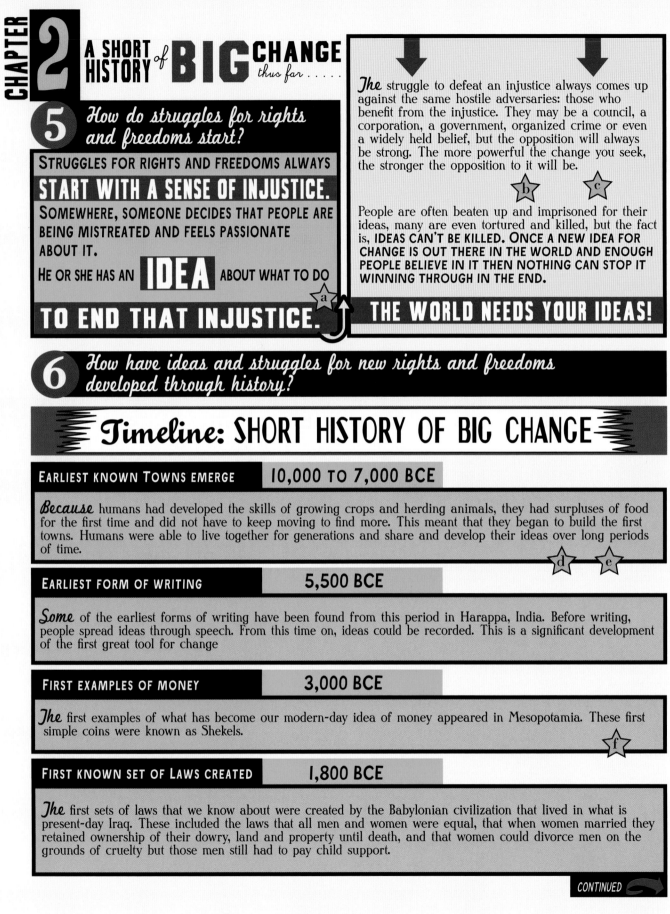

The struggle to defeat an injustice always comes up against the same hostile adversaries: those who benefit from the injustice. They may be a council, a corporation, a government, organized crime or even a widely held belief, but the opposition will always be strong. The more powerful the change you seek, the stronger the opposition to it will be.

People are often beaten up and imprisoned for their ideas, many are even tortured and killed, but the fact is, IDEAS CAN'T BE KILLED. ONCE A NEW IDEA FOR CHANGE IS OUT THERE IN THE WORLD AND ENOUGH PEOPLE BELIEVE IN IT THEN NOTHING CAN STOP IT WINNING THROUGH IN THE END.

**THE WORLD NEEDS YOUR IDEAS!**

## 6 How have ideas and struggles for new rights and freedoms developed through history?

## Timeline: SHORT HISTORY OF BIG CHANGE

**EARLIEST KNOWN TOWNS EMERGE** — 10,000 TO 7,000 BCE

*Because* humans had developed the skills of growing crops and herding animals, they had surpluses of food for the first time and did not have to keep moving to find more. This meant that they began to build the first towns. Humans were able to live together for generations and share and develop their ideas over long periods of time.

**EARLIEST FORM OF WRITING** — 5,500 BCE

*Some* of the earliest forms of writing have been found from this period in Harappa, India. Before writing, people spread ideas through speech. From this time on, ideas could be recorded. This is a significant development of the first great tool for change

**FIRST EXAMPLES OF MONEY** — 3,000 BCE

*The* first examples of what has become our modern-day idea of money appeared in Mesopotamia. These first simple coins were known as Shekels.

**FIRST KNOWN SET OF LAWS CREATED** — 1,800 BCE

*The* first sets of laws that we know about were created by the Babylonian civilization that lived in what is present-day Iraq. These included the laws that all men and women were equal, that when women married they retained ownership of their dowry, land and property until death, and that women could divorce men on the grounds of cruelty but those men still had to pay child support.

CONTINUED

# GODDESS WORSHIP

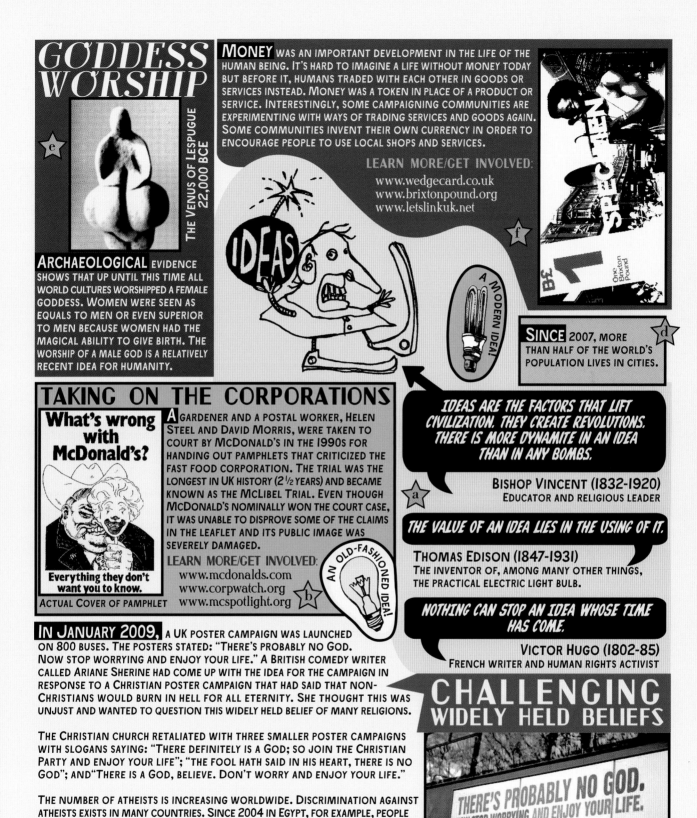

The Venus of Lespugue 22,000 BCE

e

**ARCHAEOLOGICAL** EVIDENCE SHOWS THAT UP UNTIL THIS TIME ALL WORLD CULTURES WORSHIPPED A FEMALE GODDESS. WOMEN WERE SEEN AS EQUALS TO MEN OR EVEN SUPERIOR TO MEN BECAUSE WOMEN HAD THE MAGICAL ABILITY TO GIVE BIRTH. THE WORSHIP OF A MALE GOD IS A RELATIVELY RECENT IDEA FOR HUMANITY.

**MONEY** WAS AN IMPORTANT DEVELOPMENT IN THE LIFE OF THE HUMAN BEING. IT'S HARD TO IMAGINE A LIFE WITHOUT MONEY TODAY BUT BEFORE IT, HUMANS TRADED WITH EACH OTHER IN GOODS OR SERVICES INSTEAD. MONEY WAS A TOKEN IN PLACE OF A PRODUCT OR SERVICE. INTERESTINGLY, SOME CAMPAIGNING COMMUNITIES ARE EXPERIMENTING WITH WAYS OF TRADING SERVICES AND GOODS AGAIN. SOME COMMUNITIES INVENT THEIR OWN CURRENCY IN ORDER TO ENCOURAGE PEOPLE TO USE LOCAL SHOPS AND SERVICES.

LEARN MORE/GET INVOLVED:
www.wedgecard.co.uk
www.brixtonpound.org
www.letslinkuk.net

f

IDEAS

A MODERN IDEA!

**SINCE** 2007, MORE THAN HALF OF THE WORLD'S POPULATION LIVES IN CITIES.

d

## TAKING ON THE CORPORATIONS

**What's wrong with McDonald's?**

Everything they don't want you to know.

ACTUAL COVER OF PAMPHLET

**A** GARDENER AND A POSTAL WORKER, HELEN STEEL AND DAVID MORRIS, WERE TAKEN TO COURT BY MCDONALD'S IN THE 1990S FOR HANDING OUT PAMPHLETS THAT CRITICIZED THE FAST FOOD CORPORATION. THE TRIAL WAS THE LONGEST IN UK HISTORY (2 ½ YEARS) AND BECAME KNOWN AS THE MCLIBEL TRIAL. EVEN THOUGH MCDONALD'S NOMINALLY WON THE COURT CASE, IT WAS UNABLE TO DISPROVE SOME OF THE CLAIMS IN THE LEAFLET AND ITS PUBLIC IMAGE WAS SEVERELY DAMAGED.

LEARN MORE/GET INVOLVED:
www.mcdonalds.com
www.corpwatch.org
www.mcspotlight.org

b

AN OLD-FASHIONED IDEA!

*IDEAS ARE THE FACTORS THAT LIFT CIVILIZATION. THEY CREATE REVOLUTIONS. THERE IS MORE DYNAMITE IN AN IDEA THAN IN ANY BOMBS.*

a

**BISHOP VINCENT (1832-1920)**
EDUCATOR AND RELIGIOUS LEADER

*THE VALUE OF AN IDEA LIES IN THE USING OF IT.*

**THOMAS EDISON (1847-1931)**
THE INVENTOR OF, AMONG MANY OTHER THINGS, THE PRACTICAL ELECTRIC LIGHT BULB.

*NOTHING CAN STOP AN IDEA WHOSE TIME HAS COME.*

**VICTOR HUGO (1802-85)**
FRENCH WRITER AND HUMAN RIGHTS ACTIVIST

## CHALLENGING WIDELY HELD BELIEFS

**IN JANUARY 2009,** A UK POSTER CAMPAIGN WAS LAUNCHED ON 800 BUSES. THE POSTERS STATED: "THERE'S PROBABLY NO GOD. NOW STOP WORRYING AND ENJOY YOUR LIFE." A BRITISH COMEDY WRITER CALLED ARIANE SHERINE HAD COME UP WITH THE IDEA FOR THE CAMPAIGN IN RESPONSE TO A CHRISTIAN POSTER CAMPAIGN THAT HAD SAID THAT NON-CHRISTIANS WOULD BURN IN HELL FOR ALL ETERNITY. SHE THOUGHT THIS WAS UNJUST AND WANTED TO QUESTION THIS WIDELY HELD BELIEF OF MANY RELIGIONS.

THE CHRISTIAN CHURCH RETALIATED WITH THREE SMALLER POSTER CAMPAIGNS WITH SLOGANS SAYING: "THERE DEFINITELY IS A GOD; SO JOIN THE CHRISTIAN PARTY AND ENJOY YOUR LIFE"; "THE FOOL HATH SAID IN HIS HEART, THERE IS NO GOD"; AND "THERE IS A GOD, BELIEVE. DON'T WORRY AND ENJOY YOUR LIFE."

THE NUMBER OF ATHEISTS IS INCREASING WORLDWIDE. DISCRIMINATION AGAINST ATHEISTS EXISTS IN MANY COUNTRIES. SINCE 2004 IN EGYPT, FOR EXAMPLE, PEOPLE WHO DO NOT CALL THEMSELVES MUSLIM, CHRISTIAN OR JEWISH ON THEIR IDENTITY CARDS ARE DENIED BASIC HUMAN RIGHTS. THEY HAVE NO ACCESS TO MEDICAL TREATMENT, CANNOT VOTE OR BE EMPLOYED, AND CANNOT EVEN WITHDRAW MONEY FROM THEIR OWN BANK ACCOUNTS.

c

THERE'S PROBABLY NO GOD. NOW STOP WORRYING AND ENJOY YOUR LIFE.

# CHAPTER 2

## A SHORT HISTORY of BIG CHANGE
*thus far.....*

## Timeline: SHORT HISTORY OF BIG CHANGE

### IDEA OF DEMOCRACY DEVELOPED — 507 BCE

*The* Greeks became the second nation that we know of (after the Hebrews), to have books that bound together their cultural and historical identity. These were the two epics *The Iliad* and *The Odyssey.*
In the greatest of the Greek cities, Athens, in 507 BCE, the leader Cleisthenes developed the idea of involving the people in their own governing. This became known as Demos (government by the people), which is the basis for the democracy that we live by in the UK today. In the early Greek democracy, all citizens had the right to speak about how their country should be run (though women and slaves did not qualify as citizens). The views that won the majority were the views that were accepted.

### FIRST KNOWN PROPAGANDA — 1095 CE ⓐ ⓑ

*A* huge Islamic army from Turkey took control of Palestine. As a result, the Christian world felt threatened. Pope Urban II saw this as an opportunity to unify all of the Christian nations by gathering them together to fight for the lands of Jesus Christ's birth. He may have used one of the first examples of propaganda to do this by sending out messages across Europe saying that the invading army were disembowelling Christian prisoners, desecrating churches and raping women. This had a strong effect on people's emotions and soon the first of many Crusade wars had started.

### THE SIGNING OF THE MAGNA CARTA — 1215

*In* England, powerful lords and barons confronted King John, who had been taxing them very heavily. They forced King John to sign a document called the Magna Carta. This put some controls on the King and was the first time that a king's power had been in some way moderated by the will of the people. This also marks the beginning of Parliament in the UK.

### THE BIRTH OF THE RENAISSANCE — 1350

*There* was a cultural and intellectual rebirth in Europe, partly as a result of contact with Chinese, Indian and Arabic cultures. Many ideas were learned from this, including the study of the Greek philosophers, new artistic styles and developments in science and mathematics. Most importantly, Europeans finally learned how to make paper of quality and to print books properly, even though the Chinese had been doing this for a thousand years! This period of learning and cultural growth was called the Renaissance. ⓒ ⓓ

### BOOKS BREAK THE POPE'S AUTHORITY — 1517

*Because* of the freer sharing of ideas in Europe due to the Renaissance and the flourishing of book printing, ideas began to spread that questioned the authority of the Popes as leaders of the Christian church. The most effective campaigner was a former monk in Germany called Martin Luther, who used the printing of his books to great effect. Within 60 years, most of Northern Europe had split from the power of the Pope and developed a new form of Christianity called Protestantism, based on Luther's ideas. This is an early example of how Europeans had their lives changed by the printed word.

---

## IN GROUPS

**MYSTERY GAME:** You go back 50 years in time. Describe to someone your age what a difference computers/the internet/the web are going to make to their lives. Make sure they gain a clear idea of what these technologies will actually be.

## ART ACTION
Use any of your Art Action techniques to promote the technology of the future. Of course, because you don't know what the future is, feel free to invent it now! Feed back your ideas to the class.

CONTINUED ➡

# FEEL BUT DON'T THINK

**POPE** URBAN II'S STORIES MAY NOT HAVE BEEN TRUE BUT THEY CERTAINLY AFFECTED EVERYONE WHO HEARD THEM.

ONE OF THE MOST FAMOUS EXAMPLES OF PROPAGANDA COMES FROM THE 1930S WHEN ADOLF HITLER MANAGED TO TURN THE VAST MAJORITY OF THE GERMAN PEOPLE INTO ANTISEMITES USING PROPAGANDA TECHNIQUES INCLUDING FILMS, POSTERS, BOOKS, PAMPHLETS AND RADIO BROADCASTS.

> *THE ART OF PROPAGANDA CONSISTS PRECISELY IN BEING ABLE TO AWAKEN THE IMAGINATION OF THE PUBLIC THROUGH AN APPEAL TO THEIR FEELINGS... THE BROAD MASSES OF THE PEOPLE ARE... A VACILLATING CROWD OF HUMAN CHILDREN WHO ARE CONSTANTLY WAVERING BETWEEN ONE IDEA AND ANOTHER... SUCH BEING THE CASE, ALL EFFECTIVE PROPAGANDA MUST BE CONFINED TO A FEW BARE ESSENTIALS AND THOSE MUST BE EXPRESSED AS FAR AS POSSIBLE IN STEREOTYPED FORMULAS.*

**ADOLF HITLER** IN HIS BOOK *MEIN KAMPF.*

IT'S INTERESTING FOR ACTIVE CITIZENS TO COMPARE THE TECHNIQUES USED BY TODAY'S ADVERTISING INDUSTRY AND THE IDEAS DESCRIBED ABOVE.

## THE LEGENDARY POLYMATH

**ONE** OF THE GREATEST FIGURES FROM THE RENAISSANCE WAS LEONARDO DA VINCI. HE WAS A POLYMATH, WHICH IS SOMEONE WHO IS AN EXPERT IN MANY FIELDS. HIS SKILLS INCLUDED BEING AN: ARTIST, SCULPTOR, ARCHITECT, MUSICIAN, SCIENTIST, MATHEMATICIAN, ENGINEER, INVENTOR, ANATOMIST, GEOLOGIST, BOTANIST AND WRITER! IT'S HARD TO EXPLAIN HOW ONE MAN WAS ABLE TO CREATE SO MUCH WORK OF BEAUTY AND BRILLIANCE IN ONE LIFETIME. HIS PAINTINGS *THE MONA LISA* AND *THE LAST SUPPER* ARE AMONG THE MOST FAMOUS AND MOST REPRODUCED PAINTINGS IN HISTORY. AMONG HIS MANY INVENTIONS, HE CAME UP WITH IDEAS FOR HELICOPTERS, TANKS AND FOR HARNESSING SOLAR ENERGY.

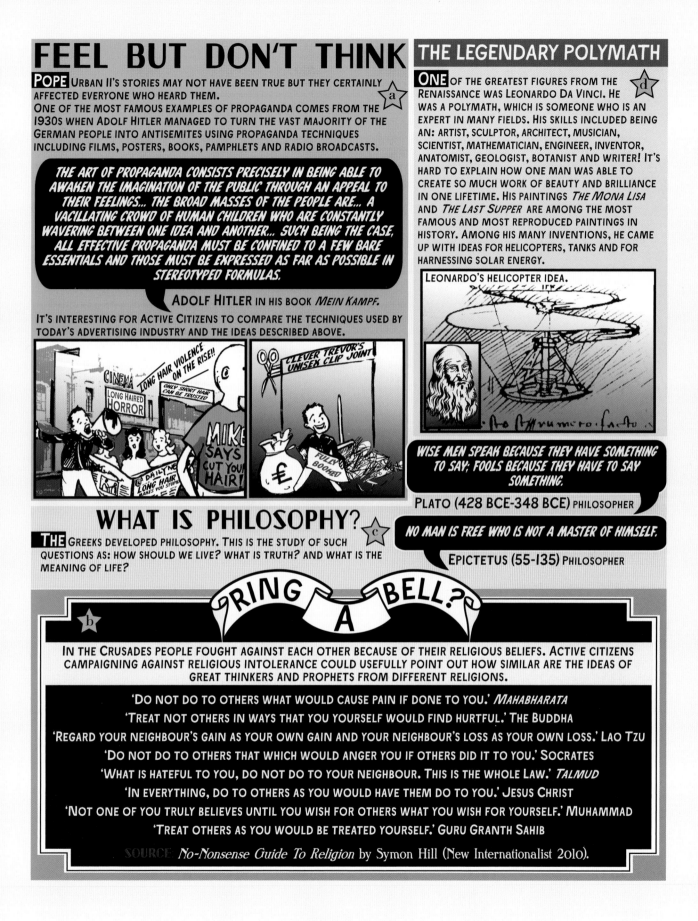

LEONARDO'S HELICOPTER IDEA.

> *WISE MEN SPEAK BECAUSE THEY HAVE SOMETHING TO SAY; FOOLS BECAUSE THEY HAVE TO SAY SOMETHING.*

**PLATO** (428 BCE-348 BCE) PHILOSOPHER

> *NO MAN IS FREE WHO IS NOT A MASTER OF HIMSELF.*

**EPICTETUS** (55-135) PHILOSOPHER

## WHAT IS PHILOSOPHY?

**THE** GREEKS DEVELOPED PHILOSOPHY. THIS IS THE STUDY OF SUCH QUESTIONS AS: HOW SHOULD WE LIVE? WHAT IS TRUTH? AND WHAT IS THE MEANING OF LIFE?

## RING A BELL?

IN THE CRUSADES PEOPLE FOUGHT AGAINST EACH OTHER BECAUSE OF THEIR RELIGIOUS BELIEFS. ACTIVE CITIZENS CAMPAIGNING AGAINST RELIGIOUS INTOLERANCE COULD USEFULLY POINT OUT HOW SIMILAR ARE THE IDEAS OF GREAT THINKERS AND PROPHETS FROM DIFFERENT RELIGIONS.

'DO NOT DO TO OTHERS WHAT WOULD CAUSE PAIN IF DONE TO YOU.' *MAHABHARATA*

'TREAT NOT OTHERS IN WAYS THAT YOU YOURSELF WOULD FIND HURTFUL.' THE BUDDHA

'REGARD YOUR NEIGHBOUR'S GAIN AS YOUR OWN GAIN AND YOUR NEIGHBOUR'S LOSS AS YOUR OWN LOSS.' LAO TZU

'DO NOT DO TO OTHERS THAT WHICH WOULD ANGER YOU IF OTHERS DID IT TO YOU.' SOCRATES

'WHAT IS HATEFUL TO YOU, DO NOT DO TO YOUR NEIGHBOUR. THIS IS THE WHOLE LAW.' *TALMUD*

'IN EVERYTHING, DO TO OTHERS AS YOU WOULD HAVE THEM DO TO YOU.' JESUS CHRIST

'NOT ONE OF YOU TRULY BELIEVES UNTIL YOU WISH FOR OTHERS WHAT YOU WISH FOR YOURSELF.' MUHAMMAD

'TREAT OTHERS AS YOU WOULD BE TREATED YOURSELF.' GURU GRANTH SAHIB

SOURCE: *No-Nonsense Guide To Religion* by Symon Hill (New Internationalist 2010).

# CHAPTER 2

## A SHORT HISTORY of BIG CHANGE *thus far* . . . . .

## Timeline: SHORT HISTORY OF BIG CHANGE

### BRITAIN BECOMES A REPUBLIC — 1641-51

*Because* the power of the Christian Church had been diminished, European rulers began to think that they represented God on earth instead, including the British King, Charles I. A group of rich Protestant landowners used new printing technology to spread their ideas of disgust at the King and this led to a civil war. King Charles was beheaded in 1649.

The leaders of this revolution changed Britain into a republic, which meant that the country was ruled by the people and not by any king or queen. However, this still meant only rich and powerful people ran the country, not ordinary men and women.

### MONARCHY REINSTATED IN BRITAIN — 1660

*Charles* II became King of Britain and the republic ended.

### THE BILL OF RIGHTS UK — 1689

*Britain's* Parliament succeeded in creating a Bill of Rights that meant that the ruling king or queen could never dissolve Parliament and take over ruling the country. Nor could they raise taxes without the agreement of Parliament. This remains the case today.

### THE AMERICAN WAR OF INDEPENDENCE — 1776

*The* American War of Independence led to the Declaration of Independence, which stated that "all men are created equal" and all have the right to "life, liberty and the pursuit of happiness".

### THE FRENCH REVOLUTION — 1789

*The* French king at the time, Louis XVI, was one of the most decadent rulers in Europe. There was an uprising of the French people, which brought about the end of the royal family in France and the establishment of a republic, which exists to this day. The mass movement used one of the first campaigning slogans in history:
*Liberté, Égalité, Fraternité,* which means 'Liberty, Equality and Brotherhood'.  〔b〕 〔c〕

### THE INDUSTRIAL REVOLUTION — 1790

*New* developments such as the steam engine and a national system of canals resulted in Britain's Industrial Revolution. Factories were built across the country and production sharply increased. All of this was fuelled mainly by coal. Britain became a mighty Empire with the new technologies giving them supremacy over most other countries. 〔d〕 〔e〕

### THE REFORM ACT — 1832

*The* Industrial Revolution changed the economic and social landscape of Britain. Relatively small towns suddenly became huge as more and more people poured in to work in the factories. There was also a vast increase in the wealth of those people profiting from new business. The electoral system in the country did not reflect these changes as towns with small populations had significant representation in Parliament whereas some large and prosperous towns had none. Through campaigns and rallies across the country, the government was put under pressure to reform the electoral process. The Reform Act was passed in 1832. This increased the number of people who could vote in elections by around 60%. Because a voter had to have property worth £10 or more and had to be a man, this excluded the working class and all women. This led to the growth of the Chartist Movement and eventually the Suffragette movement.

CONTINUED

# SHORT AND SHARP

**SLOGANS** HAVE BECOME AN IMPORTANT TOOL FOR ACTIVE CITIZENS TO USE IN THEIR CAMPAIGNS. THEY ARE A VERY EFFECTIVE WAY TO UNITE PEOPLE AND ARE OFTEN SUNG OR CHANTED ON PROTESTS AND DEMONSTRATIONS, USING SHORT AND CATCHY PHRASES THAT SOMETIMES RHYME AND OFTEN USE ALLITERATION. SLOGANS ARE ALSO WORN ON BADGES OR T-SHIRTS OR PAINTED ON BANNERS. FAMOUS EXAMPLES INCLUDE: DEEDS NOT WORDS (VOTES FOR WOMEN), POWER TO THE PEOPLE (WORKERS' RIGHTS), BAN THE BOMB (NUCLEAR DISARMAMENT), OUR BODIES OUR SELVES (WOMEN'S RIGHTS), THE PEOPLE UNITED WILL NEVER BE DEFEATED (WORKERS' RIGHTS) AND MAKE LOVE NOT WAR (ANTI-WAR CAMPAIGNS). SLOGANS ARE ALSO USED BY THE ADVERTISING INDUSTRY AND IN THE SPORTS WORLD.

# WOMEN AT THE COALFACE

**THE** INDUSTRIAL REVOLUTION MEANT THAT WOMEN, MEN AND CHILDREN WERE NEEDED IN THEIR HUNDREDS OF THOUSANDS TO WORK IN THE FACTORIES AND MINES. THE WORKING CONDITIONS WERE EXTREMELY HARSH. PEOPLE WORKED LONG HOURS IN DANGEROUS AND UNHEALTHY CONDITIONS WHILE BEING PAID LOW WAGES. WOMEN AND CHILDREN WORKED DOWN THE MINES ALONGSIDE MEN. WOMEN WHO WERE PREGNANT WOULD BE EXPECTED TO KEEP WORKING EVEN WHEN THEY WERE EIGHT-AND-A-HALF MONTHS PREGNANT AND SOME ACTUALLY GAVE BIRTH DOWN THE MINES.

# THE POWER OF WEAPONS

**IT'S** IMPORTANT FOR ACTIVE CITIZENS TO CONSIDER THAT A KEY WAY IN WHICH ONE COUNTRY GAINS POWER OVER ANOTHER IS THROUGH WEAPONS.

THERE ARE MANY CAMPAIGNS THAT SEEK TO CONTROL THE DEVELOPMENT AND USE OF MODERN MILITARY TECHNOLOGY.

LEARN MORE/GET INVOLVED:
www.caat.org.uk
www.cnduk.org
www.amnesty.org.uk

# DIGGERS AND LEVELLERS

**DURING** THIS BRIEF PERIOD OF REPUBLICANISM, OTHER STRUGGLES FOR RIGHTS AND FREEDOMS EMERGED IN BRITAIN. TWO OF THE MOST FAMOUS MOVEMENTS WERE THE DIGGERS AND THE LEVELLERS. BOTH THESE GROUPS WANTED A MORE EGALITARIAN SOCIETY, WHICH MEANS THAT THEY BELIEVED IN ALL PEOPLE BEING TREATED EQUALLY AND MORE FAIRLY. THESE ARE SOME OF THE EARLIEST EXAMPLES OF DISSENTERS, PEOPLE WHO DISAGREE WITH THE MAJORITY VIEW. IN THIS CASE, THEY HAD DIFFERENT IDEAS ABOUT HOW PEOPLE SHOULD LIVE TOGETHER AND HOW SOCIETY SHOULD BE GOVERNED. BOTH THESE GROUPS USED PRINTING, PAMPHLET MAKING AND PETITIONS TO ADVANCE THEIR IDEAS. DUE TO THEIR LOW COST AND EASE OF PRODUCTION, PAMPHLETS HAVE OFTEN BEEN USED TO POPULARIZE POLITICAL OR RELIGIOUS IDEAS.

*A DECLARATION FROM THE POOR OPPRESSED PEOPLE OF ENGLAND, DIRECTED TO ALL THOSE THAT CALL THEMSELVES, OR ARE CALLED LORDS OF MANORS, THROUGH THIS NATION; THAT HAVE BEGUN TO CUT, OR THAT THROUGH FEAR AND COVETOUSNESS, DO INTEND TO CUT DOWN THE WOODS AND TREES THAT GROW UPON THE COMMONS AND WASTE LAND.*

*PRINTED IN THE YEAR 1649.*

FOR ACTIVE CITIZENS TODAY, PETITIONS, PAMPHLETS AND PUBLICATIONS ARE CENTRAL TOOLS IN CAMPAIGNING FOR CHANGE. MUCH OF THIS CAN BE DONE MORE EFFECTIVELY BY USING 21ST-CENTURY TECHNOLOGY.

A
DECLARATION
FROM THE
Poor oppressed People
OF
ENGLAND,
DIRECTED
To all that call themselves, or are called
Lords of Manors,
through this NATION;
That have begun to cut, or that through
fear and covetousness, do intend to cut down
the Woods and Trees that grow upon the
Commons and Waste Land.

## The Storming of the Bastille

**IT** IS RARELY POINTED OUT THAT THE LEADER OF THE FIRST MASS ACTIONS TAKEN BY THE FRENCH PEOPLE WAS A WOMAN CALLED THEROIGNE DE MERICOURT. SHE LED WHAT WAS KNOWN AS THE STORMING OF THE BASTILLE (A FORTRESS THAT WAS A HATED SYMBOL OF ROYAL POWER) AND ALSO LED 8,000 WOMEN, DRESSED AS AMAZONS, ON A MARCH TO THE KING'S PALACE AT VERSAILLES. THESE EVENTS WERE CRITICAL TO THE SUCCESS OF THE FRENCH REVOLUTION BUT HISTORIANS IN THE PAST HAVE GENERALLY PAINTED THEROIGNE OUT OF THE PICTURE. DESPITE THE FACT THAT WOMEN HAD PLAYED A MAJOR PART IN THIS REVOLUTION, THEY WERE NOT GIVEN MANY RIGHTS AS CITIZENS EVEN THOUGH ONE WOMAN, OLYMPE DE GOUGES, PUBLISHED *A DECLARATION OF THE RIGHTS OF WOMAN* IN 1791. THIS WAS LARGELY IGNORED AND SHE WAS EXECUTED A FEW YEARS LATER.

# Timeline: SHORT HISTORY OF BIG CHANGE

| CAMPAIGN TO END SLAVERY | 1787-1833 | a |
|---|---|---|

*This* was the period of the campaign to end slavery. For Active Citizens there is much to learn from how this campaign was run.

### A MEETING OF LIKE-MINDED PEOPLE

*The* campaign was initially started in 1787 by like-minded people meeting to form an organization called The Society for Effecting the Abolition of the Slave Trade. These people were a mixture of Quakers, Anglicans and intellectuals. The most significant members of this group were the politician William Wilberforce and the intellectual and writer Thomas Clarkson who both went on to be campaign leaders. At the meeting, the group decided what their intentions were and planned how they would best achieve success. This marked the beginning of one of the world's first grassroots movements, in which people from all walks of life came together over one idea for change.

### GATHERING FACTS AND STATISTICS

*Thomas* Clarkson travelled the country gathering eye-witness accounts and reports as well as statistics related to the slave trade. He had already written an influential book on the subject but knew that it was important to gather as much up-to-date information and as many reliable facts as possible. This would give him the strongest and most convincing argument to win over the people and the government.

### ADVOCACY AND REPRESENTATION

*Using* the modern technologies of printing, the group created thousands of pamphlets, leaflets and posters in order to spread their message. They also used the first example of a campaign logo with a slogan, showing a picture of a slave above the words, "Am I not a man and a brother?" (see image on page 17). Clarkson and many others, including two former slaves, Ottobah Cugoano and Olaudah Equiano, began to give speeches advocating the abolition of slavery. Although women had been excluded from the original campaign group, Elizabeth Heyrick and other women set up their own supporting groups and travelled the country as advocates for the cause.

### OTHER CAMPAIGN TOOLS

*The* campaign began organizing mass petitions, rallies and boycotts. Because the sugar plantations in the West Indies were among the main exploiters of African slaves, the first boycotts were against buying sugar. A network was set up, involving groups across the country all linked together to the main campaign.

### CHANGE FROM WITHIN GOVERNMENT

*The* MP William Wilberforce represented the campaign within Parliament and gave his first campaigning speeches in 1789. He used the facts and statistics gathered by Clarkson to advocate first for the abolition of the slave trade and eventually for the abolition of slavery altogether. The famous Prime Minister William Pitt was in support of Wilberforce and this gave extra weight to the parliamentary campaign.
At that time, slaves were not seen as individuals by the slave trade but as a source of energy, a commodity to be traded. The argument against stopping the slave trade was that this source of energy was necessary to the economy of the country. Wilberforce's parliamentary campaign argued that slaves were not a commodity but were people, people with rights, people with souls who were seen as the same in the eyes of God. The parliamentary campaign led by Wilberforce ended in 1833 when the Slavery Abolition Act was passed and slavery was abolished throughout the British Empire.

### EVENTS OUTSIDE THE CAMPAIGN THAT HELPED ITS SUCCESS

*In* 1793 the British army invaded Haiti, which was part of the French Empire at the time. Haiti was a valuable resource due to its huge sugar plantations. There had been a vast slave uprising but the British were confident that they could suppress it. This was a big mistake as the war against the slaves went on for five years and more than 12,000 British soldiers died. In the end, they left the island – a rebel army of African slaves had succeeded in defeating the might of the British army. Other slave rebellions in the West Indies, as well as the success of the slave rebellion in Haiti, greatly strengthened the anti-slavery campaign in Britain. The government was forced to consider the negative effects of allowing slavery to carry on as a legal trade and practice.

CONTINUED

# MODERN-DAY CAMPAIGNS WITH HISTORICAL LINKS

**POLLY** HIGGINS IS A UK-BASED BARRISTER AND ADVOCATE FOR PLANETARY RIGHTS; SHE HAS INITIATED THREE LEGAL PLATFORMS: THE UNIVERSAL DECLARATION OF PLANETARY RIGHTS, THE PEOPLE'S DECLARATION; AND THE PLANET EARTH TRUST. SHE IS ALSO THE FOUNDER OF THE TREES HAVE RIGHTS CAMPAIGN, WHICH BROKE MEMBERSHIP RECORDS WHEN IT WAS LAUNCHED ON FACEBOOK IN 2009. THE RAX TEAM INTERVIEWED POLLY IN JANUARY 2010.

## HOW DOES YOUR CAMPAIGN RELATE TO THE ANTI-SLAVERY CAMPAIGN OF 1787-1833?

**OVER** 200 YEARS AGO WILLIAM WILBERFORCE TOOK UP THE MANTLE TO FIGHT FOR THE ABOLITION OF SLAVERY. HE REALIZED VERY EARLY ON THAT IT WAS POINTLESS TO ASK EVERYONE TO USE THEIR SLAVES A LITTLE LESS. THAT'S THE SAME AS ASKING EVERYONE TODAY TO USE A LITTLE LESS FOSSIL-FUEL-BASED ENERGY. IN WILBERFORCE'S DAY, SLAVES WERE LITERALLY A FORM OF ENERGY. HUMAN SLAVES WERE VIEWED AS THINGS, PIECES OF PROPERTY, TO BE USED AND ABUSED AS AN OWNER SO WISHED. WILBERFORCE KNEW THAT WE HAD TO CHANGE THE SYSTEM ENTIRELY, NOT MODIFY IT SLIGHTLY.

WHEN SLAVERY WAS ABOLISHED, WE REPLACED ONE FORM OF ENERGY WITH ANOTHER: INSTEAD OF USING HUMAN SLAVES, WE STARTED TO USE FOSSIL-FUELS. TODAY, INSTEAD OF ENSLAVING HUMANS, WE HAVE ENSLAVED THE PLANET. IN BOTH CASES WE HAVE TREATED THE SOURCE OF ENERGY AS A PIECE OF PROPERTY, AS A THING FOR US TO USE WITHOUT THOUGHT OF THE CONSEQUENCES. THIS CAMPAIGN IS NOT ABOUT MAKING THE FOSSIL-FUEL CORPORATIONS ILLEGAL, IT'S ABOUT MAKING THE DAMAGING PRACTICE OF USING FOSSIL FUELS ILLEGAL - IN THE SAME WAY AS WILBERFORCE DIDN'T WANT TO MAKE THE SLAVERY INDUSTRY ILLEGAL BUT RATHER TO MAKE SLAVERY ITSELF ILLEGAL.

## HOW IS YOUR CAMPAIGN PUTTING PRESSURE ON GOVERNMENTS?

**IN 1948** THE UNIVERSAL DECLARATION OF HUMAN RIGHTS WAS BORN OF THE HUMANITARIAN CRISIS OF THE SECOND WORLD WAR. NOW WE HAVE A PLANETARY CRISIS AND IT IS TIME FOR A UNIVERSAL DECLARATION OF PLANETARY RIGHTS. BOLIVIA ANNOUNCED AT COPENHAGEN THAT THEY ARE NOW GOING TO PROPOSE SUCH A DECLARATION TO THE UNITED NATIONS LATER THIS YEAR. BUT THE PROCESS DOES NOT STOP THERE. IT WILL TAKE ANOTHER TWO YEARS FOR THE DECLARATION TO BE VOTED ON. WE WILL BRING TOGETHER THE PEOPLE OF THE WORLD TO CALL ON THEIR GOVERNMENTS TO SUPPORT THE VOTE FOR THE DECLARATION.

## WHAT ADVICE WOULD YOU GIVE TO YOUNG ACTIVE CITIZENS WHO WANT TO TAKE INFORMED AND RESPONSIBLE ACTION?

**BE CREATIVE.** WORK OUT WHAT KIND OF WORLD YOU WOULD WANT TO LIVE IN. WHAT WOULD YOU LIKE THAT TO LOOK LIKE? WHAT WILL TRAVEL OF THE FUTURE LOOK LIKE? WHAT WILL OUR HOMES LOOK LIKE? WHAT WILL OUR CITIES LOOK LIKE? WHAT IS IT THAT GETS YOU REALLY EXCITED? ONCE YOU WORK THAT OUT, YOU CAN MAKE IT HAPPEN! IF YOU CAN DREAM IT, YOU WILL FIND ALL THE HELP YOU REQUIRE IS RIGHT BY YOU TO MAKE IT A REALITY.

THE UNIVERSAL DECLARATION OF *Planetary* **Rights**

**LEARN MORE/GET INVOLVED:**
www.treeshaverightstoo.com

## Timeline: SHORT HISTORY OF BIG CHANGE

**ACTIVITY**

**IN GROUPS**

**HEADS TOGETHER**

*You* have **FIVE MINUTES** for your group to come up with a list of responses to this idea:

**HOW WOULD THE USE OF 21ST-CENTURY TECHNOLOGY HAVE HELPED THE ANTI-SLAVERY CAMPAIGN?**

Feed back your ideas to the class.

*TICK TOCK*

### WORKHOUSES IN BRITAIN — 1723-1948

*The* alternative to working in the grim factories of the Industrial age was even worse. In those days there were no social services or housing benefits. Your only alternative was to go to a Workhouse. These were places where people were given very basic food and a place to stay in return for hard work under extremely harsh conditions. Workhouses existed in the UK right up until they were abolished in 1948. *a*

*b*

### THE CHARTIST MOVEMENT — 1838 *c*

*Chartism* was the first significant mass movement for social and political reform led by the working class in the world. The Chartists took their name from the 1838 People's Charter, a document that had been drawn up by a meeting of 12 like-minded men: six MPs and six working-class campaigners. These included: the right for every man over 21 to vote; the payment of a wage to MPs so that working-class people could stand for election; and Parliament to be elected every year so that corrupt MPs could be easily removed.
The Chartist movement caught on across the country, mass rallies were held and petitions of over a million signatures were signed. However, it was not until 1918 that all but one of the original demands of the Charter were met. The last demand, that Parliament be elected every year in order to avoid corruption, has never been met.

### THE CHILDREN ACT — 1908

*d*

*This* is one of the most significant Acts related to children in British parliamentary history. Children were made 'protected persons', which meant: anybody who abused them would be breaking the law; employers couldn't make children work in dangerous conditions; it was illegal for anyone to give children alcohol or sell them tobacco; and local authorities were given the powers to protect young people from abuse and to keep them out of the workhouses. Special prisons were set up so that young offenders did not have to go to the same prisons as adults and an early system of fostering was set up to ensure a better life for orphans. *e*

*f*

### THE RUSSIAN REVOLUTION — 1917

*The* Russian Revolution was the largest of the movements for social and political justice at that time. It was led and won by the working people of Russia and led to the formation of the first Communist state in the world. As so often before in history, a book inspired this revolution. This was *Das Kapital* written by Karl Marx and published in 1867. Marx had written *The Communist Manifesto* with Friedrich Engels while they lived in England. It was published in 1848 and had a major influence on the British Chartist Movement. The ideas of Marx and Engels also led to the formation of the biggest Communist country in the world, The People's Republic of China, in 1949. Today, the People's Republic of China has a population of 1.3 billion, which represents one fifth of the population of the world.

# GET MY STICK!

**IN** 2008, A POLL OF 6,162 TEACHERS IN THE UK SHOWED THAT 22% OF THEM WOULD BACK THE RETURN OF CANING AS A PUNISHMENT IN SCHOOLS. GOVERNMENT RESEARCH SHOWS THAT MANY UK CITIZENS THINK THAT THE REMOVAL OF CORPORAL PUNISHMENT IN SCHOOLS IS ONE OF THE REASONS FOR THE DECLINE IN STUDENT BEHAVIOUR.

IT'S THE CANE FOR YOU..

WHATEVER, NO BIG DEAL

..AND MR HARDMAN THE PE TEACHER HAS OFFERED TO HELP

YIKES!

**PUBLIC WARNING.**

CHILDREN ACT, 1908

Among other provisions of the Children... Parents or other persons having the ch... Children are made liable to fines... ...alties for

**BIRCHING** WAS A COMMON WAY OF PUNISHING YOUNG PEOPLE RIGHT UP UNTIL 1948. IT INVOLVED HOLDING OR TYING A BOY OR GIRL DOWN AND THEN WHIPPING THEM WITH A BUNDLE OF THIN BRANCHES. PHYSICAL PUNISHMENT LIKE THIS IS CALLED CORPORAL PUNISHMENT.

**THE** RSPCA (ROYAL SOCIETY FOR PREVENTION OF CRUELTY TO ANIMALS) WAS FORMED IN 1824 BUT THE NSPCC (WHICH PROTECTED CHILDREN) WAS NOT FORMED UNTIL 1884. AS A RESULT, THE FIRST CASE THAT PROTECTED A YOUNG PERSON FROM CRUELTY WAS BROUGHT BY THE RSPCA AS THE CHILD WAS CONSIDERED TO BE A LITTLE ANIMAL!

**WORKHOUSE** JOBS INCLUDED OAKUM PICKING, WHICH MEANT UNRAVELLING OLD, TAR-COVERED ROPE. THIS WOULD RUB THE FINGERS RAW. ANOTHER JOB WAS BREAKING UP BONES TO BE USED AS FERTILIZER. SOME CHILDREN WERE SO HUNGRY THAT THEY WOULD GNAW THE RANCID MEAT OFF THE BONES AND SUCK THE MARROW OUT OF THEM AS THEY BROKE THEM UP. BECAUSE WATER WAS SO POLLUTED IN THOSE DAYS, PEOPLE GENERALLY DRANK BEER OR GIN, EVEN CHILDREN! CHILDREN IN THE WORKHOUSE WERE SEPARATED FROM THEIR PARENTS AND BOYS WERE SEPARATED FROM GIRLS. USUALLY, YOU WOULD NEVER SEE YOUR FAMILY AGAIN!

# CHARLES DICKENS

**IN** 1838 CHARLES DICKENS WROTE HIS SECOND NOVEL, *OLIVER TWIST*. IT WAS THE FIRST NOVEL IN THE ENGLISH LANGUAGE TO HAVE A CHILD AS THE MAIN CHARACTER. DICKENS DREW UPON HIS OWN CHILDHOOD EXPERIENCES TO SHOW WHAT LIFE WAS LIKE FOR YOUNG PEOPLE IN WORKHOUSES AS WELL AS SHOWING HOW CRIMINALS RECRUITED CHILDREN TO WORK FOR THEM. THE BOOK CAUSED A SENSATION IN THE UK AND PEOPLE BEGAN TO CAMPAIGN FOR CHILDREN'S RIGHTS.

CHARLES DICKENS (1812-70)

PAWNBROKERS m... London and Liverpool, und... DEALERS IN OL... TOBACCONISTS... cigarette papers (mor... the use of the person... ...this does no... uniform employed... Persons g... hundred child... a sufficient... children in the... The...

SCENE IN A WORKHOUSE FROM *OLIVER TWIST*

# E-PROTEST! SHE PROTEST! I PROTEST!

**THE** CHARTISTS HAD TO TRAVEL UP AND DOWN THE COUNTRY TO ADVOCATE FOR THEIR CAUSE AND GATHER SIGNATURES FOR PETITIONS. 21ST-CENTURY TECHNOLOGY HAS MADE A SIGNIFICANT DIFFERENCE TO THIS PROCESS. 'E-PROTEST' IS A NEW WAY OF ALLOWING THE PUBLIC TO ACT FOR CHANGE, WHERE DEDICATED WEBSITES CONTACT THOUSANDS OF PEOPLE ABOUT CAMPAIGNS AND PROVIDE THEM WITH AN EASY WAY TO SIGN PETITIONS AND MAKE THEIR OPINIONS HEARD. ONE OF THE FIRST UK SITES TO OPERATE IN THIS WAY IS '38 DEGREES'.
"38 DEGREES IS THE ANGLE AT WHICH AN AVALANCHE HAPPENS. IN THE UK, 38 DEGREES WILL ENABLE PEOPLE TO ACT TOGETHER, TO CREATE AN AVALANCHE FOR CHANGE."

LEARN MORE/GET INVOLVED:
www.38degrees.org.uk
www.power2010.org.uk

THERE IS ANOTHER WEBSITE CAMPAIGN WITH A NEW PEOPLE'S CHARTER FOR THE 21ST CENTURY:
LEARN MORE/GET INVOLVED:
www.thepeoplescharter.com

RUMBLE

38 DEGREE people, power cha...

## Timeline: SHORT HISTORY OF BIG CHANGE

| CAMPAIGN FOR WOMEN'S SUFFRAGE | 1893-1928 |
|---|---|

**This** was the period of the campaign for women to win the vote. For Active Citizens there is much to learn from how this campaign was run.

### WITHIN THE PROCESS OF GOVERNMENT

**Within** the process of government, the campaign for women's suffrage (the right to vote) goes back to the middle of the 19th century. A series of Bills advocating the cause continually failed to win enough votes. Even women winning the vote in New Zealand in 1893 made no difference. As a result, a central campaign was formed called the National Union of Women's Suffrage Societies (NUWSS). This organization used petitions, public meetings and the lobbying of government as its main tools for change. The government remained uninterested in accepting their arguments and the media lost interest and rarely printed letters or articles discussing the issue.

### A MEETING OF LIKE-MINDED PEOPLE

**In** 1903, a group of women met in a house in Manchester to discuss how they could change campaigning tactics to raise public awareness. The most famous campaigners at this meeting were Emmeline Pankhurst and her daughter Christabel. The group decided that the new tactics should be more extreme and this was reflected in their slogan, "Deeds Not Words". Frustrated by the failure of the process within government, they chose to use actions, instead of words, to get across their point. This has since become known as 'direct action'.

The group formed a new organization, the Women's Social and Political Union (WSPU). There remained many other organizations that did not accept the use of direct action and they continued to campaign in more peaceful ways. These included the Women's Freedom League (WFL) and the NUWSS. This is an important example of how campaigns for the same cause can differ in their ideas about tactics.

### ADVOCACY AND REPRESENTATION

**The** women's suffrage campaigns created a great number of pamphlets and ran their own regular papers and magazines. Advocates gave speeches at rallies and held debates. One activist, Muriel Matters, organized a Votes For Women caravan tour of the country where advocates gave speeches in the towns that they visited, raising awareness and establishing new local groups of the WFL. This is an important tool for change, where a central group networks with different areas of the country to establish local branches.

### OTHER CAMPAIGN TOOLS

**Pankhurst's** WSPU group managed to gain a high level of attention using direct action. Their actions included damaging public property by smashing windows, setting fire to buildings and slashing a famous painting as well as going on hunger strike when the police arrested them. Although such actions raised their profile, they were strongly criticized and many believe that these tactics damaged the campaign. Public sympathy was gained, however, once the authorities started to force-feed the prisoners on hunger strike, a very painful and distressing process. Realizing this, the government brought in The Cat and Mouse Act, whereby prisoners were released once they became ill and arrested again as soon as they had recovered.

The WFL used less violent methods, such as refusing to pay taxes, refusing to fill in official forms and chaining themselves to objects in the Houses of Parliament. On 13 October 1908, 100,000 campaigners gathered outside the Houses of Parliament and tried to rush the gates of the building. This action attracted wide media coverage.

### EVENTS OUTSIDE THE CAMPAIGN THAT HELPED ITS SUCCESS

**When** World War One broke out across Europe in 1914, women suddenly became the heroes at home. While millions of British men went to war, women kept the country running. They took on all the jobs that were usually done by men, running the factories, making ammunition and running the farms, as well as nursing the sick and wounded. By the time the War had finished, women had proved that they should be treated as equals to men. The government accepted the case for women's suffrage. At first, only women who had property or a comfortable income qualified but in 1928 all women won the right to vote.

 **IN GROUPS/WHOLE CLASS**
**FIGHT YOUR CORNER**
**MOTION:** THIS HOUSE BELIEVES THAT DIRECT ACTION INVOLVING DAMAGE TO PUBLIC PROPERTY DOES MORE HARM THAN GOOD TO A CAMPAIGN.

CONTINUED

# MODERN-DAY CAMPAIGNS WITH HISTORICAL LINKS

**TAMSIN** OMOND IS A YOUNG ENVIRONMENTAL ACTIVIST WHO HAS APPEARED IN THE MAINSTREAM MEDIA MANY TIMES AS AN ADVOCATE FOR TAKING ACTION ON CLIMATE CHANGE. IN 2008, SHE FOUNDED THE CAMPAIGNING ORGANIZATION CLIMATE RUSH, WHICH LED A RUSH OF 1,000 PEOPLE ON THE HOUSES OF PARLIAMENT TO MARK THE CENTENARY OF THE SUFFRAGETTES DOING THE SAME THING. THE RAX TEAM INTERVIEWED TAMSIN IN JANUARY 2010.

### WHY DID YOU CHOOSE TO HOLD A CLIMATE RUSH ON THE HOUSES OF PARLIAMENT ON 13 OCTOBER 2008?

**I READ** ABOUT THE ORIGINAL SUFFRAGETTE RUSH ON 13 OCTOBER 1908 ABOUT SIX WEEKS BEFORE ITS CENTENARY. THEIR MODEL OF NON-VIOLENT DIRECT ACTION INSPIRED ME. I DECIDED THAT BY CELEBRATING THIS SUFFRAGETTE ANNIVERSARY WE MIGHT TALK TO AND INVOLVE A DIFFERENT AUDIENCE IN THE ENVIRONMENTAL MOVEMENT. WE HOPED TO INSPIRE THE RADICAL SUFFRAGETTE SPIRIT AND GIVE IT A NEW FOCUS: SUSTAINABILITY. WE ALSO INVITED PARTICIPANTS TO DRESS IN AN EDWARDIAN STYLE SO THAT THEY MIGHT FEEL INSPIRED BY THE HISTORICAL CAMPAIGN THAT WE WERE IMITATING, A CAMPAIGN THAT REALLY DID CHANGE THE WORLD.

### WHAT IS YOUR VIEW ABOUT THE DIFFERENT TYPES OF DIRECT ACTION USED BY THE WOMEN'S SUFFRAGE MOVEMENT?

**I THINK** THAT DIRECT ACTION IS A RESPONSE TO FRUSTRATION. DECADES WERE SPENT CAMPAIGNING WITHIN THE SYSTEM AND VERY LITTLE GROUND WAS WON. DIRECT ACTION CAN DO MANY THINGS. IT ATTRACTS PUBLICITY AND GIVES A FOCUS TO DEBATE AND IT OFFERS A DIFFERENT VISION OF HOW SOCIETY COULD BE STRUCTURED. THE SUFFRAGETTES LIVED AN ALTERNATIVE VISION OF WHAT WOMEN COULD DO, SAY AND BE IN A PATRIARCHAL SOCIETY. THEY NOT ONLY CHALLENGED WHAT MEN THOUGHT WOMEN COULD BE, THEY ALSO CHALLENGED WHAT WOMEN BELIEVED THEY SHOULD BE. I CAN ONLY HOPE THAT THE DIRECT ACTION TACTICS OF THE PRESENT ENVIRONMENTAL MOVEMENT WILL ACHIEVE THE SAME FOR OUR SOCIETY.

*CLIMATE RUSH PICNIC AT HEATHROW AIRPORT*

**THE** STRUGGLE TO WIN THE VOTE FOR WOMEN CONTINUED AROUND THE WORLD FOR A LONG TIME AFTER EMMELINE PANKHURST. WOMEN DID NOT GET THE VOTE UNTIL 1971 IN SWITZERLAND & 2007 IN KUWAIT. THE FIRST COUNTRY TO GIVE WOMEN THE VOTE WAS NEW ZEALAND IN 1893.

### WHAT IS YOUR CAMPAIGN, WHAT ISSUES ARE YOU ADDRESSING AND WHAT INSPIRED YOU TO GET INVOLVED?

**MY CAMPAIGN** IS TO RAISE AWARENESS OF THE REALITY OF GLOBAL WARMING AND TO LET NORMAL PEOPLE KNOW WHAT THEY CAN DO TO BECOME PART OF THE SOLUTION, RATHER THAN PART OF THE PROBLEM. I AM CONCERNED THAT EVEN IF WE ALL MADE OUR LIFESTYLES A LITTLE GREENER WE WOULD BE NO CLOSER TO STOPPING CLIMATE CHANGE. I HOPE THAT THE CLIMATE RUSH, WITH ITS LINKS TO THE SUFFRAGETTES, REMINDS PEOPLE THAT INJUSTICES CAN BE RECOGNIZED AND RELIEVED, BUT THAT WE MUST DO MORE THAN CHANGE OUR LIGHT-BULBS. MY HOPE IS THAT OTHERS WILL BE INSPIRED BY LIVING AT THIS HISTORIC TIME AND THAT TOGETHER WE WILL TAKE ACTION IN OUR OWN LIVES, WITHIN OUR COMMUNITIES, ON OUR HIGH STREET AND AT THE MOST PUBLIC AND POLITICAL LEVELS.

### WHAT OTHER KINDS OF ACTIONS HAVE YOU CREATED AND WHY DID YOU CHOOSE THEM?

**ON** THE EVENING BEFORE THE GOVERNMENT WAS TO ANNOUNCE ITS DECISION ON WHETHER IT WOULD BUILD A THIRD RUNWAY AT HEATHROW AIRPORT, CLIMATE RUSH ORGANIZED AN EDWARDIAN PICNIC IN THE TERMINAL ONE BUILDING AT HEATHROW AIRPORT. THIS ACTION WAS TO SHOW PEOPLE THAT IT COULD BE FUN AND INSPIRING TO TAKE RADICAL ACTION ON CLIMATE CHANGE. IT WAS ALSO TO WARN THE GOVERNMENT ABOUT THE LEVEL OF ACTIVISM THEY COULD EXPECT IF THEY WERE TO EXPAND HEATHROW AIRPORT. OVER 600 PEOPLE PARTICIPATED IN THE EDWARDIAN PICNIC AND DANCE, AND MANAGED TO FORCE THE CLOSURE OF TERMINAL ONE.

**LEARN MORE/GET INVOLVED:** www.climaterush.co.uk

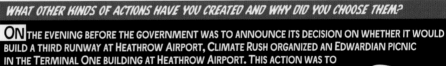

# A SHORT HISTORY *of* **BIG** CHANGE *thus far . . . . .*

## Timeline: SHORT HISTORY OF BIG CHANGE

### FIRST NEWS BROADCAST ON THE RADIO — 1920 ⓐ

*Although* scientists such as Marconi and Edison had been developing the radio since the late 19th century, the first radio news programme was broadcast on 31 August 1920 by station 8MK in Detroit, Michigan, USA. This was another technology that allowed the free flow of ideas across the world as radio not only provided entertainment but also meant that great speakers representing new ideas could have their voices heard in your own living room.

### FIRST LARGE-SCALE TELEVISION BROADCAST — 1929

*Although* the idea of television had been around since the late 19th century, regular television broadcasts began in Germany in 1929 and in 1936 the Olympic Games in Berlin were broadcast live to television stations in Berlin and Leipzig. Television was a new tool to spread ideas and became more and more important for campaigners. Adolf Hitler used the televising of the Berlin Olympic Games as a tool to show off the power and glory of his Nazi regime, which was soon to bring the world into another war.

### GANDHI AND INDEPENDENCE FOR INDIA — 1930 ⓑ ⓒ

*One* of history's most famous campaigners for new rights and freedoms was Mahatma Gandhi, who led the movement to win Indian independence from British rule. His campaign used all the tools for change that we have seen before and the Suffragettes also inspired him. Gandhi developed the idea of Satyagraha, which meant resistance through non-violent civil disobedience. Not only was Gandhi's campaign to win independence for India successful but he also left to the world a great message, that non-violence, non-cooperation, civil disobedience and mass people's movements can succeed in changing the history of an entire nation. ⓓ

### FIRST SIGNIFICANT IMMIGRATION TO BRITAIN — 1945

*After* World War Two, the UK saw the beginning of a significant influx of immigrants from Africa, the Caribbean and South Asia. At first, many of these immigrants suffered severe racism at the hands of the British people. Over the next 30 years, however, campaigns for racial equality succeeded in establishing laws to protect people from racism. Today, the UK is one of the most racially mixed countries in the world. ⓔ

### UNICEF ESTABLISHED — 1946

*The* United Nations Children's Fund (UNICEF) was set up to provide emergency food and healthcare to children in countries that had been devastated by World War Two. Today, UNICEF provides long-term humanitarian and developmental assistance to children and mothers in developing countries. In 1965, UNICEF won the Nobel Peace Prize.

### APARTHEID IN SOUTH AFRICA — 1948-94 ⓕ ⓖ

*The* National Party, the ruling white political party in South Africa, established the apartheid system in 1948. This involved racial segregation where black Africans had no national citizenship, and only had access to inferior public services. Black South Africans were made to live as second-class citizens by the white ruling class. The anti-apartheid movement in South Africa was huge and often violent, although it also involved all the tools of change we have seen before, including strikes, boycotts and civil disobedience. The movement had a great leader and advocate named Nelson Mandela who was imprisoned for 27 years until 1990. After huge international support for the campaign to end apartheid, the first multi-racial democratic elections were held in 1994. Nelson Mandela became the first black President of South Africa and won the Nobel Peace Prize in 1993.

CONTINUED ➤

**5 NOBEL PEACE PRIZE WINNERS** STATED THAT THE WORK AND IDEAS OF MAHATMA GANDHI HAD BEEN A MAJOR INFLUENCE ON THEM. DESPITE THIS, GANDHI NEVER WON THE PRIZE HIMSELF. **b**

US CIVIL RIGHTS LEADER AND ADVOCATE FOR NON-VIOLENT PROTEST.

SPIRITUAL LEADER OF TIBETAN PEOPLE AND PEACE ACTIVIST.

LEADER OF THE NON-VIOLENT MOVEMENT FOR HUMAN RIGHTS AND DEMOCRACY IN BURMA.

POLITICAL LEADER OF SOUTH AFRICA AND FIGHTER AGAINST RACIAL OPPRESSION.

ARGENTINIAN HUMAN RIGHTS ACTIVIST AND ADVOCATE FOR NON-VIOLENT PROTEST.

MARTIN LUTHER KING | DALAI LAMA | AUNG SAN SUU KYI | NELSON MANDELA | ADOLFO PEREZ ESQUIVEL

*GENERATIONS TO COME WILL SCARCELY BELIEVE THAT SUCH A MAN AS THIS WALKED THE EARTH IN FLESH AND BLOOD... I BELIEVE THAT GANDHI'S VIEWS WERE THE MOST ENLIGHTENED OF ALL THE POLITICAL MEN IN OUR TIME. WE SHOULD STRIVE TO DO THINGS IN HIS SPIRIT: NOT TO USE VIOLENCE IN FIGHTING FOR OUR CAUSE BUT BY NON-PARTICIPATION IN ANYTHING YOU BELIEVE IS EVIL.* **c**

ALBERT EINSTEIN (1879-1955) NOBEL PRIZE-WINNING SCIENTIST, HUMANIST & ADVOCATE FOR PEACE

# SATYAGRAHA

**AN** EXAMPLE OF SATYAGRAHA WAS WHEN GANDHI DECIDED TO CREATE AN EVENT THAT WOULD CONFRONT WHAT HE BELIEVED TO BE AN UNJUST TAX ON SALT. IN 1930, HE LED HUNDREDS OF THOUSANDS OF INDIANS ON A MARCH TO THE SEA WHERE HE AND EVERYONE ELSE BEGAN TO MAKE THEIR OWN SALT. THIS WAS ILLEGAL AT THE TIME AND WAS AN ACT OF CIVIL DISOBEDIENCE. EVEN THOUGH 60,000 PEOPLE WERE ARRESTED, THE TAX ON SALT WAS DESTROYED – WITHOUT THE CAMPAIGNERS USING ANY VIOLENCE. **d**

**IN** 2009, THE FASTEST-GROWING ETHNIC CATEGORY FOR NEW-BORN BABIES IN THE UK WAS 'MIXED RACE'. **e**

# PURPLE RAIN

**IN** SEPTEMBER 1989, IN SOUTH AFRICA, A LARGE CROWD OF ANTI-APARTHEID PROTESTERS TOOK TO THE STREETS IN AN ACT OF CIVIL DISOBEDIENCE. THEY WERE CONFRONTED BY HUNDREDS OF POLICE AND A POLICE WATER CANNON SPRAYING JETS OF WATER SO STRONG THAT IT KNOCKED PEOPLE OFF THEIR FEET. THE WATER HAD BEEN FILLED WITH PURPLE DYE SO THAT THE POLICE COULD EASILY ARREST ANYONE WHO HAD BEEN THERE BECAUSE THEY HAD TURNED PURPLE! AN ACTIVIST JUMPED ON TO THE CANNON, WRESTLED IT AWAY **f** FROM THE POLICE AND TURNED IT ON NEARBY WHITE-WALLED GOVERNMENT BUILDINGS. THE ANTI-APARTHEID MOVEMENT HAD BEEN USING THE SLOGAN, "THE PEOPLE SHALL GOVERN." BUT THE NEXT DAY, NEW SLOGANS APPEARED ON WALLS EVERYWHERE.

*THE PURPLE SHALL GOVERN!*

**FAKE RADIO 'WAR' STIRS TERROR THROUGH US**

**THE** NOBEL PRIZES HAVE BEEN AWARDED EVERY YEAR SINCE 1901. THERE ARE FIVE CATEGORIES: PHYSICS, CHEMISTRY, MEDICINE, LITERATURE & PEACE. THEY WERE INTRODUCED BY SWEDISH CHEMIST ALFRED NOBEL. A FRENCH NEWSPAPER HAD PUBLISHED AN ARTICLE ABOUT NOBEL, CALLING HIM "THE MERCHANT OF DEATH" BECAUSE HE HAD INVENTED DYNAMITE. SO HE CREATED THE NOBEL PRIZES TO LEAVE A BETTER LEGACY TO THE WORLD. **g**

**IN** 1938 THE POWER OF RADIO AND THE INFLUENCE THAT MODERN MEDIA CAN HAVE ON A POPULATION WAS SHOWN TO GREAT EFFECT WHEN THERE WAS A RADIO BROADCAST OF A FAMOUS SCIENCE FICTION STORY CALLED *THE WAR OF THE WORLDS*. THE FAMOUS ACTOR ORSON WELLES CREATED THE SHOW AS IF IT WERE A SERIES OF LIVE NEWS BULLETINS, DESCRIBING HOW ALIENS WERE INVADING THE PLANET. SO BELIEVABLE WERE THE BROADCASTS THAT MUCH OF AMERICA WENT INTO A PANIC, ACTUALLY THINKING THAT THEY WERE BEING INVADED BY BEINGS FROM ANOTHER PLANET! **a**

# A SHORT HISTORY of BIG CHANGE
*thus far . . . . .*

## ⟩⟩⟩ *Timeline:* SHORT HISTORY OF BIG CHANGE ⟨⟨⟨

### UNIVERSAL DECLARATION OF HUMAN RIGHTS — 1948

*Shortly* after World War Two, 51 countries joined together to form the United Nations (UN). In 1948, the UN created the Universal Declaration of Human Rights (UDHR). These 30 rights included the rights to education, to a fair trial, to freedom of expression and to freedom of thought, conscience and religion.

### EUROPEAN CONVENTION ON HUMAN RIGHTS — 1950

*The* countries of Europe followed the UDHR with a body of similar laws to cover their continent. This was called the European Convention on Human Rights (ECHR). Although the UK helped to write the ECHR, it did not allow its own citizens to use these laws in UK courts until 1998 when The Human Rights Act was passed.

### "I HAVE A DREAM" — 1963

*The* great civil rights campaign leader, Martin Luther King, delivered his famous, "I have a dream" speech to hundreds of thousands of campaigners who had marched to the US capital, Washington DC. His speech raised public awareness of the civil rights movement across the US and the world.

THERE ARE TWO ASPECTS OF MARTIN LUTHER KING'S SPEECH WHICH ARE IMPORTANT TO ACTIVE CITIZENS TODAY. FIRST, HE DELIVERED A BRILLIANT SPEECH IN A POWERFUL WAY. THESE SKILLS OF ORATORY ARE CENTRAL TO THE SUCCESS OF CAMPAIGNS. SECOND, NEW TECHNOLOGY MEANT THAT HIS SPEECH WAS FILMED AND RECORDED, WHICH MEANT THAT PEOPLE COULD WATCH WHAT HE HAD TO SAY ON TELEVISION OR LISTEN TO HIM ON THE RADIO. EVEN TODAY, PEOPLE CAN STUDY THE EVENT THROUGH FILMS OR RECORDINGS. **(a)**

### THE POWER OF TELEVISION — 1966

*The* power of television to influence struggles for new rights and freedoms was beginning to grow in the 1960s. A realistic television drama called *Cathy Come Home* shocked the British nation when it was broadcast in 1966. Around 12 million people, a quarter of the country's population at the time, watched the powerful film, which showed the harsh life suffered by a young mother trying to raise her children in poverty. The film raised awareness of many issues, including homelessness, unemployment and the rights of a mother to keep her **(b)** children. As a result, there was a huge increase in public support for campaigns that addressed these issues and influenced governments. This influenced new laws being made in government. The effect on the nation of *Cathy Come Home* was similar to that of Charles Dickens' *Oliver Twist* a hundred years before.

### BEATLEMANIA AND THE RISE OF TEEN CULTURE — 1967   **(c) (d) (e)**

*A* pop band called The Beatles released an album called *Sergeant Pepper's Lonely Hearts Club Band* in 1967. This was considered to be one of their most influential albums. The band are the most successful pop band of all time and are included in this list as they represented the rise of the voice of youth. At the time, this was called a 'youthquake'. When any member of the Beatles became an advocate for a campaign, that campaign received enormous publicity. The power of the celebrity and of the youth voice were things that were here to stay.

### THE SEXUAL OFFENCES ACT, UK — 1967   **(f)**

*After* 60 years of campaigning, sex between men was made legal (sex between women had never been illegal). The Sexual Offences Act ensured that gay men would never be prosecuted again for their sexuality. Although this was a landmark change for gay men, it did not mean the end of campaigning for gay rights or the end of persecution by homophobic people. However, members of the LGBT (Lesbian, Gay, Bisexual and Transsexual) community have since won many more freedoms to enjoy equality and justice within their work and social lives as UK citizens.

*CONTINUED* ➔

# CELEBRITY ADVOCATES

THERE ARE PLENTY OF EXAMPLES OF PEOPLE WHO HAVE USED THEIR FAME TO BE ADVOCATES FOR CAMPAIGNS. ONE RECENT EXAMPLE OF A CELEBRITY MAKING A DIFFERENCE TO A CAMPAIGN WAS WHEN THE BRITISH ACTOR JOANNA LUMLEY GAVE HER SUPPORT TO A CAMPAIGN TO GIVE UK CITIZENSHIP RIGHTS TO NEPALESE PEOPLE WHO HAD FOUGHT AS GURKHAS IN THE BRITISH ARMY.

LEARN MORE/GET INVOLVED: www.gurkhajustice.org.uk

# LIVESTRONG

ANOTHER EXAMPLE OF CELEBRITIES USING THEIR FAME TO BE AN ADVOCATE FOR A CAMPAIGN IS THE WORK OF LANCE ARMSTRONG, THE GREATEST ROAD RACING CYCLIST OF ALL TIME. HE WON THE FAMOUS TOUR DE FRANCE A RECORD BREAKING SEVEN TIMES IN A ROW FROM 1999 TO 2005. AFTER SUFFERING FROM PROSTATE CANCER, LANCE SET UP A VERY SUCCESSFUL CAMPAIGN TO HELP RAISE AWARENESS AND GIVE RESOURCES AND SUPPORT TO PEOPLE WITH CANCER. THERE ARE 28 MILLION PEOPLE IN THE WORLD WITH CANCER TODAY.

LEARN MORE/ GET INVOLVED: www.livestrong.org

## THE YOUTHQUAKE FOR DIGITAL NATIVES IS BEING CALLED A

# TECHQUAKE

THE ENTIRE SPHERE OF YOUTH CULTURE IS HAPPENING BEHIND CLOSED DOORS. IT HAS NOTHING TO DO WITH ADULTS ANY MORE. THIS IS THE KEY SOCIAL REVOLUTION IN THE LAST 50 TO 100 YEARS... WHAT WE ARE SEEING NOW IS YOUNG PEOPLE WHO CAN ACTUALLY IMPACT IN A TANGIBLE WAY ON SOCIETY AND WHO CAN SET TRENDS THEMSELVES.

JULIA MARGO – DEMOS

TECHQUAKE P*****S OVER ALL YOUTHQUAKES PUT TOGETHER!

MICK WALL – MUSIC JOURNALIST

QUOTED IN THE BBC SERIES *STORY OF THE NOUGHTIES.*

LEARN MORE/GET INVOLVED: www.demos.co.uk

MARTIN LUTHER KING (1929-68) CLERIC, ACTIVIST AND PROMINENT LEADER OF THE AMERICAN CIVIL RIGHTS MOVEMENT.

THE TIME HAS COME FOR US TO CIVILIZE OURSELVES BY THE TOTAL, DIRECT AND IMMEDIATE ABOLITION OF POVERTY.

# SEXUAL RIGHTS

AN EARLY CAMPAIGNER AND ADVOCATE FOR GAY RIGHTS WAS THE GREAT IRISH WRITER OSCAR WILDE (1854-1900). HIS BRILLIANT LITERARY WORK HAS MADE HIM ONE OF THE MOST QUOTED WRITERS IN HISTORY. HE WAS IMPRISONED FOR HOMOSEXUAL ACTS IN 1895 AND SENTENCED TO TWO YEARS' HARD LABOUR. HE DESCRIBED HOW LONG AND HARD THE CAMPAIGN FOR GAY RIGHTS WOULD BE:

"YES, WE SHALL WIN IN THE END; BUT THE ROAD WILL BE LONG AND RED WITH MONSTROUS MARTYRDOMS."

HE WAS QUITE RIGHT. EVEN TODAY, THERE ARE STILL MANY ADVOCATES AND CAMPAIGNS FOR LGBT (LESBIAN, GAY, BISEXUAL, TRANSSEXUAL) RIGHTS ACROSS THE WORLD. IN MANY COUNTRIES, HOMOSEXUALITY CAN BE PUNISHED BY THE DEATH SENTENCE. THESE COUNTRIES INCLUDE: MAURITANIA, IRAN, SAUDI ARABIA, UNITED ARAB EMIRATES AND SUDAN.

LEARN MORE/GET INVOLVED:
www.stonewall.org.uk www.reprieve.org.uk www.amnesty.org.uk

# SHELTER

UP UNTIL THE TIME *CATHY COME HOME* WAS MADE, THE CAMPAIGNS TO HELP THE HOMELESS HAD BEEN SMALL AND RELATIVELY UNKNOWN. ONE EFFECT OF THE DRAMA WAS A REMARKABLE INCREASE IN SUPPORT FOR AN ORGANIZATION CALLED SHELTER. SHELTER HAS GONE ON TO BECOME ONE OF THE BIGGEST ORGANIZATIONS CARING FOR THE HOMELESS IN THE UK TODAY.

LEARN MORE/GET INVOLVED:
www.shelter.org.uk

# ANSWERS TO THE QUESTIONS ON PAGE 22

| | |
|---|---|
| SLEEPING | 30 YEARS |
| WORKING | 15 YEARS |
| EATING | 4 YEARS |
| AT SCHOOL | 3 YEARS |
| SHOPPING | 2 YEARS (FOR WOMEN) 1 YEAR (FOR MEN) |
| GOING TO THE TOILET | 6 MONTHS (FOR WOMEN) 3 YEARS (FOR MEN) |
| QUEUING | 6 MONTHS (FOR WOMEN AND MEN) |

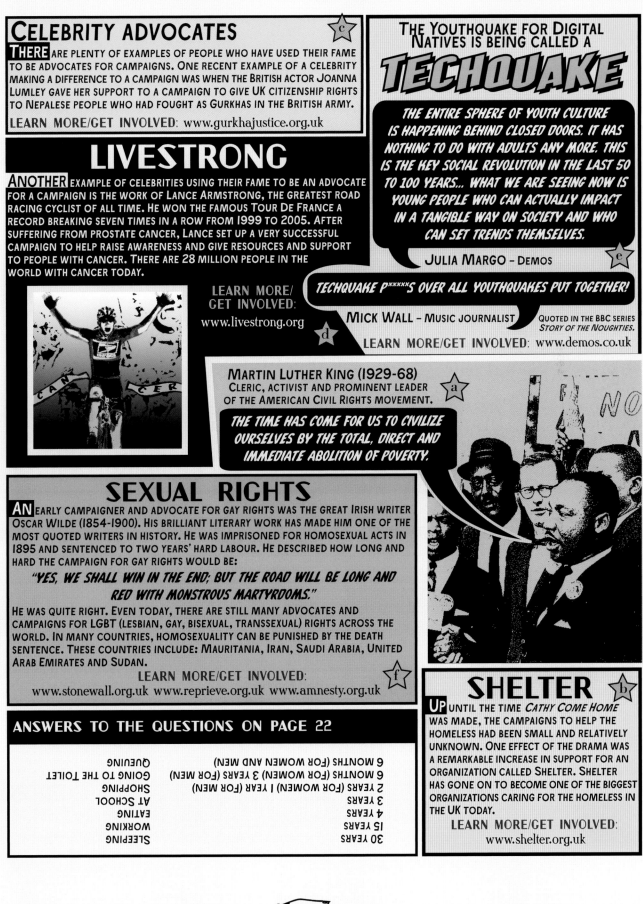

# A SHORT HISTORY of BIG CHANGE thus far.....

## Timeline: SHORT HISTORY OF BIG CHANGE

### THE YEAR OF STUDENT PROTEST — 1968

*This* year is famous in history for being a year of protests not just in Europe but across the world. These protests campaigned for many different ideas, from peace to women's rights, and were almost entirely led by students. It was the first time that younger generations had taken to the front lines of struggles for new rights and freedoms in such a major way. Many workers' unions in France went on strike in support of the huge student protests in Paris. Television news had become a major new tool for campaigners. By creating the kinds of events that would get on to the news, campaigners were able to get their message across to millions.

### MANY RIGHTS AND FREEDOMS WON BY CAMPAIGNING — 1970-79

*By* now in the UK, campaigning for change was a significant part of life for thousands of ordinary Active Citizens. As a result of many campaigns, in the 1970s a series of laws were passed that gave many new rights and freedoms:

EQUAL PAY ACT (1970) — This made it law that women had to be paid equally to men.

HEALTH AND SAFETY ACT (1974) — This made it law that workers had to be able to work in safe and healthy conditions.

⭐a SEX DISCRIMINATION ACT (1975) — This made it law that women could not suffer discrimination at work or in applying for jobs.

RACE RELATIONS ACT (1976) — This made it law that whatever your race or religion, you could not suffer discrimination at work or in applying for jobs.

SALE OF GOODS ACT (1979) — This made it law that the consumer was protected when purchasing a product or service.

### ARRIVAL OF PERSONAL COMPUTERS INTO THE UK — 1977 ⭐b ⭐c

*The* first home computers arrived in Britain. By 2008 68% of homes in the UK had a personal computer. ⭐d

### ARRIVAL OF MOBILE PHONES INTO THE UK — 1983 ⭐e

*The* 1G network was launched in the UK with the first commercial mobile phone made by Motorola. ⭐f

### THE EDUCATION ACT — 1996

*The* Education Act made it the responsibility of parents in the UK to make sure that their children receive an education between the ages of 5 until 16. This is a good example of how a right (in this case to education) comes with responsibilities.

### THE KYOTO PROTOCOL — 1997

*Hundreds* of the most powerful countries in the world met in Kyoto, Japan, to discuss the problems of climate change, pollution and abuse of the world's natural resources. On 11 December 1997, the Kyoto Protocol was created. This was a series of guidelines for countries to limit their emissions and try to stop the increase in pollution of the environment. By 2009, 187 countries had signed the agreement.

---

**IN GROUPS/WHOLE CLASS**

**FIGHT YOUR CORNER**

MOTION: THIS HOUSE BELIEVES THAT CORPORAL PUNISHMENT SHOULD BE RETURNED TO UK SCHOOLS.

CONTINUED ➤

# MORALS AND ETHICS IN THE WORLD OF DISCOVERY

FOR ACTIVE CITIZENS IT IS USEFUL TO CONSIDER THAT SCIENTIFIC DEVELOPMENTS ARE NEUTRAL; THESE DISCOVERIES CAN BE USED IN NEGATIVE OR POSITIVE WAYS. ONE OF THE MOST IMPORTANT CAMPAIGNS TODAY IS TO ENSURE THAT MORALS AND ETHICS ARE USED TO GUIDE THIS RAPIDLY EXPANDING WORLD OF DISCOVERY.

NANOTECHNOLOGY IS A GOOD EXAMPLE OF A SCIENTIFIC DEVELOPMENT THAT CAN BE USED IN POSITIVE WAYS BUT ALSO HAS THE POTENTIAL TO BE USED IN MORALLY AND ETHICALLY QUESTIONABLE WAYS. EITHER WAY, IT IS A MAJOR TECHNOLOGICAL DEVELOPMENT AND WILL HAVE A PROFOUND EFFECT ON HUMANITY. A VERY BASIC DEFINITION OF THIS NEW SCIENCE IS THAT IT INVOLVES THE CREATION OF MACHINES ON A MOLECULAR SCALE. FOR THE WORLD OF MEDICINE, THIS MAY BE A MAJOR BREAKTHROUGH, ALLOWING MINUSCULE MACHINES TO ENTER PEOPLE'S BODIES AND CLEAR CANCERS OR REPAIR HEARTS. HOWEVER, THE MILITARY USES OF NANOTECHNOLOGY MAY BE VERY DESTRUCTIVE, WITH MACHINES DESIGNED TO KILL THAT ARE INVISIBLE TO THE HUMAN EYE AND COULD BE RELEASED FROM THE AIR TO SETTLE UPON AN OPPOSING ARMY.

ACTIVE CITIZENS MIGHT SEE THIS AS AN OPPORTUNITY TO CAMPAIGN FOR ETHICALLY BASED LAWS THAT WOULD ENSURE HUMANITY BENEFITS RATHER THAN SUFFERS FROM MAJOR SCIENTIFIC DEVELOPMENTS.

**LEARN MORE/GET INVOLVED:**
www.foe.org/healthy-people/nanotechnology-campaign
www.safecosmetics.org/article.php?id=307

## ELEMENTAL SLAVERY

THERE IS A RARE EARTH MATERIAL (REM) CALLED COLTAN WHICH IS NECESSARY TO MAKE MOBILE PHONES AND IT IS CURRENTLY ONLY FOUND IN THE DEMOCRATIC REPUBLIC OF THE CONGO. AS A RESULT, THERE IS A GREAT DEAL OF PRESSURE TO EXTRACT THIS REM AND MANY PEOPLE SUFFER AS A CONSEQUENCE. THERE ARE MANY CAMPAIGNS TO ENCOURAGE PEOPLE TO RECYCLE THEIR PHONES AS WELL AS CAMPAIGNS DESIGNED TO PUT PRESSURE ON THOSE RESPONSIBLE FOR CAUSING SUFFERING IN THE DEMOCRATIC REPUBLIC OF THE CONGO.

**LEARN MORE/GET INVOLVED:**
www.globalwitness.org

## AHEAD OF SCIENCE

IN SCIENCE AND TECHNOLOGY LIES ONE OF OUR BEST CHANCES OF SOLVING WORLD PROBLEMS. A GREAT PLACE TO KEEP UP TO DATE WITH NEW DEVELOPMENTS IS THE *NEW SCIENTIST*.

**LEARN MORE/GET INVOLVED:**
www.newscientist.com

## THE WALLET-LESS SOCIETY

TEENAGERS IN SOUTH KOREA ARE THE MOST ADVANCED USERS OF MOBILE PHONES IN THE WORLD. IN FACT, MANY YOUNG SOUTH KOREANS SEE COMPUTERS AS SOMETHING FOR GRANDAD TO USE AS THEY DO EVERYTHING ON THEIR MOBILE PHONES. THEIR PHONES WAKE THEM IN THE MORNING WITH THEIR FAVOURITE TUNES. ON THE WAY TO SCHOOL, THEY WILL USE THEIR PHONE TO TAP THEM THROUGH THE TICKET MACHINE IN THE UNDERGROUND OR ON THE BUS. WHILE ON THE BUS OR TRAIN, THEY WILL CHECK IF A BOOK HAS ARRIVED IN THE SCHOOL LIBRARY, WATCH SOME TV, UPDATE THEIR BLOGS, FINISH SOME HOMEWORK, PAY SOME BILLS AND PLAY A FEW GAMES ALL ON THEIR MOBILES. WHEN THEY ARRIVE AT SCHOOL, THEY USE THE PHONES TO TAP IN AT THE ENTRANCE GATE SO THAT THEY ARE REGISTERED AND THEN USE THEIR PHONES TO RESEARCH WORK OR CREATE DOCUMENTS DURING THEIR LESSONS. THEY MAY EVEN BLUETOOTH WORK TO THEIR TEACHERS. IT'S NOT UNUSUAL FOR TEACHERS TO HAVE WEB PAGES SO THAT STUDENTS CAN CONTACT THEM WITH QUESTIONS ABOUT WORK AND THERE ARE PLENTY OF FORUMS WHERE STUDENTS MEET TO DISCUSS THEIR WORK. ALL ON THEIR MOBILE PHONES. IN 2008 SOUTH KOREANS PAID NEARLY A BILLION POUNDS' WORTH OF THEIR BILLS OR PURCHASES THROUGH THEIR MOBILE PHONES. THE AIM IS TO HAVE A 'WALLET-LESS' SOCIETY.

HOMELESS AND OUT OF WORK PLEASE BLUETOOTH SOME CREDIT

## IT'S A WIRED WIRED WORLD

AS YOUNG ACTIVE CITIZENS AND DIGITAL NATIVES, YOU HAVE THE POWER TO BRING ABOUT CHANGE IN WAYS THAT HAVE NEVER EXISTED ON THE PLANET BEFORE. 21ST-CENTURY COMMUNICATIONS TECHNOLOGY IS PRESENTING US WITH A NEW WORLD WHERE IDEAS AND RESEARCH CAN BE ACCESSED AND CONSIDERED WITH EASE AND YOUR OPINIONS CAN BE SENT OUT TO THE WORLD IN SECONDS. YOU CAN SET UP YOUR OWN BLOG, PODCAST OR SOCIAL NETWORK SITE IN MINUTES, YOUR OWN WEBSITE IN A MATTER OF HOURS AND REACH OUT TO LIKE-MINDED PEOPLE ACROSS THE WORLD IN THEIR THOUSANDS. THIS IS CREATING THE POTENTIAL FOR A GLOBAL DEMOCRACY.

**LEARN MORE/GET INVOLVED:**
www.tigweb.org www.blogger.com www.wordpress.org www.linux.org

DESPITE THE SEX DISCRIMINATION ACTS, WOMEN ARE STILL NOT BEING PAID ON AN EQUAL BASIS TO MEN.

WOMEN WORKING FULL TIME EARN ON AVERAGE

# 17% LESS

PER HOUR THAN MEN

**LEARN MORE/GET INVOLVED:**
www.fawcettsociety.org.uk

## Timeline: SHORT HISTORY OF BIG CHANGE

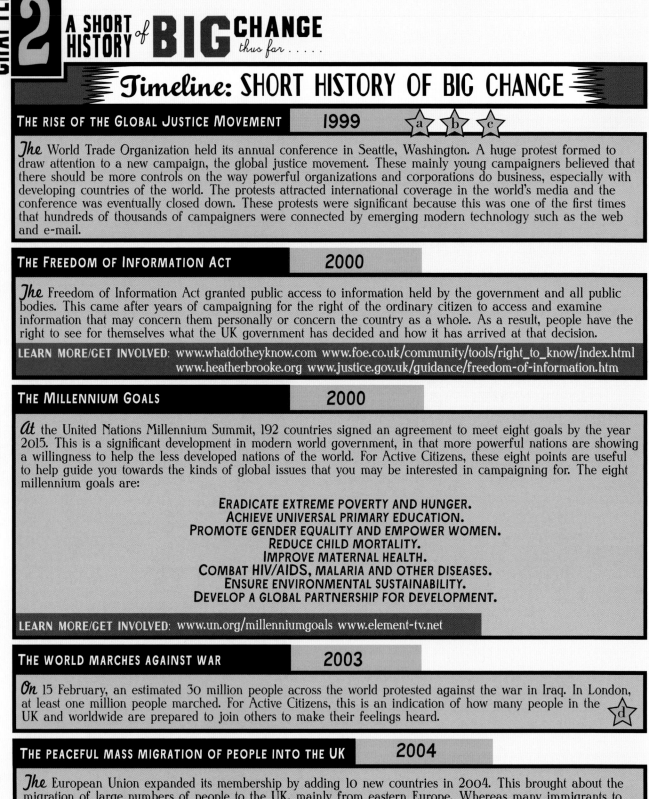

### THE RISE OF THE GLOBAL JUSTICE MOVEMENT — 1999 — a b c

The World Trade Organization held its annual conference in Seattle, Washington. A huge protest formed to draw attention to a new campaign, the global justice movement. These mainly young campaigners believed that there should be more controls on the way powerful organizations and corporations do business, especially with developing countries of the world. The protests attracted international coverage in the world's media and the conference was eventually closed down. These protests were significant because this was one of the first times that hundreds of thousands of campaigners were connected by emerging modern technology such as the web and e-mail.

### THE FREEDOM OF INFORMATION ACT — 2000

The Freedom of Information Act granted public access to information held by the government and all public bodies. This came after years of campaigning for the right of the ordinary citizen to access and examine information that may concern them personally or concern the country as a whole. As a result, people have the right to see for themselves what the UK government has decided and how it has arrived at that decision.

LEARN MORE/GET INVOLVED: www.whatdotheyknow.com www.foe.co.uk/community/tools/right_to_know/index.html
www.heatherbrooke.org www.justice.gov.uk/guidance/freedom-of-information.htm

### THE MILLENNIUM GOALS — 2000

At the United Nations Millennium Summit, 192 countries signed an agreement to meet eight goals by the year 2015. This is a significant development in modern world government, in that more powerful nations are showing a willingness to help the less developed nations of the world. For Active Citizens, these eight points are useful to help guide you towards the kinds of global issues that you may be interested in campaigning for. The eight millennium goals are:

ERADICATE EXTREME POVERTY AND HUNGER.
ACHIEVE UNIVERSAL PRIMARY EDUCATION.
PROMOTE GENDER EQUALITY AND EMPOWER WOMEN.
REDUCE CHILD MORTALITY.
IMPROVE MATERNAL HEALTH.
COMBAT HIV/AIDS, MALARIA AND OTHER DISEASES.
ENSURE ENVIRONMENTAL SUSTAINABILITY.
DEVELOP A GLOBAL PARTNERSHIP FOR DEVELOPMENT.

LEARN MORE/GET INVOLVED: www.un.org/millenniumgoals www.element-tv.net

### THE WORLD MARCHES AGAINST WAR — 2003

On 15 February, an estimated 30 million people across the world protested against the war in Iraq. In London, at least one million people marched. For Active Citizens, this is an indication of how many people in the UK and worldwide are prepared to join others to make their feelings heard. d

### THE PEACEFUL MASS MIGRATION OF PEOPLE INTO THE UK — 2004

The European Union expanded its membership by adding 10 new countries in 2004. This brought about the migration of large numbers of people to the UK, mainly from eastern Europe. Whereas many immigrants to the UK in the 1940s and 1950s met with racism, this time, the immigration was peaceful and largely welcomed by many UK citizens. The UK has become one of the most multicultural countries in the world. In London alone, there are more than 50 ethnic minorities with at least 10,000 members. e

CONTINUED

# DO YOU KNOW WHAT I MEAN?

**AS** A RESULT OF THE MIX OF RACES IN THE UK, YOUNG PEOPLE HAVE DEVELOPED A STREET SLANG THAT CHANGES RAPIDLY. NOBODY KNOWS WHERE THE WORDS HAVE COME FROM AS THEY MIX UP SLANG FROM ALL AROUND THE WORLD. DO YOU KNOW WHERE 'NANG', 'CREPS', 'BUFF', 'BATTIES' OR 'BARE' CAME FROM ORIGINALLY? THIS BOOK IS BEING WRITTEN IN 2010. MAYBE BY THE TIME YOU COME TO USE THE TOOLKIT, THERE WILL BE MANY MORE SLANG WORDS USED BY YOUNG PEOPLE AND YOU WILL HAVE NEVER HEARD OF 'NANG' OR 'BUFF'!  ⭐e

## THE LARGEST ANTI-WAR RALLY OF ALL TIME

**ON** 15 FEBRUARY 2003, MILLIONS OF PEOPLE PROTESTED AGAINST THE IMMINENT INVASION OF IRAQ IN APPROXIMATELY 800 CITIES AROUND THE WORLD. IT IS THOUGHT THAT BETWEEN SIX AND TEN MILLION PEOPLE TOOK PART IN PROTESTS IN UP TO 60 COUNTRIES OVER THE WEEKEND OF 15 AND 16 FEBRUARY. IN ROME ALONE, THREE MILLION PEOPLE PROTESTED AND THE *GUINNESS BOOK OF RECORDS* REGISTERED THIS AS THE LARGEST ANTI-WAR RALLY OF ALL TIME.

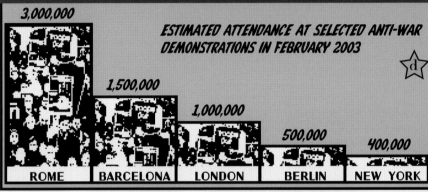

*ESTIMATED ATTENDANCE AT SELECTED ANTI-WAR DEMONSTRATIONS IN FEBRUARY 2003* ⭐d

| ROME | BARCELONA | LONDON | BERLIN | NEW YORK |
|------|-----------|--------|--------|----------|
| 3,000,000 | 1,500,000 | 1,000,000 | 500,000 | 400,000 |

# LIFE AFTER SHOPPING

**THE** GLOBAL JUSTICE MOVEMENT LED TO AN UPSURGE OF CAMPAIGNS CONNECTED TO THESE EARLY PROTESTS AND DEMONSTRATIONS. FOR THE FIRST TIME, MAJOR CAMPAIGNS WERE BEING BUILT AROUND THE WAY GLOBAL ECONOMICS WERE AFFECTING THE DEVELOPING WORLD AS WELL AS THE LIVES OF PEOPLE IN RICH COUNTRIES. PEOPLE BEGAN TO QUESTION THE MORALS AND ETHICS BEHIND WHAT THEY BOUGHT AND BEHIND THE WAY MAJOR CORPORATIONS BEHAVED, PARTICULARLY IN THE DEVELOPING WORLD.

ONE OF THE MANY CAMPAIGNS ASSOCIATED WITH THIS MOVEMENT USES HUMOUR IN ORDER TO GET ACROSS A SERIOUS MESSAGE. THE CAMPAIGN GROUP IS MADE TO LOOK LIKE A CHURCH MOVEMENT AND IS CALLED: REVEREND BILLY AND THE CHURCH OF LIFE AFTER SHOPPING. THE REVEREND BILLY IS A CHARACTER WHO IS AN ADVOCATE FOR REJECTING CONSUMERIST SOCIETY. ONE OF HIS MORE FAMOUS CAMPAIGN IDEAS HAS BEEN TO CREATE A 'BUY NOTHING DAY' WHERE HE ENCOURAGES PEOPLE ACROSS THE WORLD TO BUY NOTHING ON ONE DAY IN THE YEAR, USUALLY IN NOVEMBER.  ⭐c

LEARN MORE/GET INVOLVED:
www.revbilly.com

## THE CORPORATION

**IN** 2003, A FILM CALLED *THE CORPORATION* WAS RELEASED THAT CAPTURED THE IDEAS OF THE NEW GLOBAL JUSTICE MOVEMENT.

LEARN MORE/ GET INVOLVED: ⭐a
www.thecorporation.com

## NO LOGO

**THE** FIRST BOOK TO CAPTURE THE IDEAS OF THE NEW GLOBAL JUSTICE MOVEMENT WAS *NO LOGO* (PUBLISHED 2000) BY THE CANADIAN AUTHOR AND ACTIVIST, NAOMI KLEIN. SHE HAS GONE ON TO BE ONE OF THE MOST RECOGNIZED ADVOCATES FOR THIS GRASSROOTS CAMPAIGN. ⭐b

LEARN MORE/GET INVOLVED:
www.naomiklein.org

# A SHORT HISTORY of BIG CHANGE *thus far.....*

## Timeline: SHORT HISTORY OF BIG CHANGE

### YOUTH POWER IN FRANCE — 2006

*Over* three million people demonstrated throughout France against a new law that affected the employment rights of young people. This day of mass action was only one of many that had gone on for months in the country. As in 1968, the young people of France found that the country and the country's workers were in full support of the cause and the law was finally crushed.

ⓐ ⓑ

### THE UNITED NATIONS CLIMATE CHANGE CONFERENCE — 2009

*This* conference was held in Copenhagen, Denmark, and was the largest meeting on Climate Change that the world had ever seen. Government leaders and global Non-Governmental Organizations (NGOs) met to discuss ways to combat the continual negative effects of pollution and abuse of the world's resources. Campaigners from around the world descended on Copenhagen to make their ideas heard and an estimated 100,000 people marched through the streets. The decisions made at the end of the conference were not legally binding and although some world leaders claimed that the meeting had been a success, many others stated that it had been a failure.

ⓒ

### 2010

### THE CHILCOT INQUIRY — JANUARY – FEBRUARY

*Several* well-known figures from government – including former Prime Minister Tony Blair and Prime Minister Gordon Brown – gave evidence in public to the Chilcot Inquiry, which had been set up to assess the UK's role in the 2003 invasion of Iraq. Many people praised the government for establishing the Inquiry, which sought to investigate whether the second Gulf War was legal. However, the Chilcot Inquiry came in for some criticism both in Britain and abroad. On 12 January, for example, an independent panel of seven judges in the Netherlands ruled that the invasion of Iraq was in fact illegal and therefore declared that all Dutch support of the war should immediately cease. Philippe Sands QC – a professor of international law who gave evidence to the Dutch inquiry – also questioned the legality of the Chilcot Inquiry itself, suggesting that nobody on the Chilcot panel was legally qualified for the task. Other critics doubted the independence of the Chilcot Inquiry by pointing out that all the members of the panel had been picked by Prime Minister Gordon Brown himself. Publication of the Inquiry's conclusions was suspended until after the General Election on 6 May 2010.

### CABS FOR HIRE — MARCH ⓓ

*An* undercover team of investigators for Channel 4 TV recorded four major UK politicians apparently stating that, in return for large sums of money, they would be willing to use their political positions to influence government decisions on behalf of private companies. This was known as the 'cabs for hire' scandal as one of the politicians said that the way he worked was similar to being a "cab for hire".

### THE PEOPLE'S WORLD CONFERENCE ON CLIMATE CHANGE AND MOTHER EARTH RIGHTS — APRIL

*In* response to the Climate Change Conference in Copenhagen where many felt that the richer, industrialized nations held too much power – the President of Bolivia, Eva Morales, decided to hold a people's conference in the Bolivian city of Cochabamba. The aim of the conference was to represent the views of indigenous peoples and developing countries on climate change. Although volcanic ash from Iceland had stopped flights taking off from Europe, over 30,000 people from around the world attended. The conference concluded that a global referendum should be held over the issue of climate change. It also recommended that an international climate and environmental justice court should be set up with binding legal power to restrain, prosecute and punish states, companies and individuals. Many climate activists see this as the beginning of a new global grassroots movement for climate justice that will ultimately result in crimes against the environment being comparable to crimes against humanity.

# FIRST LIVE TV PRIME MINISTERIAL DEBATE IN UK GENERAL ELECTION

ON 15 APRIL 2010, NICK CLEGG (LIBERAL DEMOCRAT), GORDON BROWN (LABOUR) AND DAVID CAMERON (CONSERVATIVE) WENT HEAD-TO-HEAD IN THE FIRST OF THREE LIVE TELEVISION DEBATES. THIS WAS SEEN AS A STEP FORWARD FOR DEMOCRACY IN THE UK AND PRESENTED THE PUBLIC WITH AN OPPORTUNITY TO DECIDE FOR THEMSELVES WHAT THE THREE MAIN CANDIDATES WERE LIKE AND WHAT THEY STOOD FOR. BECAUSE OF RECENT POLITICAL DISGRACES SUCH AS THE 'CABS FOR HIRE' AND 'EXPENSES SCANDAL', THE MAIN PARTIES ALL STRESSED THAT CLEANING UP PARLIAMENT WOULD BE A TOP PRIORITY.

## Active French Youth 1

IN NAZI-OCCUPIED FRANCE DURING WORLD WAR TWO, THE FRENCH RESISTANCE HAD A GREAT MANY TEENAGERS AMONGST THEM. SUZANNE DAVID HALL, AT THE AGE OF 13, JOINED AFTER SHE WITNESSED A MOTHER AND HER BABY BEING BLOWN TO BITS BY A NAZI BOMB. BECAUSE SHE WAS A TALENTED OPERA SINGER, SHE TRAVELLED THE COUNTRY ON A REGULAR BASIS. AS A RESULT, HALL WAS A VALUABLE AGENT FOR THE RESISTANCE AS SHE WAS ABLE TO PASS SECRET MESSAGES TO OTHER AGENTS. SHE WAS GIVEN THE CODE NAME 'AGENT 22'. NEAR THE END OF THE WAR, SHE WAS RESPONSIBLE FOR PASSING ON MESSAGES ABOUT THE PLANNED 'D-DAY' INVASION. THE NAZIS FINALLY DID CATCH HALL AND INTERROGATED HER FOR DAYS. SHE GAVE NOTHING AWAY AND SURVIVED THE INTERROGATION, ALTHOUGH MANY OTHER SPIES WHO HAD BEEN CAUGHT WERE EXECUTED.

## Active French Youth 2

IN 1990, A 16-YEAR-OLD SCHOOL STUDENT, MANDARINE MARTINON, DISCOVERED THAT HUGE GOVERNMENT CUTS HAD BEEN MADE TO THE BUDGETS OF SCHOOLS ACROSS FRANCE, INCLUDING HER SCHOOL IN THE WORKING-CLASS SUBURB OF VILLEURBAINE. SHE ORGANIZED A GROUP OF TEENAGERS TO DEMONSTRATE AGAINST THESE CUTS IN HER OWN SCHOOL. MANY OTHER TEENAGERS DID THE SAME IN THEIR SCHOOLS AND QUICKLY, THIS TEEN GRASSROOTS MOVEMENT CAUGHT ON. THIS LED TO 100,000 TEENAGERS MARCHING IN PARIS AND CONFRONTING THE GOVERNMENT WITH THEIR WISHES. AS A RESULT, THE GOVERNMENT GAVE IN AND ADDED €68,602,050 TO THEIR SCHOOLS BUDGET. MARTINON STATED THAT THE POLITICIANS WERE "VERY CUNNING, GIVING THE IMPRESSION THAT THEY UNDERSTOOD EVERYTHING, BUT WE WERE NOT TAKEN IN".

# COPENHAGEN/HOPENHAGEN?

THE CLIMATE CONFERENCE IN COPENHAGEN WAS MATCHED BY HUGE DEMONSTRATIONS BY CAMPAIGNERS FROM ALL OVER THE WORLD. THE 10 DAYS OF ACTIONS, RALLIES AND ALTERNATIVE CONFERENCES SHOWED THAT THE PEOPLE OF THE WORLD ARE EXTREMELY CONCERNED ABOUT THE DANGERS OF CLIMATE CHANGE. THIS LED TO PLANS TO HOLD A 'PEOPLE'S WORLD CONFERENCE' IN BOLIVIA IN ORDER TO HURRY UP PLANS TO COMBAT CLIMATE CHANGE AND POLLUTION CAUSED MAINLY BY INDUSTRIALIZED NATIONS. THE BOLIVIAN CONFERENCE WAS ALSO SET UP TO INCREASE THE PRESSURE ON POWERFUL GOVERNMENT LEADERS WHO MAY BE MORE INTERESTED IN PROTECTING THEIR COUNTRIES' ECONOMIC VESTED INTERESTS THAN IN PROTECTING THE PLANET.

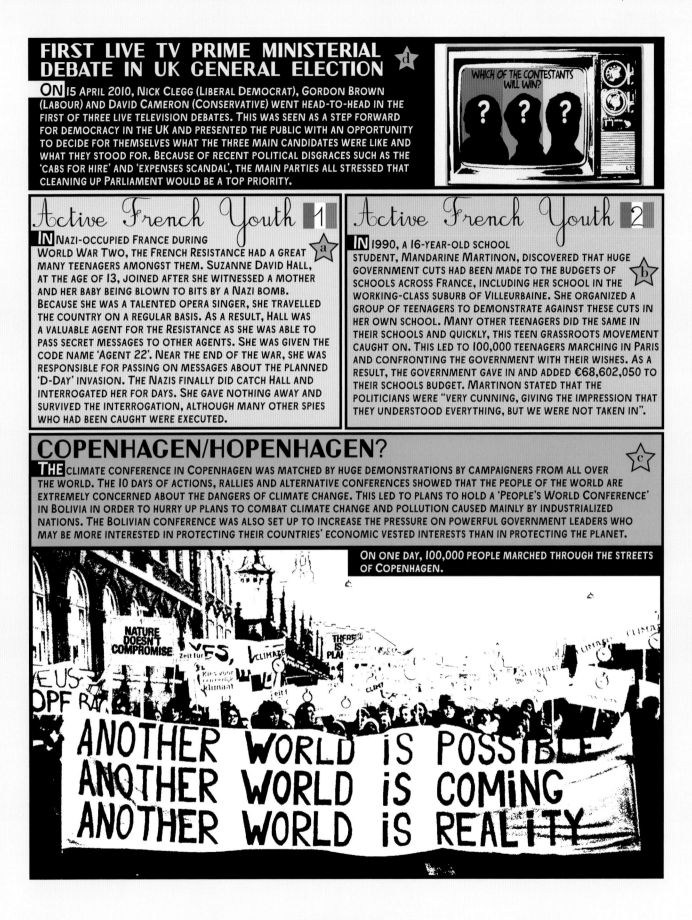

ON ONE DAY, 100,000 PEOPLE MARCHED THROUGH THE STREETS OF COPENHAGEN.

## 7 I'm only a teenager, what can I do?

**Young** people have often been a major part of movements for change in the past and definitely are today. Your voice is not only protected and valued but it is law that what you have to say must be taken seriously and acted upon where appropriate. Everything is in place to encourage young people to make change happen on a local, national and global scale.

**YOUR HELP IS NOT ONLY VALUED BUT NEEDED.**

## AFTER ALL, IT'S YOUR FUTURE!

### THE UNITED NATIONS CONVENTION ON THE RIGHTS OF THE CHILD (CRC)

*The* UK signed up to the CRC in 1990. Today, there are 194 countries that have signed up to these 54 articles of law. The only two UN countries not to have signed up to this are the US and Somalia. For Active Citizenship, the two most important ones are Article 12 and Article 13.

## ARTICLE 12

*"States* Parties shall assure to the child who is capable of forming his or her own views the right to express those views freely in all matters affecting the child, the views of the child being given due weight in accordance with the age and maturity of the child."

## ARTICLE 13

*"The* child shall have the right to freedom of expression; this right shall include freedom to seek, receive and impart information and ideas of all kinds, regardless of frontiers, either orally, in writing or in print, in the form of art, or through any other media of the child's choice."

**SOURCE/FIND OUT MORE**: www.unicef.org/crc/

### REMEMBER: WITH RIGHTS COME RESPONSIBILITIES.

**FOR EXAMPLE** the CRC grants you the right to an education but with that comes the responsibility not to abuse that right by disrupting your school or lessons. Also, don't forget the difference between needs and wants. The CRC provides laws to protect basic needs such as clean water and food. A young person may want Rogan Josh curry and milkshakes but those aren't to do with your basic needs, they are your personal wants!

---

**ACTIVITY IN GROUPS**
**3.9.27**
*You* have 10 MINUTES to COME UP WITH A 3.9.27 FOR EACH OF THESE TWO ARTICLES OF LAW. (BELOW LEFT)
**YOU MUST COMMUNICATE CLEARLY WHAT THEY MEAN.**
Feed back your ideas to the class.
Vote on the clearest one for each Article of Law.
Make a note of them.

*TICK TOCK*

## 8 Rax Interview with Craig Kielburger

AT THE AGE OF 12, CANADIAN CRAIG KIELBURGER SAW A STORY IN THE PAPERS ABOUT A 12-YEAR-OLD PAKISTANI BOY WHO HAD BEEN MURDERED FOR SPEAKING OUT AGAINST CHILD LABOUR FACTORIES. CRAIG STARTED A CHILDREN'S RIGHTS CAMPAIGN (FREE THE CHILDREN) THE NEXT DAY WITH TWO FRIENDS AT HIS SCHOOL. FREE THE CHILDREN HAS GONE ON TO BE ONE OF THE MOST SUCCESSFUL YOUTH RIGHTS CAMPAIGNS IN THE WORLD. IN 2006, RAX STUDENTS AT SWANLEA SCHOOL IN EAST LONDON HAD THE OPPORTUNITY TO INTERVIEW HIM.

*RABBEY: DID YOU EVER MISS OUT ON YOUR CHILDHOOD?*

*Childhood* is a lot more than video games, TV, hanging around shopping malls. A lot of adults say that's all there is to youth. I don't believe it. I think that even if you're young and you find an issue that you're passionate about, you take action about it now. Why just be an adult in waiting?

*IMRAN: WHAT KIND OF OBSTACLES DID YOU COME UP AGAINST?*

*Everything* from dictators in developing countries to factory owners who didn't want us taking kids out of their factories. But the greatest obstacle wasn't overseas, it was back home. Adults who looked at us kids and said, "Nice idea, you're dreaming." Ten years later, we support over a million kids around the world. 625,000 families, every day, use our clean water projects, our health clinics and co-operatives for women. We have set up 420 primary schools in developing countries... That's all because a group of Year Seven students didn't listen when those adults said, "You're dreaming".

*AYESHA: DID THE RESPONSIBILITY EVER BECOME A NUISANCE TO YOU AT SUCH A YOUNG AGE?*

*I* think what was the greatest responsibility was that we met a lot of kids whom we couldn't help at the time. There was an eight-year-old girl whom I met in India

CONTINUED ⟶

"I REALLY BELIEVE THAT THE MOST POWERFUL FORCE IN THE WORLD TODAY IS YOUNG PEOPLE BECAUSE THEY ARE AN UNTAPPED FORCE."

**CRAIG KIELBURGER** - YOUTH RIGHTS CAMPAIGNER, FOUNDER OF FREE THE CHILDREN (AT THE AGE OF 12) AND NOMINEE FOR THE NOBEL PEACE PRIZE. (SEE INTERVIEW ON PAGE 50)

I RUN ALL DAY AND NEVER WALK. I TELL YOU SOMETHING, BUT I DO NOT TALK. WHAT AM I? ANSWER ON PAGE 53.

ANSWERS TO LATERAL THINKING EXERCISE ON PAGE 23

INFLATE THE TYRES AND CHOOSE ANOTHER ROUTE! SIMPLY LET THE TYRES DOWN, SHE CAN REVERSE OUT OF THE TUNNEL,

HE'S A PRIEST AND HE'S MARRYING THEM TO OTHER PEOPLE, NOT HIMSELF!

and she worked in a recycling factory. She was taking apart used syringes and needles for their plastics but she had no gloves. I could see that her hands were cut and she'd never heard of AIDS. We were rushed out because we were told that if her master saw her talking to us he would beat her. I've gone back to India four times to that same village trying to find her but I never have. I feel a sense of responsibility, that I should have done something. But this is a responsibility I think we all have. Whenever we see an injustice, we should speak out. We do human rights work not because it's easy but because it's necessary.

### DEBORAH: HAVE YOU CHANGED YOUR LIFESTYLE?

*There's* a phrase that I always try to live by, it's the words of Mahatma Gandhi: "Be the change that you want to see in the world." It's about how we live our lives every day. When I shop, I ask, "Where's the product made? Under what working conditions?" I'll never miss an election – you make your voice heard. It's about how we spend our free moments – go and volunteer in your own neighbourhood. We can't all be Gandhi but we can at least try and be true to ourselves.

### HODDEN: HOW DO YOU MOTIVATE PEOPLE TO MAKE A CHANGE AROUND THE WORLD?

*There's* poverty going on in the world and we spend $1 trillion on arms, $400 billion on cigarettes, $140 billion drinking beer and $40 billion playing golf a year when all it would take to put every child into school is $10 billion a year.

### SO HOW DO WE MOTIVATE PEOPLE TO TAKE ACTION?

#### IT STARTS WITH CARING.

① EDUCATE YOURSELF, KNOWLEDGE IS POWER.
② FIND OUT HOW YOU CAN TAKE ACTION.
③ WHATEVER YOUR GIFT IS, FIND YOUR GIFT.
FIND YOUR ISSUE AND YOUR TALENT AND MATCH THEM TOGETHER. IT'S THE EQUATION FOR SOCIAL CHANGE.

### LILLY: YOU FOCUS ON CHILD EDUCATION BUT WHAT CAN WE DO ABOUT GLOBAL WARMING?

*Every* issue is interconnected. For example, in Kenya, a US agricultural business was growing flowers for export. It drilled massive bore wells that were sucking all the water out of the ground. As a result, the local farmers' crops didn't grow and they had to send their children to the streets to beg for money. All this so that we could buy flowers for Mothers' Day back home. Climate change has the same effect. When you start asking questions, you learn that all of these issues are interconnected: kids end up in child labour, young girls end up in prostitution and young boys end up making bricks. So it doesn't matter what your passion is – environment, animal rights, child labour, education, racism, sexism, you name it – just take action! Because they're all interconnected.

WE SPEND $1 TRILLION ON ARMS, $400 BILLION ON CIGARETTES, $140 BILLION DRINKING BEER AND $40 BILLION PLAYING GOLF WHEN ALL IT WOULD TAKE TO PUT EVERY CHILD INTO SCHOOL IS $10 BILLION A YEAR.

### SOUVIK: AS ADULTS DON'T TAKE US SERIOUSLY, WHAT CAN WE DO TO IMPROVE THE WORLD?

*Well,* the adults have left the world in a pretty good place, don't you think? Nuclear weapons, poverty, discrimination, global warming... How about we don't take the adults seriously? How about, instead, we do what we want to do, which is to create a better world?

I really believe that the most powerful force in the world is young people because it's an untapped force. The people who faced the brunt of the water cannons in the time of Dr Martin Luther King were students. In India, you had 10 and 11 year olds who were arrested in their hundreds on Gandhi's Salt March. In China, in Tiananmen Square, it was students who stood in front of the tanks. In South Africa it was students against the apartheid regime who were shot as they marched. In every great social justice movement, students have been at the forefront. So, the answer to adults who don't take us seriously? Don't take them seriously in turn. Do the research, have your statistics and have the answers because knowledge is power. At the end of the day, NOTHING, NOTHING, NOTHING SHOULD HOLD YOU BACK IF YOU HAVE A DREAM. FOLLOW IT!

> **IN EVERY GREAT SOCIAL JUSTICE MOVEMENT, STUDENTS HAVE BEEN AT THE FOREFRONT.**
>
> CRAIG KIELBURGER

HUNDREDS OF THOUSANDS OF PEOPLE JOINED GANDHI ON THE SALT MARCH IN 1930. MANY OF THEM WERE YOUNG PEOPLE.

# LEARN MORE/GET INVOLVED:

THERE ARE SEVERAL ORGANIZATIONS CONNECTED TO THE ISSUES CRAIG DISCUSSES. HERE IS A SELECTION:

### ORGANIZATIONS THAT RAISE AWARENESS ABOUT THE ETHICAL BACKGROUND TO PRODUCTS:

www.peopleandplanet.org/wearfair
www.cleanclothes.org/home
www.unionvoice.org/studentsagainstsweat

### ORGANIZATIONS THAT FOCUS ON CHILDREN'S RIGHTS TO EDUCATION:

www.oxfam.org/en/campaigns/health-education
www.amnesty.org/en/children
www.campaignforeducation.org
www.sendmyfriend.org

### ORGANIZATIONS THAT RAISE AWARENESS OF THE ETHICAL PRACTICES OF CORPORATIONS:

www.corpwatch.org
www.transparency.org

## THE 10 COUNTRIES WITH THE HIGHEST PROPORTION OF CHILD WORKERS.

| COUNTRY | PERCENTAGE OF 7– 14 YEAR OLDS AT WORK |
|---|---|
| 1. MALI | 70.9 |
| 2. GUINEA-BISSAU | 67.5 |
| 3. CENTRAL AFRICAN REPUBLIC | 67.0 |
| 4. SIERRA LEONE | 65.0 |
| 5. CHAD | 60.4 |
| 6. ETHIOPIA | 56.0 |
| 7. NEPAL | 52.4 |
| 8. CAMBODIA | 52.3 |
| 9. BURKINA FASO | 50.0 |
| 10. GUINEA | 48.3 |

SOURCE: World Bank, World Development Indicators 2008/International Labour Organization.

# WHAT HAPPENED BECAUSE A 12 YEAR OLD HAD AN IDEA FOR CHANGE

OVER 500 SCHOOLS HAVE BEEN BUILT, PROVIDING ACCESS TO EDUCATION FOR OVER 50,000 CHILDREN IN DEVELOPING COUNTRIES.

650,000 PEOPLE HAVE IMPROVED ACCESS TO CLEAN WATER, SANITATION AND HEALTH CARE.

£10 MILLION WORTH OF ESSENTIAL MEDICAL SUPPLIES HAVE BEEN SENT TO OVER 512,000 PEOPLE.

23,500 WOMEN ARE ECONOMICALLY SELF-SUFFICIENT BECAUSE OF MICROFINANCE SCHEMES.

207,000 SCHOOL AND HEALTH KITS HAVE BEEN SENT TO CHILDREN IN NEED.

3,500 LOCAL BRANCHES OF FREE THE CHILDREN HAVE BEEN SET UP.

350,000 CHILDREN A YEAR ATTEND FREE THE CHILDREN ADVOCACY WORKSHOPS AND PROGRAMMES.

**LEARN MORE/GET INVOLVED:**
Craig Kielburger's organizations: www.freethechildren.com
www.metowe.com

LOCAL FARMERS

INDUSTRIAL FLOWER FARM

EXPORT PROFITS

KENYA

NO S

CAMPAIGN HQ

"ALL THIS SO THAT WE COULD BUY FLOWERS FOR MOTHERS' DAY BACK HOME."

WATER TABLE

FLORIST

EUROPE

# CHAPTER 3 The MIRROR ЯΟЯЯIM

## 1 Why is this chapter important?

ONE OF THE KEYS TO THE SUCCESS OF AN ACTIVE CITIZENSHIP CAMPAIGN IS MAKING SURE THAT YOU KEEP A RECORD OF EVERYTHING THAT YOU DO, COLLATE ALL THE EVIDENCE THAT YOU GATHER, REFLECT ON THE PROCESS OF YOUR CAMPAIGNS AND ASSESS THE IMPACT YOU HAVE HAD.

### THIS CHAPTER WILL HELP ENSURE THAT:

- YOU HAVE THE EASIEST BUT MOST THOROUGH WAYS OF KEEPING A RECORD.
- YOU HAVE ALL THE RESEARCH THAT YOU HAVE GATHERED AT YOUR FINGERTIPS.
- YOU HAVE A SIMPLE BUT EFFECTIVE WAY TO ASSESS AND EVALUATE YOUR WHOLE CAMPAIGN PROCESS.
- YOU HAVE A CLEAR MEANS OF MONITORING THE IMPACT OF YOUR CAMPAIGNS.
- YOU HAVE EVIDENCE THAT YOU HAVE DONE WHAT YOU SAY THAT YOU HAVE DONE.
- (IF YOU ARE TAKING A GCSE) YOU CAN GET THROUGH THE CONTROLLED ASSESSMENT TASK WITH FLYING COLOURS.

IN OTHER WORDS, YOU WILL USE THE SKILLS OF COLLATING, EVALUATION AND ASSESSMENT TO A VERY HIGH LEVEL IN ORDER TO CREATE SUCCESSFUL ACTIVE CITIZENSHIP CAMPAIGNS.

*Active* Citizenship is very different from all your other subjects because it is about you making a real change to your world. As a result, the Toolkit has been specially constructed to encourage you to follow your own path through the Active Citizenship experience. This is called self-directed learning.

### YOU ARE IN CHARGE OF YOUR OWN LEARNING.

This chapter is going to give you a few more ideas about how to get the best out of the Toolkit and the Active Citizenship experience. The Toolkit is going to make you look at yourself, what you do and how you do it. That's why this chapter is called *The Mirror.*

## 2 What is self-directed learning?

*The* main aim of the Toolkit is to give you the skills to work with others to make a change happen in your world. The Toolkit will never tell you what issues you should work on but will give you as many different ideas as possible.

Most of the right-hand pages in the Toolkit are full of ideas, facts and quotations connected to the process of change. Many of these panels also include websites that you can visit to find out more. The Toolkit tries to cover as many different ideas for change as possible. However, you are in charge – the material is there to help you to choose which areas you want to pursue.

### THE RIGHT-HAND PANELS ARE PLACES WHERE YOU CAN BEGIN YOUR OWN JOURNEYS.

CONTINUED

# YOUR RIGHT TO KNOW

**THE** FREEDOM OF INFORMATION ACT (2000) HAS HAD A SIGNIFICANT EFFECT ON HOW CITIZENS CAN INTERACT WITH GOVERNMENT AT ALL LEVELS. HAVING ACCESS TO OFFICIAL RECORDS ALLOWS ORDINARY CITIZENS TO INFORM THEMSELVES ABOUT KEY ASPECTS OF PUBLIC LIFE THAT ALWAYS USED TO BE HIDDEN. IT ALSO ENABLES ACTIVE CITIZENS TO ACCESS INFORMATION THAT CAN HELP THEM RESEARCH THEIR CAMPAIGNS. THERE IS SOMETIMES A NOMINAL FEE TO PAY FOR THIS SERVICE AND CERTAIN INFORMATION – CONNECTED TO SECURITY OF THE NATION – WILL REMAIN SECRET.

HEATHER BROOKE, AN AWARD-WINNING JOURNALIST AND ACTIVIST, HAS BEEN AN EARLY CHAMPION FOR THE USE OF THE FREEDOM OF INFORMATION ACT TO BRING ABOUT CHANGE. SHE RAN A FIVE-YEAR CAMPAIGN TO FORCE FULL DISCLOSURE OF MPS' EXPENSES, WHICH BECAME A MAJOR STORY IN 2009. HER WEBSITE DETAILS HOW CAMPAIGNERS CAN USE THE ACT TO FURTHER THEIR OWN WORK.

**LEARN MORE/GET INVOLVED:** www.heatherbrooke.org
www.whatdotheyknow.com

> THINK OF AN EDUCATION NOT AS SOMETHING YOU GET, BUT AS SOMETHING YOU TAKE... THE PROCESS OF TAKING CONTROL OF YOUR OWN EDUCATION... IS THE LIFEBLOOD OF DEMOCRACY.

**CHARLES D HAYES** – US AUTHOR.

# BE THE INSPECTORS

## A THE WEB ARCHIVE

**THE** COPYRIGHT ACT OF 1911 MADE IT STATUTORY THAT A COPY OF EVERY UK PUBLICATION BE KEPT IN THE BRITISH LIBRARY – AND THIS INCLUDES PAMPHLETS AND NEWSPAPERS AS WELL AS BOOKS. BUT WHAT ABOUT WEB PAGES? THE LEGAL DEPOSIT LIBRARIES ACT, PASSED IN 2003, HAS BEEN DESIGNED SO THAT THE SAME COPYRIGHT LAWS APPLY TO NON-PRINT PUBLICATIONS SUCH AS WEBSITES, ALTHOUGH THE ACT IS STILL ONLY A FRAMEWORK AND REQUIRES FURTHER WORK BEFORE IT BECOMES LEGALLY BINDING.

ACCORDING TO RESEARCHERS AT THE BRITISH LIBRARY, THE AVERAGE LIFE EXPECTANCY OF A WEBSITE IS BETWEEN 44 AND 75 DAYS, WHICH MEANS THAT A VAST AMOUNT OF MATERIAL IS CREATED AND THEN LOST FOREVER. BASED ON A US MODEL, THE BRITISH LIBRARY HAS CREATED THE 'WEB ARCHIVE' PROJECT, WHICH SEEKS TO KEEP A COPY OF EVERY WEB PAGE EVER CREATED. IT IS A VERY INTERESTING SITE TO VISIT, OFFERING AN INSIGHT INTO HOW WEBSITES HAVE CHANGED AND DEVELOPED SINCE THEY WERE FIRST CREATED.

**LEARN MORE/GET INVOLVED:**
www.webarchive.org.uk

**A KEY** ORGANIZATION FOR SUCCESSFUL YOUNG ACTIVE CITIZENSHIP CAMPAIGNERS IS THE BRITISH YOUTH COUNCIL (BYC). THEIR MEMBERS ARE ALL UNDER 25 AND MANY OF THEM ARE TEENAGERS. THEIR CENTRAL VISION IS THAT "ALL YOUNG PEOPLE ACROSS THE UK WILL HAVE A SAY AND BE HEARD". BYC HAVE LOCAL YOUTH COUNCILS RIGHT ACROSS THE UK, RUN BY YOUNG PEOPLE FOR YOUNG PEOPLE. THESE OFFER YOU THE OPPORTUNITY TO BE INSPECTORS OF YOUR OWN LOCAL SERVICES, EVALUATING WHETHER THESE SERVICES ARE SUFFICIENT FOR YOUNG PEOPLE AND WORK PROPERLY.

THE ORGANIZATION STARTED IN 1948 AND IN 2008 IT CELEBRATED 60 YEARS OF CAMPAIGNING FOR THE VOICE OF YOUNG PEOPLE TO BE HEARD AND ACTED UPON. MANY YOUNG ACTIVISTS FROM BYC HAVE GONE ON TO BECOME POLITICIANS, AS IT IS A FIRM STARTING PLACE FOR YOUNG PEOPLE WHERE THEY LEARN THE SKILLS OF LEADERSHIP, RESPONSIBILITY, ADVOCACY AND TAKING INFORMED AND RESPONSIBLE ACTION.

IN THE LEAD-UP TO THE 2010 GENERAL ELECTION, THE BYC CAMPAIGNED ON FIVE ISSUES:

> LOWERING THE VOTING AGE TO 16
> CREATING A NATIONAL YOUTH TRANSPORT CARD THAT ALLOWS YOUNG PEOPLE A THIRD OFF PUBLIC TRANSPORT FARES.
> MAKING THE NATIONAL MINIMUM WAGE EQUAL FOR EVERYONE OVER 16.
> ENDING CHILD POVERTY IN THE UK BY 2020.
> INVESTING IN MENTAL HEALTH SERVICES FOR YOUNG PEOPLE.

**LEARN MORE/GET INVOLVED:** www.byc.org.uk

TWO PEANUTS WALKED INTO A BAR, ONE WAS A SALTED.

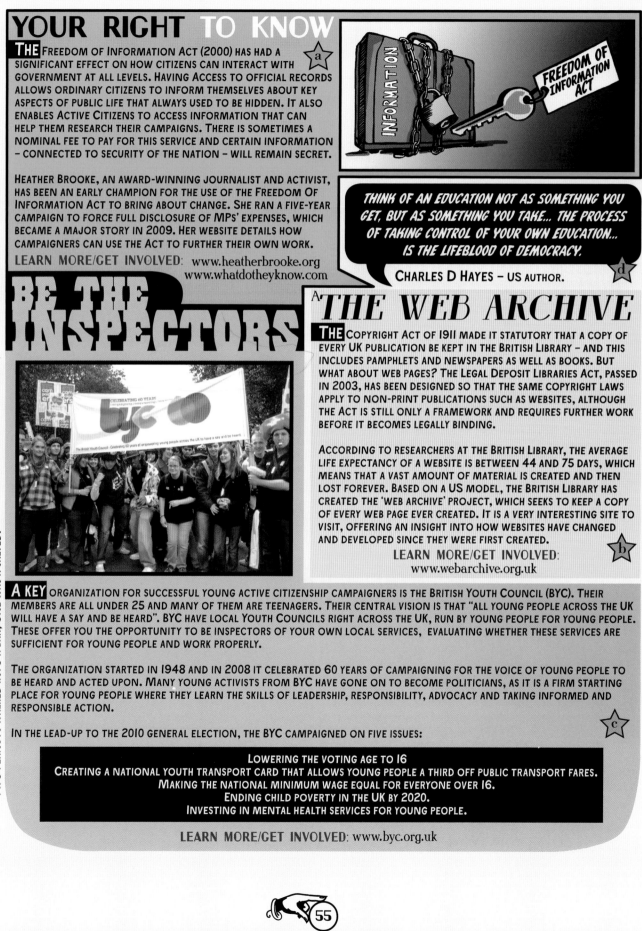

# The MIRROR

The Rax team has been able to interview famous people from the worlds of politics, activism and popular culture. Their voices will show you their own points of view about change. The Rax team has also included many young voices. They are young people who have made changes to their world already through Active Citizenship. Again, these people are talking about their own outlook on the world and it's up to you to decide on your own path and develop your own point of view.

## ALL OF THE VOICES IN THE BOOK ARE OFFERING THEIR IDEAS ABOUT HOW YOUNG PEOPLE CAN CHANGE THEIR WORLD BUT THE MOST IMPORTANT VOICE IS YOUR OWN.

Throughout the Toolkit there will be feedback sessions after all the activities and games. These can develop into major discussions if ideas come up that you are interested in talking about at more length. This should be encouraged, as it is in sessions like these that the class can find its way to new and interesting ideas, conclusions and solutions.

## SELF-DIRECTED LEARNING IS ABOUT YOU DECIDING WHAT YOU WANT TO LEARN MORE ABOUT, WHAT YOU WANT TO INVESTIGATE, WHAT YOU WANT TO BECOME INVOLVED IN AND WHAT YOU WANT TO CHANGE. ONCE YOU HAVE CHOSEN YOUR DIRECTION, THEN IT'S UP TO YOU TO FOLLOW YOUR INTEREST AND LEARN MORE.

### GROUP ACTIVITY
### FIGHT YOUR CORNER
MOTION:

**THIS HOUSE BELIEVES THAT SCHOOL DOESN'T GIVE YOU ANYTHING MORE THAN YOU COULD LEARN YOURSELF FROM THE WEB.**

  *What is the Record Book?* a

*It's* important that you use a Record Book to keep a record of everything that happens in your lessons and in your campaigns. You will see that in the Toolkit there are numerous occasions when you are asked to fill in your Record Books, usually at the end of a lesson. You will also need to be using your Record Book when you are outside your lessons. The Toolkit includes several examples from students' Record Books to give you an idea of what kind of thing to include.

## USING YOUR RECORD BOOK
### RECORD

*The* Toolkit is going to provide you with many ideas connected to change and allow you to experiment with new skills through the activities and games as well as through your actual campaigns. The best way to benefit from this is by keeping a record of everything.

### FOR EXAMPLE,

there are feedback sessions after most of the activities. It is important that you write notes on how they went. Include notes on any discussions that were sparked off, what happened in them, what different points of view emerged, what conclusions were reached and how they were reached. You will also be researching many different issues as well as ways of campaigning. It's important that you keep a record of all the new areas that you come across. b

### REFLECT

*The* Record Book should be like a diary, too, where you reflect on how you have felt about an experience. It is also like a diary in that nobody in your class will read what you have written. This means you can be as honest as you wish when you reflect upon how other people in the class have contributed during activities, discussions and the campaigning process itself. c

You also need to reflect upon every aspect of your campaigns. Be critical of yourself and others, pointing out what was done well and what could have been done better and why. By evaluating everything in detail, you will be improving your citizenship skills rapidly. You will also be adding to your basic life skills because learning from your mistakes is a powerful way to increase your understanding of life and how you can take part in it. d

### GROUP ACTIVITY
### HEADS TOGETHER

*In* groups, you have **10 MINUTES** to **WRITE AS MANY POINTS AS YOU CAN THAT SUM UP THE DEBATE YOU HELD ABOUT WHETHER SCHOOL GIVES YOU ANY MORE THAN STAYING AT HOME AND USING THE WEB.** Your points should record what happened and reflect on how it happened.

Feed back your ideas to the class.

TICK TOCK

IN 1983, THE WELL-KNOWN GERMAN MAGAZINE *STERN* PUBLISHED EXTRACTS FROM WHAT WERE CLAIMED TO BE ADOLF HITLER'S DIARIES. THE DIARIES HAD BEEN BROUGHT TO THE MAGAZINE UNDER A GREAT DEAL OF SECRECY AND EXPERTS WERE BROUGHT IN TO ANALYSE THE HANDWRITING AND DETAILS IN THE EXTRACTS TO MAKE SURE THAT THE DIARIES WERE AUTHENTIC.

DETAILS OF THE SENSATIONAL DISCOVERY WERE ANNOUNCED BY SEVERAL MEDIA OUTLETS WORLDWIDE. HOWEVER, ONCE THE DIARIES WERE MADE PUBLIC, SEVERAL MORE EXPERTS WERE ASKED TO EXAMINE THE WORK AND IT WAS QUICKLY REVEALED THAT IT WAS A FORGERY. SOME EXPERTS WENT SO FAR AS TO SAY THAT THE FORGERY WASN'T EVEN THAT GOOD AS THERE WERE FACTUAL MISTAKES IN THE WRITING AND THE PAPER USED WAS MADE IN MODERN TIMES. THE EDITORS OF *STERN* MAGAZINE RESIGNED AND THE REPUTATION OF THE EXPERTS WHO HAD ORIGINALLY SAID THAT THE DIARIES WERE AUTHENTIC WAS GREATLY DAMAGED.

IN *THE PROCESSING PLANT*, YOU WILL LEARN SKILLS TO HELP YOU IDENTIFY WHETHER A SOURCE OF INFORMATION IS RELIABLE OR NOT.

# HITLER'S DIARIES

## EXTRACT FROM BATMAN'S SECRET DIARY

**TUESDAY 7th**
Woke up this morning by being ejected through the window again. Landed on Robin, who was turning up for martial arts training. Alfred came to our aid by removing glass, stitching a few cuts and calming Robin down.
Note to self
Must fix sonic ejector on the utility belt.

## EXTRACT FROM HAMISH'S RECORD BOOK

NOTES OF FEEDBACK SESSION ABOUT AN ART ACTION AROUND THE CLOTHING AND TEXTILES INDUSTRY.

We had a discussion that went right up until the end of the lesson because Jake had said that campaigns to force companies to pay the workers in the factories more fairly could be damaging because those companies might stop using those factories and then the workers would lose their jobs. Everyone disagreed with Jake, saying that the most important thing was to support the workers. But that caused a real argument because Jasmine then said that she has an uncle who runs a clothing factory in Bangladesh. She said that her uncle pays the workers the minimum wage and about two hundred families live from those wages. If he was forced to pay them more, he might have to close the business down and they would all be unable to support their families. In the end, we decided that there were two things to do: research what the effects are when campaigns have forced factory owners to pay their workers more fairly; and also, to make up some questions that we can e-mail Jasmine's uncle so that we can get his point of view. We also found two great campaigning sites worth looking at in more detail:
www.lovefashionhatesweatshops.org
www.cleanupfashion.co.uk

# GANDHI IN LONDON

GANDHI KEPT CAREFUL DIARIES THROUGHOUT HIS LIFE AND NEVER STOPPED WRITING. IN THEM, IT IS POSSIBLE TO TRACK THE WAY THAT HIS IDEAS ABOUT CHANGE GREW AND HOW HE DEVELOPED HIS METHODS OF CAMPAIGNING. FOR ANY CAMPAIGNER FOR CHANGE, THEY ARE A GREAT SOURCE OF INSPIRATION.

GANDHI VISITED LONDON IN 1888. AN ENTRY IN HIS DIARY FROM THAT TIME, DESCRIBING HIS FIRST VISIT TO A GRAND HOTEL, SHOWS HOW DIFFERENT MODERN LONDON LIFE WAS FROM THE LIFE THAT HE HAD BEEN USED TO:

"I WAS ALL THE WHILE SMILING WITHIN MYSELF. THEN WE WERE TO GO TO THE SECOND FLOOR BY A LIFT. I DID NOT KNOW WHAT IT WAS. THE BOY AT ONCE TOUCHED SOMETHING WHICH I THOUGHT WAS THE LOCK OF THE DOOR. BUT, AS I AFTERWARDS CAME TO KNOW, IT WAS THE BELL WHICH RANG IN ORDER TO TELL THE WAITER TO BRING THE LIFT. THE DOORS WERE OPENED AND I THOUGHT THAT WAS A ROOM IN WHICH WE WERE TO SIT FOR SOME TIME. BUT TO MY GREAT SURPRISE WE WERE BROUGHT TO THE SECOND FLOOR."

LEARN MORE/GET INVOLVED:
www.mkgandhi.org
www.gandhiserve.org

# WHEN RECORD KEEPING has negative effects

AS WITH ALL SIGNIFICANT INVENTIONS IN THE WORLD, THERE IS ALWAYS A POSITIVE AND NEGATIVE SIDE TO HOW THEY CAN BE USED BY HUMANITY. IN THE CASE OF THE WEB, THE NEGATIVE ASPECTS ARE NOT IMMEDIATELY OBVIOUS.

EVEN THOUGH THEY CLAIM TO BE FREE, WHEN YOU SIGN UP TO USE SERVICES SUCH AS GOOGLE OR YOUTUBE, YOU ARE PAYING A PRICE – NOT IN MONEY BUT IN INFORMATION ABOUT YOURSELF. BY USING 'BEHAVIOURAL TARGETING' SOFTWARE, YOUR BROWSING HABITS ARE TRACKED AND WITH CERTAIN E-MAIL SERVICES SUCH AS GOOGLE, THE TEXT IN ALL YOUR E-MAILS IS ANALYSED. THIS INFORMATION IS THEN USED TO PLACE ADVERTISEMENTS IN YOUR PAGES TARGETING YOU SPECIFICALLY. MANY CAMPAIGNING ORGANIZATIONS SEE THIS RECORD OF DATA BASED ON YOU AS AN INVASION OF YOUR PRIVACY AND ARGUE STRONGLY TO MAKE THIS BEHAVIOUR ILLEGAL.

CAMPAIGNING TO KEEP THE WEB FREE OF ANY FORMS OF CONTROL HAS BECOME A GLOBAL EFFORT INVOLVING HUNDREDS OF THOUSANDS OF PEOPLE AND DIGITAL NATIVES MIGHT CONSIDER THIS AN IMPORTANT AREA FOR CAMPAIGNING.

LEARN MORE/GET INVOLVED: www.eff.org www.democraticmedia.org www.cdt.org

## COLLATE

*You* will be learning how to research your campaign issues thoroughly in the next chapter. This is vital if your campaign is to be successful. One of the most important ways to ensure the strength of your research is to collate all the evidence that you gather so that you can access it easily if anybody wants you to prove what you are saying. One important tool to help you do this is to create computer bookmarks so that, when you come across an important site or useful article, you keep the link to it. You are going to be doing this often so it's better to create new bookmark folders for each different issue or idea rather than stuffing every link into the same bookmark folder.

There will be other forms of evidence that you gather or create in your research, such as newspaper cuttings, films, presentations from experts, minutes from meetings, screen grabs showing correspondence with campaigning groups or people in positions of power, charts, graphs and surveys. You need to keep these sources organized in your Record Book or a separate folder, too.

### FOR EXAMPLE,

as part of an activity, you might come across an article in a newspaper about mental health. You would need to write down the title of the article, the page the article is on, the name of the newspaper and the date. In this way, you will be able to go back through your Record Book and use your notes to access that article again easily. When you are giving a speech or writing a letter to argue for your issue, it's a lot more convincing to be able to say, "In an article titled New Campaign to Support Mental Health, from the *Daily Mail* dated 11th April this year" than to say, "In a paper I looked at a few months ago".

**THE RECORD BOOK IS FOR TRACKING EVERY STEP OF YOUR ACTIVE CITIZENSHIP JOURNEY.**

## IN GROUPS
## NEWSPAPER GAME

*In* groups, you have **10 MINUTES** to **GO THROUGH YOUR NEWSPAPERS OR ONLINE NEWS SOURCES TO FIND AS MANY STORIES AS YOU CAN THAT ARE CONNECTED TO TEENAGERS.** Make sure you write down the title and page of the article or the web address each time. The winner is the group that has found the most stories, once they have been verified by the rest of the class.

Feed back your answers to the class.

TICK TOCK

## RECORD BOOK

*Report* on the class activities under the headings:
**USING THE RECORD BOOK:**
**NOTES ON HOW WE RECORDED AND REFLECTED UPON THE DEBATE ABOUT WHETHER SCHOOL GIVES YOU ANY MORE THAN STAYING AT HOME AND USING THE WEB.**
**NOTES ON COLLATING STORIES CONNECTED TO TEENAGERS.**
Notes on any class feedback sessions.

## 4. How do I keep a record of my campaign?

*When* you are creating and running your Active Citizenship campaigns, you need to use a few extra ways of recording what happens. As well as keeping up with the normal ways of recording, reflecting and collating in your Record Book, you also need to assess the impact of what you do and gather testimonials and evidence to prove you have done what you say you have done.

## ASSESS THE IMPACT

*You* need to use your Record Book as a way of assessing the impact or the outcomes of your campaigns. There are many different ways of doing this, depending on what kind of campaign you are running.

### FOR EXAMPLE,

if you were raising awareness of an issue in your school, it would be useful to give out evaluation forms so that people could fill in what they thought of the way you communicated your ideas, what they felt that they had learned, whether they were going to take part in whatever follow-up actions you might have suggested and how you might have made the campaign more effective.

Other forms of assessment might include: tables and graphs showing the impact that your campaign has had; petitions that show the amount of support you have gathered; letters and e-mails from people in positions of power; messages from members of the public who are showing support; films of campaign events that you have organized; and media cuttings from papers or other news sources that have covered or supported your campaign.

Assessment also includes self-assessment. What have been the outcomes of a campaign or an activity for you in personal terms? This also includes assessing the impact that the process has had on your group or partner – or on the class as a whole.

**ASSESSING THE IMPACT OF YOUR CAMPAIGN IS THE BEST WAY OF MEASURING YOUR SUCCESS AND LEARNING HOW TO DO IT BETTER NEXT TIME.**

# FAIR DEAL FOR ETHIOPIAN COFFEE FARMERS

**ETHIOPIA** IS FAMOUS FOR ITS FINE COFFEE AND MORE THAN 15 MILLION PEOPLE MAKE A LIVING FROM THE COFFEE-GROWING INDUSTRY. IN 2007, THE INTERNATIONAL CAMPAIGNING GROUP, OXFAM, USED A SERIES OF HIGH-PROFILE ACTIONS TO RAISE AWARENESS ABOUT THE FACT THAT ETHIOPIAN FARMERS WERE NOT BEING PAID A FAIR PRICE FOR THEIR COFFEE BY THE WELL-KNOWN COFFEE SHOP CHAIN STARBUCKS. THE CAMPAIGN USED A POWERFUL TOOL FOR CHANGE, WHICH IS TO ENCOURAGE ORDINARY CONSUMERS TO CONTACT A BUSINESS AND PUT PRESSURE ON THEM TO CHANGE. AFTER HUNDREDS OF THOUSANDS OF CONSUMERS WROTE TO STARBUCKS, THE COMPANY CHANGED ITS POLICY AND SIGNED A BUSINESS DEAL THAT COMMITTED THEM TO PAYING A FAIRER PRICE FOR THE COFFEE THEY BOUGHT FROM ETHIOPIA.

THE IMPACT OF THIS CAMPAIGN WAS THAT THE AVERAGE ETHIOPIAN COFFEE GROWER RECEIVED A BETTER DEAL FOR THEIR WORK BUT A LONG-TERM IMPACT WAS THAT MAJOR BUSINESSES REALIZED HOW THE CONSUMER CAN BE A FORCE FOR CHANGE. TODAY, THIS REMAINS ONE OF THE MOST POWERFUL WAYS THAT COMPANIES CAN BE MADE TO CHANGE THEIR WAYS – IF ENOUGH PEOPLE THREATEN TO STOP BEING THEIR CUSTOMERS THEN THEY HAVE TO REACT.

LEARN MORE/GET INVOLVED: www.oxfam.org.uk **b**

## EXTRACT FROM FIONA'S RECORD BOOK

Pie chart showing survey of the reactions of 40 people who attended a community event to raise awareness about the need for more facilities for young people.

- 2 DON'T KNOW
- 4 NOT INTERESTED
- 8 I AM STILL NOT SURE BUT WOULD LIKE TO LEARN MORE
- 26 I AM BEHIND THE IDEA AND WILL SUPPORT IT

## EXTRACT FROM PATRICE'S RECORD BOOK

### I GOT A LETTER BACK FROM MY MP TODAY. **a**

I e-mailed my MP three weeks ago and got a letter in the post this morning. The address was actually from the Houses of Parliament! The first paragraph talked about how she was really glad to get a letter from me and wished that more young people got in touch with their MPs. I could tell that this wasn't one of those letters that they just make up and send to everyone, this was specially to me. She's a busy woman so her taking the time meant a lot to me. She described the things that the government are trying to do about the energy crisis and said that she had voted for a new plan which is getting energy from the heat in the desert. I'd never heard about that. She gave me a website that has more details about the project. It was so weird, getting a letter in the post from an MP. Mum thought I was in trouble or something when she saw the envelope but then couldn't believe it when I showed her who it was!

**IF YOU DON'T COMPLY THEN WE WON'T BUY!**

**WE DEMAND COMPANIES HAVE BETTER ETHICAL POLICIES!**

**CONSUMER POWER**

YIKES **BIG BUSINESS**

**c**

**THE DIFFERENCE IS THAT NOW THERE IS A COMMUNITY THAT LOOKS OUT FOR EACH OTHER AND WHICH CARES. IT'S VERY HARD TO FIND A COMMUNITY THAT WILL HELP PEOPLE WHO ARE IN NEED AND WILL LOOK OUT FOR YOUR FAMILY.**

SOPHIE BARDY (SEE RAX INTERVIEW ON PAGE 138). **d**

**NOW EVERYONE KNOWS EACH OTHER, EVERYONE IS TOGETHER AND IT'S GREAT. IT'S PEACEFUL. IT'S A FRIENDLY ENVIRONMENT, AND THAT'S WHAT YOU WANT SOCIETY TO BE. YOU WANT IT TO BE FRIENDLY, YOU WANT IT TO BE COMFORTABLE, NO MATTER HOW OLD YOU ARE.**

NELU MIAH (SEE RAX INTERVIEW ON PAGE 134).

## IN GROUPS
### HEADS TOGETHER

IMAGINE THAT YOU ARE GOING TO HOLD A YEAR SEVEN ASSEMBLY, CAMPAIGNING FOR THE VOTING AGE TO BE BROUGHT DOWN TO 16. IN YOUR ASSEMBLY, YOU WILL ALSO MENTION WAYS IN WHICH YEAR SEVEN STUDENTS CAN TAKE ACTION TO SUPPORT YOUR CAMPAIGN.

*In* groups, you have **FIVE MINUTES** to **COME UP WITH FIVE QUESTIONS THAT COULD BE INCLUDED IN AN EVALUATION SHEET** assessing the impact your assembly has had on a group of Year Seven students.

*TICK TOCK*

Feed back your ideas to the class.

## GATHER EVIDENCE AND TESTIMONIALS

*Although* you will already be collating all your research in your Record Book as well as in well-ordered web bookmark folders, you will also need to collect evidence of your actions and events.

### THESE CAN BE IN MANY FORMS, INCLUDING:

QUESTIONNAIRES;
SURVEYS;
MINUTES OF MEETINGS;
INTERVIEW NOTES;
VIDEO OR AUDIO RECORDINGS;
PHOTOGRAPHS; CORRESPONDENCE WITH ORGANIZATIONS; PROMOTIONAL PAMPHLETS; AND ARTICLES FROM MEDIA OUTLETS, WHETHER ONLINE, BROADCAST OR ON PAPER.

⭐a
⭐b

### YOU ARE COLLECTING HARD EVIDENCE OF ANY KIND THAT SHOWS WHAT YOU HAVE ACHIEVED.

A further way that you will need to give evidence of your campaigning activities is to have **A SIGNED TESTIMONIAL FROM SOMEONE IN A POSITION OF AUTHORITY WHO HAS WITNESSED WHAT YOU HAVE DONE.** Your teacher can do this, for example – or any other person in authority who has been involved.

## ACTIVITY — IN PAIRS
### ART ACTION

*In* pairs, you have **10 MINUTES** to use any of the art action skills to **CREATE FIVE CLEAR ICONS** that represent different ways that you can gather evidence of a campaigning action.

*TICK TOCK*

Feed back your ideas to the class.

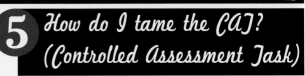

## 5 *How do I tame the CAT? (Controlled Assessment Task)*

*If* you are taking a GCSE in Citizenship Studies, you will have to take Controlled Assessment Tasks where you write about your active citizenship projects and campaigns under supervised conditions, probably in your classroom with your teacher.

Take guidance from your teacher about when and how often you will have to take a CAT and make sure you are clear about what evidence you can include in the task.

Active Citizenship campaigns are always great fun. You will be doing hard work but it won't feel like it at all. The CAT will be a place for you to show off the great work you have been doing. So there is no need to panic at all. It's not an exam, it's a chance for you to shine!

⭐c

IF YOU FOLLOW ALL THE IDEAS IN *THE MIRROR,* YOU WILL TAME THE CAT EASILY AND HAVE IT PURRING AT YOUR FEET, LICKING YOUR TOES.

### RECORD BOOK

*Report* on the class activities under the headings:

IMPACT AND EVIDENCE FOR CAMPAIGNS:

NOTES ON DEVELOPING FIVE QUESTIONS TO EVALUATE THE IMPACT OF A YEAR SEVEN ASSEMBLY.

NOTES ON USING ART ACTION SKILLS TO CREATE FIVE ICONS SHOWING DIFFERENT WAYS OF GATHERING EVIDENCE.

Notes on any class feedback sessions.

THIS IS A COPY OF THE LETTER WE GOT BACK FROM KENNY'S SHOE SHACK.

# SHOE SHACK

Dear Michele,

I am very impressed by the pamphlet you and your group handed to me last week. Here at Kenny's Shoe Shack we are always keen to support the local community and especially the young community as you are the future of this country. I grew up in this area and there did used to be a youth club but it was closed down. We'd like to support your campaign for more youth facilities. You are welcome to leave a stack of pamphlets in the shop and if you have a poster we'd happily put it up in our window.

Make sure you stay in touch and tell me about your next meeting.

Good luck!

Kenny

This is a copy of Ms Vijayakar's Testimonial, showing that we had our meeting at the Community Hall on December 4th.

## TESTIMONIAL

This is to certify that I witnessed Kamran, Clare, Alistair and Roxanne hold a debate in the Tompion Community Hall with about 20 people from the community attending on the evening of 4th December. They organized it really well. The subject of the debate was whether the community should make more efforts to overcome racial and religious differences and become unified. This was a very contentious subject but they pulled it off by ensuring that everyone had the chance to be heard and remained respectful to each other. I think the community started to improve tonight because of what they have done!

Anita Vijayakar
Tompion Community Hall Committee Chair

# CHAPTER 4 The **PROCESSING** PLANT

## 1 Why is this chapter important?

ONE OF THE KEYS TO THE SUCCESS OF AN ACTIVE CITIZENSHIP CAMPAIGN IS HAVING A WELL-RESEARCHED AND BALANCED ARGUMENT.

**TO HELP YOUR CAMPAIGNS, THIS CHAPTER WILL HELP YOU MAKE SURE OF THE FOLLOWING:**

YOU CAN FIND AN ISSUE THAT YOU FEEL CONNECTED TO.
YOU HAVE THE MOST RELIABLE INFORMATION TO SUPPORT YOUR IDEA FOR CHANGE.
YOU HAVE CONSIDERED YOUR ARGUMENT FROM MANY DIFFERENT POINTS OF VIEW.

*In* other words, you will use the skills of **CRITICAL THINKING** and **ENQUIRY** to a very high level in order to create a winning campaign that you feel strongly about.

## 2 How do I find an issue that I feel connected to?

*By* using the ideas and links we have given to you in the Toolkit so far, you've already got a good picture of what's happening out there in the world of change. Through the rest of the Toolkit, you will be given links to many more ideas for change.
But the Toolkit can't include everything. Only you can find what you care about the most.

**YOUR CAMPAIGN FOR CHANGE WILL NOT SUCCEED IF YOU DON'T CARE ABOUT IT.**

### GROUP ACTIVITY

#### NEWSPAPER GAME:

*In* groups, you have **10 MINUTES** to **SEARCH THROUGH YOUR NEWSPAPERS OR WEB NEWS SOURCES TO CHOOSE THE SIX ISSUES THAT YOU FEEL ARE MOST IMPORTANT TO YOU.** Consider issues that make you feel an injustice is being done. They can be small stories or front-page news and should include at least one local, one national and one global issue. You will need to hold a group vote to choose the top six.

Feed back your answers to the class (including why your group chose the issues that it did).

### PAIR ACTIVITY

#### ART ACTION:

*In* pairs, you have **15 MINUTES** to use any of the Art Action skills to **CREATE THREE PIECES OF ART, BASED ON THE ISSUES THAT HAVE COME FROM THE NEWSPAPER GAME ABOVE.** They must show one local (in your village, town or city), one national and one global issue.

Feed back your work to the class.

*TICK TOCK*

**TELEVISION'S** CHANNEL 4 HAVE HAD A CAMPAIGN RUNNING SINCE 2008 THAT FOCUSES ON SUPPORTING YOUNG PEOPLE WHO HAVE COME INTO CLOSE CONTACT WITH AN ISSUE THAT THEY FEEL CONNECTED TO AND WANT TO DO SOMETHING ABOUT. THESE INCLUDE CAMPAIGNS ABOUT HOMOPHOBIA, BULLYING, GANGS, SMOKING AND ISLAMOPHOBIA. ONE CAMPAIGN FEATURES A TEENAGER WHO WAS SUFFERING FROM A KIDNEY DISEASE. SHE HAD TO MAKE REGULAR THREE-HOUR VISITS TO HOSPITAL TO GO ON A DIALYSIS MACHINE WHILE SHE WAITED FOR AN ORGAN DONOR. SHE AND HER FRIENDS STARTED A CAMPAIGN TO ENCOURAGE MORE PEOPLE TO SIGN UP AS ORGAN DONORS. THE CAMPAIGN MANAGED TO GET NATIONAL PRESS COVERAGE AS WELL AS A LETTER OF SUPPORT FROM PRIME MINISTER GORDON BROWN. **(b)**

THE SITE IS FULL OF EXCELLENT CAMPAIGNS AS WELL AS PLENTY OF HELPFUL ADVICE ABOUT HOW TO START YOUR OWN.

**LEARN MORE/GET INVOLVED:** www.battlefront.co.uk

# BATTLEFRONT
## YOU'RE ALREADY INVOLVED

### A FLAG ON THE POOP DECK

> *DO THE RESEARCH, HAVE YOUR STATISTICS, AND HAVE THE ANSWERS BECAUSE KNOWLEDGE IS POWER.* **(a)**

**CRAIG KIELBURGER**
(SEE RAX INTERVIEW ON PAGE 50).

> *IT'S CRUCIAL TO HAVE YOUR FACTS STRAIGHT WHEN EMBARKING ON A CAMPAIGN. IF YOU ARE GOING TO BE CHALLENGING SOME OF THE MOST POWERFUL CORPORATIONS AND GOVERNMENTS IN THE WORLD, YOU CAN'T GIVE THEM ANY EXCUSE TO DISMISS WHAT YOU'RE SAYING OR UNDERMINE YOU IN PUBLIC.*

**JESS WORTH** (SEE RAX INTERVIEW ON PAGE 200). **(a)**

> *WE ALL NEED TO DEVELOP OUR OWN THINKING SKILLS TO QUESTION AND CHALLENGE THE PEOPLE IN CHARGE.*

**ROBBIE GILLETT** (SEE RAX INTERVIEW ON PAGE 159).

**IN** THE MID-NINETIES, ONE LOCAL CAMPAIGN, RUN BY AN ANONYMOUS USER OF A PARK IN LONDON CALLED HAMPSTEAD HEATH, CAUSED QUITE A STIR IN THE COMMUNITY. TIRED OF TIPTOEING THROUGH ALL THE DOG FAECES, THIS IMAGINATIVE PERSON CAME UP WITH A NOVEL ART ACTION WAY OF DRAWING ATTENTION TO THE PROBLEM. THIS MAN OR WOMAN MADE HUNDREDS OF LITTLE FLAGS STUCK TO COCKTAIL STICKS, WITH A MESSAGE ON THEM READING, "THE OWNER OF THIS DOG IS IRRESPONSIBLE". HE OR SHE THEN STUCK THEM IN ALL THE DOG FAECES THEY COULD FIND IN THE PARK. AS A RESULT, THE PATHS SOMETIMES LOOKED LIKE LITTLE STREAMS WITH HUNDREDS OF SAIL BOATS IN THEM. BECAUSE THIS WAS AN ENTERTAINING IMAGE, THE LOCAL MEDIA SOON HAD PICTURES OF THIS AND THE CAMPAIGN GAINED A HIGH ENOUGH PROFILE FOR LOCAL COUNCILS TO INCREASE THEIR ATTENTION TO THE PROBLEM. **(e)**

> *DO YOUR RESEARCH. ENSURE THAT YOUR POINT OF VIEW IS WELL REASONED, EVIDENCE-BASED AND BACKED UP BY PEOPLE WHO KNOW WHAT THEY'RE TALKING ABOUT... AND BE SURE TO CAREFULLY EVALUATE WHERE YOUR EVIDENCE IS COMING FROM.* **(a)**

**LAURIE PYCROFT** (SEE RAX INTERVIEW ON PAGE 100).

# BLACK LIKE ME

**IN** 1959, WHITE AMERICAN JOURNALIST JOHN HOWARD GRIFFIN CAME UP WITH A BRAVE AND IMAGINATIVE WAY TO RAISE AWARENESS ABOUT CIVIL RIGHTS ISSUES AND RACISM IN THE US. HE CHECKED IN TO A HOTEL AND, WITH THE HELP OF AN ULTRAVIOLET SUNLAMP, VARIOUS DYES AND A DERMATOLOGIST WHO GAVE HIM A SERIES OF DRUGS, JOHN HOWARD GRIFFIN WALKED OUT A BLACK MAN. **(c)**

HE SPENT THE NEXT MONTHS TRAVELLING THE STATES AND EXPERIENCING AT FIRST HAND EXACTLY WHAT IT FELT LIKE TO BE TREATED IN A RACIST WAY BY THE PREDOMINANTLY WHITE POPULATION. HE TALKED ABOUT GETTING USED TO "THE HATE STARE". EVEN FRIENDS DIDN'T RECOGNIZE HIM. HE RECORDED HIS EXPERIENCES IN A BOOK, *BLACK LIKE ME*. THE BOOK CAUSED A SENSATION. GRIFFIN FOUND THAT AT FIRST, HUNDREDS OF PEOPLE WERE FURIOUS AT WHAT HE HAD DONE BUT EVENTUALLY THE REACTION HE HAD STIRRED BECAME A TOOL FOR PEOPLE TO QUESTION ASSUMPTIONS THAT THEY HAD BEEN LIVING BY FOR A LONG TIME. GRIFFIN BECAME A LEADING ADVOCATE FOR THE CIVIL RIGHTS MOVEMENT IN THE US.

A FILM OF THE BOOK, WITH THE SAME TITLE, WAS RELEASED IN 1964.

# MATCH THE IMAGE TO THE CAUSE

**HERE** ARE SOME EXAMPLES OF CAMPAIGN LOGOS THAT SUM UP THEIR CAUSE IN A SIMPLE PICTURE. THE BETTER THE IMAGE IS, THE MORE IT TELLS THE VIEWER ABOUT THE IDEA OF THE CAMPAIGN JUST AT A GLANCE. **(d)**

## SOME TIPS ABOUT FINDING AN ISSUE THAT YOU FEEL CONNECTED TO AND CARE ABOUT:

*Look* at your personal life, your family life, your school life and your community life. You may find issues that are already affecting you about which you feel strongly.

*Take* time to look at the issues that this Toolkit has brought to your notice already. Are there any issues that you already care about and feel connected to?

*You* may want to campaign on issues such as war, poverty and global warming but feel they are so big that there is nothing you can do. Remember that you are not one voice but one of many. There will be many organizations and campaigns already working for those changes and it's often easy to start up your own branch and connect it to a campaign that is already running.

*Follow* your heart and your imagination. There may be new ideas for change that nobody has come up with yet. You may see things in a different way and have a unique solution to old problems. If that's the case, follow your instincts and shape something new.

THERE WILL BE THE OPPORTUNITY TO CREATE THREE CAMPAIGNS USING THIS TOOLKIT. YOU WILL NOT BE STARTING YOUR FIRST CAMPAIGN UNTIL THE END OF *THE GIFT OF THE GAB* SO YOU STILL HAVE SOME TIME. THE IMPORTANT THING IS TO START THINKING NOW ABOUT WHAT ISSUES YOU ALREADY CARE ABOUT AND TO LOOK OUT FOR NEW ISSUES THAT GRAB YOUR ATTENTION.

## RECORD BOOK

*Report* on the last two activities under these headings:
USING NEWS SOURCE TO FIND ISSUES.
USING ART ACTION TO SHOW DIFFERENT TYPES OF ISSUES.
Notes on any class feedback sessions.

## 3 *What is critical thinking?*

*When* you hear an opinion about something, in a few split seconds, your mind will draw upon the vast reservoir of stuff in your brain before an opinion pops out. But how does your brain do that?  SEE OVERLEAF

### IN PAIRS/GROUPS

## HEADS TOGETHER:

*In* pairs or groups, you have FIVE MINUTES to discuss and decide whether your group agrees or disagrees with this statement:

### "KILLING ANIMALS IS WRONG."

Feed back your answers to the class.

TICK TOCK

### ON YOUR OWN

## ON YOUR OWN:

*On* your own, you have FIVE MINUTES to list as many points as you can in answer to this question:

### "WHAT BELIEFS, EXPERIENCES AND FACTS DID YOU PERSONALLY USE TO COME TO A DECISION WITH YOUR GROUP?"

Dig deep, THINK ABOUT YOUR THINKING!
Feed back your answers to your group or class.

# INSTIGATE DEBATE

IN 2008, A GROUP OF YOUNG WRITERS, ACTIVISTS AND POP STARS CAME TOGETHER TO ADDRESS THE ISSUE THAT YOUNG PEOPLE FEEL DISENGAGED FROM THE POLITICAL PROCESS AND LET DOWN BY THE MAINSTREAM MEDIA. THEIR IMAGINATIVE SOLUTION WAS TO SET UP A SITE ENCOURAGING YOUNG PEOPLE TO USE 'GUERRILLA' FILM-MAKING TECHNIQUES (SUCH AS USING PHONE CAMERAS) TO INTERVIEW PROMINENT PEOPLE IN THE UK ABOUT PROMINENT ISSUES. IF A YOUNG PERSON SUCCESSFULLY CONDUCTS AN INTERVIEW, THEY CAN POST IT ON THE SITE AND WILL THEN BE IN WITH A CHANCE OF A FAMOUS BAND COMING TO PLAY IN THEIR LIVING ROOM!

SO FAR, AMONG THE ARTISTS WHO HAVE TURNED UP TO PLAY IN SOMEONE'S LIVING ROOM HAVE BEEN MEMBERS OF THE LIBERTINES, BAABA MAAL, BABYSHAMBLES, GET CAPE. WEAR CAPE. FLY, KIERAN LEONARD AND REVEREND AND THE MAKERS. THE FILMED INTERVIEWS HAVE INCLUDED ACTORS, POLITICIANS AND POP STARS BEING PUT ON THE SPOT.

LEARN MORE/GET INVOLVED: www.instigate-debate.blogspot.com

**YOUTH POWER**

IN 2009, A 10-YEAR-OLD BOY WAS SAVED FROM DEPORTATION BY HIS SCHOOL FRIENDS STARTING OFF A FACEBOOK CAMPAIGN. ADRIAN ATKINSON'S MOTHER HAD SEPARATED FROM HIS BRITISH FATHER AND WHEN HER VISA HAD RUN OUT, THE HOME OFFICE HAD SAID THAT SHE AND HER SON WOULD BE DEPORTED TO THE DEMOCRATIC REPUBLIC OF THE CONGO, THE MOTHER'S ORIGINAL HOME. ADRIAN'S PRIMARY SCHOOL FRIENDS DECIDED TO TRY AND DO SOMETHING ABOUT IT AND SET UP A FACEBOOK SITE. THEIR CAMPAIGN GATHERED INTEREST FROM THE LOCAL MEDIA AND SOON THEY HAD 5,000 NAMES ON THEIR WEB PETITION. AS A RESULT, THE HOME OFFICE REVERSED ITS DECISION AND ADRIAN AND HIS MOTHER WERE ALLOWED TO STAY IN THE UK.

# THE CHILDREN'S PEACE PRIZE

NKOSI JOHNSON, A SOUTH AFRICAN BOY BORN HIV POSITIVE, SPENT HIS SHORT LIFE ADVOCATING FOR THE RIGHTS OF THE MILLIONS OF AFRICANS SUFFERING FROM THE AIDS PANDEMIC. HE WAS THE FIRST WINNER OF THE CHILDREN'S PEACE PRIZE, AN ORGANIZATION THAT WAS SET UP BY PREVIOUS WINNERS OF THE NOBEL PEACE PRIZE. THE WINNER IN 2009 WAS 16-YEAR-OLD BARUANI NDUME (PICTURED ABOVE), A REFUGEE FROM THE DEMOCRATIC REPUBLIC OF THE CONGO. HE SET UP HIS OWN RADIO STATION, BROADCASTING FROM HIS TANZANIAN REFUGEE CAMP. THIS SERVES AS A FORUM FOR YOUNG REFUGEES TO DISCUSS THEIR PROBLEMS. IT ALSO HELPS TO LINK UP PARENTS AND CHILDREN WHO BECAME SEPARATED AS THEY FLED FROM THEIR COUNTRY.

LEARN MORE/GET INVOLVED:
www.unhcr.org
www.amnesty.org.uk
www.africaaction.org
www.one.org
www.worldaidscampaign.org

**THE BIG ISSUE**

## TALKING ABOUT CANNABIS — FRANK

IN 2007, A UK MOTHER BECAME DEEPLY CONCERNED ABOUT HER TEENAGE SON'S CANNABIS ADDICTION AND THE WAY THAT IT HAD CHANGED HIM AS AN INDIVIDUAL. DEBRA BELL DECIDED TO SET UP A WEBSITE FOR PARENTS WHO WERE IN A SIMILAR SITUATION AND STARTED TAC, TALKING ABOUT CANNABIS. SOON, THOUSANDS OF OTHER PARENTS WERE JOINING THE SITE AND SHARING THEIR EXPERIENCES AND ADVICE. THE CAMPAIGN BECAME NATIONAL NEWS AND MRS BELL BECAME A WELL-KNOWN ADVOCATE FOR FAMILIES COPING WITH CHILDREN WITH CANNABIS PROBLEMS.

HER CAMPAIGN HAD SUCH A HIGH PROFILE THAT IT MAY HAVE AFFECTED THE GOVERNMENT'S DECISION TO RECLASSIFY CANNABIS AS A CLASS B DRUG INSTEAD OF A CLASS C DRUG – THIS MEANT THAT THE PUNISHMENT FOR POSSESSION AND DEALING BECAME FAR MORE SERIOUS. MRS BELL STATED THAT HER INTENTION HAD BEEN TO "CREATE AN ENERGY FOR CHANGE, NOT TO CREATE HYSTERIA".

LEARN MORE/GET INVOLVED:
www.talkingaboutcannabis.com
www.talktofrank.com

IN 1991 TWO MEN CAME TOGETHER TO ADDRESS THE ISSUE OF HOMELESSNESS AND STREET BEGGING. THEY CAME UP WITH A SOLUTION THAT NOBODY ELSE HAD THOUGHT OF BEFORE IN THE UK. GORDON RODDICK AND JOHN BIRD FOUNDED *THE BIG ISSUE*, A MAGAZINE THAT HOMELESS PEOPLE COULD SELL ON THE STREETS, KEEPING A PORTION OF THE PROFITS FOR THEMSELVES. THEIR IDEA WAS TO HELP PEOPLE TO HELP THEMSELVES AND GIVE THEM AN ALTERNATIVE TO HAVING TO BEG TO GET BY. THIS HAS HELPED THOUSANDS OF HOMELESS PEOPLE AND SINCE 1995, THE BIG ISSUE FOUNDATION HAS WORKED TO HELP HOMELESS PEOPLE GET OFF THE STREETS – AS WELL AS TACKLING THE KINDS OF ISSUES THAT END UP FORCING PEOPLE TO LIVE ON THE STREETS.

LEARN MORE/GET INVOLVED: www.bigissue.com

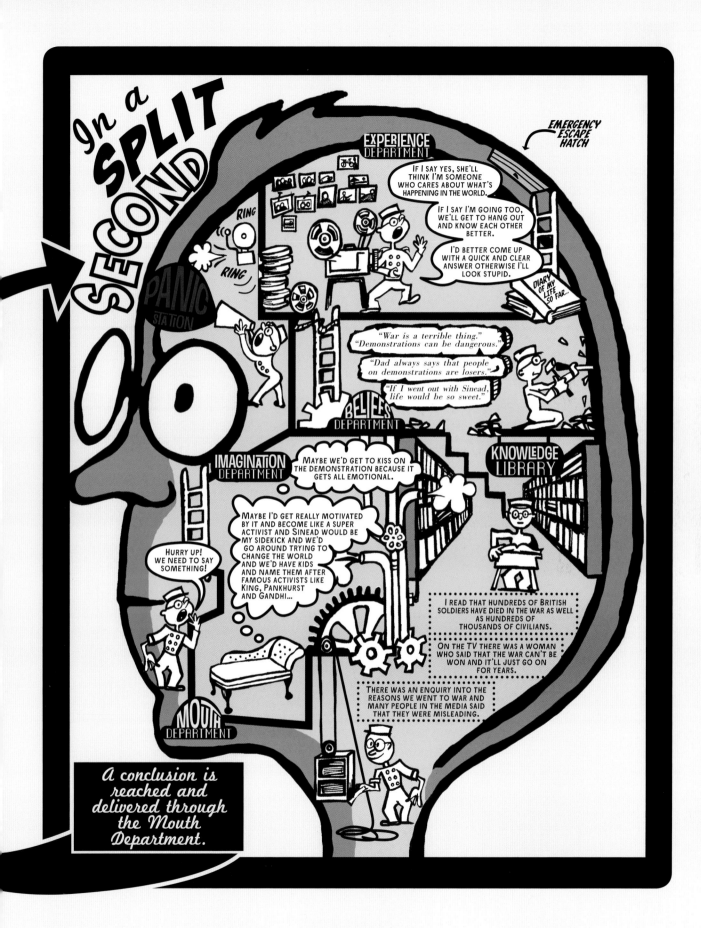

# CHAPTER 4 — The PROCESSING PLANT

**When** people decide what their opinions are about the statement "Killing animals is wrong", many different reactions happen in their mind. These depend on what beliefs they have been brought up with, what experiences they have had, what facts they know about the subject and whether they have ever thought about this before.

| | |
|---|---|
| **YOUR BELIEFS:** | *You* may have been brought up a vegetarian or vegan and believe that harming animals is wrong. **(a)** <br><br> On the other hand, you may have been brought up with the belief that animals are for humans to use. |
| **YOUR EXPERIENCES:** | *You* may be someone who has a pet that you love and you hate the idea of anyone harming it. **(b)** <br><br> On the other hand, you may have grown up on a farm and believe that killing animals for meat and killing rabbits to stop them damaging crops is a normal part of life. **(c)** |
| **YOUR KNOWLEDGE:** | *You* may have read an article in a science journal arguing that, if bees disappeared from the earth, our ecosystem would collapse. <br><br> On the other hand, you may have read a story on a website arguing that thousands of people have had their lives saved by medicines that were tested on animals first. **(d)** |
| **NEVER THOUGHT ABOUT IT BEFORE:** | *You* may have listened to what the other people in your group had to say and then made up your own mind. But have you genuinely arrived at your own view or have you made do with other people's opinions? |

**We** used this example as it is a famously complex question to find an answer to. As you can see, there are all sorts of beliefs, personal viewpoints and statistics on both sides related to whether it is wrong or right to harm animals – and that's without researching the argument in any depth. It is the kind of question that would need a thorough process of critical thinking and enquiry before you were able to reach an opinion that you could feel was complete. **(e)**

## CRITICAL THINKING AND ENQUIRY: INVESTIGATION OF AN ISSUE, USING A RANGE OF INFORMATION FROM A VARIETY OF SOURCES.

You need to evaluate and interpret those sources of information, weighing up the different values and beliefs they may represent as well as the different viewpoints they may come from. You need to be able to identify any form of bias that those sources may hide.

## THE SKILLS OF CRITICAL THINKING AND ENQUIRY ARE CENTRAL TO CREATING A SUCCESSFUL CAMPAIGN. THEY WILL HELP YOU DEVELOP A STRONG ARGUMENT THAT WILL CONVINCE PEOPLE THAT YOUR IDEA FOR CHANGE IS RIGHT.

This skill is not only vital to Active Citizenship, you will find that, as you practise it, it will improve your performance in all other school subjects as well as the way you come to understand the world around you.

## RECORD BOOK

**Report** on the class activities under the headings:

WHAT KINDS OF CRITICAL THINKING DID I USE?
CLASS REACTIONS TO THE STATEMENT "KILLING ANIMALS IS WRONG".
WHAT BASIC CRITICAL THINKING DID I USE PERSONALLY?

Notes on any class feedback sessions.

# WHERE HAVE ALL THE BEES GONE?

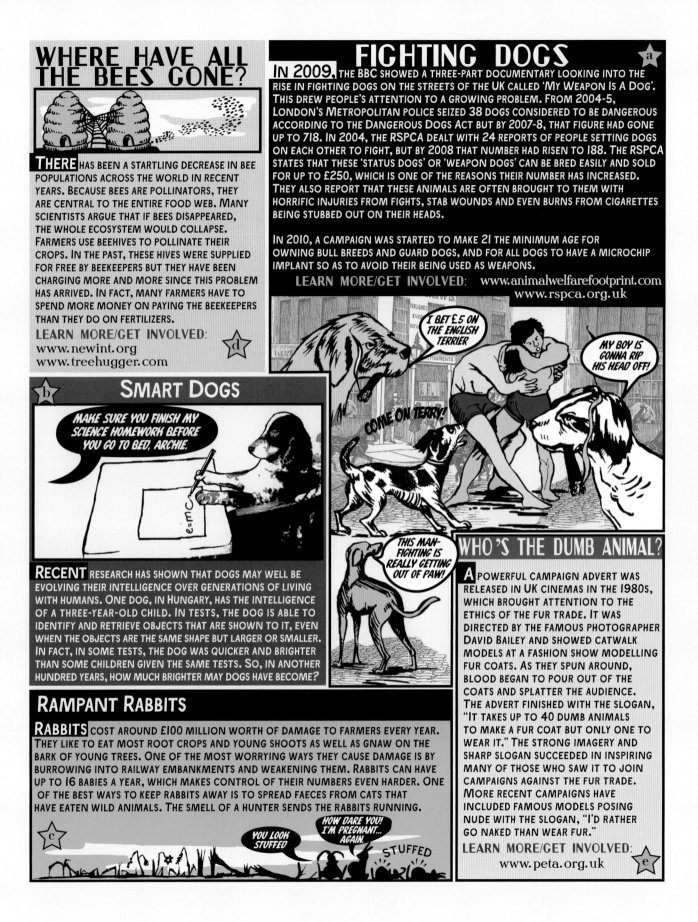

**THERE** HAS BEEN A STARTLING DECREASE IN BEE POPULATIONS ACROSS THE WORLD IN RECENT YEARS. BECAUSE BEES ARE POLLINATORS, THEY ARE CENTRAL TO THE ENTIRE FOOD WEB. MANY SCIENTISTS ARGUE THAT IF BEES DISAPPEARED, THE WHOLE ECOSYSTEM WOULD COLLAPSE. FARMERS USE BEEHIVES TO POLLINATE THEIR CROPS. IN THE PAST, THESE HIVES WERE SUPPLIED FOR FREE BY BEEKEEPERS BUT THEY HAVE BEEN CHARGING MORE AND MORE SINCE THIS PROBLEM HAS ARRIVED. IN FACT, MANY FARMERS HAVE TO SPEND MORE MONEY ON PAYING THE BEEKEEPERS THAN THEY DO ON FERTILIZERS.

**LEARN MORE/GET INVOLVED:**
www.newint.org
www.treehugger.com

## FIGHTING DOGS

**IN 2009,** THE BBC SHOWED A THREE-PART DOCUMENTARY LOOKING INTO THE RISE IN FIGHTING DOGS ON THE STREETS OF THE UK CALLED 'MY WEAPON IS A DOG'. THIS DREW PEOPLE'S ATTENTION TO A GROWING PROBLEM. FROM 2004-5, LONDON'S METROPOLITAN POLICE SEIZED 38 DOGS CONSIDERED TO BE DANGEROUS ACCORDING TO THE DANGEROUS DOGS ACT BUT BY 2007-8, THAT FIGURE HAD GONE UP TO 718. IN 2004, THE RSPCA DEALT WITH 24 REPORTS OF PEOPLE SETTING DOGS ON EACH OTHER TO FIGHT, BUT BY 2008 THAT NUMBER HAD RISEN TO 188. THE RSPCA STATES THAT THESE 'STATUS DOGS' OR 'WEAPON DOGS' CAN BE BRED EASILY AND SOLD FOR UP TO £250, WHICH IS ONE OF THE REASONS THEIR NUMBER HAS INCREASED. THEY ALSO REPORT THAT THESE ANIMALS ARE OFTEN BROUGHT TO THEM WITH HORRIFIC INJURIES FROM FIGHTS, STAB WOUNDS AND EVEN BURNS FROM CIGARETTES BEING STUBBED OUT ON THEIR HEADS.

IN 2010, A CAMPAIGN WAS STARTED TO MAKE 21 THE MINIMUM AGE FOR OWNING BULL BREEDS AND GUARD DOGS, AND FOR ALL DOGS TO HAVE A MICROCHIP IMPLANT SO AS TO AVOID THEIR BEING USED AS WEAPONS.

**LEARN MORE/GET INVOLVED:** www.animalwelfarefootprint.com
www.rspca.org.uk

## SMART DOGS

**RECENT** RESEARCH HAS SHOWN THAT DOGS MAY WELL BE EVOLVING THEIR INTELLIGENCE OVER GENERATIONS OF LIVING WITH HUMANS. ONE DOG, IN HUNGARY, HAS THE INTELLIGENCE OF A THREE-YEAR-OLD CHILD. IN TESTS, THE DOG IS ABLE TO IDENTIFY AND RETRIEVE OBJECTS THAT ARE SHOWN TO IT, EVEN WHEN THE OBJECTS ARE THE SAME SHAPE BUT LARGER OR SMALLER. IN FACT, IN SOME TESTS, THE DOG WAS QUICKER AND BRIGHTER THAN SOME CHILDREN GIVEN THE SAME TESTS. SO, IN ANOTHER HUNDRED YEARS, HOW MUCH BRIGHTER MAY DOGS HAVE BECOME?

## RAMPANT RABBITS

**RABBITS** COST AROUND £100 MILLION WORTH OF DAMAGE TO FARMERS EVERY YEAR. THEY LIKE TO EAT MOST ROOT CROPS AND YOUNG SHOOTS AS WELL AS GNAW ON THE BARK OF YOUNG TREES. ONE OF THE MOST WORRYING WAYS THEY CAUSE DAMAGE IS BY BURROWING INTO RAILWAY EMBANKMENTS AND WEAKENING THEM. RABBITS CAN HAVE UP TO 16 BABIES A YEAR, WHICH MAKES CONTROL OF THEIR NUMBERS EVEN HARDER. ONE OF THE BEST WAYS TO KEEP RABBITS AWAY IS TO SPREAD FAECES FROM CATS THAT HAVE EATEN WILD ANIMALS. THE SMELL OF A HUNTER SENDS THE RABBITS RUNNING.

## WHO'S THE DUMB ANIMAL?

**A** POWERFUL CAMPAIGN ADVERT WAS RELEASED IN UK CINEMAS IN THE 1980s, WHICH BROUGHT ATTENTION TO THE ETHICS OF THE FUR TRADE. IT WAS DIRECTED BY THE FAMOUS PHOTOGRAPHER DAVID BAILEY AND SHOWED CATWALK MODELS AT A FASHION SHOW MODELLING FUR COATS. AS THEY SPUN AROUND, BLOOD BEGAN TO POUR OUT OF THE COATS AND SPLATTER THE AUDIENCE. THE ADVERT FINISHED WITH THE SLOGAN, "IT TAKES UP TO 40 DUMB ANIMALS TO MAKE A FUR COAT BUT ONLY ONE TO WEAR IT." THE STRONG IMAGERY AND SHARP SLOGAN SUCCEEDED IN INSPIRING MANY OF THOSE WHO SAW IT TO JOIN CAMPAIGNS AGAINST THE FUR TRADE. MORE RECENT CAMPAIGNS HAVE INCLUDED FAMOUS MODELS POSING NUDE WITH THE SLOGAN, "I'D RATHER GO NAKED THAN WEAR FUR."

**LEARN MORE/GET INVOLVED:**
www.peta.org.uk

## ④ How do I research an issue?

*It's* very easy to run to the internet to find information on any subject. However, this can be a problem, as simply typing "get people to recycle their phones more" or "stop global warming" into a search engine such as Google will throw up millions of pages.

There is no doubt that the internet is a useful way to research an issue but it's not always the best place to start.

### ONCE YOU HAVE FOUND AN ISSUE YOU FEEL CONNECTED TO, TAKE THE FOLLOWING SEVEN STEPS BEFORE DOING ANYTHING ELSE.

① *Write* down, in one sentence, the change that you would like to see.

② *List* what you know so that you gain a clear picture of what you don't know and need to find out.

③ *Talk* about the issue with friends. By doing this, you will find that you encounter new ideas and opinions about the issue as well as filling a few gaps in your knowledge.

④ *Talk* about the issue with your family. They will have their own ideas about it. You may learn more facts and encounter further different points of view.

⑤ *Talk* about the issue with a teacher in your school or a responsible adult in some other organization outside school.

⑥ *Use* your school library or local library. If you are browsing through books, it's easy to find material that is specifically about your issue.

⑦ *You* will find that once you have chosen your issue, you will start noticing things that are connected to it. You may see them in newspapers, on the television or in a film, or hear them in the lyrics of a song. Even the label on a tin of food may suddenly make an idea pop into your head!

### DEVELOPING YOUR KNOWLEDGE STARTS WITH TALKING (OR LOOKING AT THE LABEL ON A TIN).

### RECORD BOOK

*Spend* FIVE MINUTES on your own constructing one sentence that describes a change that you would like to see.

Write this in your Record Book under the heading:

ONE IDEA FOR CHANGE.

Underneath this, write a second heading:

WHAT I LEARNED FROM TALKING WITH OTHERS.

### IN PAIRS/GROUPS

### HEADS TOGETHER:

*In* groups, spend **5-10 MINUTES** reading out your sentences describing your ideas for change.

Note down in your Record Book three points that have come from the rest of the group's reaction to your sentence. These may be facts, different points of view, personal experiences or ideas for campaign tools that you could use.

Then swap your groups around and repeat this activity with different people.

Now swap your groups around again and repeat this activity.

Each time, write notes in your Record Book showing the comments from group members on your idea for change.

Feed back to your class at least six points which you have learned from listening to others.

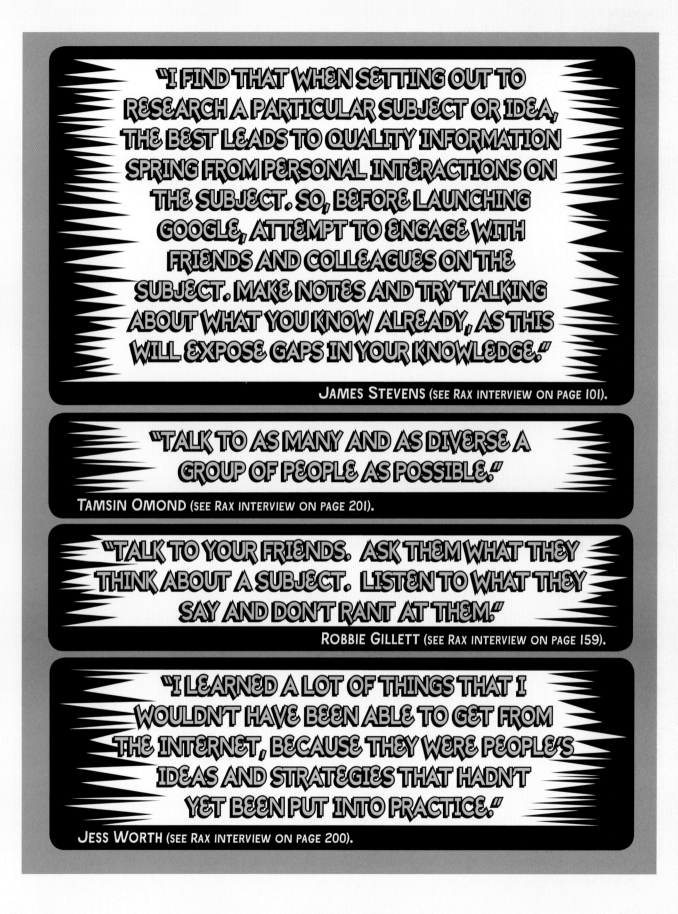

"I FIND THAT WHEN SETTING OUT TO RESEARCH A PARTICULAR SUBJECT OR IDEA, THE BEST LEADS TO QUALITY INFORMATION SPRING FROM PERSONAL INTERACTIONS ON THE SUBJECT. SO, BEFORE LAUNCHING GOOGLE, ATTEMPT TO ENGAGE WITH FRIENDS AND COLLEAGUES ON THE SUBJECT. MAKE NOTES AND TRY TALKING ABOUT WHAT YOU KNOW ALREADY, AS THIS WILL EXPOSE GAPS IN YOUR KNOWLEDGE."

JAMES STEVENS (SEE RAX INTERVIEW ON PAGE 101).

"TALK TO AS MANY AND AS DIVERSE A GROUP OF PEOPLE AS POSSIBLE."

TAMSIN OMOND (SEE RAX INTERVIEW ON PAGE 201).

"TALK TO YOUR FRIENDS. ASK THEM WHAT THEY THINK ABOUT A SUBJECT. LISTEN TO WHAT THEY SAY AND DON'T RANT AT THEM."

ROBBIE GILLETT (SEE RAX INTERVIEW ON PAGE 159).

"I LEARNED A LOT OF THINGS THAT I WOULDN'T HAVE BEEN ABLE TO GET FROM THE INTERNET, BECAUSE THEY WERE PEOPLE'S IDEAS AND STRATEGIES THAT HADN'T YET BEEN PUT INTO PRACTICE."

JESS WORTH (SEE RAX INTERVIEW ON PAGE 200).

# CHAPTER 4
# The PROCESSING PLANT

*Here* is an example from the Record Book of a school student from Sheffield, Max, who used the seven steps recommended in the Toolkit to research his idea for change. The work took place over a week and was the first stage of a campaign that his group had chosen. Each member of the group had been following the same seven steps.

## EXTRACT FROM MAX'S RECORD BOOK

### THE CHANGE I WOULD LIKE TO SEE

I would like to see more respect and praise for teenagers in the media rather than negative stories all the time.

### WHAT I DO KNOW

Every week, there are at least five stories in the news about teen gang violence or crime. Even though there are some teenagers who are violent and cause trouble, they are really in the minority but this is never pointed out. When I am out with my friends, sometimes old people cross the road if we are walking towards them, that's specially when we are wearing our hoods.

I heard on TV that there are something like five deaths from knife crime every week of the year but I can't remember if that was for adults as well or just teenagers and it was about a year ago so I need to find out the recent statistics. I know that some papers and news programmes go on about teen violence more than others. Need to find out which are the worst ones. I don't know how many teenagers are in the country, I need to find that out as then I could see what fraction are violent.

### TALKING WITH FRIENDS

Met with Izzy and Eva and talked with them about this. They made me think about how girls aren't usually involved in violent crime and it's usually boys. Need to look into the facts about this. Izzy told me a story she had read about a teenager who had done some really positive work on raising money for the Heart Foundation and that had been a little story on the website but then the main story had been about some teen violence. She said she would send me the site.

We also talked about a fight that had happened outside school last term and why it had happened. I'd forgotten about this and I know one of the boys who had been involved. I can have an interview with him. Eva told me that in her school, there's a gang that are always fighting but the next day they are always best friends. Sometimes, violence isn't always violence like they make out in the news. Need to look at the reasons these things happen.

### TALKING WITH FAMILY

I spoke with my mum about this idea. She had loads to say as she is a nurse. I should have gone to her first. She's full of statistics about youth crime and real stories. Will definitely interview her properly and maybe make it into a podcast. She made a really good point about how much adult violence happens all the time and it's hardly ever reported. She reckons adult violence is about ten times as big if not more. She'll get some facts on this. She also reminded me that uncle Vikram is a journalist for the local paper and he'd be really good to interview and to use for getting facts.

### TALKING WITH A TEACHER OR ANOTHER RESPONSIBLE ADULT

I spoke to Sascha, my Taekwondo teacher. He told me that a really good campaign to do would be to highlight how martial arts and boxing classes are really good ways to help young people to learn to control their aggression. He gave me a pamphlet about classes he does on Thursdays with young offenders and it's full of facts about how young people who have been violent can change their ways. Even better, he told me that Robbie, the youth worker who comes in sometimes, used to be someone

who got into gang fighting and now he's got a job in youth work so that he can help get kids out of gang culture and he'll be happy to let me interview him.

I'm not sure if this is going away from my first idea for change though because now I'm thinking about how to deal with teen violence instead of do something about the fact that it seems to be everywhere in the news but not in real life.

## VISIT A LIBRARY

This is really weird. I went to the library and there was a fight between the security guard and some drunk man! Made me think about what my mum had said about how much more adult violence there is than teen violence but also how much alcohol and drugs has to do with everything. The man really stank and had peed in his trousers.

Anyway, I asked the librarian to help me and she came out with this word I had never heard of before. Ephebiphobia. This means the fear and hate of teenagers. She gave me a couple of books on the subject. One of them was really complicated but the other one was like a history of the subject and it had loads of great pictures and headlines which I can use. It also made me think of the history of the subject.

I haven't read the whole book yet but already it's pretty clear that there's always been teen violence and it's always been a minority. But the weird thing is that sometimes it's made a big deal about in the media and sometimes it's not. In the 1950s the papers were full of it and then they stopped reporting it but it hadn't got any better or worse. It just stays the same.

## MAKE CONNECTIONS

It is weird but I keep seeing stuff to do with this project all the time now. Not only was there a fight in the library but whenever there's a fight at school I chase anybody who knew about it and write down why the fight had started. Most of the time it's about someone saying that someone else had said something bad about someone! Who cares? It just makes me think that most of these fights don't need to happen. Usually, that person hadn't said the bad thing anyway.

I watched a film in English called The Outsiders, it's all about teen gangs in the old days. The book's really famous and the writer was a teenager. Also, I check two news websites and one paper every day now and have started writing down the stories that are anti-teen and the stories that are pro-teen. I'm five days in to this and so far there's about 10 stories anti for every pro story. After two days, I decided to actually measure the headlines and note where in the news the story was. Eva also texted me and said she'd just seen two girls having a fight over a comb!

I reckon that there's a whole load to do in this campaign. It was really good to do all these things first because there's loads I'd never have thought of. Now I have a much better idea of how to use the internet and what to search for. Going to write a list of search words and phrases now. On Monday, in Citizenship Studies, going to start making a plan with the rest of the group and find out all the stuff they found out this week. Must remember to bring that book into class and to ask Ayesha if her phone has a good recording microphone on it so we can start doing interviews.

## RECORD BOOK

*Report* on the class activities under the headings:
EARLY STAGES OF LOOKING INTO AN ISSUE:
WHAT ISSUE I CHOSE FOR THE ACTIVITY AND WHY.
WHAT I LEARNED FROM TALKING TO OTHERS IN THE CLASS.
LIST THE SEVEN STAGES OF RESEARCHING WITHOUT THE INTERNET.
Notes on any class feedback sessions.

## SOURCES FOR RESEARCH

*You* have looked at the importance of starting your research by talking with different kinds of people, taking a look in the library and just looking out for signs to light your way.

Now it's time to look at how to use advanced critical thinking skills and skills of enquiry to find the best facts, statistics and ideas for you to research your idea for change in the most useful ways possible.

 **THE INTERNET** TIPS 'n' HINTS

*Information* technology is changing rapidly and Digital Natives will often be ahead of those changes. So this Toolkit will not be too specific about techniques to help you use the internet for research. Here are just a few basic tips, many of which you will already have come across.

### WIKIPEDIA

*Wikipedia* is a great place to start and gives you many links to follow up. For example, if you are interested in a campaign to raise awareness about the rights of people with mental illness, the Wikipedia page will give you many key words and ideas to think about as well as many links at the bottom of the page such as 'References', 'Further Reading' and 'External Links'. All of these are worth clicking on and you will soon find yourself locating many other different sites, giving you access to organizations, medical papers, media coverage and much more.

### YOUTH

*'Youth'* is a great word to put into the search bar of individual campaigning sites. Often you'll find that there are pages dedicated to young campaigners or pages dedicated to how young people are affected by the issues related to a particular campaign.

### COMMENTS PAGES AND FORUMS

*Comments* pages and forums are fantastic shortcuts to understanding the various opinions people have on an issue. The comments pages on large news sites are best as they show a wide spectrum of opinions. Always make a note of the type of news site or forum it is, as this will determine the kind of people who are visiting and leaving comments.

### LINKS

*Links* are a useful feature on websites as they can take you down different routes of enquiry or make connections you hadn't seen before when you click on them and follow them to the sites or other pages that they will open up for you.

Links can appear within a text you are reading or in groups to the side of a document or listed at the bottom of a page. Links that lead you to the sources used by a document are always important to follow.

### TAG CLOUDS

*Tag clouds* are a new development in linking which involve a cloud of tags in one place on a web page. These are headings that will take you to different areas. Rather than being links within a document or at the end of a document, these tag clouds stand on their own. The size of the tag usually means it is more commonly clicked on or that more information will be provided if you click on it.

### ANSWER ENGINES

*Answer* engines or knowledge engines are a useful system of internet research where you can type in a full question and specific answers will be offered instead of a million pages being thrown at you. For statistics, one of the best answer engines is www.wolframalpha.com Its sources are highly reliable, including scientific data from respected organizations as well as records from the US government's international database. There will be many more answer engines in the future and Google is also developing similar technology. Type 'answer engines' into a search engine and see what comes up.

### ADVANCED SEARCH

*'Advanced* search' and 'show options' are really useful tools that can result in more focused answers. Exploring the Google advanced settings shows you how you can narrow down your searches and if you click on 'show options', you'll see easy ways to arrange and filter your answers. Using Google 'trends' will show you how popular an issue has been, when interest has peaked and when it is at its lowest. Google Labs will keep you up to date on new systems that they are using and are worth checking too (www.googlelabs.com).

### NEWS WEBSITES

*News* websites provide news stories related to an issue. They generally offer links to their own stories as well as 'external links' that are relevant. Most news websites have a search bar so use it to get quickly to the issues you want to research. Always remember to use the 'News' icon on major search engines such as Google. This will lead you to all the news stories on your issue. Remember to use the preferences to make the stories chronological, starting with most recent first (unless you want to go back in time).

### BOOKMARK FOLDERS

*Bookmark* folders are important, as it's easy to race through great web pages full of information and then forget where they were. Always bookmark the pages you find. Even if at the time you don't think they are important, you may realize later that you need them. To help you sort out your

CONTINUED

# a ☆ IT'S A WIKIWIKI WORLD

**AMERICANS** JIMMY WALES AND LARRY SANGER LAUNCHED WIKIPEDIA IN 2001. THE WORD WIKI IS HAWAIIAN FOR 'FAST' AND WAS FIRST USED BY SOFTWARE DEVELOPER WARD CUNNINGHAM TO DESCRIBE HIS EARLY APPLICATION THAT INSPIRED WIKIPEDIA. THERE ARE CURRENTLY 14 MILLION PAGES ON WIKIPEDIA, IN HUNDREDS OF LANGUAGES AND WITH MILLIONS OF CONTRIBUTORS AND EDITORS. THE FACT THAT ANYONE CAN PUT UP A PAGE DOES ALLOW FOR MISTAKES AND MISLEADING INFORMATION TO APPEAR SOMETIMES BUT THE FACT THAT THERE ARE SO MANY EDITORS LIMITS THIS DANGER.
**LEARN MORE/GET INVOLVED:**
go to www.ted.com and type in Jimmy Wales.

**WIKILEAKS** IS AN OFFSHOOT FROM WIKIPEDIA THAT WAS LAUNCHED IN 2006. IT HAS ACHIEVED NOTORIETY BY THE FACT THAT IT FOCUSES ON PUBLISHING SECRET INFORMATION ABOUT GOVERNMENTS AND COMPANIES. IT WAS TAKEN OFFLINE IN 2009 AS IT HAD RUN OUT OF FUNDS BUT RETURNED IN 2010, WITH SENSATIONAL NEW 'LEAKS' FOR THE WORLD.
LEARN MORE/GET INVOLVED: www.wikileaks.org

b

**WIKILEAKS**

We are PURE, CLEAN AND GOOD FOR YOU

# d ☆ YOUTH MOVING UP

**MOVEMENTS** AND CAMPAIGNS FOR CHANGE THAT ARE YOUTH LED ARE GROWING RAPIDLY IN THIS COUNTRY. ALTHOUGH YOU WILL FIND MANY CAMPAIGN SITES THAT INCLUDE A YOUTH SECTION, THERE ARE NOW MANY UK SITES WHICH ARE RUN BY YOUNG PEOPLE AND FOR YOUNG PEOPLE.

21ST-CENTURY TECHNOLOGY IS ALLOWING YOUNG PEOPLE THE OPPORTUNITY TO CONNECT ABOUT ISSUES IN A FAR GREATER WAY THAN EVER BEFORE AND FOR MANY YOUNG PEOPLE, THAT MEANS ADDRESSING THESE ISSUES IN THEIR OWN WAY, WITHOUT ADULTS BEING INVOLVED.

TWO GREAT EXAMPLES ARE www.ukycc.org (ADDRESSING CLIMATE ISSUES) AND
www.globalforum40.com (ADDRESSING THE GLOBAL ISSUE OF HIV AND AIDS).

YOU WILL FIND THE AVERAGE AGE OF THESE CAMPAIGNERS IS IN THE LATE TEENS AND EARLY TWENTIES. THEY ARE CONNECTING NATIONALLY WITH EACH OTHER AND NETWORKING WITH GLOBAL MOVEMENTS THAT ARE ALSO YOUTH LED.
**LEARN MORE/GET INVOLVED:**
SEE INTERVIEW WITH UKYCC ON PAGE 104 AND GLOBAL FORUM 40 ON PAGE 195

# c ☆ HOW OLD WILL YOU BE IN 2050?

**KIRSTY** SHEEBURGER, FROM UKYCC, CREATED A STIR WHEN SHE PUT A VERY IMPORTANT QUESTION TO ONE OF THE DELEGATES AT AN INTERNATIONAL MEETING DURING THE COPENHAGEN CLIMATE CONFERENCE IN 2009. KIRSTY STOOD UP DURING THE PLENARY AND POLITELY ASKED THE MIDDLE-AGED CHAIR OF THE MEETING THE SIMPLE QUESTION: "HOW OLD WILL YOU BE IN 2050?" THE QUESTION WON A ROUND OF APPLAUSE AND BY THE NEXT DAY, HUNDREDS OF PEOPLE RETURNED TO THE MEETING WEARING A T-SHIRT WITH THAT QUESTION ON IT. THIS INCLUDED THE CHAIR OF THE MEETING HIMSELF, WHO BEGAN BY ADDRESSING KIRSTY, SAYING THAT HE WOULD BE 110 IN 2050 BUT HIS MANY CHILDREN WOULD BE IN THEIR FIFTIES.

KIRSTY'S POINT WAS MADE AND GAINED WIDE ATTENTION. BY ASKING ONE SIMPLE QUESTION, SHE HAD DRAWN ATTENTION TO THE FACT THAT IF SOMETHING WAS NOT DONE ABOUT THE WAY HUMANS POLLUTE THE PLANET AND ABUSE OUR NATURAL RESOURCES, THEN HER GENERATION WILL BE THE ONES TO SUFFER, NOT THE GENERATION THAT HAS CAUSED THE DAMAGE.

# f ☆ CUT AND PASTE JOURNALISM

**IN** 2007, AN ANONYMOUS CONTRIBUTOR MADE A HOAX ADDITION TO THE WIKI PAGE DEDICATED TO A RECENTLY DECEASED BRITISH COMPOSER, RONNIE HAZLEHURST. THE ENTRY CLAIMED THAT HE HAD WRITTEN A HIT FOR THE MODERN POP BAND S CLUB SEVEN. THIS WAS HIGHLY UNLIKELY, AS MR HAZLEHURST HAD MAINLY WORKED IN THE 1960S AND 1970S. DESPITE THIS, A NUMBER OF MAINSTREAM JOURNALISTS INCLUDED THIS INFORMATION WHEN THEY WROTE THEIR OBITUARIES TO MR HAZLEHURST. MANY PEOPLE SUSPECT THAT THIS WAS A TRICK TO REVEAL THE LACK OF SERIOUS RESEARCH AND CARE TAKEN BY SOME JOURNALISTS, WHO HAD JUST CUT AND PASTED FROM WIKIPEDIA WITHOUT STOPPING TO THINK. SOMETHING THAT ALL STUDENTS NEED TO BEAR IN MIND, TOO!

# e ☆ THE 50 CENT ARMY

**COMMENTS** PAGES ARE A USEFUL WAY TO GAUGE DIFFERENT POINTS OF VIEW ON AN ISSUE. HOWEVER, BE CAREFUL, SOME PEOPLE ARE NOT WHO THEY APPEAR TO BE! IN CHINA, FREEDOM OF EXPRESSION IS TIGHTLY CONTROLLED AND PEOPLE WHO OPPOSE THE RULING COMMUNIST PARTY ARE OFTEN TAKEN AND PUT IN CAMPS FOR 'CORRECTION'. THE WEB IS A PROBLEM FOR A STATE TRYING TO MAINTAIN THIS KIND OF CONTROL. AS A RESULT, THERE ARE AN ESTIMATED 300,000 PEOPLE PAID BY THE STATE TO PUSH PRO-PARTY IDEAS ON THEIR OWN BLOGS AND OTHER PEOPLE'S SITES – AS WELL AS MONITOR ANYONE WHO MAY BE DISCUSSING 'DANGEROUS' IDEAS. THESE PEOPLE ARE PAID 50 CENTS, OR 5 MAO, FOR EVERY ARTICLE OR COMMENT THAT THEY POST. THEY ARE CALLED THE '50 CENT ARMY'.

THIS IS AN IMPORTANT WARNING ABOUT THE WEB. CHINA CONTROLS PEOPLE NOT ONLY BY BLOCKING SITES BUT ALSO BY GUIDING USERS TOWARDS CERTAIN OPINIONS AND IDEAS.

# 4 The PROCESSING PLANT

bookmarked web pages, create many bookmark folders with different headings. These will be vital aids as you create a great Record Book to provide evidence of all the work you have done.

## CONTACT DETAILS

*Contact* details on websites give you the chance to send questions directly to people associated with a campaign, an issue or an area of study. Before doing so, however, you must read the Internet Security section below.

## SOCIAL NETWORKING

*Social* networking sites may put you in touch with groups running campaign sites that cover your issue. Like comments pages, they can give you a good idea of the various points of view on an issue. Again, read the section on Internet Security below before contacting anyone.

## SITES DEDICATED TO ONE ISSUE

*Sites* dedicated to one issue and informing people with up-to-date research and statistics in order to support their campaigns are another useful tool for you to search out. Good examples are:

www.climatesafety.org
www.pirc.info
www.ukycc.org

Sites that deal with climate change issues.

Or

www.notforsalecampaign.org
www.freetheslaves.net
www.antislavery.org

Sites that deal with campaigning to end modern-day slavery.

Often you will be able to make contact with sites like this and ask specific questions, although usually all the information you need will be presented to you.

## WARNING

PEOPLE TELLING YOU THINGS TO SELL YOU THINGS ARE A COMMON PROBLEM WITH INTERNET RESEARCH. BE SUSPICIOUS OF SITES THAT GIVE YOU INFORMATION BUT AT THE SAME TIME SEEM TO BE SELLING PRODUCTS LINKED TO THAT INFORMATION. THE MORE ADVERTS ON THE PAGE, THE LESS TRUSTWORTHY THE INFORMATION.

## IN PAIRS/GROUPS

### HEADS TOGETHER:

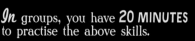

*In* groups, you have **20 MINUTES** to practise the above skills.

### CHOOSE AN ISSUE BY VOTING

Access the internet and use at least 10 of the points above to experiment with how you can research your issues.

For each point, create a screen grab of a page you have found.

Copy and paste a page that shows a list of the bookmarks you made as well as the various bookmark folders that you created.

This is just a practice run. Under no circumstances are you to contact anyone yet. You must read the 'internet security' section below before you contact anyone.

Feed back your work to the class.

## RECORD BOOK

*Either* print your screen grabs and put them in your Record Book or create a file on your computer where you save a set of screen grabs. Put this work under the title:

### PRACTISING INTERNET RESEARCH ON... (FILL IN THIS SPACE WITH THE ISSUE YOUR GROUP CHOSE)

Write notes under the following two headings:
### USEFUL INTERNET RESEARCH TECHNIQUES I HAVE LEARNED, WITH EXAMPLES.

Notes on any class feedback sessions.

## B INTERNET SECURITY TIPS 'n' HINTS

*You* will know how dangerous the internet can be. By law, your school has to have in place a strict code to ensure your security when using the internet. It is vital that you stick to the school code on this. In addition, here are a few other ideas:

*Create* a set of e-mail addresses just for your campaign work, which don't have anyone's personal names in the wording. Even better, create e-mail addresses using language which reflects your campaign. Use these e-mail addresses if you need to contact a site or an individual connected to your campaign.

Another way of keeping secure is if your teacher allows you to create a school e-mail address for contacting people connected to your campaigns.

Never give out any personal details. If an organization or individual wants to send you hard copy material, always use your school address.

CONTINUED

# TROLLS, SOCKPUPPETS AND MEATPUPPETS

**COMMENTS** PAGES FROM MAINSTREAM MEDIA, INDEPENDENT MEDIA, BLOGS, WEB FORUMS AND NETWORKING SITES ARE INDEED USEFUL WAYS TO GET AN IDEA OF PEOPLE'S OPINIONS ABOUT AN ISSUE. BUT THERE ARE A FEW IMPORTANT DANGERS TO BE AWARE OF. EVEN THOUGH THESE CHARACTERS ALL SOUND LIKE SOMETHING FROM A *LORD OF THE RINGS* FILM, THEY ARE INFLUENTIAL AND YOU NEED TO KNOW ABOUT THEM.

*WE WILL CREATE A CIVILIZATION OF THE MIND INSIDE OF CYBERSPACE. MAY IT BE MORE HUMANE AND FAIR THAN THE WORLDS YOUR GOVERNMENTS HAVE MADE BEFORE.*

JOHN PERRY BARLOW – ONE OF THE FOUNDING MEMBERS OF THE ELECTRONIC FRONTIER FOUNDATION **LEARN MORE/GET INVOLVED:** www.eff.org

## TROLLS:

**BASED** ON THE OLD FISHING TERM FOR SLOWLY DRAGGING A BAITED LINE THROUGH THE WATER IN ORDER TO GET A BITE FROM A FISH ('TRAWL'). TROLLS ARE PEOPLE WHO USE THE INTERNET IN A NEGATIVE WAY, TO CAUSE TROUBLE IN DISCUSSIONS OF ISSUES, TAKING ADVANTAGE OF THEIR ANONYMITY. THIS IS ONE OF THE INTERESTING ASPECTS OF MEETING SOMEONE IN THE VIRTUAL WORLD OF 'CYBERSPACE' COMPARED TO MEETING SOMEONE IN THE REAL WORLD. IN THE REAL WORLD, YOU CAN LOOK THEM IN THE FACE WHEN THEY TALK TO YOU AND YOU CAN REACT TO WHAT THEY HAVE TO SAY, PERSON TO PERSON. THE FACT THAT ON-LINE COMMUNITIES ARE DIFFERENT ALLOWS FOR MANIPULATION OF OPINIONS AND IDEAS.

## CONCERN TROLLS:

**THESE** ARE PEOPLE WHO JOIN USER SITES, PRETENDING TO AGREE WITH THEIR CONCERNS BUT IN REALITY HAVE THE OPPOSING OPINION. THEY WILL TRY TO SOW SEEDS OF UNCERTAINTY AND DOUBT AMONGST THE WEB COMMUNITY THEY ARE INFILTRATING.

*I AGREE WITH YOU BUT I DON'T THINK IT WILL WORK, DO YOU?*

*I THINK I AM...I MEAN.. DANIEL IS GREAT*

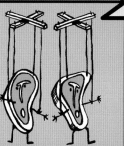

## SOCKPUPPETS:

**THESE** ARE WEB USERS WHO INVENT AN IDENTITY WHEN THEY JOIN A SITE, ONLY TO POST CONTINUAL PRAISE FOR THEIR REAL SELVES. THERE HAVE BEEN EXAMPLES OF POLITICIANS AND AUTHORS WHO HAVE JOINED SITES ANONYMOUSLY AND THEN SPENT THEIR TIME USING THEIR INVENTED IDENTITY TO PRAISE THEMSELVES. THEY ARE CALLED SOCKPUPPETS BECAUSE THEY ARE INVENTED CHARACTERS OPERATED BY REAL PEOPLE.

## MEATPUPPETS:

**THESE** ARE PEOPLE WHO HAVE BEEN PERSUADED BY AN INDIVIDUAL PERSON TO JOIN SITES TO POST COMMENTS THAT PRAISE THAT PERSON. THEY ARE CALLED MEATPUPPETS BECAUSE THEY ARE ACTUALLY REAL PEOPLE AS OPPOSED TO INVENTED CHARACTERS.

**IT'S** WORTH WONDERING HOW MANY TROLLS, SOCKPUPPETS AND MEATPUPPETS ARE BEHAVING LIKE THIS ON THE INTERNET WITHOUT BEING CAUGHT. IT IS DIFFICULT TO IDENTIFY THEM AND PROVE WHAT THEY ARE DOING BUT IT DOES HAPPEN AND YOU CAN FIND OUT MANY EXAMPLES WITH A LITTLE RESEARCH.

# ASTROTURFING AND FALSE FLAGS

**ASTROTURFING** IS DEVELOPMENT OF THE IDEA OF TROLLS AND SOCKPUPPETS WHERE BUSINESS INTERESTS, POLITICAL MOVEMENTS AND INDEPENDENT GROUPS USE THE COMMENTS PAGES AND FORUMS ON VARIOUS SITES TO CREATE THE IDEA OF A GRASSROOTS MOVEMENT WHEN THERE ISN'T ONE. A CLOTHING COMPANY MAY PAY PEOPLE TO ENTER A WIDE VARIETY OF SITES JUST TO MENTION HOW MUCH THEY 'LOVE' THE COMPANY'S PRODUCTS. THESE METHODS ARE CALLED ASTROTURFING BECAUSE ASTROTURF IS THE NAME FOR MANUFACTURED OR FAKE GRASS.

**FALSE FLAGS** COMES FROM THE MILITARY TERM DESCRIBING THE PRACTICE OF SHOWING A FALSE FLAG, PRETENDING TO BE THE ENEMY. IN THE WORLD OF THE INTERNET, THIS IS WHEN AN INDIVIDUAL OR GROUP OF INDIVIDUALS PRETEND TO BE SUPPORTERS OF A MOVEMENT OR PERSON BUT THEN MAKE STATEMENTS OR TELL OUTRIGHT LIES THAT PUT THAT MOVEMENT OR PERSON IN A BAD LIGHT. THERE ARE SEVERAL EXAMPLES OF THIS, PARTICULARLY IN THE WORLD OF POLITICS.

LEARN MORE/GET INVOLVED: www.globalwitness.org/pages/en/conflict_diamonds.html

The only time you can allow an individual to send a letter to your home address is when you have contacted a Member of Parliament. Only do this if you have contacted them through:

www.writetothem.com or www.parliament.uk

 ## IN PAIRS
### BE THE BARD:

*In* pairs, IMAGINE YOU CAN CHOOSE ANY NAME FOR A WEBSITE ADDRESS.

Use inspiring language to capture the idea of your campaign. If possible, check that the name is not being used already.

For example: www.streetstuck.com could suit a local campaign that is raising awareness about the damage and cost of chewing gum being dropped on the pavement.

www.38degrees.org.uk cleverly shows that the organization is interested in causing an 'avalanche' of opinion – 38 degrees is the angle at which a heavy load of snow will become an avalanche.

**COME UP WITH AT LEAST THREE DIFFERENT IDEAS FOR THREE DIFFERENT CAMPAIGNS. YOU HAVE 10 MINUTES.**

Feed back your three ideas for website names to the class and see if they can guess what the campaign stands for. Do they think these are effective names which will inspire the average internet surfer?

## Ⓒ NEWSPAPERS, MAGAZINES AND OTHER REGULAR PUBLICATIONS  **TIPS 'n' HINTS**

*There* are many publications specializing in areas that may be connected to your campaign ideas.

### FOR EXAMPLE,

you may be interested in a campaign that aims to raise awareness about the idea that cycling is better for the environment than driving cars. If so, you would do well to look in your library to see if they stock the many different magazines that focus on cycling.

There are some magazines that focus on a cross-section of the many different campaigns and ideas for change around the world. One of the best ones to start with is the *New Internationalist* (www.newint.org).

Often, if a library does not stock a magazine it can order it from other libraries. You may have to wait a few days but it's usually worth it and you have nothing to lose by putting in the request.

Your school library will have copies of the daily newspapers and usually someone at home will buy a paper a day. Get into the habit of looking through a paper every day but make sure you sample a variety of newspapers. Don't just read the same paper every day as they all have different approaches to the news.

If you are using newspapers that other people have finished with or that you have bought yourself, get into the habit of cutting out stories that interest you or that are connected to an issue that concerns you. It's easy to keep a folder of these in some kind of order and this will become a really useful resource.

 ## IN GROUPS
### NEWSPAPER GAME:

*In* groups, use newspapers and/or magazines to find a story connected to the following list of issues. There is **NO TIME LIMIT** as the winner is the first group to have found a story connected to all of the issues on this list:

**HUMAN RIGHTS**
**TRANSPORT**
**EDUCATION**
**TEENAGERS**

The first group to finish must feed back to the class for checking before being crowned the winners.

## Ⓓ BOOKS  **TIPS 'n' HINTS**

*Books* remain one of the best sources for research. You can hold a book, flick through it quickly, check the headings and the pictures easily and use the index at the back. Of course, you can do most of these things with websites but books still remain a useful tool. Although there may be well over a trillion pages on the web, very often a simple book will help you find what you want to know considerably more easily.

Use your library to access books that may be of use to you. Libraries will often check subjects for you, make recommendations and order books from other libraries if their branch doesn't have the one you are after.

Sitting in front of a pile of books is frightening to some people but it's a really easy way to browse and flick through information. You will often be surprised with what pops out of a page and slaps you in the face with a great new idea.

# GET LOCAL ATTENTION

**THERE** ARE 1,300 LOCAL NEWSPAPERS IN THE UK AND 1,500 WEBSITES THAT COVER LOCAL NEWS. THEY ARE AN EXCELLENT WAY FOR YOU TO GET PUBLICITY FOR YOUR ACTIVE CITIZENSHIP CAMPAIGNS OR RAISE AWARENESS ABOUT ISSUES.

LOCAL PAPERS WILL ALWAYS BE LOOKING FOR STORIES THAT ARE DIFFERENT AND ENTERTAINING, WHICH ALSO OFFER THE OPPORTUNITY FOR A GOOD PHOTOGRAPH. STORIES ABOUT YOUNG PEOPLE DOING SOMETHING POSITIVE IN THE COMMUNITY ARE VERY ATTRACTIVE FOR LOCAL PAPERS AND NEWS SITES.

IN THE CHAPTER CALLED *THE PROJECTOR ROOM*, YOU WILL BE LEARNING ABOUT HOW TO DEAL WITH THE MEDIA SO THAT YOU CAN GET THEM WORKING FOR YOU.

LEARN MORE/GET INVOLVED:
www.thepaperboy.com/uk www.newspapersoc.org.uk and www.mediauk.com OFFER YOU DETAILS ABOUT ALL THE NATIONAL AND LOCAL NEWSPAPERS AND WEBSITES IN THE UK.

# An Expert In Your Hand

**EVEN** THOUGH THERE ARE OVER A TRILLION PAGES ON THE WEB AND IT IS ONE OF THE MOST IMPORTANT INVENTIONS IN HUMAN HISTORY, IT IS MISLEADING TO THINK THAT IT IS A GOOD ENOUGH RESOURCE TO USE FOR EVERYTHING. WHEN YOU ARE USING YOUR CRITICAL THINKING SKILLS TO UNDERSTAND AN ISSUE IN DEPTH, CONSULTING A BOOK THAT IS DEDICATED TO IT IS THE SAME AS CALLING IN AN EXPERT. THE BOOK WILL USUALLY BE THE RESULT OF SOMEONE ELSE HAVING DONE YEARS OF RESEARCH ON THE SAME ISSUE AND THEN OFFERING IT UP TO YOU IN A VERY HANDY, EASILY ACCESSED WAY. THE WEB IS ESSENTIAL TOO BUT IT OFFERS OTHER LEVELS OF INFORMATION AND RESEARCH.

# The New Internationalist

**STARTED** OVER 30 YEARS AGO, *THE NEW INTERNATIONALIST* HAS GROWN INTO ONE OF THE LEADING PUBLICATIONS REPORTING ON WORLD POVERTY AND CAMPAIGNING FOR GLOBAL JUSTICE. IT CARRIES THE KIND OF STORIES – ESPECIALLY ABOUT THE LIVES OF PEOPLE IN POOR COUNTRIES – THAT RARELY APPEAR IN MAINSTREAM NEWSPAPERS AND MAGAZINES. THE MAGAZINE HAS WON THE UTNE INDEPENDENT MEDIA AWARD FOR BEST INTERNATIONAL COVERAGE EIGHT TIMES. IT IS PRODUCED BY AN EQUAL-PAY CO-OPERATIVE BASED IN OXFORD BUT ALSO HAS OFFICES IN CANADA, AUSTRALIA AND NEW ZEALAND.

WHEN YOU COME TO RESEARCH YOUR GLOBAL CAMPAIGN, THIS IS A GOOD PLACE TO START – EITHER BY USING THE MAGAZINE ITSELF OR THE WEBSITE, WHICH HAS A LARGE ARCHIVE OF ARTICLES THAT ARE EASILY SEARCHED FOR AND ACCESSED.

LEARN MORE/GET INVOLVED: www.newint.org

# GOING TO THE TRUBRARY

**TRUBRARY** IS A JAMAICAN PATOIS WORD USED TO DESCRIBE A LIBRARY. IT SHOWS THE SUSPICION OF A PLACE OF TRUTH THAT HAS ITS NAME BEGINNING WITH THE WORD 'LIE'. THE WORD IS A WARNING ABOUT THE IMPORTANCE OF USING CRITICAL THINKING.

THE WORD LIBRARY COMES FROM THE LATIN WORD *LIBER*, WHICH DESCRIBED THE THIN LAYER FOUND BETWEEN THE BARK AND THE WOOD OF A TREE. ANCIENT ROMANS USED THIS TO WRITE ON BEFORE THE DEVELOPMENT OF THE FIRST PARCHMENT AND PAPER.

LIBRARIES ARE AN EXCELLENT RESOURCE FOR YOUR CRITICAL THINKING AND ENQUIRY. LIBRARIANS ARE OFTEN VERY WILLING TO HELP YOU FIND WHAT YOU ARE LOOKING FOR AS WELL AS SUGGEST OTHER AREAS OF STUDY THAT YOU HADN'T REALIZED WERE CONNECTED TO YOUR ISSUE. THERE ARE ALSO SPECIALIST LIBRARIES, WHICH FOCUS ON JUST ONE ISSUE.

### LEARN MORE/GET INVOLVED:

THE BRITISH LIBRARY IS THE SECOND BIGGEST LIBRARY IN THE WORLD AND CONTAINS 18 MILLION BOOKS. IT HAS AN EXCELLENT ONLINE RESOURCE TOO: www.bl.uk

THE BRITISH LIBRARY SITE ALSO INCLUDES USEFUL CAMPAIGNING TIPS AND RESOURCES:
www.bl.uk/learning/citizenship/campaign/campaignhome.html
www.bl.uk/learning/citizenship/takingliberties/tlinteractive.html

SOME SPECIALIST LIBRARIES WITH EXCELLENT ONLINE RESOURCES:

THE PEOPLE'S HISTORY MUSEUM, MANCHESTER: www.phm.org.uk
THE WOMEN'S LIBRARY, GLASGOW: www.womenslibrary.org.uk
THE WORKING CLASS MOVEMENT LIBRARY, SALFORD: www.wcml.org.uk
THE WOMEN'S LIBRARY, LONDON: www.londonmet.ac.uk/thewomenslibrary

# MEGAMAGAZINE

**THERE** ARE MAGAZINES ON EVERY KIND OF SUBJECT YOU CAN THINK OF. THERE ARE SEVEN DIFFERENT MAGAZINES DEDICATED TO CROSS STITCHING, FOR EXAMPLE, AND EVEN A MAGAZINE ALL ABOUT HOW TO BUILD GARDENS FOR MODEL RAILWAY SETS. FOR YOUR RESEARCH, ONE USEFUL SITE IS: WWW.MAGPORTAL.COM. THIS SITE ALLOWS YOU TO ENTER A SUBJECT AND THE SEARCH ENGINE WILL FIND ARTICLES FROM MAGAZINES THAT HAVE COVERED IT. THIS CAN LEAD YOU TO MAGAZINE SOURCES AS WELL AS TO ORDERING MAGAZINES AT YOUR LIBRARY.

# 4 The PROCESSING PLANT

## E FILM AND TELEVISION DOCUMENTARIES AND MAINSTREAM FICTION
TIPS 'n' HINTS

### FILM AND TELEVISION DOCUMENTARIES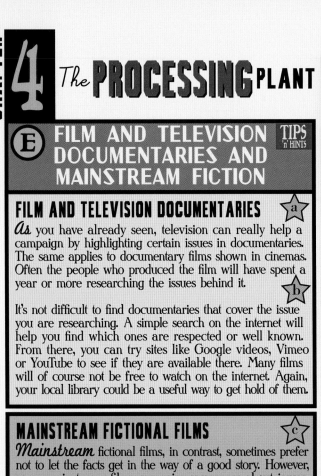

*As* you have already seen, television can really help a campaign by highlighting certain issues in documentaries. The same applies to documentary films shown in cinemas. Often the people who produced the film will have spent a year or more researching the issues behind it.

It's not difficult to find documentaries that cover the issue you are researching. A simple search on the internet will help you find which ones are respected or well known. From there, you can try sites like Google videos, Vimeo or YouTube to see if they are available there. Many films will of course not be free to watch on the internet. Again, your local library could be a useful way to get hold of them.

### MAINSTREAM FICTIONAL FILMS

*Mainstream* fictional films, in contrast, sometimes prefer not to let the facts get in the way of a good story. However, some mainstream films can raise awareness about issues.

#### FOR EXAMPLE,

*Avatar* brought millions of people to consider the environmental and social damage caused by the mining industry and *The Day After Tomorrow* made its viewers think about the possible results of climate change.

### IN GROUPS

### HEADS TOGETHER:

*In* your groups, you have **SIX MINUTES** to **LIST AS MANY FILMS AS YOU CAN, WHICH COVER ISSUES THAT COULD BE CAMPAIGNS.**

List the film title and the issues connected to it.

Feed back to the class. The winning group is the one with the longest list – once it has been verified by the rest of the class.

## RECORD BOOK

*Report* on the class activities under the headings:

COMING UP WITH CAMPAIGN WEBSITE NAMES.

SPEED SEARCHING NEWSPAPERS OR MAGAZINES.

LISTING NAMES OF FILMS WHICH COVER CAMPAIGNING ISSUES.

Make sure you include notes on any class feedback sessions.

## F INDEPENDENT MEDIA SOURCES
TIPS 'n' HINTS

*Most* newspapers, magazines, television programmes, films and books need to make money. They have to target their audiences and work out exactly how to sell to that market. This is their priority. That's why celebrities, gossip, scandal, crime, sex, funny or shocking stories dominate many newspapers and television channels. These are the kinds of stories that most people want to consume.

'Independent media' often have different priorities. These can range from blogs and films covering events posted by ordinary citizens (Citizen Journalism) or whole news stations which do not exist primarily to make money. These websites may be independent enough to report the news without having to focus on celebrities or providing stories designed to shock or make you laugh.

Of course, these independent sites can have their own bias but this is often not hidden. They generally show their bias by focusing on the stories that they believe are most important.

There are:

## 1. ORGANIZATIONS WHICH COVER NEWS INTERNATIONALLY.

*These* websites run as a normal international news service but operate on a not-for-profit basis. A good example is www.democracynow.org which is based in the US but broadcasts across the web. This station is sophisticated in that its news shows and podcasts sound and look like regular news channels. The difference is in what they report and how they report it. These sites are much more focused on questioning government policies, exposing corruption and pursuing stories related to human rights, the environment and grassroots movements.

CONTINUED

## Docs-On-Line

**THERE** ARE SEVERAL DEDICATED SITES WHICH YOU CAN USE TO ACCESS DOCUMENTARIES. FROM ARCHIVE FOOTAGE OF CHARLIE CHAPLIN AND GANDHI VISITING THE EAST END OF LONDON TO RECENT SCIENTIFIC DOCUMENTARIES COVERING RESEARCH INTO WATER BEING USED AS A SOURCE OF CLEAN FUEL.

**LEARN MORE/GET INVOLVED**:
www.documentary-film.net
www.britishpathe.com
www.newsplayer.com
www.factualtv.com

THE BRITISH FILM INSTITUTE PROVIDES ANOTHER EXCELLENT SERVICE AND YOUR SCHOOL CAN EASILY JOIN UP SO THAT YOU CAN ACCESS ITS LARGE COLLECTION:

www.screenonline.org.uk

AS WELL AS THESE RESOURCES FOR DOCUMENTARIES, 21ST-CENTURY TECHNOLOGY HAS ALLOWED FOR A WEALTH OF INDEPENDENTLY MADE FILMS BEING MADE AVAILABLE ON THE INTERNET. MANY OF THESE ARE SHORT FILMS THAT DOCUMENT POINTS OF VIEWS ON ISSUES AS WELL AS EVENTS THAT ARE POSTED ON THE WEB LIVE OR VERY SHORTLY AFTERWARDS.

**LEARN MORE/GET INVOLVED**:
www.reelnews.co.uk
www.undercurrents.org
http://visionon.tv

## IN THE PAST

**THE** FIRST PUBLIC SHOWING OF A FILM WAS HELD IN PARIS IN 1895 BY THE LUMIERE BROTHERS, USING THEIR INVENTION CALLED THE CINEMATOGRAPHE. ALTHOUGH THE 10 FILMS WERE ALL UNDER A MINUTE LONG AND SHOWED NORMAL EVERYDAY EVENTS LIKE PEOPLE LEAVING THEIR FACTORY AFTER WORK AND A MAN WATERING HIS GARDEN, THEY CAUSED AN ABSOLUTE SENSATION. WHEN THE BROTHERS SHOWED A FILM OF A TRAIN ARRIVING AT A STATION, THE AUDIENCE OFTEN RAN OUT, TERRIFIED THAT THEY WERE ABOUT TO BE RUN OVER BY A REAL TRAIN!

\* TRANSLATION: HELP!

## PRESENT

**WE'VE** COME A LONG WAY SINCE THE LUMIERE BROTHERS IN 1895. SEVERAL TELEVISION-MANUFACTURING COMPANIES ARE NOW DEVELOPING HOLOGRAPHIC TELEVISIONS. EXPECTED IN 2020, THESE TELEVISIONS WILL PROVIDE A FULL HOLOGRAPHIC EXPERIENCE. RESEARCHERS SUGGEST THAT THE TELEVISIONS WILL ALLOW THE VIEWER TO HAVE A THREE-DIMENSIONAL IMAGE FLOATING IN THEIR ROOM, SO THAT IT WILL BE POSSIBLE TO WALK AROUND IT, LOOKING AT IT FROM ALL ANGLES.

## MAKE ME LAUGH, MAKE ME CRY, MAKE ME THINK?

**THERE** HAVE BEEN NUMEROUS FILMS THAT HAVE DONE MORE THAN SIMPLY ENTERTAIN PEOPLE AND HAVE HAD A DEEP IMPACT, CHALLENGING PEOPLE'S POINT OF VIEW ON ISSUES.

IN THE SAME WAY THAT CHARLES DICKENS' BOOKS MADE PEOPLE LOOK AT THE REALITIES OF PEOPLE LIVING IN POVERTY, CHARLIE CHAPLIN'S FILMS MADE PEOPLE QUESTION THE INJUSTICES OF IMPOVERISHED PEOPLE SUFFERING THROUGH THE GREAT DEPRESSION OF THE 1930S IN AMERICA. IN THE 1970S, *APOCALYPSE NOW* DEPICTED SUCH A GRAPHIC DESCRIPTION OF THE VIETNAM WAR THAT MANY CAME AWAY FROM THE FILM HATING THE IDEA OF WAR EVER BEING WAGED AGAIN. IN A SIMILAR WAY *NETWORK* (1976) EXPOSED THE THINKING BEHIND MAINSTREAM TV, LEADING VIEWERS TO QUESTION WHETHER GETTING HIGH RATINGS HAD BECOME MORE IMPORTANT THAN TELLING THE TRUTH. A MORE RECENT FILM THAT HAS AFFECTED THE WAY THAT PEOPLE THINK ABOUT ISSUES IS *AVATAR* (2009). THE DIRECTOR STATED THAT IT WAS HIS WAY OF GETTING PEOPLE TO CONSIDER THE EFFECTS OF MILITARY INTERVENTION IN THE MIDDLE EAST AND CORPORATIONS EXTRACTING THE NATURAL RESOURCES OF POOR COUNTRIES.

THE KEY PRESENTER FOR DEMOCRACY NOW!, AMY GOODMAN

## DEMOCRACY NOW!

**AS** AN INTRODUCTION TO THEIR SITE, DEMOCRACY NOW! STATE THE FOLLOWING:

*"FOR TRUE DEMOCRACY TO WORK, PEOPLE NEED EASY ACCESS TO INDEPENDENT, DIVERSE SOURCES OF NEWS AND INFORMATION."*

THIS REFLECTS THE MAIN AIM OF INDEPENDENT MEDIA SOURCES, TO PROVIDE AN ALTERNATIVE TO THE MAINSTREAM AND TO BRING A GREATER DIVERSITY OF STORIES, VIEWPOINTS AND ISSUES TO THE USER'S ATTENTION. THE NAME OF THE SITE SHOWS THAT THEY VIEW MAINSTREAM MEDIA AS BEING UNDEMOCRATIC AS THEY BELIEVE IT DOES NOT REFLECT THE WIDER RANGE OF NEWS AND ISSUES THAT EXIST IN THE WORLD, BUT ONLY A SELECTION. THE EXCLAMATION MARK ADDS STRENGTH TO THEIR NAME, AS IF IT IS AN URGENT DEMAND.

ALTHOUGH DEMOCRACY NOW! IS AN AMERICAN SITE, IT COVERS WORLD NEWS AND REMAINS ONE OF THE MOST FAMOUS AND RESPECTED INDEPENDENT MEDIA SOURCES IN THE WORLD.

**LEARN MORE/GET INVOLVED**:
www.democracynow.org

I'M READING A BOOK ABOUT GLUE AT THE MOMENT... I CAN'T PUT IT DOWN.

# 4 The PROCESSING PLANT

Another large independent media organization is www.indymedia.org, which has been running since the early days of the web and has branches in most of the world's countries. It is possible for anyone to be trained by Indymedia and become one of their world reporters. It provides written reports which often have films and podcasts attached to them. It is a multilingual website and, in addition to the main site, there are branch sites belonging to individual countries which themselves are often broken down by city.

As with Democracy Now! Indymedia covers stories which often never make the mainstream news. The site also focuses on issues like the environment, human rights, corruption and grassroots movements.

Both sites have a worldwide network through the internet and both exist mainly on donations. This allows them to be free of any 'vested interests', which might affect what they report and, more importantly, what they don't report.

**LEARN MORE/GET INVOLVED:**
www.democracynow.org
www.medialens.org
www.indymedia.org
www.informationclearinghouse.info
www.counterpunch.org
www.opendemocracy.net

## 2. SITES WHICH USE NEWS SELECTION AND ANALYSIS.

*These* sites are also known as 'aggregation' sites. They sift through news from around the world and filter out everything except the issues they are targeting. Again, as with Indymedia and Democracy Now! many of these sites focus on grassroots movements, human rights issues, corruption, the environment and questioning government policies. As with the other sites, these sites mostly survive thanks to donations by their web users.

**A GOOD EXAMPLE** of this kind of site is
www.commondreams.org

Common Dreams collects news from around the world, from well established and respected news sources, and regroups them on the site. Alongside this ever-changing feed of selected news, there are articles written by bloggers, recognized experts, commentators and activists which lead the reader to look at news stories and analyse them in more depth.

There are also thousands of 'blogger' news sites where individuals or small groups post their own news or analysis. Again, they are worth exploring to find alternative points of view on various issues.

These are just a few examples from a wide selection of 'independent news' sources. They can be a valuable resource to help you look at stories from other points of view. **LEARN MORE/GET INVOLVED:**
www.commondreams.org www.medialens.org

### ARGUMENTS FOR AND AGAINST INDEPENDENT MEDIA

#### FOR

INDEPENDENT MEDIA SITES OFTEN OPEN UP A WHOLE NEW APPROACH TO ISSUES. THEY FOCUS ON STORIES THAT DO NOT INTEREST THE MAINSTREAM MEDIA AND ENCOURAGE CAMPAIGNING JOURNALISM. THEY ARE FREE FROM ANY CORPORATE CONTROL.

#### AGAINST

INDEPENDENT MEDIA SITES ARE OFTEN HIGHLY CRITICAL OF GOVERNMENTS AND CORPORATIONS AND AS A RESULT, THEIR STORIES CAN CREATE A SENSE THAT GOVERNMENTS AND CORPORATIONS ARE IN SOME WAY THE 'ENEMY'. THEY OFTEN SEEK OUT STORIES THAT CONFIRM THEIR OWN WORLDVIEW AND IGNORE STORIES THAT APPEAR IN THE MAINSTREAM MEDIA.

## IN PAIRS/GROUPS

### HEADS TOGETHER:

*In* groups or pairs, you have **15 MINUTES** to **USE THE INTERNET TO LOOK AT THE FOLLOWING NEWS SOURCES. THEY ARE A MIXTURE OF MAINSTREAM AND INDEPENDENT NEWS SITES.**

For each one:

**NOTE DOWN THE MAIN SIX STORIES ON THE SITE.**

**IF THERE ARE ANY STORIES THAT ARE COVERED BY BOTH MAINSTREAM AND INDEPENDENT SITES, NOTE DOWN THE DIFFERENCE IN THE WAY THEY ARE REPORTED.**

Overall:

**NOTE DOWN SIX KEY DIFFERENCES THAT YOU CAN SEE BETWEEN MAINSTREAM AND INDEPENDENT SITES.**

**MAINSTREAM MEDIA SOURCES**
www.thesun.co.uk
www.skynews.com
www.guardian.co.uk

**INDEPENDENT MEDIA SOURCES**
www.democracynow.org
www.indymedia.org
www.commondreams.org

Feed back your findings to the class.

# INVESTIGATIVE JOURNALISM BRINGS DOWN THE MIGHTY

**ON** A NATIONAL SCALE, THERE HAVE BEEN MANY SUCCESSFUL CAMPAIGNS RUN BY NEWSPAPERS. A RECENT EXAMPLE IS A CAMPAIGN THAT HAD BEEN HEADED BY *THE GUARDIAN* NEWSPAPER. THE NATIONAL PAPER HAD ACCUSED THE GLOBAL ARMS AND AERONAUTICS MANUFACTURERS BAE OF FRAUD AND CORRUPTION. ALTHOUGH THE COMPANY HAD STATED THAT THE CLAIMS WERE FALSE, INVESTIGATIVE JOURNALISM FINALLY PROVED THEM WRONG IN FEBRUARY 2010, WHEN BAE ADMITTED GUILT. THE PAPER HAD CONTINUED WITH THIS CAMPAIGN FOR 20 YEARS, MAKING IT FRONT-PAGE NEWS AND DRAWING THE ATTENTION OF THE UK PUBLIC TO THE ISSUE.

LEARN MORE/GET INVOLVED:

www.guardian.co.uk
www.corpwatch.org
www.transparency.org

## LOCAL PAPER POWER

**NEWSPAPERS** CAN BE POWERFUL INGREDIENTS IN THE SUCCESS OF A CAMPAIGN AND OFTEN RUN THEIR OWN CAMPAIGNS, BOTH ON A LOCAL AND NATIONAL SCALE.

IN 2009, *THE SOUTHERN DAILY ECHO*, BASED IN SOUTHAMPTON, RAN A LOCAL CAMPAIGN TO QUESTION WHY THE LOCAL COUNCIL HAD AN ART COLLECTION WORTH £180 MILLION BUT MOST OF THE PAINTINGS WERE NOT AVAILABLE FOR THE PUBLIC TO VIEW. AFTER MONTHS OF CAMPAIGN JOURNALISM, RAISING AWARENESS, GATHERING SUPPORT AND ASKING TOUGH QUESTIONS TO THE COUNCIL, THE CAMPAIGN SUCCEEDED. THE COUNCIL AGREED TO SELL OFF A MAJORITY OF THE PAINTINGS AND USE THE MONEY TO BUILD A TITANIC MUSEUM. THIS HAD BEEN THE WISH OF THE MAJORITY OF THE PEOPLE IN THE AREA AND THE PAPER HELPED GIVE THE CAMPAIGN ENOUGH PROFILE TO SUCCEED.

BECAUSE THE ART WORK THAT THE COUNCIL HAD STORED AWAY INCLUDED A PAINTING BY MONET, THE NEWSPAPER'S SLOGAN WAS...

SHOW US THE MONET
Local News

## Indymedia

**THE** INDEPENDENT MEDIA CENTRE (WWW.INDYMEDIA.ORG) WAS LAUNCHED IN 1999 AS A RESULT OF SEVERAL SMALLER ALTERNATIVE MEDIA GROUPS FROM EUROPE AND US COLLABORATING TOGETHER. THE ORIGINAL INTENTION WAS TO PROVIDE GRASSROOTS COVERAGE OF THE SEATTLE GLOBAL JUSTICE PROTESTS OUTSIDE THE WORLD TRADE ORGANIZATION'S CONFERENCE IN THE CITY. NOT ONLY WERE THESE PROTESTS THE BEGINNING OF A WORLDWIDE MOVEMENT BUT THEY ALSO MARKED THE BEGINNING OF THE LARGEST INDEPENDENT MEDIA NETWORK IN THE WORLD.

THE FIRST EVER POSTING ON THE SITE, ON 24 NOVEMBER 1999, STATES THEIR INTENTION:

"THE WEB DRAMATICALLY ALTERS THE BALANCE BETWEEN MULTINATIONAL AND ACTIVIST MEDIA. WITH JUST A BIT OF CODING AND SOME CHEAP EQUIPMENT, WE CAN SET UP A LIVE AUTOMATED WEBSITE THAT RIVALS THE MAINSTREAM."

LEARN MORE/GET INVOLVED: www.indymedia.org

# BE THE MEDIA

**CITIZEN** JOURNALISM IS A MODERN PHENOMENON THAT HAS COME AS A RESULT OF 21ST-CENTURY TECHNOLOGY ALLOWING ORDINARY PEOPLE TO DOCUMENT EVENTS OR PROMOTE THEIR IDEAS AND OPINIONS REGARDING ISSUES AND POST THEIR MATERIAL ON TO THE WEB. IN 2003, A REPORT CALLED 'WE MEDIA: HOW AUDIENCES ARE SHAPING THE FUTURE OF NEWS AND INFORMATION' WAS PUBLISHED BY AUTHORS BOWMAN AND WILLIS. THEY STATED THAT "THE INTENT OF THIS PARTICIPATION IS TO PROVIDE INDEPENDENT, RELIABLE, ACCURATE, WIDE-RANGING AND RELEVANT INFORMATION THAT A DEMOCRACY REQUIRES."

ONE STRIKING EXAMPLE OF CITIZEN JOURNALISM WAS A FILM TAKEN ON A MOBILE PHONE, WHICH WAS RELEASED TO THE PRESS, SHOWING CIRCUMSTANCES LEADING TO THE DEATH OF UK CITIZEN IAN TOMLINSON IN 2009 DURING A PROTEST IN LONDON. WHILE SOME NEWSPAPERS HAD SUGGESTED THAT TOMLINSON HAD DIED NATURALLY AND HAD NOT BEEN THE VICTIM OF POLICE ACTIONS, THE FILM SHOWED OTHERWISE AND LED TO AN INVESTIGATION INTO THE WAY THE PROTEST HAD BEEN HANDLED.

ACTIVE CITIZENS NOW HAVE THE OPPORTUNITY TO ACTUALLY BE THE MEDIA THEMSELVES. AS MORE AND MORE PEOPLE BEGIN TO ACCESS INDEPENDENT MEDIA SOURCES IN ORDER TO WIDEN THEIR CRITICAL THINKING, IT WILL BECOME LESS LIKELY THAT THE VIEWS HELD BY MAINSTREAM MEDIA WILL BE SO READILY ACCEPTED AS THE ONLY VIEW TO HAVE.

LEARN MORE/GET INVOLVED:
www.mediatrust.org
www.communitychannel.org
www.digiactive.org
http://hub.witness.org
www.tacticaltech.org

## G OTHER MEDIA SOURCES

TIPS 'n' HINTS

### MICRO BLOGGING

Another increasingly influential source of news and opinion is the Twitter social networking micro-blogging site. Invented in 2006, it has been picked up by millions of people worldwide. By using SMS technology, users are able to send out messages no longer than 140 characters long. These messages can include links to sites. People around the world are able to follow these 'tweets'. As a result, some major news events have been first described by ordinary people who are actually on the scene. Of course, tweets can easily lie or mislead, and in several cases people have been prosecuted as a result of messages that they sent out via Twitter.

This system of micro blogging is another example of Citizen Journalism, where ordinary people can write their own news and have it read around the world within seconds. There is no doubt that over the years, there will be many other technological developments in this area.

### SOCIAL NETWORKING SITES

One of the most popular uses of the internet has become social networking sites such as Facebook or Digg. These can help you discover if there are any other groups campaigning on the same issues as you are. They can also provide you with a clear picture of people's views on an issue. You can also set up your own campaigning group to connect with other people who care about the issue.

There are many varieties of social networking sites and there will be many more as the years go on.

SOME FOCUS ON MUSIC – www.myspace.com
OTHERS FOCUS ON PHOTOGRAPHS – www.flickr.com
OR FILMS – www.flixster.com
SOME ARE MORE YOUTH ORIENTATED – www.hi5.com
OTHERS REVOLVE AROUND RACIAL GROUPS – www.blackplanet.com
OR MOTHERS – www.cafemom.com

Once again, it is vital that all Active Citizenship work using these sites sticks closely to your school rules on internet security. Think about setting up sites and user names that don't include personal names and instead signal the campaign issues. Follow the guidance of your teacher on this matter.

## ACTIVITY – IN PAIRS

### ALIEN'S EYES:

In pairs, you have 5 MINUTES to

WORK OUT A THREE-POINT REPORT TO YOUR ALIEN LEADER DESCRIBING WHAT SOCIAL NETWORKING SITES ARE AND WHAT EFFECT THEY HAVE HAD ON THE PEOPLE OF EARTH.

Feed back to the class.

## RECORD BOOK

Report on the class activities under the headings:

THE DIFFERENCE BETWEEN MAINSTREAM AND INDEPENDENT MEDIA SITES WITH EXAMPLES.

HOW SOCIAL NETWORKING SITES HAVE AFFECTED PEOPLE'S LIVES.

Make sure you include notes on any class feedback sessions.

## H MISTAKES, BIAS AND DOWNRIGHT LIES

TIPS 'n' HINTS

### MISTAKES

There is no such thing as a completely reliable source of information.

Scientific data itself is often questioned. A good example of this is scientific data collected in the 1950s which seemed to show that smoking was not bad for you. This is connected to the fact that data can be interpreted in many different ways, particularly if research is sponsored by an organization with a vested interest in a particular result.

Although Wikipedia can be an excellent internet resource as you start researching an issue, it also includes many mistakes, as you will see from the various symbols and comments which sometimes appear, questioning information given.

Mistakes can be down to information which has become out of date or information which has been taken from a source which is itself incorrect. Information can also be faked or manipulated for many reasons, including individuals protecting their own reputations, campaigners hostile to any view but their own, or organizations and corporations protecting their vested interests.

CONTINUED

## False Flags On Twitter

**DURING** US ELECTIONS IN 2009, MEMBERS OF THE REPUBLICAN PARTY SET UP 33 FAKE TWITTER ACCOUNTS IN THE NAMES OF DEMOCRATIC PARTY MEMBERS IN ORDER TO MAKE THOSE CANDIDATES LOOK LIKE A BAD CHOICE. THIS DECEPTION WAS UNCOVERED AND TWITTER SHUT DOWN THE FAKE ACCOUNTS. TWITTER STATED THE PART OF THEIR POLICY THAT TRIES TO DETER THIS KIND OF BEHAVIOUR:

*"A PERSON MAY NOT IMPERSONATE OTHERS THROUGH THE TWITTER SERVICE IN A MANNER THAT DOES OR IS INTENDED TO MISLEAD, CONFUSE OR DECEIVE OTHERS."*

THE ORIGINS OF THE WORD MAY GO BACK TO A FAMOUS SCENE BY THE BRITISH COMEDY TEAM MONTY PYTHON, WHO CREATED A LEGENDARY SKETCH WHERE PEOPLE VISITING A CAFÉ WERE UNABLE TO BUY ANYTHING BUT SPAM. THE TINNED MEAT WAS PREVALENT THROUGHOUT BRITAIN AFTER WORLD WAR TWO AND FAMOUS FOR BEING BLAND. SOME INTERNET HISTORIANS STATE THAT THIS SUITED THE ACTION OF SPAMMING PERFECTLY, WHERE YOU ARE FLOODED WITH SOMETHING YOU DON'T WANT.

# SPAM! SPAM! SPAM!

**ONE** OF THE NEGATIVE SIDE-EFFECTS OF USING THE WEB IS 'SPAM'. WEB USERS CAN HAVE THEIR E-MAIL BOXES, CHAT ROOMS, COMMENTS PAGES OR MOBILE DEVICES FLOODED BY MESSAGES, OFTEN ADVERTISING SOMETHING. AN EARLY EXAMPLE OF INTERNET SPAMMING IS AN ADVERTISEMENT SENT OUT BY A COUPLE TRYING TO FIND CUSTOMERS FOR THEIR LAW BUSINESS. THE COUPLE WERE FLOODED BY FURIOUS USERS FROM THE WIRED WORLD, THREATENING THEM, SAYING THAT THEY WOULD HAVE THEIR OFFICES BURNED DOWN, JAMMING THEIR INTERNET SERVER AND THE FAX MACHINE. DESPITE THIS, THE COUPLE CLAIMED THAT THEY HAD ALSO MADE GOOD BUSINESS. ANOTHER EARLY EXAMPLE OF SPAMMING INVOLVED *STAR WARS* FANS SPAMMING *STAR TREK* CHAT ROOMS AND VICE VERSA BUT RAX ARE UNABLE TO TRIANGULATE THAT PARTICULAR 'TRUTH'.

## BE MY FRIEND

**MARK** ZUCKERBERG AND CO-FOUNDERS DUSTIN MOSKOVITZ, CHRIS HUGHES AND EDUARDO SAVERIN LAUNCHED FACEBOOK IN FEBRUARY 2004. THEY CREATED THE NETWORK IN THEIR STUDENT ROOMS AT HARVARD UNIVERSITY IN THE US SO THAT THEY COULD LINK UP WITH OTHER STUDENTS. BY DECEMBER OF THE SAME YEAR, THERE WERE OVER ONE MILLION USERS. BY DECEMBER 2009, THERE WERE 350 MILLION USERS!

**THE AVERAGE USER SPENDS 55 MINUTES A DAY CHECKING THEIR FACEBOOK SITE. HAS 130 FRIENDS AND SENDS 8 FRIENDS REQUESTS A MONTH.**

# THE POLITICS OF SOCIAL NETWORKING SITES

**CHRIS** HUGHES, ONE OF THE CO-FOUNDERS OF FACEBOOK, WAS EMPLOYED BY PRESIDENT BARACK OBAMA IN 2008 TO HELP HIS CAMPAIGN TO BECOME PRESIDENT. MANY POLITICAL ANALYSTS STATE THAT THIS MOVE WAS FUNDAMENTAL TO OBAMA WINNING THE ELECTION AS HE WAS ABLE TO CONNECT WITH THE YOUNGER VOTE MORE EASILY AND WAS ABLE TO RAISE MORE FUNDS THAN HIS COMPETING CANDIDATES. IN ONE MONTH, HE RAISED $45 MILLION OVER THE INTERNET.

CURRENTLY, THE PRESIDENT HAS 7,361,681 FANS ON HIS FACEBOOK SITE. FOR THE WIRED GENERATION, THIS IS A REVOLUTIONARY WAY TO FEEL TO SOME EXTENT CONNECTED TO THE LEADER OF YOUR COUNTRY. THIS IS BACKED UP BY HIS PRIMARY WEBSITE WHICH IS INTERACTIVE, INCLUSIVE AND OPERATES IN MANY WAYS LIKE A CAMPAIGNING SITE. DURING THE LEAD-UP TO THE UK GENERAL ELECTION IN MAY 2010, THE LEADERS OF THE MAJOR POLITICAL PARTIES HAD STUNNINGLY LOW NUMBERS OF FANS IN COMPARISON.

LEARN MORE/GET INVOLVED: www.barackobama.com

## FACEBOOK CAMPAIGNS

**CAMPAIGNS** FROM UP AND DOWN THE UK ARE USING FACEBOOK TO RAISE AWARENESS AND GATHER SUPPORT. FROM CAMPAIGNS TO SAVE LOCAL GRAFFITI IN NEWCASTLE TO STUDENTS IN CHELTENHAM FIGHTING CUTS TO THEIR STAFF, IT HAS BECOME ONE OF THE FIRST STEPS WHEN SOMEONE HAS AN IDEA FOR CHANGE.

HOWEVER, IT IS JUST AS EASY FOR AN ADVERTISING COMPANY TO RAISE AWARENESS ABOUT A NEW PRODUCT THROUGH SOCIAL NETWORKING SITES. OFTEN, YOU WILL FIND YOURSELF BEING ADVERTISED TO WITHOUT KNOWING IT. PERHAPS A FUNNY FILM THAT FEATURES A BABOON FALLING OVER WILL TICKLE YOUR FANCY AND YOU'LL SEND IT TO ALL YOUR FRIENDS. IT MAY BECOME VIRAL BEFORE YOU HAVE REALIZED THAT AT THE END OF THE FILM THERE IS THE LOGO FOR A COMPANY OR A CHARACTER IN THE FILM IS SWIGGING BACK A NEW FIZZY DRINK.

AS WELL AS THIS NEGATIVE ASPECT TO SOCIAL NETWORKING SITES, IT'S WORTH BEARING IN MIND THAT THE GREAT CAMPAIGNS FOR CHANGE IN HISTORY HAVE BEEN MADE UP OF HUNDREDS OF THOUSANDS OF PEOPLE UNITING UNDER ONE GRASSROOTS MOVEMENT. 21ST-CENTURY TECHNOLOGY ALLOWS YOU TO START A CAMPAIGN IN THE TIME IT TAKES TO BOIL AN EGG. AS A RESULT, THERE ARE HUNDREDS OF CAMPAIGNS FOR ALMOST EVERY CAUSE AND A LACK OF UNITY CAN OFTEN DESTROY ANY CHANCES OF SUCCESS.

# CHAPTER 4 *The* PROCESSINGPLANT

*This* is something that needs to be taken into account when you are engaging in critical thinking and enquiry connected to your campaigning issues. There are ways to deal with this, though, as you will see in the section overleaf called 'Triangulate the Truth'.

## BIAS

**WHEN YOU ARE USING CRITICAL THINKING AND ENQUIRY TO RESEARCH YOUR CAMPAIGNING ISSUES, ONE OF YOUR BIGGEST OBSTACLES IS TO MAKE SURE YOU HAVEN'T BEEN FOOLED BY BIAS.**

*Bias* can affect any information that you come across and it comes in many different forms as well as for many different reasons. The key question to ask yourself is:

## WHAT IS THE MOTIVATION BEHIND THIS SOURCE OF INFORMATION?

### TO MAKE MONEY

*Many* sources of information exist to persuade people to buy something. A magazine dedicated to natural remedies as a way of healing people will focus on information and stories that back up the view that natural remedies work. If people are encouraged to believe in natural remedies, they are more likely to keep buying the magazine. On the other hand, sources of information which condemn natural remedies might be created by the major pharmaceutical companies, which stand to lose money if people buy natural remedies instead.

**A FAMOUS EXAMPLE** of a company using information in a biased way to make money happened in the first half of the 20th century when the alcohol firm Guinness used research that showed the iron content in their product could be considered to be good for you. As a result, the slogan 'Guinness is good for you' was used on a regular basis in their advertising. Of course, this was a very distorted view as, even though iron is good for the human system, alcohol definitely isn't.

### TO INFLUENCE YOUR OPINION

*Individuals* or organizations can often use information to influence the way you think about an issue. For example, in the lead-up to the Copenhagen Climate Change Conference in 2009, some scientists and researchers released reports claiming that climate change is not caused by humans. This could have been to protect the interests of gas and oil companies or it could have been simply to resist changes to existing Western lifestyles that are based on the exploitation of fossil fuels. But the reports were clearly released to influence opinion at a critical time.

#### ANOTHER EXAMPLE

of this could be a campaigning website which uses information to encourage people to have a negative opinion about CCTV use in the UK. That site will use statistics and arguments which focus on the negative aspects of CCTV surveillance. It will not mention CCTV's contributions to solving crimes, tracking terrorists or catching drug dealers.

### TO PROMOTE A PUBLIC IMAGE

*The* way information is used can often affect people's views of the public image of an individual or an organization. An obvious example of this is in politics where a spokesperson from one party may publicly provide information that concentrates on the negative aspects of an individual from another party, ignoring evidence that might cast them in a positive light.

You might stumble upon another example of this if you were researching the issue of pollution by a large oil corporation. You might come across sources of information highlighting the good work that the corporation does – pointing out how it supports local communities as well as investing large sums of money in developing green technologies. With a little research you might find that the oil corporation itself is behind these sources of information. They exist to persuade the public that the corporation has a green and caring side to it and distract attention from any negative effects it may have on society or on the environment.

**THERE ARE TWO SIDES TO EVERY STORY. IF YOU FEEL LIKE YOU ARE ONLY GETTING ONE SIDE THEN YOU'RE NOT GETTING THE WHOLE STORY.**

### TO LEAVE AN ASSUMPTION UNQUESTIONED

*The* long and often violent campaign for women to win the vote at the beginning of the 20th century was necessary because it was countering what people had assumed for hundreds, or even thousands, of years – that women were inferior to men. This assumption had existed for so long that it was simply accepted as fact and wasn't even questioned. This meant that there was a bias built into people's everyday lives, from influential politicians to the average person in the street. Even most women themselves accepted that assumption.

Questioning these kinds of deep-rooted assumptions, which are a form of bias, is a useful way for Active Citizens to find new campaigns and issues. For example, magazines, books, television shows, films and adverts are full of lifestyles that encourage you to believe that, to be happy, you need to look a certain way, live a certain way and buy certain things. Yet this can cause unhappiness for people who can't afford that lifestyle

CONTINUED ➡

# How To MANIPULATE a POPULATION

**IN 1954,** THE WEIGHT OF SCIENTIFIC EVIDENCE LINKING SMOKING TO LUNG CANCER THREATENED US TOBACCO COMPANIES' ABILITY TO MAKE HUGE PROFITS FROM CIGARETTES. THIS LED TO ONE OF THE FIRST EXAMPLES OF MANIPULATION OF THE WAY MILLIONS OF PEOPLE THOUGHT IN THE INTERESTS OF MAKING MONEY. IT IS A CLASSIC EXAMPLE OF BIAS INTERFERING WITH SOLID FACTS.

THE TECHNIQUES ARE STILL USED TODAY TO INFLUENCE YOUR OPINION, PROMOTE A PUBLIC IMAGE OR LEAVE ASSUMPTIONS UNQUESTIONED.

THE TOBACCO COMPANIES GROUPED TOGETHER AND EMPLOYED A MAJOR PUBLIC RELATIONS (PR) COMPANY TO HELP THEM. THE RESULT WAS A FULL-PAGE ADVERTISEMENT, PUBLISHED THROUGHOUT MOST OF THE MEDIA OUTLETS OF THE TIME, WHICH WAS MADE TO LOOK LIKE AN OFFICIAL DOCUMENT. IT WAS ENTITLED, 'A FRANK STATEMENT TO CIGARETTE SMOKERS'.

## The Illusion

ONE OF THE FIRST STRATEGIES THE PR COMPANY SUGGESTED WAS TO CREATE AN ORGANIZATION WITH THE WORD 'RESEARCH' IN ITS TITLE AND THEN SAY THAT THE STATEMENT WAS BEING MADE BY THAT ORGANIZATION. THE WORD 'RESEARCH' WAS THERE TO CONVINCE PEOPLE THAT SCIENTISTS WERE SOMEHOW INVOLVED. AS A RESULT, THE 'TOBACCO RESEARCH INDUSTRY COMMITTEE' WAS FOUNDED AND LISTED AS THE AUTHORS OF THE STATEMENT, LENDING THE DOCUMENT A SPURIOUS SENSE OF AUTHORITY.

THE FIRST SENTENCE IN THE STATEMENT SAID:

*"RECENT REPORTS ON EXPERIMENTS WITH MICE HAVE GIVEN WIDE PUBLICITY TO A THEORY THAT CIGARETTE SMOKING IS IN SOME WAY LINKED WITH LUNG CANCER IN HUMAN BEINGS."*

PEOPLE CAN BE INFLUENCED BY THE WAY LANGUAGE IS USED. IN THIS SENTENCE, THE USE OF 'THEORY' AND 'IN SOME WAY' CREATES DOUBT. THE WAY THAT 'MICE' IS USED AT THE BEGINNING AND 'HUMAN BEINGS' AT THE VERY END OF THE SENTENCE, CREATES A SENSE OF DISTANCE BETWEEN THE TWO.

THE 'FRANK STATEMENT' FOCUSED ON A NUMBER OF CAREFULLY CONSTRUCTED POINTS. THE FIRST WAS:

*"THAT MEDICAL RESEARCH OF RECENT YEARS INDICATES MANY POSSIBLE CAUSES OF LUNG CANCER."*

THIS SENTENCE AGAIN USES 'MEDICAL RESEARCH' TO SUGGEST THE WEIGHT OF SCIENCE BEHIND WHAT THEY ARE SAYING. THE WORD 'INDICATES' IS VERY DIFFERENT FROM THE WORD 'PROVES' BUT IF YOU ARE NOT USING YOUR CRITICAL THINKING SKILLS, IT CAN SOUND ALMOST THE SAME. THE SENTENCE SETS UP THE IDEA THAT THE LINK BETWEEN SMOKING AND CANCER COULD BE A MISTAKE AND THAT THERE COULD BE OTHER CAUSES INSTEAD. IT SEEKS TO CONFUSE THE ISSUE AND SOW SEEDS OF DOUBT.

THE FINAL 'FRANK STATEMENT' POINT WAS:

*"THE VALIDITY OF THE STATISTICS THEMSELVES IS QUESTIONED BY NUMEROUS SCIENTISTS."*

THIS SENTENCE ALSO SOUNDS LIKE IT SAYS A LOT BUT IT SAYS VERY LITTLE. THERE WERE THOUSANDS OF SCIENTISTS AT THE TIME AND FEW OF THEM KNEW THE RESEARCH IN DEPTH, SO IT WOULD NOT BE A LIE TO SAY THAT SOME DOUBTED THE RESEARCH. IN ANY EVENT, THERE HAVE BEEN MANY CASES IN HISTORY AND IN THE PRESENT WHERE COMPANIES HAVE BEEN FOUND GUILTY OF FUNDING SCIENTISTS TO PERFORM RESEARCH THAT SEEMED TO PROVE EXACTLY WHAT THE COMPANIES WANTED. TO THE ORDINARY PERSON, THIS SENTENCE IMPLIED THAT SCIENCE DID NOT SUPPORT THE LINK BETWEEN SMOKING AND CANCER. AGAIN, DOUBT AND CONFUSION WAS CREATED BY CAREFUL USE OF LANGUAGE.

PEOPLE READ THIS STATEMENT AND WERE MANIPULATED BY IT. ONCE DOUBT WAS CREATED AND SCIENCE WAS MADE TO SEEM TO BACK UP THAT DOUBT, THEN THE TOBACCO COMPANIES HAD WON AND THE PR COMPANY HAD EARNED ITS MONEY. A KEY ASPECT OF THIS KIND OF BIAS IS THAT PEOPLE ARE MANIPULATED WITHOUT EVEN KNOWING IT. THEY CAN WALK AWAY THINKING THAT THEY HAVE MADE THEIR OWN MIND UP WHEN, IN FACT, THEY HAVE HAD THEIR MINDS MADE UP FOR THEM.

CRITICAL THINKING AND ACTIVE CITIZENSHIP IN GENERAL IS ABOUT ASKING QUESTIONS. A KEY QUESTION TO ASK IN RELATION TO THE 'FRANK STATEMENT' WOULD BE: "DOES IT STATE ANYWHERE THAT SCIENCE PROVES CLEARLY THAT SMOKING DOESN'T CAUSE CANCER?" THAT QUESTION ALONE WOULD SUCCESSFULLY BREAK THE SPELL THAT THE MAGICIANS AT THE PR COMPANY HAD CAST.

(a) **The Reality**

**DYING TO SMOKE?**

**SMOKING KILLS**

I WENT INTO THE WOODS AND GOT IT. I SAT DOWN TO SEEK IT. I BROUGHT IT HOME WITH ME BECAUSE I COULDN'T FIND IT. WHAT IS IT? ANSWER ON PAGE 93.

# The PROCESSING PLANT

or whose appearance will never match that of a supermodel. This can be seen in recent research which suggests that people in the UK and Europe, with all their material goods and luxury lifestyles, are less happy than they were 50 years ago.

## QUESTIONING ASSUMPTIONS IS KEY TO UNDERSTANDING HOW YOUNG ACTIVE CITIZENS CAN MAKE A BETTER WORLD FOR ALL.

 **ACTIVITY**

## IN GROUPS

## MYSTERY GAME:

The head of the richest advertising company in the world earns a fortune, has Hollywood stars on speed dial, owns a Premier League football team and occasionally has dinner with the prime minister.

But she is also nearing retirement age and wakes up one morning feeling that she has wasted her life and talents selling stuff to people that they don't really need. She decides to do something to balance out everything she has done before.

She goes in to work and calls her top creative team together. When they are all seated and paying attention, she announces that their wages will be tripled while they do the best work they have ever done. She tells them:

### "YOU HAVE A WEEK TO MAKE THE WORLD BELIEVE THAT YOU DON'T NEED TO BUY ANYTHING TO BE HAPPY."

In groups, be that team: create a campaign that uses all the methods of normal advertising as well as all the connections and influence that your boss has, to do what she has asked you. Be biased but don't lie.

You have **15 MINUTES TO COME UP WITH IDEAS, PLANS, STORY BOARDS, ART WORK, SCRIPTS, SLOGANS AND AS MANY UNEXPECTED ANGLES TO YOUR CAMPAIGN AS YOU CAN THINK OF.**

Feed back your campaigns to the class.

## ① TRIANGULATE THE TRUTH
**TIPS 'n' HINTS**

Now you have a much firmer understanding of the importance of critical thinking and enquiry. You have learned how to access a variety of sources and how to be aware of mistakes and bias.

The best way of identifying reliable evidence, facts and statistics to back up your arguments is this simple technique called 'Triangulate the Truth'.

### WHATEVER RESEARCH YOU USE, CHECK IT THREE TIMES USING THREE DIFFERENT SOURCES.

Once you have made sure that your material isn't heavily biased in any way then you still need to check your information by finding other sources that give the same information. When you have found three reliable sources that tell you the same information, then you can be pretty sure that you have something that will stand up in an argument or be useful to help you when you come to be an advocate for your issue.

Remember, always keep the evidence for your research. When you are using the internet, keep your links and bookmarks in folders and clearly mark these folders so that you can easily access your sources. When you are using books and publications, note the page number, the title and the writer's name. Keep all this information well organized as you will need it as evidence of the work you have done.

### RESEARCH MUST COME FROM A VARIETY OF SOURCES.

Ultimately it's detective work you are doing here but if you are thorough enough with your skills of critical thinking and enquiry, you will have a firm basis on which to build a campaign.

Here is an example from the Record Book of a student who used critical thinking and enquiry in researching a campaign about the issue of slavery in the world today.

### EXTRACT FROM MARLON'S RECORD BOOK

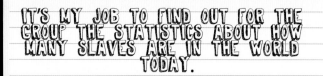
IT'S MY JOB TO FIND OUT FOR THE GROUP THE STATISTICS ABOUT HOW MANY SLAVES ARE IN THE WORLD TODAY.

① I started with WIKIPEDIA by putting in 'slavery'. Right at the top it said that there were 27 million slaves in the world today. That's an amazing number, they said it's more than twice the amount of people who were slaves back in history when slavery was legal.

# CHAPTER 4 The PROCESSING PLANT

(2) It made me wonder how that number compares with the population of the UK. So I checked that using the WOLFRAM ALPHA site and we have 61.2 million people in the UK so that means that the amount of people who are slaves today in the world is nearly half the population of the whole of the UK which is a really shocking way of putting that fact.

I made sure I was keeping all the links from the sites I was using so I made a folder called 'SLAVERY – STATISTICS'.

The Wikipedia page said that the figure of 27 million came from a group called Free The Slaves and the number had been said in 1999. I checked out their site and it's really useful, there is a map where you can see where most slavery happens and there's ten facts to learn about slavery including the fact that the average price to buy a slave is $90, which is about £53. Free the Slaves is a really good site and I'll get the group to look at it next lesson. But it doesn't say where that figure comes from.

I made another folder called 'SLAVERY – USEFUL SITES' and put the Free The Slaves link in to it.

## (3) EXPERT'S OPINION

I put 'how many slaves in the world today' in to Google and got an article from 2001 saying there were over 20 million slaves in the world. The article was from a site called 'Info Please' and was written by Manuel Lopez. I put his name in to Google and kept his blog site address, he's a successful journalist who's written for many different papers and journals as well as published many books so that makes him fairly reliable. I reckon that because he wrote that article in 2001, then the number of slaves going up to 27 million by now seems possible.

## (4) CAMPAIGN WEBSITES

I put slavery campaigns in to Google and found another really useful site called The Anti Slavery Society. They have been going since the times when slavery was legal and they also have an excellent website although it's a bit old fashioned. There's loads on that site that we can use. They did say something really useful, which is that saying how many slaves there are in the world depends on how you define what a slave is. That's crucial for us to look at.

They said that there are 2.7 million slaves in the world today because their definition doesn't include bonded labour and forced labour. So we really need to look at what the actual definition of a slave is for us. Right at the bottom of their page they said something really important, though, which is that deciding whether there are 27 million slaves or 2.7 million slaves doesn't matter and we won't free one slave by arguing over the number.

CONTINUED

89

# CHAPTER 4 The PROCESSING PLANT

⑤ STATISTICS TO DO WITH LABOUR IN THE WORLD

Then I found a site that was interviewing an expert on slavery and this man said that the figure of 27 million slaves come from research by the head of Free The Slaves and the International Labour Organization ( ILO ). So I'm now going to try putting that into Google and see what happens.

I used the search bar on the ILO site to get articles on slavery and found that their research in 2005 said that there were around 12 million slaves in forced labour. This is beginning to look like the number 27 million, which I have found in six sites now, includes all different types of slavery, that's trafficking, bonded slavery, debt slavery and forced labour. It turns out that these are the different ways of dividing slavery up.

## THESE ARE THE MAIN THINGS THAT MY RESEARCH HAS FOUND OUT:

**a** 27 MILLION SLAVES OVERALL.
That's made up from:
**b** 12 MILLION IN FORCED LABOUR.
13 MILLION IN BONDED OR DEBT LABOUR which means that they are paying off debts by being slaves.
**c** 1.8 MILLION ARE TRAFFICKED.
I started out checking a statistic and found loads more to look at, how to think about what the word slavery actually means and three great sites that already have campaigns going which we can become members of.

## I USED THESE DIFFERENT KINDS OF SOURCES:
Wikipedia, Wolfram Alpha, interviews with experts, campaign websites and a website that focuses on statistics to do with labour in the world.

---

*If* Marlon had just checked once, he'd have come up with the number 27 million slaves. This would have been dangerous because if he was representing his campaign, someone more knowledgeable on the subject might have said that there aren't necessarily 27 million slaves and they might have questioned how that figure is broken down into different types of slavery. This example shows how being thorough in your research and using techniques like Triangulate the Truth, where you check with three different kinds of sources, can make all the difference to having a wider and clearer picture about your issue and having a strong argument when you come to advocate for your campaign.

---

## IN GROUPS
### HEADS TOGETHER:

*In* groups, you have **10 MINUTES** to **USE THE INTERNET TO FIND THREE DIFFERENT KINDS OF SOURCES WHICH GIVE YOU INFORMATION ABOUT THE EFFECTS OF ENERGY DRINKS ON TEENAGERS.**
For each, make a record of the website address, the kind of website it is and a few basic facts that you learned.
Feed back to the class.

---

## RECORD BOOK

*Report* on the class activities under the headings: **d**

**USING ADVERTISING TECHNIQUES TO MAKE PEOPLE BELIEVE THEY DON'T NEED TO SPEND MONEY TO BE HAPPY.** **e**

**USING A VARIETY OF SOURCES ON THE INTERNET TO GATHER INFORMATION ABOUT THE EFFECTS OF ENERGY DRINKS ON TEENAGERS.**

Make sure you include notes on any class feedback sessions.

> *IF I KNEW THEN WHAT I KNOW NOW... I WOULD HAVE TRIED TO UNDERSTAND THAT MY OBSESSION AND SOCIETY'S OBSESSION WITH MATERIAL VALUES WAS/IS A COMPLETE WASTE OF TIME AND ENERGY. I WAS BREAKING MY NECK AT 14 TO CLOTHE MYSELF IN ARMANI, VERSACE AND D&G... OUR FIXATION WITH FIXING WHAT IS ON THE OUTSIDE IS A DOWNWARD, NEVER-ENDING SPIRAL AND THE LONGER WE FOCUS ON WHAT'S OUTSIDE WE ARE DEPRIVING OURSELVES OF THE TRUE REMEDY: EVERLASTING, SOLID, TRUE LOVE INSIDE!*

Ms Dynamite
(SEE RAX INTERVIEW ON PAGE 135)

# CHILD SLAVERY

HUMAN TRAFFICKING IS THE THIRD LARGEST AND FASTEST-GROWING CRIMINAL ACTIVITY IN THE WORLD AND IT HAS INCREASED IN THE UK BY 90% SINCE 2006. EVERY YEAR, AROUND 2.4 MILLION PEOPLE ARE TRAFFICKED ILLEGALLY AND HALF OF THEM ARE CHILDREN. OFTEN, THEY ARE GIVEN TO CRIMINAL GANGS BY THEIR FAMILY IN ORDER TO PAY OFF A DEBT OR THEY ARE LURED ABROAD BY THE PROMISE OF A BETTER LIFE. INSTEAD, THEY ARE VERY OFTEN FORCED INTO THE DRUG OR SEX INDUSTRY AS WELL AS KEPT AS SLAVES TO DO HARD WORK FOR NOTHING. THE UK POLICE OR ORGANIZATIONS LIKE THE NSPCC AND UNICEF HAVE SAVED HUNDREDS OF CHILDREN. THERE ARE MANY CAMPAIGNS THAT FOCUS ON THIS ISSUE AND TO WHICH YOU CAN EASILY GIVE YOUR SUPPORT.

**LEARN MORE/GET INVOLVED:**
www.unicef.org.uk (TYPE 'SLAVE BRITAIN' INTO THEIR SEARCH BAR)
www.nspcc.org.uk

# SUPPORTING TRAFFICKING WITHOUT KNOWING IT

A 2009 SURVEY BY ECPAT, ONE OF THE LEADING CAMPAIGN GROUPS AGAINST CHILD TRAFFICKING, REVEALED THAT 89% OF UK CITIZENS DID NOT KNOW THAT THERE WAS A CLEAR LINK BETWEEN HUMAN TRAFFICKING AND PURCHASING FAKE DVDS, BUYING HOME GROWN-CANNABIS OR PROSTITUTION. ALL OF THESE INDUSTRIES USE TRAFFICKED CHILDREN WHO ARE KEPT AS SLAVES AND FORCED TO BREAK THE LAW. A THIRD OF PEOPLE ASKED DID NOT REALIZE THE EXTENT OF HUMAN TRAFFICKING AND A THIRD DID NOT REALIZE THAT IT WAS HAPPENING IN THE UK.

**LEARN MORE/GET INVOLVED:**
www.ecpat.org.uk

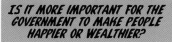

ARE YOU HAPPY?

52% — 1950
36% — 2005

# Active Citizens Have An Impact

IN 2008, A CLASS OF YEAR NINE STUDENTS, FROM NEWENT COMMUNITY SCHOOL IN GLOUCESTERSHIRE, CREATED AN ACTIVE CITIZENSHIP PROJECT BASED ON HUMAN TRAFFICKING. AFTER USING CRITICAL THINKING AND ENQUIRY TO RESEARCH THE SUBJECT, INCLUDING A PRESENTATION GIVEN BY AN OFFICER FROM THE POLICE'S ANTI-TRAFFICKING UNIT, THEY CAME UP WITH A REMARKABLE SOLUTION. TO RAISE AWARENESS OF THE ISSUE, THEY CREATED POSTERS TO BE PUT UP ON THE INSIDE OF AIRPORT TOILETS, WRITTEN IN SEVERAL LANGUAGES, INFORMING PEOPLE THAT IF THEY THOUGHT THAT THEY HAD BEEN TRAFFICKED, THEY COULD RING THE NUMBER GIVEN ON THE POSTER AND BE RESCUED. THE CAMPAIGN WAS SO SUCCESSFUL THAT THE POSTERS ARE NOW USED IN A NUMBER OF UK AIRPORTS, THE POLICE USE THE PROJECT AS PART OF THEIR TRAINING OF SPECIALIST OFFICERS, THE UN PRAISED THE PROJECT AND THE CAMPAIGN WON A DIANA AWARD.

IS IT MORE IMPORTANT FOR THE GOVERNMENT TO MAKE PEOPLE HAPPIER OR WEALTHIER?

**81% PREFER HAPPIER**

**19% PREFER WEALTHIER**

# THE SECRET OF HAPPINESS

IN THE 1950S, RESEARCH SHOWED THAT 52% OF UK CITIZENS CONSIDERED THEMSELVES TO BE 'VERY HAPPY'. IN 2005, THAT HAD FALLEN TO 36%, DESPITE THE FACT THAT PEOPLE WERE THREE TIMES RICHER ON AVERAGE. THE SAME SURVEY ASKED PEOPLE WHETHER THEY THOUGHT IT WAS MORE IMPORTANT THAT THE GOVERNMENT MADE PEOPLE RICHER OR HAPPIER. 81% STATED THAT GREATER HAPPINESS WAS MORE IMPORTANT THAN GREATER WEALTH. SO DOES BEING WEALTHIER ACTUALLY MAKE YOU HAPPIER AND, IF NOT, THEN WHAT IS THE SECRET OF HAPPINESS?

# 5 How do I get to speak to an expert?

*You* will have realized that to run a good campaign for change it's very important that you know what you are talking about. Many campaigners recommend that you also make use of experts to inform you about your chosen issue.

## FOR EXAMPLE,

you may have decided to focus on the issue of energy drinks in schools. In a week of research backed up by critical thinking, you will have gathered a substantial amount of information, but what about speaking to someone whose job it is to know about this topic?

There will be people who have spent years researching the same area. This will include scientists who have created their own experiments and tests on the effects of energy drinks as well as members of health organizations who have gathered their own research. In addition to these people, what about contacting the energy drinks companies directly to see what experts they may be able to put you in contact with? As with all forms of critical thinking and enquiry, you need to be on your guard for possible bias. An expert working for an energy drinks company will have a very different motivation from one who is independent!

## BRINGING IN AN EXPERT WILL ADD TO THE STRENGTH OF YOUR ARGUMENT ENORMOUSLY.

### TIPS 'n' HINTS — SOME TIPS TO HELP YOU CONTACT AN EXPERT

*People* are usually very keen to help the younger generation advance their understanding of an issue.

### ALWAYS MAKE IT CLEAR THAT YOU ARE SCHOOL STUDENTS ENGAGED IN AN ACTIVE CITIZENSHIP PROJECT.

There will often be campaigns already associated with the issues you are interested in. They will usually be very supportive to young people who want to become involved. The organization may not only be able to answer your questions and help you with your research but may even provide an expert to visit your school and make a presentation.

If you are campaigning about something local – connected to social, health, crime or housing issues, for example – there will be experts on that subject working for the local council. Contact those people and see if they are willing to answer your questions or to give a talk at your school.

If your campaign is connected to a business or a large corporation, they may have a department that focuses on media and publicity. These departments are usually happy to answer any questions you send them and may provide an expert willing to make a presentation at your school.

If there has been a documentary on your issue or an article written about your issue, then contact the people behind this and see if they are prepared to answer questions or come in to your school.

Use your imagination and your detective skills to come up with unusual ways of contacting experts. For example, one Active Citizenship student had been researching the effects of energy drinks on teenagers and came across an article that quoted a particular scientist. The student put the man's name into a search engine and found a university e-mail address for him, which made it possible to organize an interview.

Make sure you use the adults around you too: they may know an expert or may have a friend who knows one. Remember, people are often prepared to go out of their way if it means helping the younger generation to learn more and develop their ideas for change.

## ALWAYS BE POLITE AND CLEAR WHEN CONTACTING PEOPLE. NEVER CONTACT THEM UNTIL YOU KNOW EXACTLY WHAT YOU WANT AND WHAT YOUR CAMPAIGN IS SEEKING TO ACHIEVE.

## PEOPLE ARE USUALLY VERY KEEN TO HELP THE YOUNGER GENERATION ADVANCE THEIR UNDERSTANDING OF AN ISSUE.

### TIPS 'n' HINTS — SOME TIPS ABOUT WHAT TO DO WHEN YOU HAVE CONTACTED AN EXPERT

*If* you have found an expert who can visit your school, you need to make sure that they are made to feel welcome and looked after properly. Your teacher will help you with organizing this but the more effort you put into this, the more rewarding the experience will be for the expert.

### WHEN AN EXPERT COMES TO YOUR SCHOOL, IT IS VERY IMPORTANT THAT YOU RECORD THE EVENT.

Film their presentation or interview, make a voice recording and take photographs of the whole event. Make sure that you also find out what the experience was like for the expert, either by interviewing them afterwards or by giving them an evaluation form.

### PREPARATION IS VITAL IF A VISIT BY AN EXPERT IS TO BE SUCCESSFUL.

Not only must you organize where and how the presentation or interview will happen but you must also prepare clear and effective questions to ask. The chapter called *The Projector Room* will help with many of these points.

Some experts are extremely busy so they may not have time to travel to your school. Web technology like Skype will enable you to hold live interviews with the expert over the web. If this is the case, then make sure you organize someone to film the Skype interview so that you have a record of the event. The Rax interview between students in Swanlea School in London and Craig Kielburger on page 50 used similar technology as he was in Sri Lanka at the time.

CONTINUED ➡

"STATISTICS CAN BE USED AND ABUSED. I HAVE BEEN IN DEBATES WHERE THE CLIMATE CHANGE DENIERS JUST REEL OUT STATISTICS THAT YOU HAVE NEVER HEARD AND HAVE NO TIME TO CHECK, THUS DERAILING ANY CONSTRUCTIVE DEBATE. HOW USEFUL! STATISTICS ARE THE FAVOURITE WEAPON OF CHOICE BY PR FIRMS AND NEWSPAPERS. CLIMATE CHANGE IS A PARTICULARLY HECTIC ONE BECAUSE THERE IS SO MUCH TECHNICAL SCIENCE AND IT IS SUCH AN EMOTIVE SUBJECT WITH PEOPLE DESPERATE TO BE TOLD IT AIN'T TRUE."

THOM YORKE (SEE RAX INTERVIEW ON PAGE 165).

"THE WORD 'EXPERTS' DOESN'T JUST MEAN SCIENTISTS OR ACADEMICS. RIGHT FROM THE START I HAVE WORKED VERY CLOSELY WITH INDIGENOUS PEOPLE WHO LIVE IN THE TAR SANDS REGION. THEY, MORE THAN ANYONE, ARE IN A POSITION TO EXPLAIN HOW THE TAR SANDS ARE CHANGING THE ENVIRONMENT AROUND THEM, AND CAUSING SUFFERING TO HUMANS AND ANIMALS... I THINK PEOPLE ARE MUCH MORE LIKELY TO TAKE OUR CAMPAIGN SERIOUSLY WHEN OUR SPOKESPEOPLE ARE TALKING FROM DIRECT EXPERIENCE."

JESS WORTH (SEE RAX INTERVIEW ON PAGE 200).

# The PROCESSING PLANT

ACTIVITY

**IN PAIRS/GROUPS**

**HEADS TOGETHER:**

If you are interviewing an expert over the phone, make sure that you use a system where the expert's voice is amplified so that everybody can hear (for example, switching your mobile from handset to speaker). In a situation like this, it is important that you have a quiet room and that nobody interrupts the expert speaking. It is also important that you make a recording of the interview.

**IMAGINE YOU ARE RESEARCHING THE ISSUE OF HUMAN TRAFFICKING AND YOU HAVE BEEN ABLE TO ORGANIZE AN INTERVIEW WITH A POLICE OFFICER WHO IS PART OF THE TEAM IN CHARGE OF COMBATING THIS CRIMINAL ACTIVITY.**

**"EXPERT ADVICE IS AN ESSENTIAL PART OF RUNNING A GOOD CAMPAIGN AND I RELY HEAVILY ON THE KNOWLEDGE OF THOSE BETTER INFORMED THAN ME."**

LAURIE PYCROFT (SEE RAX INTERVIEW ON PAGE 100)

**You have FIVE MINUTES TO COME UP WITH FIVE QUESTIONS THAT YOU WOULD ASK THE OFFICER.**

**EXTRACT FROM BONNIE'S RECORD BOOK**

Feed back your ideas to the class.

## 15 JUNE

### The change I would like to see:

*I WOULD LIKE TO SEE ALL CHILDREN IN THE WORLD HAVE THE OPPORTUNITY TO GO TO SCHOOL*

**WE** have been researching the issue of children's rights to an education across the world. Yesterday we looked at the website for the [United Nations] Millennium Development Goals as one of them is to provide education for all children by 2015. At home yesterday evening, I started doing more research about them and found out about a website for a film company making films about the Millennium Goals. So I went to their website and they have a film where they interviewed Craig Kielburger, who is a famous campaigner and advocate for children's rights to education.

I clicked on the contact option at the top of the page and went to a page that gave me an e-mail address. Using our campaign e-mail address, I wrote to them asking if they could help our campaign by letting us get in contact with an expert. I looked through the whole site and it had some brilliant short films. I then made the e-mail really polite and let them know the kind of questions that we would like to ask an expert.

Today, I got a reply from Joanna, who is a director and producer with the organization. She was really friendly and supportive and told me that she was really pleased I had found the site and liked the films. She said that her company is based in London but she will be working on a new film that would be shot in Devon next week. I hadn't said anything about asking if we could get an expert to come in to the school but she offered to come to our school without me asking.

CONTINUED

# The PROCESSING PLANT

_24 JUNE_

_Joanna, the lady from the production company, is coming in tomorrow._

## We spent this afternoon preparing for her visit:

☐ CHECK ROOM IS BOOKED

☐ CHECK THE SCHOOL RECEPTION KNOWS THAT WE HAVE A VISITOR COMING IN

☐ CHECK THAT OUR TEACHER WILL BE THERE WITH US TO MEET JOANNA

☐ CHECK THAT WE HAVE VEGETARIAN FOOD AND HERBAL TEAS

☐ CHECK THAT WE WILL HAVE A SCHOOL VIDEO CAMERA _and that it is charged and that we have spare films to use_

☐ CHECK THAT WE WILL HAVE A SCHOOL CAMERA TO TAKE PICTURES _and that it is charged and has a memory card in it_

☐ CHECK THAT WE HAVE TEN QUESTIONS TO ASK JOANNA

☐ CHECK THAT WE HAVE A CLEAR FIVE-MINUTE PRESENTATION _to show Joanna what our ideas are for a raising awareness campaign_

☐ CHECK THAT WE HAVE AN EVALUATION SHEET TO GIVE JOANNA AFTERWARDS SO THAT SHE CAN FEED BACK TO US ABOUT THE EVENT _(this includes things like were the questions clear and effective? and do you think our ideas for our raising awareness campaign will be successful? and did you feel welcome and comfortable when you came to our school?)_

---

## IN GROUPS

## HEADS TOGETHER:

_In_ groups, USE THE INTERNET TO FIND CONTACT DETAILS FOR FIVE DIFFERENT ORGANIZATIONS THAT MIGHT BE ABLE TO PROVIDE YOU WITH ACCESS TO EXPERTS CONNECTED TO THE ISSUE OF RACISM. Try to contact people from different fields. For example, a police source and a governmental source as well as campaigning sources.

You have 10 MINUTES.
Feed back your answers to the class.

---

## RECORD BOOK

_Report_ on the class activities under the headings:

COMING UP WITH QUESTIONS TO ASK A POLICE EXPERT ON HUMAN TRAFFICKING.

RESEARCHING CONTACT DETAILS FOR FIVE DIFFERENT SOURCES THAT MAY PROVIDE EXPERT HELP ON THE ISSUE OF RACISM.

Make sure you include notes on any class feedback sessions.

## 6 Why is it important to understand different points of view?

*There* is one last skill that will really help you with researching your campaigns for change. That is, the importance of seeing an issue from different points of view.

### FOR EXAMPLE,

the political situation in Gaza is seen very differently from the point of view of a Palestinian than from the point of view of an Israeli. A Palestinian might consider their people to be oppressed by the Israeli government and military, whereas an Israeli might see Palestinians as potential terrorists who need to be controlled. Both will consider that they have rights to the land that is in dispute. If you were to organize an awareness-raising campaign on this issue but only took into consideration one point of view, you would not have a balanced argument and your campaign would suffer as a result.

### BALANCED ARGUMENTS THAT TAKE INTO ACCOUNT MANY POINTS OF VIEW ARE FAR MORE LIKELY TO SUCCEED.

### IN PAIRS/GROUPS
### HEADS TOGETHER:

*In* pairs, COME UP WITH TWO 3.9.27 SPEECHES. BOTH SPEECHES ARE REACTING TO PLANS FOR A NEW AIRPORT TO BE BUILT IN THE UK.

The first speech is from the point of view of a climate activist who is against the plans.

The second should be from the point of view of the owner of a major aviation company.

You have 10 MINUTES.

Feed back your answers to the class.

*As* you will have already realized, there are always at least two sides to every argument and there may be several points of view from which an issue can be considered.

WHEN YOUR CAMPAIGN TAKES INTO ACCOUNT THE MANY POINTS OF VIEW AROUND AN ISSUE AND IS ABLE TO INCLUDE AS MANY OF THEM AS POSSIBLE IN THE SOLUTION, THEN YOU ARE CREATING AN ARGUMENT WITH A BROAD APPEAL.

It's also important to realize that people's points of view change through their lives as they experience different events. For example, you may have had a very negative attitude towards people who are mentally ill until a relative was diagnosed with a mental illness. The ability to put yourselves in other people's shoes and understand their different experience of the world and the reasons for their different points of view will make you a far more understanding individual as well as a far more convincing advocate.

This does not mean that your campaign should lack a focused argument. But people should be able to see that you have taken into account the differing views on the issue while reaching your conclusions.

### IN GROUPS OF SIX
## P.O.V

*In* groups of six, ROLL THE DIE TO FIND YOUR CHARACTERS. Take 10 MINUTES TO USE THE INTERNET TO RESEARCH YOUR ROLE (the names of the organizations have been made up).

You then have at least 20 MINUTES FOR THE MAIN ACTIVITY. Remember that all people have to remain in role throughout and everyone has to have the chance to be heard.

## SITUATION:

A PUBLIC MEETING IN A TOWN HALL WHERE VARIOUS REPRESENTATIVES ARE DISCUSSING PLANS FOR A MAJOR CORPORATION, WELLBEING PHARMACEUTICALS, TO BUILD A MEDICAL RESEARCH LABORATORY ON THE OUTSKIRTS OF THE TOWN. THE BUILDING WILL TAKE TWO YEARS TO CONSTRUCT AND THERE WILL BE A FOCUS ON USING A VARIETY OF ANIMALS, FROM MICE TO PRIMATES, IN THEIR MEDICAL RESEARCH.

*The six characters to pick from are as follows...*

**1** You are very keen to have the building plan accepted, as you believe that it will make a positive contribution to the local community.

## WILL RUSSELL
### NEW BUILDINGS MANAGER

**1** # WILL RUSSELL
### NEW BUILDINGS MANAGER
### FOR THE LOCAL AUTHORITY.

### YOUR KEY POINTS TO MAKE ARE:

**1.** The new building plan will mean lucrative business for local construction companies.
**2.** It will result in employment and business for local people in specialized industries such as cleaning, maintenance, security, accommodation and catering.
**3.** You think that testing on animals for medical research is entirely acceptable as it saves human lives.
**4.** Wellbeing Pharmaceuticals, the international corporation that is financing the project, has offered to provide work experience for 50 school students every year.
**5.** If a large corporation like Wellbeing Pharmaceuticals brings its business to the town then many other big companies may invest in the town too.

### YOUR KEY SENTENCE:

"This building project will bring jobs, money and a higher profile to our town."

**2** You are against the use of animals for medical research and your organization will mount a mass campaign to protest against these plans.

## SHEILA MUIRY
### SPOKESPERSON FOR HUNTED

**2** # SHEILA MUIRY
### SPOKESPERSON FOR HUNTED,
### A NATIONAL ANIMAL RIGHTS CAMPAIGN.

### YOUR KEY POINTS TO MAKE ARE:

**1.** Testing on animals is a barbaric practice, which causes unnecessary harm and distress to animals.
**2.** Last year, over 3.5 million animals were used in scientific experiments and if that number included the amount of animals that died on their way to the research laboratories, it would be much higher.
**3.** Many scientists have stated that using animals in research is useless as they have such different biological systems to human beings.
**4.** The laboratory will be using primates such as chimpanzees. These are the closest species to humans and will feel pain and terror in exactly the same way that humans would.
**5.** If the plans go ahead, your group will mount a national campaign against the building plans and there will be daily protests for the entire time of the construction.

### YOUR KEY SENTENCE:

"Why should millions of animals be made to suffer and die just so that a major corporation can add to its wealth when a massive proportion of the animals will die without any new cures being developed?"

**3** *You* are for the new building and reassure the people at the meeting that the animals will be looked after well. You remind them that you will be saving lives with your research.

**DIANA GOMEZ**
**HEAD SCIENTIST**

## 3 DIANA GOMEZ
### HEAD SCIENTIST FOR THE RESEARCH TEAM.

### YOUR KEY POINTS TO MAKE ARE:

**1.** Medical research saves lives and ends suffering for millions of people.
**2.** Testing on animals is the only way to be sure that new medicines are safe.
**3.** The living conditions for the animals used in research are clean, healthy and comfortable.
**4.** Most of the animals used will be rats and mice and most people consider them to be vermin. Why don't the animal rights organizations focus on chasing pest exterminators instead?
**5.** You will guarantee that the young people of the town will benefit greatly from the research laboratory being built as 50 of them every year will have a carefully planned programme of work experience.

### YOUR KEY SENTENCE:

"Medical research using animals saves lives and ends suffering for millions of people."

---

**4** *You* are against the building of the laboratory as you have been investigating Wellbeing Pharmaceuticals for five years and have uncovered disturbing evidence about the organization.

**ANDREAS KYRIACOU**
**INDEPENDENT MEDIA JOURNALIST**

## 4 ANDREAS KYRIACOU
### INDEPENDENT MEDIA JOURNALIST.

### YOUR KEY POINTS TO MAKE ARE:

**1.** Wellbeing Pharmaceuticals devote 90% of their research to developing genetic treatments so that rich parents can have 'designer babies'.
**2.** You have had death threats for articles you have written against the corporation and can only assume that they have paid for this form of intimidation.
**3.** The corporation is notorious for refusing to sell the patents for life-saving medicines to developing nations that wish to manufacture them cheaply.
**4.** The corporation was found guilty of illegal practices in Africa where they tested medicines on people without their consent. When some of these patients died, they were buried secretly as part of a cover-up.
**5.** The careless behaviour of the corporation will possibly result in there being a danger to the community due to possible leaks of poisonous materials. You wouldn't dream of letting any of your own children within a mile of the building.

### YOUR KEY SENTENCE:

"Wellbeing Pharmaceuticals is not what it appears to be and is in fact a ruthless and dangerous organization devoted to nothing other than making vast profits."

## 5 You are for the new building as you had a life-threatening disease three years ago but survived due to new medicines that had been tested on animals.

**ROBERT TAYLOR**
LOCAL TEENAGER

## 5 ROBERT TAYLOR
LOCAL TEENAGER.

### YOUR KEY POINTS TO MAKE ARE:

**1.** You would be dead now if it weren't for new drugs, which saved you.
**2.** If these drugs had not been tested on animals then the process of testing them would have gone on for many years longer and you would not have lived long enough to use them.
**3.** You understand the arguments against the harm to animals but to you, those arguments are saying that it would be better that you were dead than some animals were dead.
**4.** You question why animal rights activists don't focus on the slaughter of millions of animals by the meat industry. You are a vegan, not only to save harm to animals but because the meat industry causes an enormous amount of pollution and is a major contributor to global warming.
**5.** You have two younger sisters and know that work experience in the laboratories would really help their future career prospects.

### YOUR KEY SENTENCE:

"If it weren't for testing on animals, I wouldn't be here today. I'd have died of a painful illness."

## 6 You are against the new building because your council block will be demolished for it, you distrust the pharmaceutical corporations and fully support the animal rights campaigners.

**SANGEETA SHARMA**
CHAIR OF LOCAL RESIDENTS' ASSOCIATION

## 6 SANGEETA SHARMA
CHAIR OF LOCAL RESIDENTS' ASSOCIATION.

### YOUR KEY POINTS TO MAKE ARE:

**1.** The local authority doesn't care about its residents and just cares about making money and looking good.
**2.** Forty council flats will be demolished and although you will all be rehoused, the block is in perfectly good order and the community is very close.
**3.** You think that this pharmaceutical corporation will have given some fat backhanders to members of the local authority so that the building will happen anyway, whatever anyone says against it.
**4.** You distrust pharmaceutical corporations and think that all modern medicines do is cure one problem which then becomes a worse problem somewhere else in the body. You think this is the real reason for the massive rise in cancer worldwide.
**5.** You question why we think humans are more important than animals. Animals haven't polluted the planet, don't make wars and don't make dirty deals behind other animals' backs. Why should animals suffer and die just to help humans?

### YOUR KEY SENTENCE:

"Put people before profits for a change and scrap this deal, which stinks of greed and corruption."

# The PROCESSING PLANT

and we formed a committee through which we organized our first full-scale march, which drew nearly a thousand individuals onto the streets in support of biomedical research.

## RECORD BOOK

*Report* on the class activities under the headings:

**3.9.27 ON SEEING TWO POINTS OF VIEW AROUND THE ISSUE OF BUILDING A NEW AIRPORT.**

**AND**

**P.O.V. ACTIVITY DECIDING WHETHER TO BUILD A MEDICAL RESEARCH LABORATORY WHICH WILL TEST ITS DRUGS ON ANIMALS.**

Make sure you include notes on any class feedback sessions.

### IN WHAT WAYS IS 21ST-CENTURY TECHNOLOGY IMPORTANT FOR CAMPAIGNING?

*Online* communication is, I believe, fostering a renaissance in political activism. It's easier than ever to attract like-minded people and make your voices heard. A massive variety of tools for publicizing your message exists, many of which were inconceivable even a decade ago – Facebook pages, YouTube, blogging – all these services mean that there's no excuse not to actively engage with the issues you think are important.

## 7 Rax Interview with Laurie Pycroft

AT THE AGE OF 16, LAURIE PYCROFT SAW AN ANIMAL RIGHTS PROTEST OUTSIDE A BUILDING SITE WHERE A NEW MEDICAL RESEARCH UNIT WAS GOING TO BE BUILT IN 2006. HE AND TWO FRIENDS RAN ACROSS AND MADE THEIR OWN PROTEST IN SUPPORT OF ANIMALS BEING USED FOR SCIENTIFIC RESEARCH AND A NEW CAMPAIGN WAS BORN, PRO TEST. THE RAX TEAM INTERVIEWED LAURIE IN 2010.

### WHAT KIND OF WORK DID YOU DO TO INFORM YOURSELF OF THE KEY ISSUES IN YOUR CAMPAIGN?

*Before* founding Pro-Test, I was already reasonably well informed regarding animal-based research and biomedical research in general, but it's a subject which requires massive scientific knowledge so I had to spend a lot of time reading journals and articles on the subject. Probably most valuable, however, was actually visiting laboratories engaged in animal research and speaking with the scientists and technicians involved, which allowed me insight into the realities of an animal lab – an insight which ran contrary to the view of these labs promoted by anti-vivisectionists.

### WHAT WERE THE MAIN STEPS YOU TOOK IN SETTING UP YOUR CAMPAIGN?

*The* first step was an impromptu demonstration consisting of myself, two friends and a hastily scrawled placard. We spent the day standing opposite an animal rights march being shouted at while we quietly supported the construction of the new animal research laboratory in Oxford. The campaign really got going when I recorded the events of the day on my blog and, following a massively positive response, constructed a website to get the message out. I was quickly contacted by a small group of Oxford University students interested in helping me out with my proposed campaign. I met with them

### HOW DID YOU GO ABOUT RESEARCHING AND GETTING ALL THE FACTS TOGETHER?

*For* scientific papers, PubMed has been invaluable, as it enables easy searching of a huge database of biomedical literature. I also had a large degree of assistance from scientists and students involved in the area who helped gather relevant evidence for use in debates.

## WHAT TIPS WOULD YOU GIVE YOUNG CAMPAIGNERS IN THIS VITAL STAGE OF CRITICAL THINKING AND ENQUIRY?

*Be* sure to evaluate carefully where your evidence is coming from. The internet provides unprecedented access to information, and tools like Wikipedia can be wonderful ways of discovering new knowledge, but always be sceptical of where the information is coming from. A website selling homeopathy products, for example, is unlikely to be the best place to find objective, unbiased analysis of the efficacy of alternative medicines.

## DID YOU EVER USE EXPERTS TO BACK UP YOUR CAUSE OR INFORM YOUR CAUSE?

*Expert* advice is an essential part of running a good campaign and I rely heavily on the knowledge of those better informed than me. Quite a few members of the Pro-test committee are professional scientists, and it wouldn't have been possible to maintain our credibility without them. Of course, it's important to take advice from a variety of experts in order to get a wider view of the issue so that one can decide upon a well-reasoned course of action.

LEARN MORE/GET INVOLVED: www.pro-test.org.uk

## 8 Rax Interview with James Stevens

JAMES STEVENS HAS BEEN ON THE CUTTING EDGE OF NEW TECHNOLOGIES SINCE THE EARLY DAYS OF THE WEB. WHEN THE FIRST INTERNET SITES WERE EMERGING, HE WAS CONTRACTED BY LEVI'S JEANS AND *NATURE* MAGAZINE TO MAKE THEIR FIRST UK WEBSITES AND ALSO HELPED TO DEVELOP INDYMEDIA. HE IS A HIGHLY RESPECTED NEW MEDIA ADVISOR TO MANY CAMPAIGNING GROUPS AND ADVOCATE FOR THE USE OF OPEN-SOURCE SOFTWARE. THE RAX TEAM INTERVIEWED HIM IN 2010.

## IS THE WEB THE BEST PLACE TO START RESEARCHING AN ISSUE FOR A CAMPAIGN?

*The* web is such a compelling source that it's always tempting to start there! However, I find that when setting out to research a particular subject or idea, the best leads to quality information spring from personal interactions on the subject. So, before launching Google, attempt to engage with friends and colleagues on the subject. Make notes and try talking about what you know already, as this will expose gaps in your knowledge.

## HOW CAN YOU EVALUATE THE AUTHENTICITY OF INFORMATION AND RESEARCH THAT YOU GATHER FROM THE WEB?

*Research* subjects using a variety of internet-based resources, such as Newsgroups, Web Encyclopedias and search engines to cross-reference and verify sources. In the end we have to trust sources which we can verify with our peers and communities.

## ARE THERE OTHER WAYS OF USING THE INTERNET THAT WOULD GIVE USEFUL RESULTS WHEN RESEARCHING AN ISSUE?

*Get* access to or set up your own user groups and forums on the subject. You will find a mine of observation and experience-based accounts will inform and expand your information base, plus you can ask questions. Break down the subject into a set of related components to investigate before getting locked into one train of thought. Use the 'advanced' search options!

> BREAK DOWN THE SUBJECT INTO A SET OF RELATED COMPONENTS TO INVESTIGATE BEFORE GETTING LOCKED INTO ONE TRAIN OF THOUGHT.

## WHAT OTHER WAYS ARE THERE OF USING 21ST-CENTURY TECHNOLOGY THAT CAN HELP AN ACTIVE CITIZEN ACCESS RELIABLE INFORMATION RELATING TO AN ISSUE THEY ARE INTERESTED IN?

*The* position of newsgathering and reporting on the world has been radically transformed by mobile technologies. Not only can we easily carry high-quality TV cameras anywhere we go but we can relay the materials we collect in real or next to real time using an array of personal, community and commercial communication networks.

This democratization of media has fostered a huge range of 'people' reporting. In news, as consumers, as advocates and as a challenge to the voice of authority. Swarming and tagging, collaborative writing and the success of open-source software are testament to this sea change.

## 9 Rax Interview with Media Lens

DAVID CROMWELL AND DAVID EDWARDS ARE THE EDITORS OF A BRITISH MEDIA ANALYSIS WEBSITE CALLED MEDIA LENS, FOUNDED IN 2001. THEY ENCOURAGE THE CRITICAL STUDY OF CURRENT NEWS, BY COMPARING THE WAY ALTERNATIVE MEDIA SOURCES COVER STORIES WITH THE WAY THEY ARE COVERED IN THE MAINSTREAM MEDIA. IN 2007, MEDIA LENS WAS AWARDED THE GANDHI INTERNATIONAL PEACE AWARD. THE RAX TEAM CAUGHT UP WITH THEM EARLY IN 2010.

**WHAT DOES AN ORGANIZATION LIKE MEDIA LENS PROVIDE FOR THE YOUNG CRITICAL THINKER THAT THEY CANNOT ACCESS FROM MAINSTREAM MEDIA?**

We do something very simple: we compare examples of journalism from the corporate media with reporting, analysis and commentary from 'alternative sources': human rights groups, environmental campaigners, peace activists, and so on. We aim to highlight what are often glaring gaps between the two: the corporate media, for obvious reasons, all too often reports from a vantage of power; while other sources, often more knowledgeable and genuinely authoritative, report from a grassroots perspective. By presenting such contrasting views of vital issues – climate, war, and so on – we encourage the reader to pursue the links and references we provide; to make up their own minds; and, if they wish, to challenge the journalists and editors responsible for the distorted corporate media version of events. Our underlying aim is to boost the interlinked qualities of wisdom and compassion.

**WHAT ADVICE COULD YOU GIVE YOUNG CAMPAIGNERS WANTING TO USE THE SKILLS OF CRITICAL THINKING AND ENQUIRY TO FIND A RELIABLE BODY OF STATISTICS AND POINTS OF VIEW REGARDING AN ISSUE?**

It's important to access a wide range of resources and perspectives. You need to be aware of the establishment view of any particular issue as propagated across newspapers, radio and television. To challenge this view, you could then see what some of the more well-known campaign groups say on the same issue – for example, Amnesty, Human Rights Watch, Oxfam, Christian Aid, Friends of the Earth, Greenpeace and so on. However, you should bear in mind that many such groups strive to be close to government and the media – seeking access to ministers, battling to influence parliamentary affairs, trying to grab the attention of sympathetic journalists. They often end up being unable or unwilling to really criticize power, and consequently become compromised and part of the system that needs to be changed. You need to seek out voices that are, as far as possible, unfettered by any notion of seeking influence in, or access to, the corridors of power.

**HOW DO YOU THINK THAT 21ST-CENTURY DIGITAL TECHNOLOGY IS GOING TO AFFECT THE DEMOCRATIC PROCESS IN THE UK AND CAMPAIGNING?**

The impact of online social networking – sites like Facebook, for instance – has already been seen in protests against bankers, fossil fuel dinosaurs and arms companies. As with any new technology, there is a potential for good and also a risk that it will be subverted for other ends... The internet makes it much easier for people to gain access to information and ideas challenging illusions rooted in the needs of power and profit.

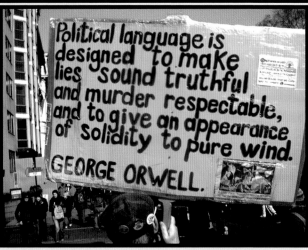

**WHAT WOULD YOUR THREE TOP TIPS BE FOR YOUNG PEOPLE SEEKING TO CREATE A POSITIVE CHANGE IN THEIR WORLD?**

Think more deeply about the standard news framework. The main problem with corporate news is that it restricts the limits of thinkable thought. On the Six O'Clock News of 20 March 2006, Diplomatic Correspondent Bridget Kendall declared solemnly: "There's still bitter disagreement over invading Iraq.

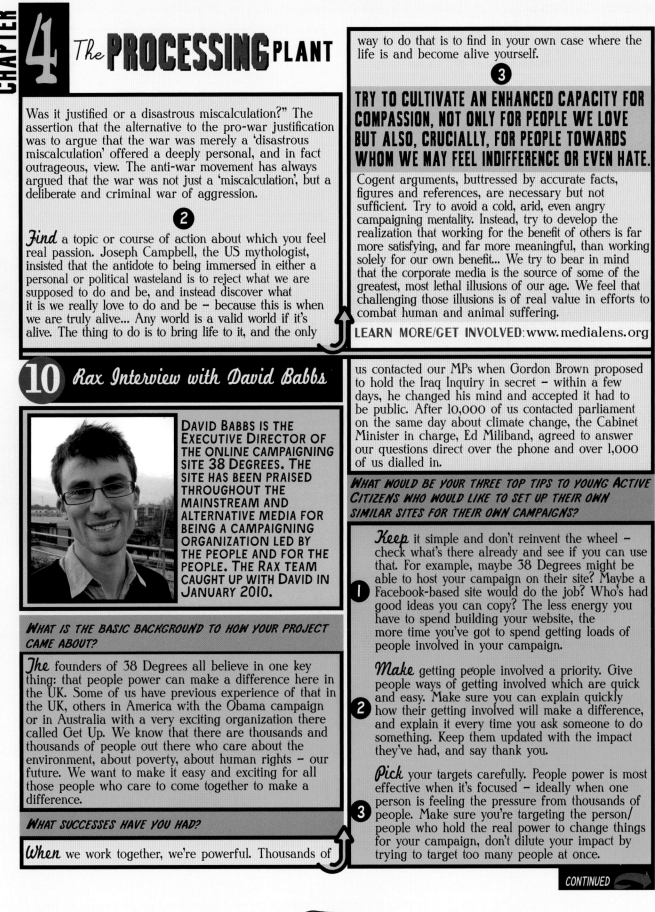

Was it justified or a disastrous miscalculation?" The assertion that the alternative to the pro-war justification was to argue that the war was merely a 'disastrous miscalculation' offered a deeply personal, and in fact outrageous, view. The anti-war movement has always argued that the war was not just a 'miscalculation', but a deliberate and criminal war of aggression.

**2**

**Find** a topic or course of action about which you feel real passion. Joseph Campbell, the US mythologist, insisted that the antidote to being immersed in either a personal or political wasteland is to reject what we are supposed to do and be, and instead discover what it is we really love to do and be – because this is when we are truly alive... Any world is a valid world if it's alive. The thing to do is to bring life to it, and the only

way to do that is to find in your own case where the life is and become alive yourself.

**3**

## TRY TO CULTIVATE AN ENHANCED CAPACITY FOR COMPASSION, NOT ONLY FOR PEOPLE WE LOVE BUT ALSO, CRUCIALLY, FOR PEOPLE TOWARDS WHOM WE MAY FEEL INDIFFERENCE OR EVEN HATE.

Cogent arguments, buttressed by accurate facts, figures and references, are necessary but not sufficient. Try to avoid a cold, arid, even angry campaigning mentality. Instead, try to develop the realization that working for the benefit of others is far more satisfying, and far more meaningful, than working solely for our own benefit... We try to bear in mind that the corporate media is the source of some of the greatest, most lethal illusions of our age. We feel that challenging those illusions is of real value in efforts to combat human and animal suffering.

**LEARN MORE/GET INVOLVED**:www.medialens.org

## 10 Rax Interview with David Babbs

**DAVID BABBS IS THE EXECUTIVE DIRECTOR OF THE ONLINE CAMPAIGNING SITE 38 DEGREES. THE SITE HAS BEEN PRAISED THROUGHOUT THE MAINSTREAM AND ALTERNATIVE MEDIA FOR BEING A CAMPAIGNING ORGANIZATION LED BY THE PEOPLE AND FOR THE PEOPLE. THE RAX TEAM CAUGHT UP WITH DAVID IN JANUARY 2010.**

### WHAT IS THE BASIC BACKGROUND TO HOW YOUR PROJECT CAME ABOUT?

**The** founders of 38 Degrees all believe in one key thing: that people power can make a difference here in the UK. Some of us have previous experience of that in the UK, others in America with the Obama campaign or in Australia with a very exciting organization there called Get Up. We know that there are thousands and thousands of people out there who care about the environment, about poverty, about human rights – our future. We want to make it easy and exciting for all those people who care to come together to make a difference.

### WHAT SUCCESSES HAVE YOU HAD?

**When** we work together, we're powerful. Thousands of

us contacted our MPs when Gordon Brown proposed to hold the Iraq Inquiry in secret – within a few days, he changed his mind and accepted it had to be public. After 10,000 of us contacted parliament on the same day about climate change, the Cabinet Minister in charge, Ed Miliband, agreed to answer our questions direct over the phone and over 1,000 of us dialled in.

### WHAT WOULD BE YOUR THREE TOP TIPS TO YOUNG ACTIVE CITIZENS WHO WOULD LIKE TO SET UP THEIR OWN SIMILAR SITES FOR THEIR OWN CAMPAIGNS?

**1** **Keep** it simple and don't reinvent the wheel – check what's there already and see if you can use that. For example, maybe 38 Degrees might be able to host your campaign on their site? Maybe a Facebook-based site would do the job? Who's had good ideas you can copy? The less energy you have to spend building your website, the more time you've got to spend getting loads of people involved in your campaign.

**2** **Make** getting people involved a priority. Give people ways of getting involved which are quick and easy. Make sure you can explain quickly how their getting involved will make a difference, and explain it every time you ask someone to do something. Keep them updated with the impact they've had, and say thank you.

**3** **Pick** your targets carefully. People power is most effective when it's focused – ideally when one person is feeling the pressure from thousands of people. Make sure you're targeting the person/people who hold the real power to change things for your campaign, don't dilute your impact by trying to target too many people at once.

CONTINUED

**WHAT EFFECT DO YOU THINK 21ST-CENTURY TECHNOLOGY WILL HAVE ON THE PROCESS OF DEMOCRACY IN THE FUTURE?**

It's too early to say, really! But clearly it's easier for lots of people to get involved and work together on big issues than it's ever been before, and that can only be a good thing. There'll be more and more opportunities to do things like campaigning and voting online. But there'll still be an important role for campaigning offline – talking to each other, working with people in your local area, your family, school or workplace.

LEARN MORE/GET INVOLVED: www.38degrees.org.uk

## 11 Rax Interview with UKYCC

THE UK YOUTH CLIMATE COALITION (UKYCC) IS THE LEADING YOUTH-LED CAMPAIGN ORGANIZATION IN THE COUNTRY ADDRESSING THE ISSUE OF CLIMATE CHANGE. THE RAX TEAM CAUGHT UP WITH ALEX FARROW (21) AND ELLIE HOPKINS (21) FROM UKYCC IN JANUARY 2010.

**WHAT IS YOUR CAMPAIGN AIMING TO ACHIEVE?**

We're really inspired by the vision of a clean, 'post-carbon' future. One where everyone can access clean energy, enough food and clean water. Where people don't fight over natural resources and with lots of great opportunities for all of us to get ahead like green jobs, public transport we can afford (the list goes on).

**WHAT KIND OF WORK DID YOU DO TO INFORM YOURSELF OF THE KEY ISSUES?**

There's a lot of stuff out there – some of it is good, some of it not so good, so the main tip is to be careful and make sure you know where it's coming from. If you're campaigning on something, there's probably an opposing group too so it is important to be clued up because it takes a lot of work to build

campaigns up, but not a huge amount to bring them down.

In the climate world, however, the science and theory is all pretty complex and while it's good to have an understanding of it, being an expert in it all doesn't necessarily mean that's going to be effective in inspiring others to act. For us it was about making it relevant on a personal, real level. If we can take a big problem and make it something that actually affects us, then we stand a much better chance of getting other people on our side and involved in our campaigns.

One of the things that we're really strong about is talking and sharing everything we do with all the Youth Climate Coalitions from around the globe. Information is crucial and to save time it's better to share the knowledge we have within the movement by talking and listening to everyone else working with us.

**HOW IMPORTANT DO YOU THINK IT IS TO USE EXPERTS TO BACK UP YOUR CAMPAIGN?**

Of course it's important to use facts, figures, statistics and quotes to back yourself up. Sometimes it can be really useful to show that adults who have researched this stuff support what you are saying. But be careful. You don't want to sound like you're just repeating what other people have said, especially if you don't know much about whom you are quoting. Often the most powerful way to express your cause is to be personal. Tell stories about how it affects you, your friends or your peers. Tell people how we are all coming together to tackle these issues, and then tell people they should join that cause too.

**WHAT KINDS OF ACTIONS HAVE YOU TAKEN PART IN AND WHY DID YOU THINK THEY WOULD BE EFFECTIVE?**

People in UKYCC have done a range of actions, from being arrested for non-violent direct action against things like the expansion of Heathrow airport or the renewal of the UK's nuclear weapons, to all calling the Prime Minister's office at the same time to tell him the

same message. As an organization we try to focus on really positive actions that show people that we are young, engaged and proactive, and that we can have fun whilst making positive change. We've become known for our flash-mob dancing outside Parliament. Recently we even managed to hire a massive projector, which we used to put a message onto the side of Parliament. Again, it's all about being fun and innovative but having a clear and understandable message. But remember: if it's not fun, it's not the right thing to do!

### WHAT KEY ADVICE WOULD YOU GIVE YOUNG PEOPLE WHO WANT TO SET UP THEIR OWN CAMPAIGNS?

Go for it! As long as you show people that you are enthusiastic, passionate and you have a good idea and the willingness to work hard, the rest will follow. Know/be clear about what your aim is, that way you'll know when you've achieved it. Don't just string random events together!

Open Sandwiches

**LEARN MORE/GET INVOLVED:**
www.ukycc.org   www.ukyouthparliament.org.uk

**12** *Rax Interview with*
*Patrick Mercer OBE MP*

PATRICK MERCER HAS BEEN CONSERVATIVE MEMBER OF PARLIAMENT FOR NEWARK SINCE 2001. BEFORE BECOMING A POLITICIAN, HE WAS A COLONEL IN THE BRITISH ARMY AND A JOURNALIST FOR BBC RADIO 4. THE RAX TEAM CAUGHT UP WITH PATRICK IN MARCH 2010.

### WHAT ISSUES DO YOU THINK ARE OF MOST CONCERN FOR YOUNG ACTIVE CITIZENS IN THE UK TO ADDRESS?

The most important issues for young people to address are, I believe: the economic recovery of this country and its place in the international community. The next generation must decide whether they want Britain to continue to be an influence outside her own borders.

### THE UK PRESS HAS BEEN ACCUSED OF EPHEBIPHOBIA. WHY DO YOU THINK THIS IS AND WHAT SOLUTIONS CAN YOU SEE TO ENDING THIS?

It is human nature for the young to challenge the old and for the old to be naturally reserved about innovation. By definition, young people are immature; the media and teachers of all types must try to be more empathetic towards youngsters. With my own son, I constantly try (and usually fail) to think of issues that interest him in the way that I might have done when I was 18.

### WHAT WOULD BE YOUR ADVICE TO YOUNG ACTIVE CITIZENS WHO WANT TO BRING ABOUT A CHANGE TO THEIR WORLDS THROUGH TAKING INFORMED AND RESPONSIBLE ACTION?

Get involved in community and nationally based activities. For instance, volunteer to be a retained firefighter or a special constable. Volunteer to fight for your nation but above all vote in local and general elections.

### WHAT ARE YOUR VIEWS ON CAMPAIGN GROUPS THAT USE NON-VIOLENT DIRECT ACTION AS PART OF THEIR STRATEGY?

Continue with what they are doing but remember the persuasiveness of courtesy and open-mindedness.

### YOUNG PEOPLE ARE LESS AND LESS ENGAGED IN THE WORLD OF POLITICS. WHY DO YOU THINK THIS IS AND WHAT CAN BE DONE ABOUT IT?

The British party political system is deeply unattractive – and I should know, as I am part of it! MPs' expenses and the constant vitriol of all parties' rhetoric are deeply unpersuasive. Until professional politicians learn to act like proper leaders and place the nation before themselves then this will continue.

[Young people] must invite councillors and MPs to discussions and debates. Most elected representatives will jump at the chance to talk to them. Politicians have got to learn that the younger generation communicate through every sort of medium. So, web and blog sites, Twitter, Facebook etc have got to be used if the older generation wishes to communicate effectively with youngsters.

**LEARN MORE/GET INVOLVED:**
www.conservatives.com

# 5 The GIFT of the GAB

## ① Why is this chapter important?

*The Processing Plant* gave you plenty of ideas about how to use the skills of critical thinking and enquiry to make sure that you have a well-researched and balanced argument to help your campaign for change.

### THE TRUTH IS OUT THERE – USING GOOD CRITICAL THINKING AND ENQUIRY, YOU WILL FIND IT!

*However,* in order to make your research work for you and make your campaign as effective as possible, there is no alternative but to develop your ability to use language well. In ancient times, words were seen as having magical power, which is why the word 'spell' is not only associated with an English lesson but also with magic. Even a full stop has drama in its use and an exclamation mark can add strength to a sentence. Words have the power to change the world and the world can also change our words.

### WORDS PROVIDE THE GLUE THAT WILL HELP YOUR ARGUMENT FOR CHANGE HANG TOGETHER.

### THIS CHAPTER WILL HELP ENSURE THAT:

YOU CAN EXPLAIN YOUR VIEWPOINT EFFECTIVELY.

YOU CAN PRESENT A CONVINCING ARGUMENT.

YOU CAN COMMUNICATE WITH A RANGE OF AUDIENCES.

YOU CAN MAKE LANGUAGE WORK FOR YOU IN A VARIETY OF DIFFERENT WAYS FROM SPEECHMAKING TO SONGWRITING, FROM LETTER WRITING TO PODCASTING.

IN OTHER WORDS, YOU WILL USE THE SKILLS OF ADVOCACY AND REPRESENTATION TO A VERY HIGH LEVEL IN ORDER TO CREATE A WINNING CAMPAIGN THAT WILL CONVINCE PEOPLE.

## ② What is advocacy and representation?

**ADVOCACY:** arguing in favour of, or supporting something; the practice of supporting someone to make his or her voice heard.

**REPRESENTATION:** the act of representing; standing in for someone or some group and speaking with authority on their behalf.

You will be using both of these skills at every level of your citizenship work. From the time you decide on your issue and work out how your campaign will be run, everything you say, write or even do is a form of advocacy and representation. **FOR EXAMPLE,** if you are campaigning against bullying but then go and pick on a Year Seven student because they laughed at your cap, then your campaign has just fallen apart!

### ADVOCACY AND REPRESENTATION ARE WHEN YOU SPEAK UP FOR WHAT YOU BELIEVE IN OR ON BEHALF OF SOMETHING THAT YOU BELIEVE IN.

# THE STONE OF ELOQUENCE

**BLARNEY CASTLE,** NEAR CORK IN IRELAND, HAS AN EXTRAORDINARY LEGEND ATTACHED TO IT. IT IS SAID THAT, IF YOU KISS A CERTAIN STONE IN THE BATTLEMENTS OF THE CASTLE, YOU WILL BE GRANTED THE GIFT OF ELOQUENCE. FROM THEN ON, YOU WILL BE ABLE TO SPEAK PERSUASIVELY ABOUT ANYTHING AND MAKE THE EXPERIENCE OF YOUR TALKING AN ACTUAL PLEASURE FOR THE LISTENER. THIS IS ALSO KNOWN AS THE 'GIFT OF THE GAB' AND IT'S WHY THIS CHAPTER HAS THAT TITLE. MILLIONS OF PEOPLE HAVE KISSED THE BLARNEY STONE, INCLUDING FILM STARS, WRITERS AND POLITICIANS. AS YOU CAN SEE FROM THE PICTURE, IT'S NOT THE EASIEST THING TO DO!

# THE ORIGIN OF SPECIES

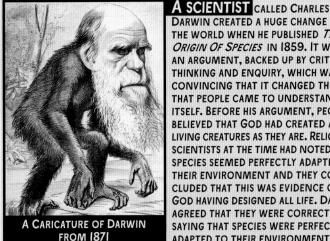

A CARICATURE OF DARWIN FROM 1871

**A SCIENTIST** CALLED CHARLES DARWIN CREATED A HUGE CHANGE IN THE WORLD WHEN HE PUBLISHED *THE ORIGIN OF SPECIES* IN 1859. IT WAS AN ARGUMENT, BACKED UP BY CRITICAL THINKING AND ENQUIRY, WHICH WAS SO CONVINCING THAT IT CHANGED THE WAY THAT PEOPLE CAME TO UNDERSTAND LIFE ITSELF. BEFORE HIS ARGUMENT, PEOPLE BELIEVED THAT GOD HAD CREATED ALL LIVING CREATURES AS THEY ARE. RELIGIOUS SCIENTISTS AT THE TIME HAD NOTED THAT SPECIES SEEMED PERFECTLY ADAPTED TO THEIR ENVIRONMENT AND THEY CONCLUDED THAT THIS WAS EVIDENCE OF GOD HAVING DESIGNED ALL LIFE. DARWIN AGREED THAT THEY WERE CORRECT IN SAYING THAT SPECIES WERE PERFECTLY ADAPTED TO THEIR ENVIRONMENTS BUT HE CHANGED THE CONCLUSION. HE SHOWED THAT SPECIES HAD EVOLVED, OVER MILLIONS OF YEARS, TO BECOME WHAT THEY ARE THROUGH A PROCESS OF NATURAL SELECTION – AND BACKED UP HIS CASE WITH EXTENSIVE SCIENTIFIC EVIDENCE. THIS IS A POWERFUL FORM OF ARGUMENT, IN WHICH YOU ACKNOWLEDGE WHAT IS CORRECT IN YOUR OPPONENTS' VIEW BUT SHOW WHY IT SHOULD LEAD THEM TO A DIFFERENT CONCLUSION.

# ANTI-BULLYING BULLY

**THE** LEAD SINGER OF A FAMOUS UK HIP HOP ACT WAS ASKED IN 2009 TO REPRESENT A GOVERNMENT-LED ANTI-BULLYING CAMPAIGN AND BE AN ADVOCATE SPEAKING OUT AGAINST BULLYING. IN JANUARY 2010, THE RAPPER TOOK PART IN A BBC RADIO SHOW, TAKING CALLS FROM LISTENERS. ONE OF THE LISTENERS SENT IN A TEXT CRITICIZING THE YOUNG SINGER. HE SECRETLY TOOK DOWN THE MOBILE PHONE NUMBER OF THE CALLER AND LATER SENT HER A SERIES OF TEXTS, THREATENING HER VIOLENTLY. WHEN THIS WAS REVEALED, THE ANTI-BULLYING CAMPAIGN QUICKLY DROPPED THE RAPPER, SAYING THAT HIS BEHAVIOUR WAS UNFORGIVABLE.

### LEARN MORE/GET INVOLVED:
www.nspcc.org.uk www.bbclic.com
www.anti-bullyingalliance.org.uk
www.bullying.co.uk

---

*I THINK THAT IT TAKES A LOT MORE THAN 'STRONG LYRICS' TO BRING ABOUT CHANGE BUT I DO BELIEVE THAT 'THOUGHTS ARE THINGS', SO THROUGH LYRICS WE CAN PROVOKE THOUGHT AND IN TURN THOSE THOUGHTS WILL MANIFEST IN WHICHEVER WAY THEY ARE RECEIVED! I LOVE TO PROVOKE THOUGHT IN MY LYRICS.*

MS DYNAMITE (SEE RAX INTERVIEW ON PAGE 135).

# SONGS THAT MAKE YOU THINK

**FOR** HUNDREDS OF YEARS, PROTEST SONGS HAVE BEEN USED TO ADVOCATE FOR PARTICULAR CAMPAIGNS OR NEW WAYS OF THINKING. IN 1824, FOR EXAMPLE, THE GREAT GERMAN COMPOSER LUDWIG VAN BEETHOVEN USED A POEM BY FRIEDRICH SCHILLER TO ADVOCATE FOR A STRONGER SENSE OF BROTHERHOOD BASED ON THE FACT THAT WE CAN ALL FEEL PAIN AND PLEASURE. THIS WAS IN THE 'ODE TO JOY', WHICH FINISHES HIS FAMOUS NINTH SYMPHONY AND IS NOW THE OFFICIAL ANTHEM OF THE EUROPEAN UNION. THE SUFFRAGETTES, THE SLAVERY ABOLITIONISTS, THE CHARTISTS, THE WORKERS' RIGHTS MOVEMENT AND THE ANTI-APARTHEID MOVEMENT HAVE ALL USED PROTEST SONGS AS PART OF THEIR CAMPAIGNS.

IN 1984, THE UK BAND 'THE SPECIALS AKA' RELEASED A SINGLE CALLED 'FREE NELSON MANDELA'. IT WAS AN UPBEAT SONG WITH A CATCHY CHORUS, WHICH MADE IT TO THE TOP TEN. IT HAD MILLIONS OF PEOPLE IN THE COUNTRY THINKING ABOUT NELSON MANDELA'S IMPRISONMENT AND QUESTIONING THE MORALS AND ETHICS OF THE APARTHEID REGIME IN SOUTH AFRICA.

LUDWIG VAN BEETHOVEN

# CHAPTER 5

## The GIFT of the GAB

### IN PAIRS

### MYSTERY GAME

*In* pairs, **DISCUSS TIMES WHEN YOU HAVE STOOD UP FOR SOMEONE.** It doesn't matter if you were successful or not. It could be when you stood up for your little sister who was in trouble with your mum or it could be when you stood up against a bully who was picking on someone. Choose which one of your stories interests you both the most.

Here's the difficult part. Replay that scene, with the two of you taking on the roles.

Write down what were the effective points that the advocate made and what could have made them better. **YOU HAVE 10 MINUTES.**

## 3 How have advocacy and representation contributed to change?

*In* the Toolkit so far, you have looked at great advocates in history such as Thomas Clarkson and William Wilberforce in the campaign to end slavery and women like Emmeline Pankhurst and Muriel Matters who helped win the vote for women. You have also looked at people who used the printed word to advocate for change such as Charles Dickens and films that have brought about change, such as *Cathy Come Home*. All these people contributed to change by presenting convincing arguments that won people over.

You will have studied speechmaking in your English lessons and, more than likely, you will have looked in

detail at the famous speeches given by the likes of Martin Luther King or Mahatma Gandhi. Both of these advocates used powerful speeches to persuade people of the justice in their cause, to gain huge support and ultimately to make a change in their worlds.

But both King and Gandhi represented mass grassroots movements. How does a teenager in a school use these models to effect change? You may be advocating for a youth club being opened in your community or more laptops to be provided to students in your school. How does that connect to Martin Luther King addressing hundreds of thousands of Americans about civil rights issues?

**WHATEVER THE CAMPAIGN, THE TECHNIQUES OF SUCCESSFUL ADVOCACY AND REPRESENTATION REMAIN THE SAME.**

### IN GROUPS

### HEADS TOGETHER

*In* groups, discuss what you know already about the basic techniques for great speechmaking.
**YOU HAVE FIVE MINUTES.**
Feed back your points to the class.

### IN PAIRS

### ART ACTION

*In* pairs, you have **10 MINUTES** to use any of the Art Action skills to show three key tips about how to make a great speech. Feed back your work to the class.

### RECORD BOOK

*Report* on the class activities under the headings:

**THINKING ABOUT ADVOCACY AND REPRESENTATION:**

**NOTES ON A TIME WHEN ONE OF US STOOD UP FOR SOMEONE ELSE.**

**HEADS TOGETHER IDEAS SHOWING BASIC POINTS ABOUT SPEECHMAKING.**

Notes on any class feedback sessions.

# LET YOUR GREATNESS BLOSSOM

☆ c

**IN** 2005, NELSON MANDELA ADDRESSED A CROWD OF 20,000 PEOPLE IN TRAFALGAR SQUARE IN LONDON. HE HAD COME TO REPRESENT THE 'MAKE POVERTY HISTORY' CAMPAIGN. MANDELA MADE IT CLEAR THAT THE MOST IMPORTANT PEOPLE TO BRING ABOUT POSITIVE CHANGE ARE THE YOUNGER GENERATIONS. HE CLOSED HIS SPEECH WITH A POWERFUL CALL TO ACTION.

## THE POWER OF A SPEECH  ☆ a

LEARN MORE/GET INVOLVED:
www.actionaid.org.uk
www.peopleandplanet.org
www.oxfam.org.uk
www.christianaid.org.uk

*AT VARYING TIMES IN HUMAN HISTORY, THE ART OF SPEECHMAKING HAS BEEN MORE POWERFUL THAN WAR, MORE POWERFUL THAN ARROWS OR GUNS OR BOMBS. BECAUSE A SPEECH CARRIES THE IDEA AND THERE IS NOTHING MORE POWERFUL THAN AN IDEA WHOSE TIME HAS COME. BOMBS CANNOT STOP IT, GUNS AND BULLETS AND SPEARS CANNOT STOP IT.*

MAYA ANGELOU – US WRITER AND POET.

SOURCE:
www.bbc.co.uk/learningzone/clips/the-power-of-speech-making

*SOMETIMES IT FALLS UPON A GENERATION TO BE GREAT. YOU CAN BE THAT GREAT GENERATION. LET YOUR GREATNESS BLOSSOM!*

NELSON MANDELA

*THE THREE PS AND A C ARE THE BEST ADVICE ONE CAN GIVE – BE PATIENT, BE PERSISTENT, KEEP PUSHING AND CHANGE WILL HAPPEN!*

SCOTT FORBES (SEE RAX INTERVIEW ON PAGE 195).  ☆ d

LEARN MORE/GET INVOLVED: www.globalforum40.com

## JUST A FEW WORDS...

**AT** THE UN SECURITY COUNCIL IN 1957, THE INDIAN POLITICIAN VK KRISHNA MENON TALKED FOR NEARLY EIGHT HOURS. THE TRANSCRIPT OF THE SPEECH RUNS TO 160 PAGES! HUGO CHAVEZ, THE CURRENT PRESIDENT OF VENEZUELA, REGULARLY BROADCASTS SPEECHES TO HIS COUNTRY THAT CAN LAST UP TO SEVEN HOURS. CHAVEZ'S RADICAL POLICIES HAVE BROUGHT ABOUT SUCH A SHIFT IN VENEZUELAN LIFE THAT HE USES HIS BROADCASTS TO INFORM PEOPLE OF THE LATEST FUNDAMENTAL CHANGES.

☆ e

*WHICH BRINGS ME NEATLY TO MY 467TH POINT....*

## DR MARTIN LUTHER KING

**DURING** HIS LIFE AS A CIVIL RIGHTS CAMPAIGNER, DR MARTIN LUTHER KING RECEIVED HUNDREDS OF DEATH THREATS, HIS HOUSE WAS BLOWN UP WHILE HE AND HIS FAMILY WERE INSIDE IT AND THE FBI BUGGED HIS PHONE AND RAN A SECRET CAMPAIGN SPREADING DAMAGING RUMOURS ABOUT THE NOBEL PEACE PRIZE WINNER. DESPITE THIS, KING REMAINED FAITHFUL TO HIS POLICY OF COMPLETELY NON-VIOLENT PROTEST.

☆ b

*LOVE IS THE ONLY FORCE CAPABLE OF TRANSFORMING AN ENEMY INTO A FRIEND.*

DR MARTIN LUTHER KING.

☆ f

*IT IS IMPORTANT TO BE PRECISE, PASSIONATE AND CLEAR ABOUT YOUR THOUGHTS AND FEELINGS. YOU WILL FIND THAT NOT EVERYBODY AGREES WITH YOUR BELIEFS BUT IF YOUR RESEARCH AND SUPPORT OF YOUR CLAIMS IS SOLID, PEOPLE ARE LEFT WITH NO CHOICE BUT TO LISTEN. COMMUNICATION IS KEY TO DEALING WITH PEOPLE IN AUTHORITY. IT'S IMPORTANT TO BE TRUTHFUL, OPEN-MINDED AND, MOST OF ALL, POLITE. TAKE ON BOARD ANY CRITICISM THAT YOU GET. IF PEOPLE IN AUTHORITY CAN SEE THAT YOU ARE WILLING TO TAKE CRITICISM AND LEARN FROM IT, THEY WILL LISTEN TO YOU MORE THAN SOMEONE WHO IS NARROW-MINDED.*

SOPHIE BARDY (SEE RAX INTERVIEW ON PAGE 138).

 **How can I make a convincing argument?**

## A MAKE SURE YOU HAVE ALL THE APPROPRIATE INFORMATION.

*For* any campaign, local or global, your first step is to inform yourself about the issue. This includes seeing the issue from many different viewpoints, having carefully evaluated research from a variety of resources, including expert opinions, making sure your information is up to date, that your understanding is balanced and that you have come to your own conclusions. All of this has been covered in *The Processing Plant.*

**YOUR RESEARCH WILL BE A KEY FACTOR IN PERSUADING PEOPLE TO SUPPORT YOUR IDEA FOR CHANGE. NOTHING IS AS EFFECTIVE AS AN ADVOCATE WHO CAN BACK UP EVERYTHING HE OR SHE HAS TO SAY WITH FACTS. THAT'S WHAT WINS ARGUMENTS.**

When using the ideas and facts from your research, however, be sure that you know them inside out. If you

are writing a letter or giving a speech and you use material that you don't understand, you are creating a weak point in your argument. Someone could call your bluff and, as a result, you could lose the respect and support of those whom you are trying to persuade.

Be sure to use your research in a way that people can understand. Don't just rattle off loads of facts and figures. Make clear what they mean, what their implications are and how they fit in with your whole argument. If you are talking to Year Seven students about ephebiphobia, then make sure you explain what the word means. If you are using recent statistics, carefully outline what they mean and how they apply to the argument. You may need to use plenty of examples and even visual aids to communicate your ideas to your audience.

> **USE YOUR RESEARCH WISELY AND MAKE SURE PEOPLE ARE ABLE TO UNDERSTAND IT CLEARLY.**

## B CAREFULLY PLAN WHAT YOU WANT TO COMMUNICATE AND PUT YOUR MAIN POINTS IN A USEFUL ORDER. c

*You* will already have a good idea of this from your English lessons. It is important here because when you are communicating with people about a campaign, you usually only have one chance to hook them in.

### FOR EXAMPLE,

you may be setting up a campaigning page on a social networking site. When people click on it, they are only going to read it once to decide if they want to support you. Another example could be if you are giving a presentation to the local community. They will want to gain a clear idea of what you are advocating

for, understand your argument completely and feel your passion for your idea.

**TIPS 'n' HINTS**

**A GOOD TIP IS TO REFINE YOUR ARGUMENT SO THAT YOU HAVE THREE MAIN POINTS. IF THIS IS FOR A SPEECH OR PRESENTATION, IT IS EFFECTIVE IF YOU CAN MAKE YOUR THREE POINTS THREE TIMES; AT THE BEGINNING OF YOUR SPEECH, IN MORE DETAIL WITHIN THE SPEECH AND AS PART OF YOUR CONCLUSION. THIS APPLIES TO WRITTEN WORK ADVOCATING FOR YOUR CAUSE, TOO.**

> **AS WITH A GOOD SONG, WHERE PEOPLE CAN'T GET THE CHORUS OUT OF THEIR HEADS, MAKE SURE YOUR THREE MAIN POINTS STICK IN YOUR AUDIENCE'S MINDS.**

# CUT AND PASTE CRUMBLE

**TEACHERS** TODAY FIND THAT SOME STUDENTS TRY TO PASS OFF COURSEWORK AS THEIR OWN WORK WHEN IN FACT THEY HAVE CUT AND PASTED THE WORK FROM WEBSITES. TEACHERS CAN SPOT THIS EASILY, EITHER BY PUTTING A SEGMENT OF THE WORK INTO A SEARCH ENGINE OR BY SIMPLY IDENTIFYING A WORD IN THE COURSEWORK AND ASKING THE STUDENT WHAT IT MEANS. IT DOESN'T WORK TO SAY, "I KNEW WHAT IT MEANT WHEN I WROTE IT BUT I FORGOT." NEW SOFTWARE IS BEING INTRODUCED THROUGHOUT THE UK THAT IS DESIGNED TO MAKE IT EVEN EASIER TO SPOT PLAGIARISM, WHICH IS THE TERM FOR COPYING THE WORK OF ANOTHER PERSON.

JUST AS YOUR COURSEWORK NEEDS TO BE YOUR OWN, YOU NEED TO UNDERSTAND AND BE ABLE TO EXPLAIN ALL THE RESEARCH AND STATISTICS THAT YOU USE IN YOUR ADVOCACY.

*SO YOUR ORIGINAL WRITING PIECE ABOUT A ROBOT WHO COMES FROM THE FUTURE TO KILL A BOY WHO WILL GROW UP TO DEFEAT THE ROBOTS IS COMPLETELY YOUR OWN IDEA?*

*OF COURSE IT'S IMPORTANT TO USE FACTS, FIGURES, STATISTICS AND QUOTATIONS TO BACK YOURSELF UP. SOMETIMES THEY CAN BE REALLY USEFUL TO SHOW THAT WHAT YOU ARE SAYING IS SUPPORTED BY ADULTS WHO HAVE RESEARCHED THIS STUFF. BUT BE CAREFUL, YOU DON'T WANT TO SOUND LIKE YOU'RE JUST REPEATING WHAT OTHER PEOPLE HAVE SAID.*

UKYCC (SEE RAX INTERVIEW ON PAGE 104).

# THE OLD GREY WHISTLE TEST

**THIS** IS AN INTERESTING LEGEND THAT GOES BACK TO THE EARLY DAYS OF POPULAR MUSIC. WHEN A BAND HAD RECORDED A NEW SONG, THEY WOULD PLAY IT A FEW TIMES TO DOORKEEPERS WHO WERE CALLED 'OLD GREYS' BECAUSE OF THE LONG GREY COATS THAT THEY USED TO WEAR. IF THESE DOORKEEPERS COULD WHISTLE THE TUNE BACK, IT WAS CATCHY ENOUGH TO BE A HIT AND THE BAND HAD PASSED 'THE OLD GREY WHISTLE TEST'. PRACTISE YOUR SPEECHES ON FRIENDS AND FAMILY. IF THEY CAN REPEAT BACK TO YOU THE THREE MAIN POINTS YOU ARE TRYING TO MAKE, YOU'VE GOT A HIT!

*I PERSONALLY BELIEVE THAT US AMERICANS ARE UNABLE TO DO SO BECAUSE, UM, SOME PEOPLE OUT THERE IN OUR NATION DON'T HAVE MAPS AND, UH, I BELIEVE THAT OUR, UH, EDUCATION LIKE SUCH AS, UH, SOUTH AFRICA AND, UH, THE IRAQ, EVERYWHERE LIKE SUCH AS, AND, I BELIEVE THAT THEY SHOULD... OUR EDUCATION OVER HERE IN THE U.S. SHOULD HELP THE U.S... UH, OR, UM, SHOULD HELP SOUTH AFRICA AND SHOULD HELP THE IRAQ AND THE ASIAN COUNTRIES, SO WE WILL BE ABLE TO BUILD UP OUR FUTURE, FOR OUR CHILDREN.*

# HOW NOT TO DO IT!

**AN** AMERICAN TEEN CONTESTANT IN A 2007 BEAUTY PAGEANT WAS ASKED THE QUESTION: "RECENT POLLS HAVE SHOWN A FIFTH OF AMERICANS CAN'T LOCATE THE US ON A WORLD MAP. WHY DO YOU THINK THIS IS?" OVERWHELMED BY BEING ON NATIONAL TELEVISION AND NOT QUITE SURE ABOUT THE QUESTION, SHE GAVE AN ANSWER THAT WAS SO CONFUSING THAT THE YOUTUBE CLIP HAS HAD MILLIONS OF HITS AND SHE HAS BECOME SOMETHING OF A CELEBRITY DUE TO HER UNFORTUNATELY RAMBLING SPEECH.

WHAT CAN RUN BUT NEVER WALKS, HAS A MOUTH BUT NEVER TALKS, HAS A HEAD BUT NEVER WEEPS, HAS A BED BUT NEVER SLEEPS? ANSWER ON PAGE 119.

# The GIFT of the GAB

## C. MAKE SURE YOU USE APPROPRIATE LANGUAGE FOR EACH DIFFERENT AUDIENCE.

*If* you were writing a letter to an MP or a member of the local council, you would use different language than you would in a Year Seven assembly. And you would use different language again in a tweet or mass text aimed at getting other teenagers excited about your campaign. You would need to choose language appropriate to each particular audience.

Although this sounds obvious, using inappropriate language is a common mistake. When you get this right, it can greatly help your success.

**ALWAYS CONSIDER YOUR AUDIENCE AND WHAT KIND OF LANGUAGE WILL MAKE IT AS EASY AS POSSIBLE FOR THEM TO UNDERSTAND YOUR IDEAS AND ARGUMENTS WHILE ALSO CATCHING SOME OF YOUR PASSION AND BEING INSPIRED.** ⓑ

### ACTIVITY

### IN GROUPS

### 3.9.27

*In* groups, **HOLD A VOTE TO FIND AN ISSUE THAT THE MAJORITY OF THE GROUP CARES ABOUT.** Then you need to **WRITE TWO DIFFERENT 3.9.27 SPEECHES.** Both speeches are to interest people in taking action on the issue but each has a different audience.

**THE FIRST SHOULD BE TARGETING TEENAGERS.**
**THE SECOND SHOULD BE TARGETING ELDERLY PEOPLE IN THE COMMUNITY.**

Feed back your ideas to the class.

## D. MAKE SURE YOU HAVE GATHERED THE VIEWS OF THE PEOPLE YOU ARE ADVOCATING FOR AS WELL AS ALL THE OTHER PEOPLE YOUR CAMPAIGN WILL AFFECT.

*It* is important that you have communicated with all the different types of people affected by the issues you are working on. You cannot advocate for or represent people if you do not have a connection to them.

You also need to be aware of everyone else who will be affected by the campaign. This should include people who do not agree with your ideas for change, as you need to be able to understand their arguments and see if you can come up with solutions that suit them in your campaign.

### IF YOU ARE DEALING WITH A LOCAL ISSUE,

then make sure that you have communicated with the people in the community who will be affected by your campaign.

### FOR EXAMPLE,

if you are campaigning for a new youth club then you need to have made contact with young people in the area and have gathered their opinions on the issue. But you will also need to have consulted other local people who will be affected by it such as tenants' and residents' associations, the local authority and other community groups.

### ANOTHER EXAMPLE

would be if you were campaigning for more laptops in your school. In this case, you would need to have gathered the opinions not only of other students but also of staff, parents, your school council, the individuals responsible for the school budget – and ideally your headteacher and board of governors too. ⓒ

### IF YOU ARE DEALING WITH A NATIONAL ISSUE,

then it is important to gather the opinions of a variety of citizens who are connected to the issue. ⓓ

CONTINUED

# ONE LAPTOP PER CHILD

**THE** NOT-FOR-PROFIT ORGANIZATION ONE LAPTOP PER CHILD (OLPC) WAS FOUNDED IN 2005. THE AIM OF THE ORGANIZATION WAS TO CREATE A CHEAP, RUGGED LAPTOP THAT COULD BE BOUGHT BY DEVELOPING COUNTRIES FOR THEIR CHILDREN. OLPC STARTED A SCHEME CALLED GIVE ONE GET ONE WHERE EVERY LAPTOP BOUGHT BY A CUSTOMER IN THE RICHER COUNTRIES OF THE GLOBAL NORTH WOULD MEAN THAT ONE WAS SENT TO A DEVELOPING COUNTRY. BY 2010, OVER A MILLION LAPTOPS HAD BEEN SUPPLIED TO A RANGE OF COUNTRIES INCLUDING URUGUAY, PERU, GHANA AND SIERRA LEONE.

ON THE OTHER HAND, WHEN 1,800 STUDENTS WERE GIVEN FREE LAPTOPS BY THEIR HIGH SCHOOL IN THE US STATE OF PENNSYLVANIA IN 2009, IT HAS BEEN ALLEGED THAT THE INBUILT CAMERAS WERE REMOTELY USED BY THE SCHOOL ADMINISTRATION TO SPY ON THE STUDENTS. A CASE HAS BEEN TAKEN UP AGAINST THE SCHOOL BY PARENTS OF THE STUDENTS. THIS INVASION OF PRIVACY BY NEW TECHNOLOGIES IS AN INTERESTING ISSUE FOR ACTIVE CITIZENS TO CONSIDER. IT'S IMPORTANT TO LOOK AT THE POTENTIAL DISADVANTAGES AS WELL AS THE OBVIOUS ADVANTAGES OF THE FREE PROVISION OF LAPTOPS.

☆c **LEARN MORE/GET INVOLVED**:
www.laptop.org  www.unesco.org
www.campaignforeducation.org

JAPANESE USERS OF NEW TECHNOLOGY DEVELOPED A NEW STYLE OF LITERATURE CALLED THE 'MOBILE NOVEL', AN EXAMPLE OF DIGITAL LITERATURE, WHERE AUTHORS USE THE FORMAT OF THE TEXT MESSAGE TO SEND STORIES OUT IN SHORT INSTALMENTS. THE WRITERS USE THE WAY TEXT MESSAGES ARE SHAPED TO ADD TO THE IMPACT OF THE STORY. IF THERE IS A FIGHT, FOR EXAMPLE, THE LETTERS AND WORDS MAY BE PACKED TOGETHER TIGHTLY. IF WATER IS FLOWING, WORDS MAY BE PLACED ONE BELOW THE OTHER. BY INSERTING WEB LINKS, THE STORIES CAN ALSO BE 'ILLUSTRATED'. IN 2007, FIVE OF THE TOP TEN SELLING NOVELS IN JAPAN HAD BEEN MOBILE NOVELS FIRST AND THE MAIN SITE FOR SHOWING COMPLETE MOBILE NOVELS HAS OVER THREE BILLION VISITS A MONTH!

WHEN YOU ARE USING MOBILE TECHNOLOGY OR SYSTEMS LIKE TWITTER TO CREATE SHORT MESSAGES ABOUT YOUR CAMPAIGN, CONSIDER NOT ONLY THE LANGUAGE YOU USE BUT ALSO THE ACTUAL LOOK OF THE MESSAGE AND WHAT LINKS YOU CAN INCLUDE.

---

*WE SPOKE TO A LOT OF THE YOUNG PEOPLE FIRST TO SEE IF THEY WOULD BE INTERESTED AND THEN WE SPOKE WITH THE OLDER PEOPLE IN THE COMMUNITY, ESPECIALLY THE PEOPLE WHO RAN THE TENANTS' AND RESIDENTS' ASSOCIATIONS. WE WERE BRINGING THEM THE IDEAS OF WHAT COULD BE POSITIVE AND CONSTRUCTIVE IN THE AREA AND BECAUSE THEY WERE THE OLDER GENERATION LOOKING AT US, TEENAGERS, WANTING TO DO THIS, THEY WERE THINKING THIS IS SOMETHING THAT'S GREAT. WE MADE SURE WE REALLY KNEW WHAT WE WERE TALKING ABOUT FIRST.*

NELU MIAH
(SEE RAX INTERVIEW
ON PAGE 134).

☆b

# VOTES AT SIXTEEN

**THE** VOTES AT 16 COALITION IS A YOUTH-LED CAMPAIGN ADVOCATING FOR A CHANGE TO THE CURRENT UK VOTING SYSTEM, WHICH ONLY ALLOWS PEOPLE 18 AND OVER TO VOTE. THE CAMPAIGN POINTS OUT THAT, AT 16, YOUNG PEOPLE CAN JOIN THE ARMY, PAY TAXES, LEAVE HOME, CHOOSE TO LEAVE SCHOOL, GET MARRIED, HAVE CONSENTING SEX, HAVE A BABY AND WORK FULL TIME BUT STILL THEY DON'T HAVE THE RIGHT TO VOTE. IN AUSTRIA, BRAZIL, NICARAGUA, CUBA, THE ISLE OF MAN, JERSEY AND GUERNSEY, PEOPLE AGED 16 AND 17 ARE ALLOWED TO VOTE.

**LEARN MORE/GET INVOLVED**: www.votesat16.org.uk  www.byc.org.uk ☆d

# The GIFT of the GAB

vote at 16 and, if possible, found out the opinions of politicians, too.

### IF YOU ARE DEALING WITH A GLOBAL ISSUE,

it is vital to gather the opinions of organizations already campaigning on the matter. You should speak to a wide variety of UK citizens – especially to people who are linked to the subject through family or experience. You will also increase your chances of success if you use 21st-century technology to consult people in the countries most affected by your issue.

### FOR EXAMPLE,

if you were campaigning for people to have the right to vote at the age of 16, then it would be important to have gathered the opinions of older people as well as young people. You would also need to have contacted organizations that are already campaigning for the

---

**WHEN YOUR ADVOCACY OR REPRESENTATION REFLECTS A WIDE VARIETY OF VIEWS ON THE ISSUE, YOU ARE SHOWING THAT YOUR CAMPAIGN IS BALANCED AND WELL THOUGHT OUT.**

---

## (E) MAKE IT PERSONAL

*Facts* and statistics give great weight to your argument, but something else that can really win people over is when you add stories that are personal. For example, if you are advocating for a campaign to raise awareness about the HIV/AIDS pandemic in Africa, use true stories and real people to bring your arguments home to people and add impact. In the same way, if you are advocating for more connection between politicians and the younger generations, say what it feels like for you personally not to have enough connection and what a difference it would make to you if you did.

**IF YOU HAVE TAKEN CARE IN CHOOSING YOUR CAMPAIGN ISSUE, THEN YOU WILL BE PASSIONATE ABOUT IT. SPEAK FROM THE HEART AND YOU WILL WIN PEOPLE OVER.**

### A RECENT EXAMPLE

of using personal material to good effect was in a Greenpeace video campaign advocating for action on climate change. The video featured a young boy describing what life in the future could be like if nothing was done about global warming. The boy was angry with all the adults in power who had so far failed to take action. He pointed out that while the politicians will not be around to suffer the severe negative effects of climate change, he will. This had enormous impact. Because the boy was talking about his own feelings and how his life would be affected, the Greenpeace campaign received a large amount of attention.

---

**A PERSONAL CONNECTION MAKES YOUR ARGUMENT REAL TO YOUR AUDIENCE AND WILL AFFECT THEM EMOTIONALLY.**

---

## IN GROUPS

## NEWSPAPER GAME

*In* groups, USE YOUR NEWSPAPERS AND MAGAZINES OR ONLINE NEWS RESOURCES TO FIND AS MANY PERSONAL STORIES AS POSSIBLE THAT COULD BE USED TO MAKE PEOPLE CARE ABOUT THE ISSUE OF POVERTY IN THE UK.

You have **FIVE MINUTES.**

The winner is the group to have found the most stories once the rest of the class has verified them.

## HOW CAN WE CONNECT TO YOUNG PEOPLE?

## HOW CAN WE CONNECT TO POLITICIANS?

# WHAT DO YOU WANT?

**OFTEN,** PEOPLE DO NOT REALIZE THAT POLITICIANS ARE VERY KEEN TO HEAR FROM THEIR CONSTITUENTS IN ORDER TO KNOW WHAT ISSUES ARE OF CONCERN TO THEM. HOW CAN AN MP REPRESENT YOU IF YOU DON'T CONNECT WITH THEM? ONE OF THE FIRST THINGS A YOUNG CAMPAIGNER MUST DO IS TO WRITE TO THEIR MP. MAKE SURE YOU ARE INFORMED ABOUT YOUR ISSUE AND ABOUT THE ISSUES THAT YOUR MP STANDS FOR.

*YOUNG PEOPLE MUST TAKE AN INTEREST IN CURRENT AFFAIRS AND IN WHAT THE POLITICIANS ARE DOING ON THEIR BEHALF AND MAKE THEIR OPINIONS KNOWN TO THOSE POLITICIANS.*

LORD PHILLIPS, PRESIDENT OF THE SUPREME COURT OF THE UK (SEE RAX INTERVIEW ON PAGE 169).

**LEARN MORE/GET INVOLVED:**
www.writetothem.com www.parliament.uk

*BE CALM BUT PASSIONATE.*
ROBBIE GILLETT (SEE RAX INTERVIEW ON PAGE 159).

# ANGRY KID

STILL FROM GREENPEACE VIDEO CAMPAIGN

*WE WON'T BE CUTE. WE WON'T BE PATRONIZED AND WE WILL NOT BE DENIED OUR FUTURE.*

**LEARN MORE/GET INVOLVED:** www.greenpeace.org

*OFTEN THE MOST POWERFUL WAY TO EXPRESS YOUR CAUSE IS TO BE PERSONAL... IF YOU CAN TELL A STORY THAT SAYS HOW SOMETHING IS AFFECTING YOU, AND HOW IT WILL AFFECT THEM TOO, YOU'LL HAVE THEIR FULL ATTENTION AND THEY'LL REALLY WANT TO DO SOMETHING.*

UKYCC (SEE RAX INTERVIEW ON PAGE 104).

# DUMP A KNIFE SAVE A LIFE

**WHEN** A 21-YEAR-OLD MAN FROM ANGLESEY, NORTH WALES, WAS STABBED TO DEATH, HIS FAMILY AND COMMUNITY RALLIED TOGETHER TO CREATE A CAMPAIGN. IN FEBRUARY 2010, 1,200 PEOPLE MARCHED WITH THE VICTIM'S FAMILY TO SHOW SUPPORT AND RAISE AWARENESS OF THE DANGERS OF CARRYING KNIVES. THE CAMPAIGN ACHIEVED MASS SUPPORT, NATIONAL COVERAGE AND OVER 5,000 NAMES ON A PETITION. THE YOUNG MAN'S FAMILY MEMBERS WERE OVERWHELMED AND SAID THAT THEY FELT HIS DEATH WAS NOT IN VAIN IF THE CAMPAIGN HAD SUCCEEDED IN EDUCATING PEOPLE ABOUT THE ISSUE AND MIGHT HAVE SAVED OTHER PEOPLE'S LIVES.

WHEN THE FAMILY AND FRIENDS OF SOMEONE AFFECTED BY AN ISSUE ORGANIZE A CAMPAIGN THEMSELVES, THEIR PERSONAL CONNECTION MAKES IT EASIER FOR THEM TO GATHER SUPPORT.

**LEARN MORE/GET INVOLVED:** www.knifecrimes.org www.itsnotagame.org www.benkinsella.org.uk www.familiesutd.com

RACE IS JUST A PIGMENT OF THE IMAGINATION. (GLEN HIGHLAND)

# The GIFT of the GAB

## (F) BE INCLUSIVE

*Letting* your audience know that you understand how they feel can be very effective. People need to feel you are connecting with them, whether you are giving a speech or writing a letter. It takes careful planning to be able to shape your words so that as many different people as possible feel included in your message.

### FOR EXAMPLE,

if you want to make a change in your community, make it clear that you have grown up there and mention aspects of the area that everyone will identify with. You will also need to show that you understand all the different viewpoints within the community.

You may have an idea for a new local skate park. For this to work, you would do well to include in your advocacy not only how young people will feel about it but also how the elderly will react. In your speeches and letters,

let the elderly know that you are speaking with them in mind too. You may assume that elderly people will be against a new skate park but, once you have spoken to them and understood their perspective, you may find that they come around to your way of thinking. They may be persuaded that young people who are occupied in doing something positive will be happier and make for a safer environment. It would be best if you made a point of including members of the elderly from the early stages of the planning for the campaign.

In the same way, your skate park campaign would have a far better chance of success if you included local businesses, community groups and the council from the outset.

**ALLOW PEOPLE THE OPPORTUNITY TO SEE HOW THEY ARE CONNECTED TO YOU, HOW THEY MAY EVEN FEEL THE SAME AS YOU AND CAN IDENTIFY WITH YOU. AFTER ALL, ADULTS KNOW WHAT IT WAS LIKE TO BE YOUNG, SO REMIND THEM OF THAT (BUT DON'T MAKE THEM TOO JEALOUS!).**

## THE MORE THAT PEOPLE FEEL THEY CAN IDENTIFY WITH YOU AND ARE BEING INCLUDED BY YOU, THE EASIER IT WILL BE TO WIN THEIR SUPPORT.

## RECORD BOOK

*Report* on the class activities under the headings:

WAYS TO USE LANGUAGE TO MAKE A CONVINCING ARGUMENT:

USING 3.9.27 TO REACH TWO DIFFERENT AUDIENCES.

SEARCHING NEWS SOURCES TO FIND PERSONAL STORIES CONNECTED TO THE ISSUE OF POVERTY IN THE UK.

Notes on any class feedback sessions.

## (G) PROVIDE SOLUTIONS

*You* always need to be clear about the change you want to see happen. It is no good saying what is wrong if you don't also state clearly your ideas for solutions to that problem.

### FOR EXAMPLE,

the issue of ephebiphobia can be very frustrating but there is no point in complaining about it and getting angry in a letter to your local MP. You should give a reasoned account of what it is, how extensive it is,

how it makes you feel and add in all the statistics showing how common it is. But that's only half of the argument; you will not start to win support until you start suggesting convincing solutions to the problem.

In the same way, it's very easy to get caught up in the negative implications of climate change but it's only when you show people what your solutions to this problem are, that they are going to support you.

## IF YOU DON'T OFFER SOLUTIONS THEN ALL YOU ARE DOING IS SHARING A PROBLEM.

# GREEN SOLUTIONS

FINDING RENEWABLE SOURCES OF ENERGY THAT ARE NON-POLLUTING AND BOUNTIFUL IS THE HOLY GRAIL FOR MUCH OF THE WORLD AT PRESENT. THERE ARE MANY DIRECTIONS TO GO IN, FROM WAVE, SOLAR AND WIND POWER TO NEW TECHNOLOGIES THAT ARE LOOKING AT WATER BECOMING A SOURCE OF POWER OR USING HUGE WINDMILLS IN THE SKY TO TAP IN TO THE JET STREAM FOR WIND ENERGY.

THIS IS A COMPLEX ISSUE AND IT IS NECESSARY TO KEEP UP TO DATE WITH ANY NEW DEVELOPMENTS AS WELL AS CHECKING YOUR SOURCES CAREFULLY. BUT IT IS ALSO AN EXCITING AREA TO LOOK AT AND HOLDS SOME PROMISE OF A BETTER FUTURE FOR ALL.

## LEARN MORE/GET INVOLVED:

www.cat.org.uk
www.zerocarbonbritain.com
www.pirc.info
www.greensolutionsmag.com
www.newscientist.com

# THE MOSQUITO

EEEEEEE

WHEN HOWARD STAPLETON WAS A CHILD, HIS FATHER TOOK HIM TO A FACTORY BUT HE HAD TO RUN OUT IMMEDIATELY AS HIS YOUNG EARS WERE BEING TORTURED BY THE HIGH-FREQUENCY SOUNDS FROM THE MACHINERY. THE ADULT WORKERS IN THE FACTORY WERE UNABLE TO HEAR THE SOUNDS AS, WHEN YOU BECOME OLDER, YOUR HEARING RANGE DIMINISHES.

YEARS LATER, WHEN STAPLETON HAD CHILDREN OF HIS OWN, HE INVENTED A DEVICE THAT EMITTED A HIGH-FREQUENCY SOUND THAT WOULD IRRITATE YOUNG PEOPLE BUT WHICH ADULTS COULD NOT HEAR. THE MOSQUITO WAS BORN AND, UP AND DOWN THE UK, THOUSANDS HAVE BEEN SOLD, MAINLY TO SHOPKEEPERS AND LOCAL AUTHORITIES, WHO USE THE MACHINES TO STOP YOUNG PEOPLE CONGREGATING.

WHAT DO YOU THINK ABOUT THIS? THERE HAVE ALREADY BEEN SOME CAMPAIGNS TRYING TO BAN THESE MACHINES, CLAIMING THAT THEY REPRESENT AN ABUSE OF YOUNG PEOPLE'S RIGHTS BUT, SO FAR, THE MOSQUITO IS SELLING WELL AND REMAINS LEGAL.

SOME YOUNG PEOPLE TURNED THE INVENTION TO THEIR ADVANTAGE. THEY RECORDED THE SOUND AND USED IT AS THEIR RINGTONES. IF THEIR PHONES RANG IN CLASS, THE TEACHER WOULDN'T HEAR IT!

## LEARN MORE/GET INVOLVED:

www.11million.org.uk
www.liberty-human-rights.org.uk/issues/young-peoples-rights

# GRAY PANTHERS

SINCE THE 1970s, THERE HAS BEEN A STEADILY GROWING AND REMARKABLY POWERFUL CAMPAIGNING GROUP IN THE US CALLED THE GRAY PANTHERS. THEY ARE 'INTERGENERATIONAL', WHICH MEANS THAT THEY REPRESENT ALL GENERATIONS, "FROM 9 TO 90". THEY HAVE HAD LAWS CHANGED, COMPANY POLICIES TRANSFORMED AND HAVE EVEN SET UP THEIR OWN CITY WHERE THEY LIVE AS MUCH BY THEIR OWN RULES AS BY THE RULES OF THE COUNTRY. THEY USE ALL FORMS OF CAMPAIGNING, FROM DIRECT ACTION, MASS RALLIES AND EVEN NUDE PROTESTS TO PETITIONS, LOBBYING THEIR REPRESENTATIVES AND USING SOPHISTICATED 21ST-CENTURY TECHNOLOGY. WHY ARE THEY CALLED 'GRAY PANTHERS'? BECAUSE THESE ACTIVISTS ARE USUALLY PEOPLE OVER 60 YEARS OLD.

PENSIONERS IN THE UK ARE ALSO ACTIVE CITIZENS, CAMPAIGNING FOR POSITIVE CHANGE. IN JANUARY 2010, THE NATIONAL PENSIONERS CONVENTION HELD A NUDE PROTEST OUTSIDE A LABOUR CONFERENCE IN BRIGHTON. BECAUSE THEY HAVE RETIRED, MANY PENSIONERS HAVE MUCH MORE TIME TO GET INVOLVED IN CAMPAIGNING. THEY ARE ALSO MORE AWARE OF THE HISTORICAL STRUGGLES FOR NEW RIGHTS AND FREEDOMS AND ARE FAR MORE LIKELY TO FIGHT TO PRESERVE THOSE FREEDOMS AS WELL AS TO WIN NEW ONES. MAKING CONTACT WITH PENSIONERS AND ADDING THEIR SUPPORT TO YOUR CAMPAIGN COULD BRING POWERFUL RESULTS. PENSIONERS ARE OFTEN KEEN TO WORK WITH YOUNG PEOPLE TO IMPROVE THEIR CHANCES OF HAVING A BETTER FUTURE BUT IT ALL COMES DOWN TO COMMUNICATING WITH THEM FIRST.

## LEARN MORE/GET INVOLVED:

www.npcuk.org www.ageuk.org www.graypanthers.org www.age-platform.org

## ACTIVITY — IN GROUPS

### HEADS TOGETHER

UK MOBILE PHONE USERS DISCARD AROUND 150 MILLION PHONES EVERY YEAR BUT ONLY 10% OF THESE ARE RECYCLED. MOBILE PHONES CONTAIN SMALL AMOUNTS OF TOXIC ELEMENTS THAT CAN BE HARMFUL TO THE ENVIRONMENT BUT, WHEN RECYCLED, THESE CAN BE USED IN NEW PHONES OR FOR OTHER ELECTRONIC DEVICES.

*In* groups, you have **TEN MINUTES** to discuss this problem and come up with three different campaign ideas that provide practical solutions.

Feed back your ideas to the class.

## H SHOW THE OUTCOMES OF TAKING ACTION

*Whatever* your campaign for change, there will be many outcomes if it is successful. A powerful way to convince people to support you is to put great emphasis on what will happen if the campaign succeeds. The outcomes of a campaign can be divided into short and long term.

### FOR EXAMPLE,

the short-term outcome of a successful campaign to provide education for all children in developing countries would be that young people would have a better chance of avoiding poverty and finding employment. The long-term outcome would be that there would be more educated young adults who are trained in a variety of skills such as law, economics, engineering and politics. This might have another result in the long run, that their country is better equipped to escape debt. These skilled young people might be able to provide better legal arguments for cancelling old debts to richer countries. They might also suggest more efficient ways of financing within their own country, how to provide a better technical infrastructure and establish a fairer political structure.

In the same way, a campaign that has successfully called for more youth provision in your community will have the short-term outcome that young people are no longer on the streets and are given something positive and constructive to do. In the long term, this might establish new ways in which the community can work together. It might also open young people up to new career paths that they did not know about before.

DRAWING YOUR AUDIENCE'S ATTENTION TO THE SHORT-TERM AND LONG-TERM OUTCOMES OF YOUR CAMPAIGN STRENGTHENS YOUR ARGUMENT AND THE CHANCES OF WINNING THEIR SUPPORT.

## I MAKE CONNECTIONS

*You* have already seen how campaigns for change are almost always interconnected. For example, Craig Kielburger showed how the flower industry in East Africa can be connected to poverty, environmental damage and child labour.

In your advocacy, it's always important to show the bigger picture in this way.

### FOR EXAMPLE,

if you are campaigning for people to recycle their clothes more then you should explain what effect this will have. In this case, you would do well to talk about how buying fewer clothes and recycling the ones you don't want might cut down on 'sweated' labour in clothing factories overseas. Recycling clothes also encourages more unwanted clothing to be donated to charitable organizations, and the money earned from selling them offers developing countries more financial support. Recycling clothes connects to environmental issues in many ways. For example, the carbon emissions involved in transporting clothes around the world would be cut. So too would the environmental damage caused by dyes and other toxic chemicals in the areas where the clothes are manufactured.

MAKING CONNECTIONS TO OTHER ISSUES SHOWS THAT SUPPORTING YOUR CAMPAIGN HAS OTHER POSITIVE EFFECTS ON TOP OF THE OBVIOUS ONES.

# FAIR PAY

**BRITISH** WORKERS' RIGHTS TO PAID HOLIDAYS, PAID SICK LEAVE AND HEALTH AND SAFETY PROTECTION ARE THE RESULTS OF HUNDREDS OF YEARS OF CAMPAIGNING. TODAY, THE TRADE UNIONS, WHICH REPRESENT MANY UK WORKERS, ARE STILL ACTIVELY CAMPAIGNING ON NEW ISSUES.

IN 2006, THE RAIL MARITIME AND TRANSPORT UNION (RMT) BEGAN A CAMPAIGN TO SUPPORT THE CLEANING STAFF IN TUBE STATIONS. THEY WERE BEING PAID LOW WAGES AND HAD MANY OF THEIR BENEFITS AND FREEDOMS CUT BY THEIR EMPLOYERS. AFTER A TWO-YEAR CAMPAIGN, INCLUDING STRIKE ACTION, RALLIES AND RAISING AWARENESS THROUGH MEDIA, THEY WON. THEIR PAY WENT FROM £5.85 AN HOUR TO £7.20 AN HOUR. THIS HAD A SIGNIFICANT IMPACT ON THE LIVES OF THESE WORKERS.

THE SHORT-TERM OUTCOME OF THIS CAMPAIGN WAS THAT THE TUBE CLEANERS RECEIVED A FAIRER WAGE. THE LONG-TERM OUTCOME HAS BEEN THAT OTHER CAMPAIGNS HAVE BEEN INSPIRED TO CALL FOR FAIRER WAGES AND FAIRER TREATMENT OF WORKING PEOPLE ACROSS THE UK.

**LEARN MORE/GET INVOLVED:**
www.rmt.org.uk
(SEE RAX INTERVIEW WITH BOB CROW ON PAGE 168)

PROTECT **OUR** PENSIONS

OFFICIAL DISPUTE: DEFEND POSTAL SERVICES

A DECENT LIVING WAGE FOR POSTAL WORKERS

NEGOTIATE **NOT** REITERATE

## THE WOMEN OF KERALA

**IF** YOU WERE TO BE ADVOCATING FOR HIGHER LEVELS OF FEMALE EDUCATION IN A COUNTRY THEN IT WOULD BE IMPORTANT TO USE THE INDIAN STATE OF KERALA AS A REFERENCE. KERALA IS AN INDIAN STATE THAT HAS HAD A SOCIALIST GOVERNMENT FOR MANY YEARS. THE LITERACY RATE OF WOMEN HERE IS HIGHER THAN IN ANY OTHER STATE IN INDIA. IT IS NO COINCIDENCE THAT KERALA ALSO HAS THE LOWEST RATES OF INFANT AND MATERNAL MORTALITY IN INDIA AS WELL AS HIGHER PROPORTIONS OF WOMEN IN POSITIONS OF POWER AND LOWER RATES OF ABUSE AGAINST WOMEN. EDUCATING GIRLS IMPROVES THE WHOLE OF SOCIETY – IT BOOSTS ECONOMIC DEVELOPMENT AND IMPROVES THE HEALTH OF THIS GENERATION AND THE NEXT.

THIS IS A GOOD EXAMPLE OF HOW A CAMPAIGN ON ONE ISSUE CAN LINK TO OTHER ISSUES.

## FROM LOCAL TO NATIONAL AND GLOBAL

**ON** A LOCAL LEVEL, YOUNG PEOPLE CAN HAVE A DRAMATIC EFFECT ON THEIR COMMUNITY IN MANY AREAS THAT AREN'T ALWAYS CLEAR AT THE TIME.

FOR EXAMPLE, NELU MIAH AND SOPHIE BARDY CREATED THEIR OWN LOCAL CAMPAIGNS FOR MORE YOUTH PROVISION WHEN THEY WERE TEENAGERS. THE LONG-TERM EFFECTS WERE THAT THE COMMUNITY WAS MORE COHESIVE, HAPPIER AND SAFER. HOWEVER, THIS HAD AN IMPACT ON MANY OTHER ISSUES TOO.

YOUNG PEOPLE TAKING AN INTEREST IN SOPHIE'S GARDENING PROJECTS BECAME MORE AWARE OF THE ENVIRONMENT AND, AS A RESULT, RECYCLING INCREASED SIGNIFICANTLY. SIMILARLY, BECAUSE YOUNG PEOPLE BECAME MORE EMPOWERED THROUGH THE YOUTH CLUB THAT NELU AND HIS FRIENDS SET UP, SOME OF THEM WENT ON TO BECOME YOUTH WORKERS. SOME OF THE YOUNG PEOPLE AFFECTED BY THESE CAMPAIGNS ALSO BECAME MORE INVOLVED WITH LOCAL GOVERNMENT, WORKING TO CREATE BETTER STANDARDS OF LIVING AND BETTER COMMUNICATION BETWEEN RESIDENTS AND LOCAL AUTHORITIES.

ALL OF THESE ACTIONS HAD AN EFFECT AT A LOCAL, NATIONAL OR GLOBAL LEVEL. YOU CAN LOOK AT YOUR OWN CAMPAIGNING ISSUE AND MAKE SIMILAR CONNECTIONS.

(SEE RAX INTERVIEWS WITH NELU AND SOPHIE ON PAGES ON PAGES 134 AND 138)

The GIFT of the GAB

## J IF YOU'RE NOT HAVING FUN THEN THERE'S SOMETHING WRONG

*If* your audience has a sense that you are not only passionate about what you are doing but you are also having fun and enjoying it, then this will have a strong positive effect on them. Genuine positive energy is infectious – it can affect everyone in the room if you are giving a speech or anyone who reads something

that you have written. Every one of the young campaigners interviewed for the Toolkit has said that campaigning for change is fun. You may not believe that but until you have run your own campaign and bring about some kind of change, you will not know how true this is.

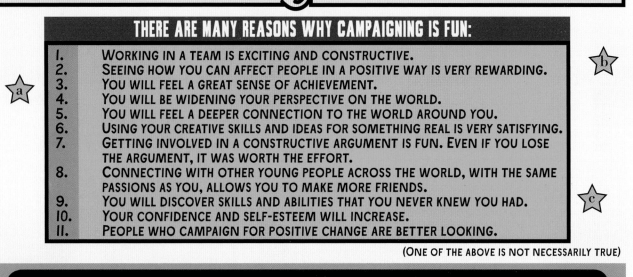

### THERE ARE MANY REASONS WHY CAMPAIGNING IS FUN:

1. WORKING IN A TEAM IS EXCITING AND CONSTRUCTIVE.
2. SEEING HOW YOU CAN AFFECT PEOPLE IN A POSITIVE WAY IS VERY REWARDING.
3. YOU WILL FEEL A GREAT SENSE OF ACHIEVEMENT.
4. YOU WILL BE WIDENING YOUR PERSPECTIVE ON THE WORLD.
5. YOU WILL FEEL A DEEPER CONNECTION TO THE WORLD AROUND YOU.
6. USING YOUR CREATIVE SKILLS AND IDEAS FOR SOMETHING REAL IS VERY SATISFYING.
7. GETTING INVOLVED IN A CONSTRUCTIVE ARGUMENT IS FUN. EVEN IF YOU LOSE THE ARGUMENT, IT WAS WORTH THE EFFORT.
8. CONNECTING WITH OTHER YOUNG PEOPLE ACROSS THE WORLD, WITH THE SAME PASSIONS AS YOU, ALLOWS YOU TO MAKE MORE FRIENDS.
9. YOU WILL DISCOVER SKILLS AND ABILITIES THAT YOU NEVER KNEW YOU HAD.
10. YOUR CONFIDENCE AND SELF-ESTEEM WILL INCREASE.
11. PEOPLE WHO CAMPAIGN FOR POSITIVE CHANGE ARE BETTER LOOKING.

(ONE OF THE ABOVE IS NOT NECESSARILY TRUE)

"IT'S ALL ABOUT BEING FUN AND INNOVATIVE BUT HAVING A CLEAR AND UNDERSTANDABLE MESSAGE. IF IT'S NOT FUN, IT'S NOT THE RIGHT THING TO DO!"

UKYCC (SEE RAX INTERVIEW ON PAGE 104).

### WHOLE CLASS/IN GROUPS

### FIGHT YOUR CORNER

MOTION:

THIS HOUSE BELIEVES THAT YOUNG PEOPLE SHOULD STEER CLEAR OF CAMPAIGNING FOR CHANGE IN THE WORLD AND LEAVE THAT TO THE ADULTS.

### RECORD BOOK

*Report* on the class activities under the headings:

MORE WAYS TO USE LANGUAGE TO MAKE A CONVINCING ARGUMENT:

COMING UP WITH SOLUTIONS TO THE AMOUNT OF MOBILE PHONES THAT ARE DISCARDED EVERY YEAR.

DEBATING WHETHER OR NOT YOUNG PEOPLE HAVE A PLACE IN CAMPAIGNING FOR CHANGE.

Notes on any class feedback sessions.

# FLASH MOB

WAITING FOR THE TEXT

SETTING UP CAMP IN A FLASH!

CLIMATE CAMP TAKES OVER THE STREET!

IN APRIL 2009, THE ENVIRONMENTAL CAMPAIGNING GROUP CLIMATE CAMP SET UP A 'FLASH CAMP' IN THE STREET OUTSIDE THE CENTRE FOR CARBON TRADING IN LONDON'S FINANCIAL DISTRICT.

**LEARN MORE/GET INVOLVED:** www.climatecamp.org.uk

THE ARRIVAL OF SMS ALLOWED FOR A NEW FORM OF CAMPAIGN EVENT CALLED 'FLASH MOBS'. THESE ARE WHEN THOUSANDS OF PEOPLE WHO HAVE SIGNED UP TO AN ORGANIZATION ARE SENT A MESSAGE SIMULTANEOUSLY TO MEET AT A CERTAIN PLACE AT A CERTAIN TIME IN ORDER TO CREATE AN EVENT. SOMETIMES THIS IS FOR FUN BUT OFTEN IT IS TO RAISE AWARENESS ABOUT AN ISSUE.

ONE OF THE EARLIEST MASS FLASH MOBS WAS AT GRAND CENTRAL STATION IN NEW YORK, WHERE HUNDREDS OF PEOPLE ALL FREEZE-FRAMED AT THE SAME MOMENT. THIS CAUSED SHOCK AND CONFUSION AMONGST ALL THE PEOPLE IN THE BUSY STATION WHO WERE NOT IN ON THE SECRET AND HIT THE HEADLINES IN THE MAINSTREAM MEDIA. OTHER FLASH MOBS HAVE INCLUDED PEOPLE MEETING IN PUBLIC SPACES TO DANCE WITH EACH OTHER, HAVE PILLOW FIGHTS, TAKE THEIR TROUSERS OFF ON THE TUBE AND HAVE THUMB FIGHTS!

THESE EVENTS ARE EXCELLENT WAYS TO ATTRACT THE MEDIA, ENGAGE THE INTEREST OF THE PUBLIC AND TO RAISE AWARENESS ABOUT ISSUES. ANOTHER VERY IMPORTANT INGREDIENT IS THAT ALL PEOPLE WHO PARTICIPATE SAY THAT IT IS ONE OF THE MOST ENJOYABLE THINGS THAT THEY HAVE EVER DONE.

THERE ARE SEVERAL SITES ON THE WEB THAT SHOW THESE ACTIONS.

# MUSIC ON THE MARCH

IN 1936, 200 MEN MARCHED 300 MILES TO LONDON IN ORDER TO DRAW ATTENTION TO THE MASS UNEMPLOYMENT IN THEIR HOMETOWN OF JARROW IN NORTHEAST ENGLAND. ONE OF THE INTERESTING FEATURES OF THE MARCH WAS THAT THE MEN INCLUDED A SMALL ORCHESTRA OF MOUTH ORGAN PLAYERS TO GIVE MUSICAL ACCOMPANIMENT TO THEIR LONG MARCH.

THIS TRADITION IS STILL COMMON IN CAMPAIGN ACTIONS TODAY WHERE SAMBA BANDS, SINGERS, MUSICIANS AND MOBILE SOUND SYSTEMS OFTEN ACCOMPANY MARCHES AND RALLIES. THERE ARE ALSO INCREASING NUMBERS OF RAPPERS WHO ACCOMPANY CAMPAIGN ACTIONS: THE EARLY DAYS OF RAP AND HIP HOP WERE CLOSELY TIED TO ACTIVISM AND CAMPAIGNING. DANCING IN THE STREET IN ORDER TO MAKE YOUR VOICE HEARD IS SOMETHING THAT MANY PEOPLE REALLY ENJOY.

**LEARN MORE/GET INVOLVED:**
www.rhythmsofresistance.co.uk
www.caledonian.ac.uk/politicalsong

# CREATIVITY TOOL

AS YOU WILL SEE IN THE CHAPTER CALLED *TOOLS FOR CHANGE*, THERE ARE ALL KINDS OF WAYS IN WHICH PEOPLE HAVE USED THEIR CREATIVITY AND SENSE OF HUMOUR IN CAMPAIGNING FOR POSITIVE CHANGE (AND HAVING GREAT FUN ALONG THE WAY!). FROM MAKING AN ARMY OF SNOWPEOPLE IN FRONT OF GOVERNMENT BUILDINGS IN ORDER TO MAKE A POINT ABOUT CLIMATE CHANGE TO HOLDING A MASS SNOWBALL FIGHT WITH BANKERS TO DRAW ATTENTION TO GLOBAL ECONOMIC ISSUES, CAMPAIGNERS ARE MORE AND MORE FOCUSED ON MAKING SURE HUMOUR IS PART OF THEIR CAMPAIGN STRATEGY.

**LEARN MORE/GET INVOLVED:**
www.spacehijackers.co.uk www.labofii.net
www.criticalmasslondon.org.uk
www.climatecamp.org.uk

SNOW TODAY GONE TOMORROW!

HELP, I'M MELTING!

SNOWPEOPLE'S RIGHTS

Here is an extract from the Record Book of Finley, a school student from Birmingham who used some of the tips recommended in the Toolkit for making a convincing argument. The work took place as Finley and his Year Ten Citizenship Studies group were preparing to give a Year Seven assembly.

## EXTRACT FROM FINLEY'S RECORD BOOK

### THE CHANGE I WOULD LIKE TO SEE

I would like to see people using their power as consumers to put pressure on the clothing industry by insisting on fairer pay and better working conditions for workers in clothing factories in Bangladesh.

12 January

### CITIZENSHIP STUDIES PERIOD FIVE

Meeting with Wayne, Maria, Stella and Luke.

We have a week from today before we are going to give a Year Seven assembly. At the meeting, we divided up the jobs for organizing the event. Maria and Stella are in charge of organizing the assembly. We all worked out a list of things for them to do. Maria even had an idea about a track to play for when we are coming on the stage. We all thought that was a good idea but it made me nervous already about something that's not happening until next week. I know they're Year Sevens but there's still a lot of them!

Wayne was put in charge of organizing all our campaign images and the short film we made for a powerpoint presentation as well as sorting out all the equipment.

Luke and I were put in charge of writing the presentation. We both agreed to meet up after school tomorrow but before then we should both write a basic outline of the speech on our own and then compare notes.

The whole group agreed to meet again on Thursday so we could have an update of how everything is going and the others can give some feedback about our draft for the speech.

12 January

### WORKING AT HOME

I started work on my ideas for the speech. I decided that I SHOULD GET THE THREE MAIN POINTS WORKED OUT FIRST AND BUILD EVERYTHING AROUND THEM. THEY SHOULD BE SHORT AND EASY TO REMEMBER. I looked through all our research for ideas.

There should be one hard-hitting fact that people can remember easily. I decided that

because we are focusing on the workers' conditions, it would be good to highlight the fact that the starting wage is £8 a month.

### MAYBE THE FIRST POINT SHOULD BE SOMETHING LIKE THIS

"Workers in the clothes factories can make as little as £8 a month, which is not enough for them to live on." I should quote the source for the research, how many people they spoke to and the date it was made, so that people know it's reliable.

<u>ANOTHER MAIN POINT</u> is that many of the workers are very young, some of them our age. That's a good point to use because that helps us make the facts personal as they affect people our age. I thought it might be even more effective if we made one section about the typical day for one of these child labourers. To make it even more real and hard-hitting.

I think the <u>THIRD POINT</u> should be about how people can help and what effect that would have, long term and short term. So I looked back at the main campaigning site we are using, that details which shops have the worst record for using slave labour or sweatshop methods. I made a list of the best shops and the worst shops near the school. I then looked at the descriptions of what has happened when people have had campaigns to put pressure on major shops to clean up their act. There are some really good descriptions from workers themselves of how things had changed in their lives. I decided to use two of these descriptions and texted Wayne telling him that he had to dig those two descriptions up for the powerpoint as they had good pictures as well.

The main thing is to get people to write letters, send e-mails and make phone calls to the companies we are targeting. I started to experiment with a poster that would show all three but gave up. I've got the ideas but Stella is a much better artist than I am.

I wanted a catch phrase or sort of slogan so that we could sum up what we wanted people to do. I came up with Consumer Power first as it's not something that people usually think of even though there's lots of examples of how companies really listen when enough consumers contact them. Then I came up with Hand Me Ups because that's playing on the phrase Hand Me Downs, which usually means giving someone old clothes that you've grown out of. With Hand Me Ups you are referring to the idea that you are helping someone by giving them a hand.

### THE THREE MAIN POINTS WE WANT TO GET ACROSS ARE

1 Bangladeshi workers in clothes factories make very little money and work under very harsh conditions.
2 Many of them are our age.
3 By joining our campaign to put pressure on clothing shops that use this kind of slave labour it will improve these people's lives.

 CONTINUED

## The GIFT of the GAB

*Tomorrow, I'm going to work on building up more examples, making sure that the language we use is right for Year Sevens, giving more details about the long-term effects of taking action as well as the short-term ones. I will also see if I can include the point of view of the clothes shops to show that I have thought of them as well. We have to get the main points down to a 3.9.27 statement too so that we can easily get it across to anyone who asks.*

## IN PAIRS

### 3.9.27

*In* pairs, **MAKE A 3.9.27 SPEECH FOR FINLEY'S CAMPAIGN.** This time, you are making your points for an adult audience.

You have **FIVE MINUTES.**

Feed back your ideas to the class.

## 5 What makes a great letter?

**THE 10 POINTS THAT YOU HAVE JUST LOOKED AT COVER ALL THE MAIN IDEAS ABOUT HOW TO MAKE LANGUAGE WORK FOR YOUR CAMPAIGNS AND THEY SHOULD BE CONSIDERED IN EVERYTHING THAT YOU DO.**

*However,* it's worth spending a bit of time looking at the kinds of letters you may have to write as part of your campaigning. You will have covered letter writing in your English lessons but it's important to consider how campaigning letters use special techniques.

### WRITING TO PEOPLE IN AUTHORITY.

**(THIS INCLUDES WRITING TO MPS AND MEMBERS OF YOUR LOCAL AUTHORITY.)**

1. AS IN ALL CAMPAIGNING SITUATIONS, BE POLITE.
2. ALWAYS POINT OUT THAT YOU ARE SCHOOL STUDENTS DOING AN ACTIVE CITIZENSHIP PROJECT. PEOPLE ARE ALMOST ALWAYS KEEN TO HELP YOUNGER PEOPLE.
3. START WITH AN INTRODUCTION ABOUT YOURSELF AND YOUR CAMPAIGN BUT KEEP IT SHORT. THEY WILL WANT TO KNOW WHAT YOU WANT OF THEM AND YOU NEED TO GET TO THAT QUICKLY RATHER THAN ON PAGE FOUR JUST AFTER THE BIT WHEN YOU HAVE GIVEN A DETAILED ACCOUNT OF WHEN YOU CUT YOUR KNEE AFTER FALLING FROM YOUR BIKE LAST WEEK.
4. IF YOU ARE ASKING QUESTIONS OR ASKING FOR HELP, THEN BE COMPLETELY CLEAR ABOUT WHAT YOU WANT.
5. ALWAYS ACKNOWLEDGE THAT THEY ARE BUSY AND THAT THEIR ATTENTION TO YOUR LETTER IS GREATLY APPRECIATED.
6. ALWAYS INCLUDE EASY WAYS FOR THE PERSON TO GET BACK TO YOU.

# MAXINE GENTLE

**IN** 2004, A 14-YEAR-OLD SCOTTISH GIRL DELIVERED A LETTER TO PRIME MINISTER TONY BLAIR AND IMMEDIATELY HIT THE HEADLINES. MAXINE'S BROTHER GORDON HAD DIED IN THE WAR IN IRAQ AND SHE WROTE A LETTER TO THE PM SAYING THAT SHE THOUGHT THE WAR WAS WRONG AND THAT HE SHOULD RECALL ALL THE TROOPS IMMEDIATELY. THE CONTENTS OF MAXINE'S PASSIONATE LETTER WERE MADE PUBLIC IN THE PRESS AND DREW SUPPORT FOR THE GROWING CAMPAIGN AGAINST THE WAR.

**LEARN MORE/GET INVOLVED:** www.mfaw.net www.stopwar.org.uk

## THE ORIGINAL TEXT MESSAGING?

**THE** PICTURE POSTCARD WAS INTRODUCED IN THE UK IN 1894. IT PROVIDED A QUICK, CHEAP AND EASY WAY FOR CITIZENS TO COMMUNICATE ACROSS THE COUNTRY. IN MAJOR CITIES, THERE WERE UP TO 10 COLLECTIONS A DAY, WHICH MEANT THAT YOU COULD POST A CARD TO SOMEONE AND THEY WOULD BE ABLE TO SEND A REPLY THAT WOULD ARRIVE WITH YOU THE SAME DAY. ALTHOUGH THIS WASN'T INSTANT, IT DID CREATE A RELIABLE NETWORK OF COMMUNICATION, WHICH WAS QUICKLY PICKED UP ON BY CAMPAIGNERS OF THE TIME SUCH AS THE SUFFRAGETTES.

JUST AS THERE ARE COMPLAINTS IN THE MEDIA TODAY THAT TEXT MESSAGING IS RUINING PEOPLE'S ABILITY TO USE ENGLISH 'CORRECTLY', THERE WERE SEVERAL ARTICLES BY EDWARDIANS COMPLAINING THAT THE INFORMAL LANGUAGE USED ON POSTCARDS WAS THE BEGINNING OF THE END FOR 'PROPER' ENGLISH. THE COUNTER-ARGUMENT BOTH THEN AND NOW IS THAT LANGUAGE IS ABOUT COMMUNICATION AND IF THE PERSON RECEIVING THE CARD OR TEXT UNDERSTANDS THE MESSAGE THEN IT HAS DONE ITS JOB.

THE IMPORTANT THING IS TO BE CAREFUL IN CHOOSING THE CORRECT LANGUAGE FOR YOUR AUDIENCE.

## BROADBAND WITH FEATHERS

**IN** 2009 AN AMAZING RACE TOOK PLACE IN SOUTH AFRICA. AN IT COMPANY IN DURBAN WANTED TO DISCOVER WHETHER USING A PIGEON CARRIER TO DELIVER A 4GB MEMORY STICK OF DATA TO A COMPANY 50 MILES AWAY WOULD BE QUICKER THAN SENDING THE DATA OVER THE WEB.

WINSTON THE PIGEON DELIVERED THE MEMORY STICK IN TWO HOURS AND THE DATA WAS SOON DOWNLOADED WHILE ONLY 4% OF THE SAME DATA HAD ARRIVED OVER THE WEB IN THE SAME TIME.

**LEARN MORE/GET INVOLVED:** www.postalheritage.org.uk

# SAMANTHA SMITH

**IN** 1982, THE UNITED STATES AND RUSSIA WERE STILL ENGAGED IN WHAT WAS KNOWN AS 'THE ARMS RACE', A DEADLY SITUATION WHERE BOTH COUNTRIES WERE ON CONSTANT ALERT FOR A NUCLEAR ATTACK. THIS CLIMATE OF POSSIBLE WORLD DESTRUCTION WITHIN MINUTES WAS VERY DISTRESSING FOR YOUNG PEOPLE. A 10-YEAR-OLD AMERICAN GIRL DECIDED TO REACT TO THIS BY WRITING TO THE NEW PRESIDENT OF RUSSIA, YURI ANDROPOV. THIS IS HER LETTER:

> Dear Mr Andropov,
> My name is Samantha Smith. I am 10 years old. Congratulations on your new job. I have been worrying about Russia and the United States getting into a nuclear war. Are you going to vote to have a war or not? If you aren't, please tell me how you are going to help to not have a war. This question you do not have to answer, but I would like to know why you want to conquer the world or at least our country. God made the world for us to live together in peace and not to fight.
> Sincerely,
> Samantha Smith

ANDROPOV REPLIED TO SMITH AT LENGTH. HIS LETTER INCLUDED THE LINES,

> Your question is the most important of those that every thinking man can pose. I will reply to you seriously and honestly. We want peace for ourselves and for all peoples of the planet. For our children and for you, Samantha.

THIS CAUSED A MEDIA SENSATION AND SMITH BECAME AN 'AMBASSADOR FOR PEACE', TRAVELLING THE WORLD, ADVOCATING FOR ALL COUNTRIES NEVER TO USE WAR AGAIN. SHE EVEN SUGGESTED A SCHEME WHEREBY US AND RUSSIAN LEADERS WOULD SEND THEIR GRANDCHILDREN TO LIVE IN EACH OTHER'S COUNTRIES ONCE A YEAR, AS EACH LEADER "WOULDN'T WANT TO SEND A BOMB TO A COUNTRY HIS GRANDDAUGHTER WOULD BE VISITING".

**LEARN MORE/GET INVOLVED:** www.samanthasmith.info

## WRITING TO GAIN SUPPORT

### (THIS INCLUDES WRITING FOR ANY WEBSITES OR BLOGS THAT YOU SET UP.)

1. BE BRIEF AND CLEAR BUT MAKE SURE YOU HAVE SOME OF YOUR PASSION IN THERE AND INSPIRE PEOPLE.
2. BE SURE TO USE THE CORRECT LANGUAGE FOR YOUR TARGET AUDIENCE.
3. GIVE SOME HARD-HITTING DETAILS AND FACTS TO SHOW YOU HAVE DONE YOUR RESEARCH AS WELL AS TO GRAB ATTENTION.
4. MAKE IT AS EASY AS POSSIBLE FOR YOUR POTENTIAL SUPPORTERS TO UNDERSTAND EXACTLY WHAT THEY CAN DO TO SUPPORT YOU.
5. BE CLEAR ABOUT WHAT EFFECT THEIR SUPPORT WILL HAVE, SHORT TERM AND LONG TERM. MAKE YOURSELF STAND OUT!

## WRITING TO ASK FOR HELP

### (THIS INCLUDES WRITING TO EXPERTS OR TO PEOPLE FROM WHOM YOU WANT ANY KIND OF HELP.)

1. BE CLEAR ABOUT WHAT YOUR CAMPAIGN IS TRYING TO ACHIEVE.
2. MAKE IT CLEAR THAT THE PERSON WILL BE HELPING THAT CAMPAIGN AND HELPING THOSE ACHIEVEMENTS HAPPEN.
3. MAKE IT CLEAR THAT YOU WILL KEEP THE PERSON IN TOUCH WITH THE PROGRESS OF THE CAMPAIGN.
4. MENTION ANYTHING THAT THE PERSON WILL GET IN RETURN FOR HELPING YOU. FOR EXAMPLE, IF IT IS AN EXPERT WHO YOU WANT TO VISIT YOUR SCHOOL, THEN STATE THAT THEY WILL BE LOOKED AFTER AND HAVE A WARM WELCOME. IF YOU ARE PRODUCING A BOOKLET OR LEAFLET, YOU CAN ALSO ADD THAT YOU WILL BE HAPPY TO MENTION EVERYONE WHO HAS HELPED YOUR CAMPAIGN.
5. ALWAYS GIVE THE PERSON AN ESCAPE ROUTE. FOR EXAMPLE, "I KNOW THAT YOU ARE TREMENDOUSLY BUSY SO IF YOU CANNOT HELP, I WILL UNDERSTAND COMPLETELY." THIS LETS THE PERSON OFF THE HOOK BUT CAN ACTUALLY MEAN THAT THEY ARE MORE LIKELY TO HELP YOU BECAUSE YOU ARE BEING ACCOMMODATING.

## IN GROUPS

### HEADS TOGETHER

*In* groups, IMAGINE YOU ARE A 50-YEAR-OLD BUSINESS MANAGER FOR A SOFT DRINKS COMPANY AND A YEAR 10 CLASS HAS PERSUADED YOU TO COME TO THEIR SCHOOL TO GIVE A PRESENTATION.

How do you expect the students to be?
What are your main fears about this visit?
What will have changed in school since you were a student?
How could your presentation help your business?

You have **TEN MINUTES.**

Feed back your ideas to the class.

# ADD YOUR VOICE ON A POSTCARD

**AMNESTY** INTERNATIONAL (AI) IS ONE OF THE LARGEST CAMPAIGNING GROUPS IN THE WORLD, WITH OVER 2.2 MILLION MEMBERS ADVOCATING FOR HUMAN RIGHTS AND JUSTICE WORLDWIDE. PETER BENENSON, A BRITISH LAWYER, FOUNDED THE GROUP IN 1961. BENENSON HAD WRITTEN AN ARTICLE IN *THE OBSERVER* NEWSPAPER DRAWING ATTENTION TO THE 'FORGOTTEN PRISONERS' IN THE WORLD. THESE WERE PEOPLE WHO HAD BEEN IMPRISONED FOR THEIR IDEAS – 'PRISONERS OF CONSCIENCE'. AI HAS SUCCEEDED IN SAVING THE LIVES OF THOUSANDS OF PEOPLE ACROSS THE WORLD WHO HAD BEEN LOCKED UP AND EVEN TORTURED FOR THEIR IDEAS. ONE OF THEIR MANY CAMPAIGNING TECHNIQUES IS TO DISTRIBUTE FREE POSTCARDS THAT DRAW ATTENTION TO ONE ISSUE. THE CARDS ARE ALREADY ADDRESSED TO A FIGURE IN AUTHORITY RESPONSIBLE FOR THE ABUSE OF HUMAN RIGHTS. IN THIS WAY, INDIVIDUALS WHO HAVE THE POWER TO STOP THE ABUSE ARE INUNDATED WITH SACKS FULL OF ACTIVE VOICES CALLING FOR JUSTICE.

CREATING YOUR OWN POSTCARDS TO GAIN SUPPORT IN THIS WAY IS AN EXCELLENT TOOL TO ADD TO YOUR CAMPAIGN STRATEGY.

## LEARN MORE/GET INVOLVED:

www.amnesty.org.uk

## FREE BINAYAK SEN

**Dear Minister**

Please bring your urgent attention to the case of human rights defender Dr Binayak Sen. Dr Sen was arrested in Chhattisgarh state in May 2007 after he brought to light human rights abuses committed by local authorities. Denied bail, he has been held in detention ever since awaiting trial proceedings which have been repeatedly delayed.

Amnesty International believes the charges against him to be politically motivated and I join the organisation in demanding Dr Sen's immediate and unconditional release.

I also call on you to take urgent steps to end the harassment of human rights defenders in Chhattisgarh state and to allow them to carry out their legitimate work free from fear.

Yours sincerely

Signed:
Name:
Address:

## RAPE IS CHEAPER THAN BULLETS

In conflict zones around the world, military commanders are using rape to terrorise, humiliate and demoralise whole communities.

Amnesty International
**PROTECT THE HUMAN**

## NINE WOMEN'S HUMAN RIGHTS DEFENDERS
### NICARAGUA

'Defending human rights in Nicaragua means taking on emotional, political and personal risks. We are going to keep on, because we believe justice is on our side.'

Luisa Molina, one of the nine human rights defenders

**PROTECT THE HUMAN**
Amnesty International

IAPL049

## 6 How can I use manifestos, slogans and songs?

THESE ARE THREE OTHER WAYS OF USING LANGUAGE THAT CAN HAVE REAL IMPACT ON THE SUCCESS OF YOUR CAMPAIGN AS WELL AS AN IMPACT ON YOUR OWN LIVES. THEY ARE ALL DIFFERENT WAYS OF REPRESENTING YOUR CAMPAIGN AND ADVOCATING FOR YOUR CAUSE.

### MANIFESTO

**A MANIFESTO IS A DECLARATION OF WHAT YOUR GROUP BELIEVES IN, YOUR PRINCIPLES, YOUR POLICIES AND YOUR INTENTIONS.**

*Although* the most popular use of the word refers to a political party's statement of its ideas and policies before an election, manifestos also have a long history in the world of art and the world of grassroots movements.

Once you have established your group and the issue you want to work on, writing your own manifesto is an excellent tool for making sure you are all focused. In the same way as you established the ground rules for how to work with each other, a manifesto helps your group to establish what it stands for. This should also be a democratic process.

A manifesto should not just include the change you would like to see in the world. It should also outline your group's broader vision and the principles it will stick to.

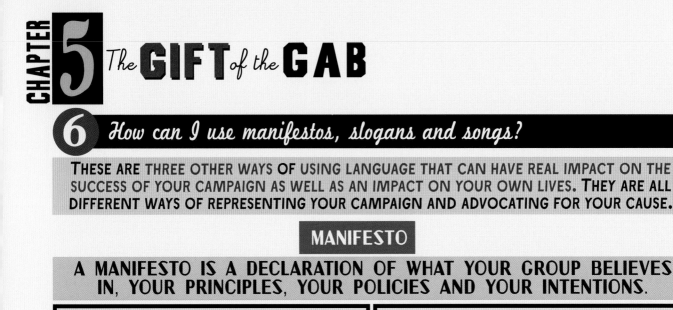

### FOR EXAMPLE,

#### OUR MANIFESTO

WE, THE UNDERSIGNED, BELIEVE IN THE FOLLOWING PRINCIPLES:

1. THAT YOUNG PEOPLE ARE THE FUTURE AND MUST BE HEARD NOW.
2. THAT WE WILL TREAT ALL PEOPLE EQUALLY, WHATEVER GENDER, AGE, RACE OR RELIGION THEY ARE AND WHETHER THEY SUPPORT OUR CAMPAIGN OR NOT.
3. THAT POSITIVE CHANGE IS TO BE SUPPORTED WHENEVER POSSIBLE.
4. THAT WE WILL RESPECT EACH OTHER IN THE GROUP AND SUPPORT EACH OTHER IN ALL OUR EFFORTS.
5. THAT WE WILL RESOLVE ALL PROBLEMS DEMOCRATICALLY.

SIGNED *Halina*       Sabina
*Gulzar*  Rud

### SLOGANS

*If* you are holding a demonstration outside your town hall and someone drives by in his or her car, a slogan painted on a placard is the only way to tell the driver what you are campaigning for. That's how slogans need to work – just a few words that sum up your campaign and hook people in. This is a difficult thing to do well but it is worth putting in the hours to get it right.

# A MANIFESTO FROM THE WORLD OF BUSINESS

A GOOD EXAMPLE OF A MANIFESTO FROM THE WORLD OF BUSINESS COMES FROM THE CO-OPERATIVE BANK. THIS HIGH STREET BANK HAS A STRICT ETHICAL POLICY, SETTING OUT THE TYPES OF BUSINESSES THE BANK WILL AND WILL NOT FINANCE, WHICH ITS CUSTOMERS ARE ABLE TO VOTE ON AND INFLUENCE. AS A RESULT OF THIS MANIFESTO, THE BANK HAS WON PRAISE FROM MANY CAMPAIGNING GROUPS FROM HUMAN RIGHTS ORGANIZATIONS TO ENVIRONMENTAL CAMPAIGNING GROUPS. HERE ARE A FEW EXAMPLES OF STATEMENTS FROM THE CO-OPERATIVE BANK'S ETHICAL POLICY – WHICH ALSO COVERS ANIMAL WELFARE AND SOCIAL ENTERPRISE – SHOWING WHAT PRINCIPLES THE CO-OPERATIVE BANK AND THEIR CUSTOMERS STAND FOR.

## HUMAN RIGHTS

We support the principles of the Universal Declaration of Human Rights. In line with this, we will not finance:
- any government or business which fails to uphold basic human rights within its sphere of influence
- any business whose links to an oppressive regime are a continuing cause for concern
- any organization that advocates discrimination and incitement to hatred
- the manufacture or transfer of armaments to oppressive regimes
- the manufacture or transfer of indiscriminate weapons, e.g. cluster bombs and depleted uranium munitions
- the manufacture or transfer of torture equipment or other equipment that is used in the violation of human rights.

## INTERNATIONAL DEVELOPMENT

We will seek to support poverty reduction. In line with this, we will not finance organizations that:
- fail to implement basic labour rights as set out in the Fundamental ILO Conventions, e.g. avoidance of child labour, or that actively oppose the rights of workers to freedom of association, e.g. in a trade union
- take an irresponsible approach to the payment of tax in the least developed countries
- impede access to basic human necessities, e.g. safe drinking water or vital medicines
- engage in irresponsible marketing practices in developing countries, e.g. with regard to tobacco products and manufacture.

We will support fair trade and the provision of finance to the working poor in developing countries, via microfinance.

## ECOLOGICAL IMPACT

We will not finance any business whose core activity contributes to:
- global climate change, via the extraction or production of fossil fuels (oil, coal and gas), with an extension to the distribution of those fuels that have a higher global warming impact (e.g. tar sands and certain biofuels)
- the manufacture of chemicals that are persistent in the environment, bioaccumulative in nature or linked to long-term health concerns
- the unsustainable harvest of natural resources, including timber and fish
- the development of genetically modified organisms where there is evidence of uncontrolled release into the environment, negative impacts on developing countries, or patenting e.g. of indigenous knowledge
- the development of nanotechnology in circumstances that risk damaging the environment or compromising human health.

Furthermore, we will seek to support: businesses involved in recycling and sustainable waste management, renewable energy and energy efficiency, sustainable natural products and services (including timber and organic produce), and the pursuit of ecological sustainability.

**LEARN MORE/GET INVOLVED**: www.goodwithmoney.co.uk

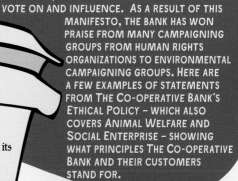

# CHAPTER 5 The GIFT of the GAB

One of our favourite slogans used by a young campaigner is 'Power In The Present, Change In The Future'. This sums up the ideas of Scott Forbes, who started the 'Global Forum 40' international campaign at the age of 19, advocating for greater awareness of HIV/AIDS and equal rights for people who are HIV-positive. The slogan conveys the idea that by acting now, we can change the future.

The Rax Team asked Scott how he came up with the slogan and what advice he could give to other campaigners.

"I spent a good few days sat at a desk scribbling ideas down on paper, getting frustrated that nothing was popping into my mind that was substantial and unique... I then decided to choose some words that I wanted to associate GF40 with. These were: knowledge, global, change, power, future, weapon and so on... I then went back to playing with these words; it becomes more easy and fruitful. I started coming out with a whole string of slogans such as:

'Knowledge is your Power', 'Knowledge is your Weapon', 'You have the Power to Change your Future', 'Global Youth. Local Knowledge'. But still nothing leaped out at me.

"Then all of a sudden something sparked; staring at those words and constantly going over them in my mind I found the perfect slogan: 'Power in the Present, Change in the Future'. This really encompasses everything GF40 sets out to do; it's fresh, punchy, youthful, strong and most of all catchy.

"So what advice would I give to young campaigners? Try not to get stressed, scribble some ideas and words down on paper, and have fun, as this really shouldn't be a boring exercise. Get some friends over to help you... But generally speaking, if your heart is in the right place and you're passionate about the topic, finding a slogan shouldn't be so difficult. Remember these three Ps – 'Be patient, be persistent, be positive – and ideas will flow."

## RECORD BOOK

*Report* on the class activities under the headings:

**MORE WAYS TO USE LANGUAGE TO MAKE A CONVINCING ARGUMENT:**

**COMING UP WITH A 3.9.27 STATEMENT FOR AN ADULT AUDIENCE, ADVOCATING FOR CONSUMERS TO INSIST THAT COMPANIES PROVIDE BETTER WORKING CONDITIONS IN THEIR CLOTHES FACTORIES.**

**IMAGINING THE POINT OF VIEW OF AN ADULT BUSINESS MANAGER VISITING A SCHOOL.**

Notes on any class feedback sessions.

## SONGS

*A song* can be a useful tool for your campaigns as music is a universal language that can speak across cultures and social divides. You can consider creating music and even a film to go with it for your campaigns but it should only be part of your overall campaign, not the campaign itself.

Underground music is often at the centre of major cultural movements. The first 'youth quakes' of the 1960s advocated peace, love and the questioning of authority. In the 1970s came the anti-racist and anti-authoritarian punk rock movement while the rave culture of the 1980s advocated alternative living and the end of class barriers. Then, in the 1990s, came the emergence of rap and hip hop, which advocated questioning authority and celebrated street culture.

For active citizens of any era, there will always be an emerging or underground music culture which forms part of your identity. You will have the ability to tap into this in order to spread your ideas for change. 21st-century digital technologies make this a far easier process than it has ever been before.

However, writing lyrics and songs for campaigns is a difficult task, as it is hard to advocate for an idea for change lyrically without sounding like you are preaching – nobody likes being told what to do.

130

SCOTT FORBES' FINAL LOGO WITH SLOGAN

ALTHOUGH THERE HAVE BEEN ATTEMPTS BY THE GOVERNMENT TO REMOVE HAW, HE HAS WON THE LEGAL RIGHT TO REMAIN IN THE SQUARE. HE ORIGINALLY HAD A LARGE DISPLAY OF PLACARDS FILLED WITH ANTI-WAR SLOGANS AND INFORMATION SHOWING THE HARM CAUSED TO CIVILIANS IN IRAQ AND AFGHANISTAN BUT, IN 2006, POLICE REMOVED A LARGE NUMBER OF THESE. HE HAS BECOME A SYMBOL OF THE ANTI-WAR MOVEMENT AND WON PRAISE AND SUPPORT FROM HUNDREDS OF THOUSANDS OF ORDINARY CITIZENS AS WELL AS FROM MANY CAMPAIGNING ORGANIZATIONS AND SOME POLITICIANS. IN 2007, HAW WON CHANNEL 4'S MOST INSPIRING POLITICAL FIGURE AWARD.

LEARN MORE/GET INVOLVED:
www.parliament-square.org.uk www.stopwar.org.uk

# BRIAN HAW

ON 2 JUNE 2001, BRIAN HAW SET UP CAMP IN PARLIAMENT SQUARE, LONDON, OPPOSITE THE HOUSES OF PARLIAMENT, AND BEGAN A ONE-MAN CAMPAIGN AGAINST THE ECONOMIC SANCTIONS IMPOSED ON IRAQ. WHEN WAR IN IRAQ WAS DECLARED, HAW'S CAMPAIGN BECAME A PRO-PEACE CAMPAIGN. MORE THAN 3,000 DAYS LATER, HE IS STILL THERE IN 2010. RIGHT FROM THE BEGINNING, HE MADE THE REASONS FOR HIS ACTION CLEAR:

"I WANT TO GO BACK TO MY OWN KIDS AND LOOK THEM IN THE FACE AGAIN KNOWING THAT I'VE DONE ALL I CAN TO TRY AND SAVE THE CHILDREN OF IRAQ AND OTHER COUNTRIES WHO ARE DYING BECAUSE OF MY GOVERNMENT'S UNJUST, AMORAL, FEAR- AND MONEY-DRIVEN POLICIES. THESE CHILDREN AND PEOPLE OF OTHER COUNTRIES ARE EVERY BIT AS VALUABLE AND WORTHY OF LOVE AS MY PRECIOUS WIFE AND CHILDREN."

131

# The GIFT of the GAB

The Toolkit includes interviews with well-known musicians and singers giving their ideas about writing songs and many of you will already be budding rappers, singers or songwriters yourselves. Below are just a few ideas to help you create songs for change.

**A** THIS IS NOT A DEBATE OR A SPEECH; RATHER THAN FOCUS ON FACTS AND STATISTICS, FOCUS ON FEELINGS. MUSIC IS A LANGUAGE THAT SPEAKS TO THE EMOTIONS.

**B** MAKE THE SONG PERSONAL; THIS CAN MEAN DESCRIBING YOUR OWN THOUGHTS AND FEELINGS ABOUT AN ISSUE OR THE THOUGHTS AND FEELINGS OF AN IMAGINED CHARACTER WHO IS AFFECTED BY AN ISSUE.

**C** USE IMAGERY TO COMMUNICATE YOUR IDEAS. STRONG METAPHORS AND SIMILES WORK WELL IN ALL LYRICS BUT WITH CAMPAIGNING SONGS THEY HELP YOU TO AVOID SOUNDING TOO OBVIOUS OR 'PREACHY'.

**D** TRY TO USE THE FIVE SENSES IN YOUR LYRICS – THINK ABOUT IMAGERY THAT RELATES TO SOUND, SMELL, TOUCH, TASTE OR SIGHT. THIS HELPS YOU TO GET UNDER THE SKIN OF THE AUDIENCE.

**E** TIGHT RHYMING THAT SEEMS EFFORTLESS DEEPLY ENGAGES AN AUDIENCE WHEREAS CLUMSY RHYMING LOSES AN AUDIENCE.

**F** A GREAT CHORUS FOR A CAMPAIGNING SONG SHOULD SUM UP THE MAIN POINT OF THE LYRICS; IT SHOULD ALSO MAKE THE AUDIENCE FEEL LIKE SINGING ALONG AND THAT THEY ARE PART OF THE MESSAGE. CHORUSES THAT ARE UPLIFTING LEAVE THE AUDIENCE FEELING HOPEFUL AND OPTIMISTIC.

**G** CARRY A NOTEPAD WITH YOU AT ALL TIMES, AS YOU NEVER KNOW WHEN A GOOD LINE WILL COME TO YOU.

## ACTIVITY — IN PAIRS/GROUPS

### BE THE BARD

In pairs or groups, you have **10 MINUTES** to **WRITE A SET OF LYRICS FOR A CAMPAIGN OF YOUR CHOICE,** use as many of the ideas above as you can. This song may be best as a rap. Beat-boxing is welcomed!

**YOU HAVE FIVE MINUTES TO PRACTISE YOUR SONG.**

Perform your song to the class.

## ACTIVITY — IN PAIRS

### ART ACTION

In pairs, you have **10 MINUTES** to **CREATE A PIECE OF ART - USING ANY OF THE ART ACTION METHODS -** to accompany one of the class's songs from the last Be The Bard activity.

Feed back your ideas to the class.

## RECORD BOOK

Report on the class activities under the headings:

**WRITING A CAMPAIGN SONG. CREATING ART TO BACK UP A CAMPAIGN SONG.**

Notes on any class feedback sessions.

"DON'T FORCE IT, DON'T TRY TO FIND WRITING! JUST GO TO WHERE, WHEN, HOW... YOU FEEL MOST INSPIRED, DIS-ATTACH, KEEP A PEN CLOSE AND LET WRITING FIND YOU!"

MS DYNAMITE (SEE RAX INTERVIEW ON PAGE 135).

## 7 Rax Interview with Nelu Miah

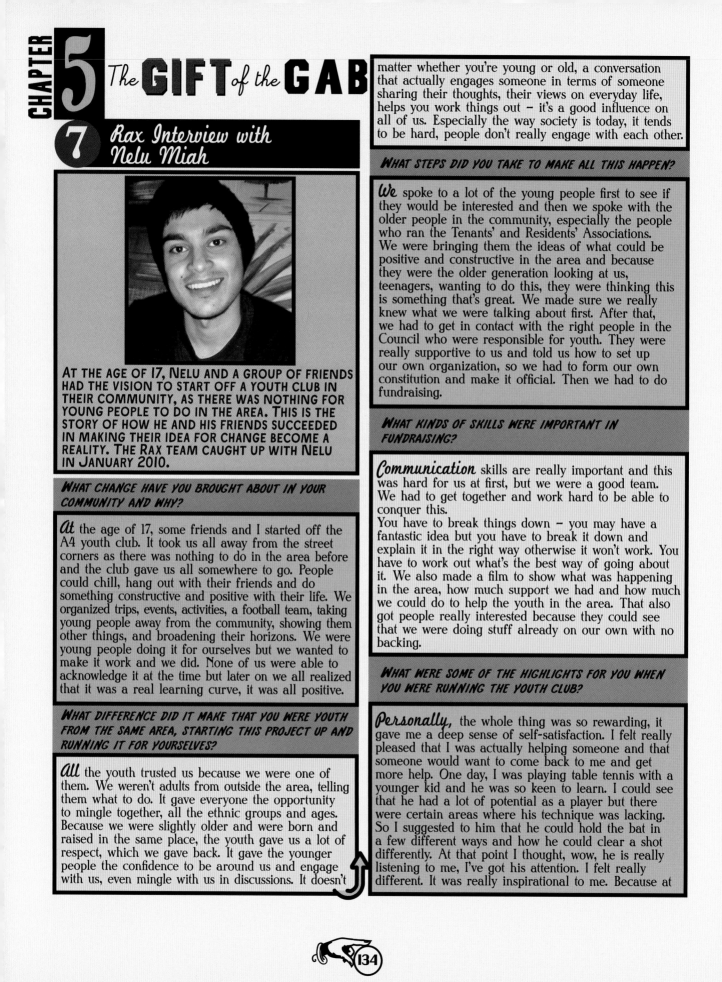

AT THE AGE OF 17, NELU AND A GROUP OF FRIENDS HAD THE VISION TO START OFF A YOUTH CLUB IN THEIR COMMUNITY, AS THERE WAS NOTHING FOR YOUNG PEOPLE TO DO IN THE AREA. THIS IS THE STORY OF HOW HE AND HIS FRIENDS SUCCEEDED IN MAKING THEIR IDEA FOR CHANGE BECOME A REALITY. THE RAX TEAM CAUGHT UP WITH NELU IN JANUARY 2010.

### WHAT CHANGE HAVE YOU BROUGHT ABOUT IN YOUR COMMUNITY AND WHY?

At the age of 17, some friends and I started off the A4 youth club. It took us all away from the street corners as there was nothing to do in the area before and the club gave us all somewhere to go. People could chill, hang out with their friends and do something constructive and positive with their life. We organized trips, events, activities, a football team, taking young people away from the community, showing them other things, and broadening their horizons. We were young people doing it for ourselves but we wanted to make it work and we did. None of us were able to acknowledge it at the time but later on we all realized that it was a real learning curve, it was all positive.

### WHAT DIFFERENCE DID IT MAKE THAT YOU WERE YOUTH FROM THE SAME AREA, STARTING THIS PROJECT UP AND RUNNING IT FOR YOURSELVES?

All the youth trusted us because we were one of them. We weren't adults from outside the area, telling them what to do. It gave everyone the opportunity to mingle together, all the ethnic groups and ages. Because we were slightly older and were born and raised in the same place, the youth gave us a lot of respect, which we gave back. It gave the younger people the confidence to be around us and engage with us, even mingle with us in discussions. It doesn't

matter whether you're young or old, a conversation that actually engages someone in terms of someone sharing their thoughts, their views on everyday life, helps you work things out – it's a good influence on all of us. Especially the way society is today, it tends to be hard, people don't really engage with each other.

### WHAT STEPS DID YOU TAKE TO MAKE ALL THIS HAPPEN?

We spoke to a lot of the young people first to see if they would be interested and then we spoke with the older people in the community, especially the people who ran the Tenants' and Residents' Associations. We were bringing them the ideas of what could be positive and constructive in the area and because they were the older generation looking at us, teenagers, wanting to do this, they were thinking this is something that's great. We made sure we really knew what we were talking about first. After that, we had to get in contact with the right people in the Council who were responsible for youth. They were really supportive to us and told us how to set up our own organization, so we had to form our own constitution and make it official. Then we had to do fundraising.

### WHAT KINDS OF SKILLS WERE IMPORTANT IN FUNDRAISING?

Communication skills are really important and this was hard for us at first, but we were a good team. We had to get together and work hard to be able to conquer this.
You have to break things down – you may have a fantastic idea but you have to break it down and explain it in the right way otherwise it won't work. You have to work out what's the best way of going about it. We also made a film to show what was happening in the area, how much support we had and how much we could do to help the youth in the area. That also got people really interested because they could see that we were doing stuff already on our own with no backing.

### WHAT WERE SOME OF THE HIGHLIGHTS FOR YOU WHEN YOU WERE RUNNING THE YOUTH CLUB?

Personally, the whole thing was so rewarding, it gave me a deep sense of self-satisfaction. I felt really pleased that I was actually helping someone and that someone would want to come back to me and get more help. One day, I was playing table tennis with a younger kid and he was so keen to learn. I could see that he had a lot of potential as a player but there were certain areas where his technique was lacking. So I suggested to him that he could hold the bat in a few different ways and how he could clear a shot differently. At that point I thought, wow, he is really listening to me, I've got his attention. I felt really different. It was really inspirational to me. Because at the time, I was only 17, it was a big step for me mentally, for me to be going out of my way to be actually helping someone else and at the same time, to be feeling good about it. When I experienced that, I thought, "this is what I really want to do".

**YOU HAVE TO REALIZE THERE WAS NOTHING FOR ANYONE YOUNG TO DO. WE WERE ALL COMING OFF THE STREETS AND THE STREET CORNERS AND THEN TO HAVE SOMEONE PICKING UP ON SOMETHING AND LEARNING SOMETHING AND DOING SOMETHING POSITIVE, IT MEANT A LOT TO ME. IT MAKES YOU FEEL REALLY GOOD ABOUT YOURSELF.**

### *WHAT KIND OF DIFFERENCE DID YOU MAKE TO THE COMMUNITY AS A WHOLE?*

**To** be honest, as soon as the youth club started, it made the community as one. Before the youth club, everyone was kind of separated, people weren't talking to each other, everyone had their own little gang. Now everyone knows each other, everyone is together and it's great. It's peaceful. It's a friendly environment, and that's what you want society to be. You want it to be friendly, you want it to be comfortable, no matter how old you are.

**AS SOON AS THE CLUB WAS OPEN, EVERYONE WAS ENGAGING WITH EACH OTHER. NOW EVERYONE KNOWS EACH OTHER, EVERYONE IS TOGETHER AND IT'S GREAT. IT'S PEACEFUL. IT'S A FRIENDLY ENVIRONMENT, AND THAT'S WHAT YOU WANT SOCIETY TO BE.**

### *WHAT WOULD BE YOUR THREE TOP TIPS FOR YOUNG PEOPLE WHO WANT TO START OFF THEIR OWN YOUTH CLUB?*

**You** have to form a team: it's very important to have the right group of people there who you can all trust and work with well; all sharing the same thoughts and all sharing the same passion. Second, get yourself around to all the local community groups, representing yourselves, letting them know what you want to do, getting their support and getting across the positive ideas you have and inspiring them with the same ideas. Finally, you need to get in touch with the right people. For us, it was the local authority. You have to have the right vision and then know how to break it down and make it clear so that anybody can understand it and will be inspired by it too.

MS DYNAMITE IS ONE OF THE MOST INFLUENTIAL HIP HOP AND RAP SINGERS IN THE UK TODAY. SHE HAS WON TWO BRIT AWARDS AND THREE MOBO AWARDS. THE RAX TEAM CAUGHT UP WITH HER IN JANUARY 2010.

### *WHAT KINDS OF ISSUES DO YOU THINK YOUNG PEOPLE SHOULD ADDRESS IN THE UK TODAY?*

**I** don't feel it's for me to 'tell' young people what they should be addressing. I actually feel that that's part of society's problem. The people in authority talk a lot but don't listen much!!! Listening is KEY in teaching, enforcing rules and laws and is absolutely paramount in trying to 'run' a productive, positive, progressive society. We are under the misconception that the more years you have, the more intelligence and rights you have, when in actual fact all that 'really/naturally' comes with age is more authority; and that's not even always true. It's down to the individual to grow and gain more knowledge and wisdom along the way. I've met many a 13 year old that could teach many a 30 year old A LOT about what 'they' should be addressing!!! (But that's another matter, lol!).

### *WHAT WOULD YOU SAY TO YOUR TEENAGE SELF, NOW THAT YOU ARE OLDER?*

**I** think I would have tried to understand that my obsession and society's obsession with material values was/is a complete waste of time and energy. I was breaking my neck at 14 to clothe myself in Armani,

CONTINUED

# The GIFT of the GAB

Versace and D&G. I carelessly watched friends sell drugs just to 'own' stuff that would be totally worthless within less than a season. I would have tried to understand that 'we' were risking our freedom (one of our most valuable birthrights) for something completely worthless!!!

Our fixation with fixing what is on the OUTSIDE is a downward, never-ending spiral and the longer we focus on what's outside we are depriving ourselves of the true remedy – everlasting, solid, true love inside!

## WHAT WOULD YOUR ADVICE BE TO YOUNG PEOPLE USING CRITICAL THINKING AND ENQUIRY TO RESEARCH AN ISSUE?

*Never* take one perspective or one person's/group's/company's opinion or information. Even when things are backed up with facts and figures, it doesn't make them correct. Statistics can be manipulated and stories can be influenced. Most people have an agenda and many people give info but are actually misinformed themselves. I would advise seeking info from numerous sources and weighing up the responses... then simply look within and 'trust you'.

## WHAT WOULD YOUR ADVICE BE TO YOUNG PEOPLE WHO WANT TO USE LYRICS AND THEIR MUSICAL TALENTS TO BRING ABOUT CHANGE?

### Ⓐ READ! READ! AND READ SOME MORE!

*Widen* your vocab, swallow a dictionary and dissect a thesaurus! Widening our vocab and giving ourselves ample ways to explain and express ourselves is where we begin.

EVERYTHING has been spoken, sung, rapped, rhymed about already, it's not really 'what' we talk about, it's 'how' we talk about it!

> **WIDENING OUR VOCAB AND GIVING OURSELVES AMPLE WAYS TO EXPLAIN AND EXPRESS OURSELVES IS WHERE WE BEGIN.**

### Ⓑ EXPLORE MOTIVATION AND INSPIRATION! WHAT MOTIVATES OR INSPIRES YOU?

*Music* inspires me, and so do beats, children, people, different cultures, eating, being active, being in the sun, being in the countryside, being in my car and being in love... So I try to surround myself with these things or indulge in these things as often as possible and then...

### Ⓒ YOU JUST OPEN UP AND LET THE MAGIC HAPPEN!

*Don't* force it, don't try to find writing! Just go to where, when, how... you feel most inspired, dis-attach, keep a pen close and let writing find you! Once you actually find the writer within you and set her/him free... Once you've connected properly just once... it becomes easy and totally natural and can be accessed at nearly any time, anywhere. Do not view writing as good or bad, do not compare or relate it to anything else, it is what it is! It's perfect, however it comes! (But there are different levels of perfection, so feel free to tweak if need be! Lol!)

## WHAT ADVICE WOULD YOU GIVE TO YOUNG PEOPLE WHO WANT TO MAKE A CHANGE IN THEIR WORLD?

*So* many people want to make a change to the world but very few want to make a change to the self! The self is all we can ever 'really' change and in changing ourselves we are changing the world! If we change the way we look at things, then the things we look at will change. For me this is about positivity, acceptance, and appreciation! It was very hard for me to see the good in my childhood and in my teenage years 'good' was non-existent. I now realize that everything comes bearing gifts. Everything has a positive side or a lesson to be learned. That is what 'my journey/story/history/past/baggage' gave me... the key... self-love.

**LEARN MORE/GET INVOLVED:** www.msdynamite.co.uk

## 8 Rax Interview with Isla Brown

ISLA IS A MUM OF FOUR YOUNG BOYS AND HAD NO CAMPAIGNING EXPERIENCE UNTIL HER LOCAL SCHOOL WAS UNDER THREAT OF CLOSURE. WORKING WITH THE OTHER PARENTS AND PLAYING TO ALL THEIR STRENGTHS, THEY HAVE CAMPAIGNED TO PERSUADE THE LOCAL COUNCIL TO FIX THE BUILDING OR BUILD A NEW ONE. THE RAX TEAM CAUGHT UP WITH ISLA IN MARCH 2010.

## WHAT IS YOUR CAMPAIGN AIMING TO ACHIEVE?

*We* are campaigning to keep our small, local, rural primary school open.
The council has decamped us to another school in the neighbouring large town because they said our school was badly in need of repair.

# The GIFT of the GAB

**6**

*The* council criticized our "lack of community" so we have formalized our social gatherings and we now have an "Outdoor Toddlers Group", a first in our county as far as we know, and are working with cutting-edge concepts with regard to pre-school development, outdoor nature play and parental engagement. We have also started up a community women's group as we felt there was a "gap in the market" for women to meet up and socialize, learn and be involved in community-based projects.

**7**

*We* ran a community survey on all households in the catchment area and asked people what they thought about their local school and their community and what they wanted from it in the future.

## WHAT CAMPAIGNING METHODS HAVE YOU USED?

### OUR CAMPAIGN HAD SEVERAL ANGLES:

**1** *Constantly* asking the council for all the legal and official documentation and evidence to back up their claims that our school was unsafe to be inhabited, which they have not been able to provide.

**2** *We* queried their costings on everything. Costs to fix the building; costs to keep our kids at another school; what the costs to put up temporary accommodation at the original site would have been; how much it would be to fix the building; how much a new building would cost. We also did our own costings on many of these points.

**3** *New* legislation had just come into force to ensure that school closures would come under closer scrutiny and a rural schools act had just been given royal assent, which meant that rural schools could not be closed on financial grounds alone, but there had to be educational advantage to be gained from the closure. Our parents know more about these Acts now than the council officers and many of the local councillors and we have proven that their consultation to shut our school is legally flawed.

**4** *We* engaged the help of a pressure / lobby group called The Rural Schools Network and they have helped us with the legal and financial issues. On our behalf they have lobbied the Minister of Education and gained his support.

**5** *We* have a "Save our School" petition page on Facebook.

## WHAT IMPACT HAS YOUR CAMPAIGNING HAD?

*Our* impact so far has been very positive. We have got backing from central government although we still have to work through the small print at local government level. We have had positive national and local press coverage. Our public meetings have changed local opinion on the issue of our school closure and we have gained increasing local support. Most significantly, it has been a character-building experience for all of those involved in the campaign.

Overall I think it will have the effect of immensely deepening our connections within the school and within the community. The potential with any campaign that involves so much commitment and effort is that it could sometimes drive people apart as well as together and I think the ultimate goal is to try and stay close to your end vision and everything else will fall into place and have the significance that it deserves.

**LEARN MORE/GET INVOLVED:**
www.facebook.com/pages/Hurlford-United-Kingdom/
SAVE-CROSSROADS-PRIMARY-SCHOOL/257861120937

**9** *Rax Interview with Simon Hughes MP*

SIMON HUGHES HAS BEEN MEMBER OF PARLIAMENT FOR NORTH SOUTHWARK AND BERMONDSEY SINCE 1983. HE LEADS THE LIBERAL DEMOCRATS' ENVIRONMENTAL TEAM. THE RAX TEAM CAUGHT UP WITH SIMON IN MARCH 2010.

CONTINUED

# The GIFT of the GAB 10 Rax Interview with Sophie Bardy

## WHAT ISSUES DO YOU THINK ARE MOST IMPORTANT FOR YOUNG PEOPLE TO ADDRESS TODAY?

*Active* young citizens in Britain can do lots of really useful things. You can help work out how best to involve many more young people in the decisions taken in your area and further away, to make our schools and colleges more successful at providing the education your generation needs for the years ahead, and to make sure as many people as possible understand the rights and responsibilities that come with being a citizen. There is also a lot of opportunity to become involved in public and community life locally. You can be elected to a council at 18 and to parliament at 21 and I heard recently of somebody appointed as a magistrate in their early twenties.

## HOW CAN YOUTH ENGAGEMENT WITH POLITICIANS BE ENCOURAGED?

*The* more young people who can meet and see the work done by councillors, and members of the assemblies and parliaments around Britain and in Europe, the more chance young people will understand how important these jobs are. We always have people coming to our office to do work experience and internships and I try and arrange regular visits of schools, colleges and youth clubs to parliament and to see what I do in Southwark, which is where I have been the MP for. Young people are normally very happy to get stuck in when they have the chance to ask questions at any event, from one in the classroom or the youth club to one at university or on the radio or TV. Some of the best people to inspire the next generation to get involved in politics are people from their own age group and charismatic and well-known public figures – especially public figures who are well known for other things!

## WHAT ARE YOUR VIEWS ON CAMPAIGN GROUPS THAT USE NON-VIOLENT DIRECT ACTION AS PART OF THEIR STRATEGY?

*Non-violent* direct action is an important and valuable method of political campaigning. I have used it myself and it can work very successfully. It should not however replace other campaigning but be additional to it. It can also be good fun!

## WHAT ADVICE WOULD YOU GIVE TO YOUNG CAMPAIGNERS?

*Join* a really good campaigning organization and work with them. Take a gap year or a year during your twenties to go abroad to a country in the developing world where you do practical work that directly saves lives. Join or support a political party near where you live to campaign on issues that matter to you.

LEARN MORE/GET INVOLVED: www.libdems.org.uk

AT THE AGE OF 18, SOPHIE BARDY DECIDED TO BRING ABOUT A CHANGE IN HER COMMUNITY BY ORGANIZING A THREE-YEAR PROGRAMME OF EVENTS AND ACTIVITIES. THIS BROUGHT HER COMMUNITY TOGETHER AND GAVE YOUNG PEOPLE ON HER ESTATE THE OPPORTUNITY TO HAVE CONSTRUCTIVE AND POSITIVE THINGS TO DO IN THEIR SCHOOL HOLIDAYS. SOPHIE WAS AWARDED A YOUNG CITIZEN AWARD IN 2007. THE RAX TEAM CAUGHT UP WITH HER IN JANUARY 2010.

## WHAT CHANGES HAVE YOU BROUGHT ABOUT IN YOUR COMMUNITY AND WHY?

*I* started off running community-based events and trips for children who were underprivileged and whose parents and carers could not afford to take them anywhere during the summer holidays. Some of these included trips to theme parks and the seaside and activities such as gardening, football training, theatre outings and summer parties where everyone brought their own food, from countries all around the world. The reason I did this was to help bring social cohesion to a community that consisted of all different ethnic groups and ages. I also did it because I grew up like those children on the estate, with parents that didn't have enough money to take us anywhere or do anything with us. My siblings and I just hung around on the streets. I didn't want the same for these children.

## WHAT STEPS DID YOU TAKE TO MAKING THESE EVENTS AND ACTIVITIES HAPPEN?

*The* first thing I did was consult the people in the community themselves to see what they actually wanted to happen and what they believed was needed. Then I put these ideas into an activity sheet and progress sheet with a breakdown of the costs and supporting evidence that these events were needed and how they would make a difference. I did some research and then applied to the right local charities that might fund these types of events. Because of my original ideas and the amount of depth and heart that went into the plans, the majority of the charities awarded the funding.

**THE REASON I DID THIS WAS TO HELP BRING SOCIAL COHESION TO A COMMUNITY THAT CONSISTED OF ALL DIFFERENT ETHNIC GROUPS AND AGES.**

# The GIFT of the GAB

## HOW CAN YOU FIND THE RIGHT PEOPLE TO TALK TO?

The most important people to talk to are the communities themselves. If big organizations see that the majority of the community supports what you are applying for, they tend to have no choice but to help. It's important to remember that, without help from local people and people that are willing to get involved, no plans will ever work. Charities and organizations are obliged to help the majority of the community, especially if you can show that they are all behind the idea.

## WHAT DIFFERENCE HAVE YOU MADE TO YOUR COMMUNITY?

The difference is that now there is a community that looks out for each other and which cares. It's very hard to find a community that will help people who are in need and will look out for your family. Crime has reduced considerably and there have been no burglaries on our estate. Adults respect the children and children respect the adults. People may not necessarily like each other but they still value each other as a member of their community. If more things occurred like my events, there would be a significant change in younger people and how people perceive youngsters. Many charitable organizations feel that what they are doing helps young people when really it doesn't. If a young person plants a tree and sees it grow the likelihood is that they will protect that tree. This is how communities are built; when young people and older people work together to build it in unison.

SOPHIE'S KIDS' GARDENING CLUB

## WHAT ARE YOUR THREE TOP TIPS TO YOUNG PEOPLE WHO WANT TO MAKE A CHANGE IN THEIR LOCAL COMMUNITY?

❶ Listen to each part of the local community, from the young to the old.

❷ Be passionate and show people that it's for an overall gain for everyone in the community, not an individual gain or for just one group.

❸ Find a way to make a difference within a community that wants to help each other because if people don't want to work together then nothing will be achieved, find people who are as passionate about your beliefs as you are.

## 11 Rax Interview with Jon Snow

JON SNOW IS A BRITISH TELEVISION PRESENTER AND JOURNALIST, AND CURRENTLY PRESENTS CHANNEL 4 NEWS. THE RAX TEAM CAUGHT UP WITH JON IN MARCH 2010, THROUGH HIS INVOLVEMENT IN A LOCAL COMMUNITY CAMPAIGN.

### WHAT ISSUES DO YOU THINK ARE MOST IMPORTANT FOR YOUNG PEOPLE TO ADDRESS TODAY?

Family and Community: both are under siege and can never be compensated for by twitter/email/games/TV/Ipod/mobile activity.

### WHAT ADVICE WOULD YOU GIVE TO YOUNG PEOPLE USING THE SKILLS OF CRITICAL THINKING AND ENQUIRY?

Start local, compare what you know with what 'they' tell you... the media is full of half-truths.

### WHAT ADVICE WOULD YOU GIVE YOUNG PEOPLE SEEKING TO ENGAGE WITH THE POLITICAL PROCESS?

Start local, build community strength and build an intranet in your street so that you can link the people who live there. Stage a local street meeting at the pub to share local issues, take local action to win improvements etc and then push out to the wider community beyond.

### WHAT EFFECT DO YOU THINK 21ST-CENTURY DIGITAL TECHNOLOGY IS GOING TO HAVE ON DEMOCRACY IN THE UK?

Positive, I guess, but then Obama was Obama and we don't have any of them. Indeed, in terms of leadership we are in a mess – hence the need to concentrate on the local.

### WHAT WOULD YOUR ADVICE BE TO YOUNG CAMPAIGNERS?

Think and act local. Don't take 'no' for an answer. Non-violent demonstration.

# FIRST Campaign LOCAL ACTION

## 1 What is the first campaign?

*You* have now reached the stage where you can engage in your first active citizenship campaign. This campaign is optional, depending on whether you are taking a GCSE in Citizenship Studies and what examination board you are using. It's for you and your teacher to decide. There will be another optional campaign opportunity at the end of *The Projector Room* and a major campaign opportunity at the end of *Tools For Change*.

For the first campaign, it's best for you to keep it simple. If all the groups in the class are working on the same campaign issue, it's easier to co-ordinate the campaign, so you may want to consider this. However, you may choose to work on several different issues in separate groups. That's for you and your teacher to decide.

For all campaigns, you need to use the ideas in *The Mirror* that show you how to record, evaluate and assess the whole campaign process. Use the checklist under the title: 'How do I keep a record of my campaign?'

IF YOU ARE TAKING THE GCSE, YOU WILL ALSO NEED TO MAKE SURE THAT YOUR CAMPAIGN IS CLEARLY CONNECTED TO THE CONTENT PART OF YOUR CITIZENSHIP STUDIES COURSE (DEMOCRACY AND JUSTICE, RIGHTS AND RESPONSIBILITIES OR IDENTITIES AND DIVERSITY).

You may be asked to focus just on using critical thinking and enquiry or advocacy and representation. You may also be asked to choose your issue from a list but you will still have plenty of freedom in taking it from there. On all matters connected to your GCSE, take your teacher's advice.

## DEMOCRACY IS ALWAYS THE BEST TOOL TO USE TO COME TO A FAIR DECISION.

## 2 What kinds of actions should you take?

YOUR FIRST CITIZENSHIP ACTION NEEDS TO ADDRESS A LOCAL ISSUE USING THE SKILLS YOU HAVE LEARNED SO FAR – CRITICAL THINKING AND ENQUIRY, AND ADVOCACY AND REPRESENTATION. THERE ARE SEVERAL KINDS OF ACTIONS YOU CAN TAKE AND THE FOLLOWING ARE JUST A FEW IDEAS. YOU SHOULD USE MORE THAN ONE OF THEM FOR YOUR CAMPAIGN.

### SCHOOL

**FOR EXAMPLE:**

- LAUNCHING AN AWARENESS-RAISING CAMPAIGN IN SCHOOL
- GIVING A YEAR SEVEN ASSEMBLY
- MAKING AND SHOWING YOUR OWN CAMPAIGN FILM SO THAT THE WHOLE SCHOOL CAN HAVE ACCESS
- CREATING A PODCAST THAT CAN BE BROADCAST ON THE SCHOOL INTRANET
- ORGANIZING A CAMPAIGN FOR CHANGE THROUGH YOUR SCHOOL COUNCIL
- SETTING UP AN EVENT TO CELEBRATE A PARTICULAR CULTURE IN YOUR SCHOOL
- CO-ORDINATING A LOCAL SCHOOL NETWORK TO ENCOURAGE OTHER SCHOOLS TO ADDRESS A PARTICULAR ISSUE
- ORGANIZING A SCHOOL CONCERT WHERE YOU CAN PLAY SOME OF YOUR OWN MUSIC CREATED TO ADVOCATE FOR AN ISSUE
- HOLDING A SCHOOL DEBATE
- SETTING UP AN EVENT WHERE EXPERTS FROM OUTSIDE THE SCHOOL COME IN TO GIVE TALKS OR PRESENTATIONS ABOUT A PARTICULAR ISSUE.

# WORK

### FOR EXAMPLE:

- MAKING LINKS WITH LOCAL WORKERS TO EXPLORE THE ROLES AND RESPONSIBILITIES OF EMPLOYERS OR EMPLOYEES.
- MAKING LINKS WITH A LOCAL UNION OR GROUP OF WORKERS TO SUPPORT A CAMPAIGN.
- MAKING LINKS WITH LOCAL SMALL BUSINESSES AND FINDING WAYS TO SUPPORT THEM.
- MAKING LINKS WITH LOCAL TRADES THAT MIGHT BE SPECIAL TO YOUR AREA AND RAISING AWARENESS ABOUT THEM.
- CONTACTING LOCAL ORGANIZATIONS THAT PROVIDE SUPPORT FOR PEOPLE SEEKING EMPLOYMENT AND CREATING A CAMPAIGN THAT RAISES AWARENESS ABOUT THE SERVICE THESE ORGANIZATIONS PROVIDE.

# THE LOCAL COMMUNITY

### FOR EXAMPLE:

- HOLDING A COMMUNITY EVENT TO RAISE AWARENESS ABOUT AN ISSUE.
- HOLDING AN EVENT TO PROMOTE COMMUNITY COHESION.
- STARTING A YOUTH-BASED COMMUNITY GROUP.
- RESEARCHING A LOCAL HISTORICAL FIGURE WHO WAS CONNECTED TO ACTIVE CITIZENSHIP ACTIVITIES AND PROMOTING AWARENESS ABOUT THIS PERSON.
- VOLUNTEERING TO WORK WITH A RECOGNIZED COMMUNITY ORGANIZATION THAT PROMOTES ACTIVE CITIZENSHIP.
- CREATING A CAMPAIGN CONNECTED TO A SPECIFIC ISSUE THAT IS AFFECTING THE COMMUNITY.
- CREATING AN EVENT THAT ALLOWS FOR A VARIETY OF VOICES AND CULTURAL OPINIONS TO BE SHARED WITHIN ONE GROUP.

# CONTACTING PEOPLE IN POSITIONS OF POWER

### FOR EXAMPLE:

- INTERVIEWING TEACHERS OR MEMBERS OF THE SENIOR MANAGEMENT TEAM IN YOUR SCHOOL ABOUT YOUR ISSUE.
- CONTACTING YOUR LOCAL MP ABOUT YOUR ISSUE.
- CONTACTING YOUR LOCAL COUNCILLOR ABOUT YOUR ISSUE.
- CONTACTING OFFICERS OF YOUR LOCAL AUTHORITY WHOSE WORK IS CONNECTED WITH YOUR ISSUE.
- INVESTIGATING YOUR LOCAL AUTHORITY'S WORK CONNECTED TO GOVERNMENT INITIATIVES LIKE EVERY CHILD MATTERS, YOUTH MATTERS OR THEIR ENVIRONMENTAL/SUSTAINABILITY/YOUTH PROVISION PROGRAMMES.
- CONTACTING LOCAL COMMUNITY LEADERS ABOUT YOUR ISSUE.
- INTERVIEWING LOCAL BUSINESS LEADERS ABOUT YOUR ISSUE.

# THE LOCAL MEDIA

### FOR EXAMPLE:

- CONTACTING LOCAL MEDIA OUTLETS SUCH AS A LOCAL PAPER OR RADIO STATION AND RESEARCHING HOW THEY COVER CAMPAIGNING ISSUES AND ACTIVE CITIZENSHIP.
- WRITING COMMENTS ON LOCAL MEDIA WEBSITES TO RAISE AWARENESS ABOUT A CITIZENSHIP ISSUE.
- PARTICIPATING IN PHONE-INS ON LOCAL RADIO STATIONS TO RAISE AWARENESS ABOUT A CITIZENSHIP ISSUE.
- CONTACTING LOCAL INDEPENDENT MEDIA SOURCES SUCH AS WEBSITES AND SMALL PUBLICATIONS TO ADVOCATE FOR YOUR ISSUE.

CONTINUED

THESE LISTS HAVE SHOWN YOU JUST A VERY FEW EXAMPLES OF WHAT YOU COULD DO. THESE ARE DECISIONS FOR YOU TO MAKE. IF YOU HAVE AN IDEA FOR A CAMPAIGN THAT'S NOT ON THE ABOVE LIST BUT IS CONNECTED TO YOUR LOCAL COMMUNITY THEN GO FOR IT!

## YOU ARE IN CHARGE. YOU ARE THE ACTIVE CITIZEN. THIS IS YOUR CHANCE TO MAKE A CHANGE THAT YOU BELIEVE IN.

 **What kinds of issues should you address?**

*You* may already have found issues that you care about. They may be ideas that have been sparked off by the Toolkit or you may have always had an idea for change burning inside you. The only restriction is that the issue you choose must be connected to your school or local community. Once you find something that you are passionate about, you're on the right path!

## IT'S YOUR CHANGE. YOU MAKE THE CHOICES. YOU'RE IN CHARGE.

**4** *What's the process?*

## FORM THE GROUP

*You* may work individually, in pairs or in groups for the first campaign – though, if you are taking a GCSE in Citizenship Studies, you and your teacher will need to follow the guidance of your examination board. But, if you have the choice, it may be best to work in a group. It's more fun, you will learn more from the experience and you will be more likely to have an impact.

You should be aiming to work with people you feel safe with and whom you can trust. It's also very useful to have a mix of skills in your group. For example, there could be someone who has strong graphic skills, someone who is talented at writing, someone who is accomplished at using IT, someone who is good at organizing and someone who isn't shy of speaking in front of people. That would be an ideal group but don't worry if your group doesn't tick all the boxes. Citizenship campaigns often lead you to discover skills you never knew you had.

## CHOOSE THE ISSUE

*You* will have understood by now that if you are not passionate about the change you would like to see then your campaign will be unlikely to work. That's the magic ingredient, so bear that in mind when you select your issue.
Vote on what issue you want to work on. Once this is done, write down the change you would like to see.

Be clear about the aims of your campaign and your intended outcomes.

If you are taking a GCSE, make sure that you are clear about how the issue you choose relates to content that you have covered in the other parts of your course.

## WRITE YOUR MANIFESTO

*As* you have learned earlier, writing a manifesto is an excellent way to focus your group and to establish exactly what you stand for.

## MAKE A PLAN

*Make* sure you spend enough time on the planning stage. The more detailed your plan is, the more smoothly your campaign will run.

Your plan should show that you have thought carefully about what steps you should take. A good plan will anticipate problems or obstacles and lay out ideas as to how to overcome them.

Divide your plan into stages. The first stage needs to be research, using critical thinking and enquiry. Everybody needs to be involved in this and you should make a separate plan covering how the research will be done. Your plan should also identify experts or people in authority whom you would like to contact to help you with your research.

Another important aspect of planning is to work out which people or authorities have the power to make the change you want to see. For example, if this were a school project aimed at providing more laptops for students, then the people who could make the change happen would include the school council, the headteacher, the governors, and the heads of year.

It's important to manage your time well in your campaign and a good plan will help you to do this. Keeping the momentum going is also really important.

There will be many hours of hard work, from the research period through to the action or event itself. You need to keep up your energy and enthusiasm. Support each other in this, and if somebody is having a hard time, help them out. Be as supportive as you can and see the project through to the end as a tight unit. In this way, problems become challenges for the whole group to deal with together, and problem solving becomes a group responsibility. Nobody has to deal with anything on his or her own.

An important part of the campaign, from the planning stage onwards, is to consider health and safety issues in everything that you do – and to show that you have done this. If you are organizing an event, then it's key that you make a risk assessment to show that you have considered exactly how to ensure the health and safety of everyone who may be taking part.

## DELEGATE THE JOBS

*Once* you have made a plan, you will know everything that needs to be done. The next step is to decide who is responsible for what. It's often a good idea to have one person responsible for a job and a second person as their support.
**YOU SHOULD DECIDE WHO DOES WHAT JOB ACCORDING TO EACH PERSON'S TALENTS. BUT EVERYTHING SHOULD ALWAYS BE VOTED ON TO KEEP THE WHOLE PROCESS FAIR.**

## THE RESEARCH

*Everybody* needs to contribute to the process of critical thinking and enquiry. Make sure you cover all the points from *The Processing Plant.* Also make sure that you all keep a record of your research. All the evidence that you gather should be well organized and kept safely.
**REMEMBER, RESEARCH DOESN'T ONLY INVOLVE LOOKING THINGS UP – IT ALSO INVOLVES TALKING WITH PEOPLE AND INCLUDING AS MANY DIFFERENT VIEWPOINTS AS YOU CAN.**

## THE ACTION

*There* are hundreds of possible ways of taking action. Make sure that you plan an action that is appropriate to the scale of change you are seeking. Organizing a mass rally outside the Houses of Parliament to campaign for Fairtrade foods to be sold at break time in your school is not going to be as effective as holding debates, creating a petition and taking assemblies within your school. Remember, this is your first campaign for change; you will be working on a bigger one later in your course.

## REFLECT AND EVALUATE

*Reflecting* and evaluating is a process that should be continuous throughout your campaign and you should stick to the advice in *The Mirror* about how to do it effectively. However, once your campaign is finished, it's useful to evaluate how it went and reflect upon how each of you did as individuals as well as how you performed as a group.
**REMEMBER, THIS IS ONLY YOUR FIRST CAMPAIGN. FOCUSING ON MISTAKES AND HOW THINGS COULD HAVE GONE BETTER WILL REALLY HELP YOU TO MAKE YOUR LATER, MAIN CAMPAIGN AS SUCCESSFUL AS IT CAN POSSIBLY BE.**

## ASSESS THE IMPACT

*The* final stage is to assess exactly what impact your campaign had. This can be done in a variety of ways and depends on the kind of action that you took. Always gather detailed feedback. Don't just ask people if they thought the action was any good – find out what effect it had, what people learned from it and what changes have happened as a result of it.

# CHAPTER 6 — The PROJECTOR ROOM

## 1 Why is this chapter important?

*The Gift of the Gab* gave you plenty of ideas about how to use language in the best way possible to win support for your campaign. *The Projector Room* looks at tools to help you project your ideas for change into the world.

**ONCE YOU HAVE FOUND YOUR VOICE, YOU NEED TO PROJECT IT SO THAT YOU CAN REACH AS MANY PEOPLE AS POSSIBLE.**

*This* chapter helps you look at other ways to use 21st-century technology: from making your own campaign films and creating memes that go viral to setting up special websites.

Using new technology for campaigning is never the be-all and end-all. Creating actions and events in the real world – as opposed to the virtual world – will have much more impact but 21st-century technology is an excellent tool to support these actions. *The Projector Room* will look at creative and often humorous ways of harnessing new technology and being active in the real world.

**YOU HAVE THE RIGHT TO EXPRESS YOURSELF AND THE RIGHT TO BE HEARD. THE FUTURE IS YOURS TO CREATE.**

### THIS CHAPTER WILL HELP ENSURE THAT:

YOU HAVE CONSIDERED A VARIETY OF WAYS TO USE 21ST-CENTURY TECHNOLOGY TO MAKE YOUR VOICE HEARD.

YOU CAN USE LOCAL AND NATIONAL MEDIA TO HELP SUPPORT YOUR CAMPAIGN.

YOU KNOW WHAT IT MEANS TO BE THE MEDIA.

YOU UNDERSTAND THE EFFECT OF THE MEDIUM ON THE MESSAGE.

YOU CAN MAKE A FILM TO ADVOCATE FOR YOUR CAMPAIGN.

YOU KNOW HOW TO WRITE A PROFESSIONAL PRESS RELEASE.

IN OTHER WORDS, YOU WILL USE ADVANCED MEDIA AND CAMPAIGNING SKILLS TO A VERY HIGH LEVEL IN ORDER TO CREATE A WINNING CAMPAIGN THAT WILL REACH THE MAXIMUM NUMBER OF PEOPLE.

## 2 In what ways can digital technology help a campaign?

*When* you are trying to communicate your ideas to a wider audience by using 21st-century technology, it is worth taking some tips from one of the biggest industries in the world, which survives by finding new and powerful ways to convey its messages to the public: the advertising industry.

CONTINUED

# WILL IT BLEND?

**ONE** OF THE MOST SUCCESSFUL VIRAL VIDEO SERIES IS BASED AROUND THE IDEA OF TESTING WHAT WILL AND WILL NOT BLEND IN A BLENDER. OBJECTS THAT HAVE BEEN BLENDED SUCCESSFULLY INCLUDE MARBLES, GOLF BALLS, AN iPHONE, A CAMCORDER, A GARDEN RAKE HANDLE – AND SIX LIGHTERS, WHICH ENDED UP IGNITING AND CAUSING A MINI-FIREBALL. WEB USERS BECAME FASCINATED BY THE SIMPLE IDEA AND 'WILL IT BLEND?' HAS HAD OVER 80 MILLION HITS SINCE THE SERIES OF SHORT CLIPS STARTED IN 2006. THE PRESENTER OF THE VIDEO CLIPS IS THE OWNER OF THE COMPANY THAT MAKES THE BLENDER. HE HAS BECOME A CELEBRITY IN THE US AS WELL AS SEEING HIS BUSINESS THRIVE – ALL THANKS TO THIS CLEVER FORM OF VIRAL PROMOTION, WHICH TURNS WEB USERS INTO UNPAID ADVERTISERS AS THEY SHARE LINKS WITH THEIR FRIENDS.

> TO STAND WITH OTHERS ON A MARCH THROUGH A CITY ABOUT SOMETHING YOU REALLY CARE ABOUT IS MORE LIKELY TO HAVE A PROFOUND EFFECT ON HOW YOU SEE THE WORLD.
>
> THOM YORKE (SEE RAX INTERVIEW ON PAGE 165)

> HISTORY IS NOT MADE UP OF PEOPLE DOING STUFF ON MSN MESSENGER. IT'S JUST A METHOD OF COMMUNICATION. REAL CHANGE HAPPENS OUTSIDE OF THE INTERNET.
>
> ROBBIE GILLETT (SEE RAX INTERVIEW ON PAGE 159).

## HUMOUR VERSUS TYRANNY

**THE** PRESIDENT OF THE ARAB REPUBLIC OF EGYPT, HOSNI MUBARAK, HAS BEEN IN POWER FOR 29 YEARS. HE HAS BEEN CRITICIZED BY SEVERAL HUMAN RIGHTS GROUPS AND SOME WORLD GOVERNMENTS WHICH ACCUSE HIS LEADERSHIP OF CORRUPTION, ABUSING BASIC HUMAN RIGHTS AND RIGGING ELECTIONS. ALTHOUGH MUBARAK AND HIS STATE SECURITY POLICE ARE A THREAT TO ORDINARY CITIZENS WISHING TO EXERCISE THEIR RIGHT TO FREEDOM OF SPEECH, YOUNG ACTIVISTS ENGAGED IN A HUMOROUS WEB-BASED CAMPAIGN. BY USING SIMPLE IMAGE MANIPULATION PROGRAMS, THE ACTIVISTS SUPERIMPOSED MUBARAK'S HEAD ON TO THE BODIES OF FAMOUS THUGS AND VILLAINS SUCH AS GOLLUM FROM *LORD OF THE RINGS* AND THE BADDIES FROM BATMAN FILMS. THESE IMAGES SPREAD THROUGHOUT THE COUNTRY IN A MATTER OF HOURS AND SOON, PEOPLE WERE LAUGHING AT THEIR LEADER. THIS SIMPLE USE OF HUMOUR HELPED TO BREAK THE SPELL OF FEAR ON WHICH THE POWER OF THE MUBARAK REGIME HAS RELIED. MANIPULATING IMAGES IN THIS WAY IS A POPULAR TECHNIQUE FOR CAMPAIGNERS.

## MATCHING POLLUTERS AND POLITICIANS

**THE** USE OF HUMOUR IS A KEY TOOL FOR MANY CAMPAIGNERS AND THIS IS OFTEN MATCHED WITH CREATIVE WAYS OF USING THE WEB. A GOOD EXAMPLE OF THIS IS A SITE THAT APPEARS TO BE AN ONLINE MATCHMAKING SERVICE BUT, WHEN YOU LOOK CLOSER, YOU REALIZE THAT IT IS DEDICATED TO "MATCHING POLLUTERS AND POLITICIANS". WITH ATTRACTIVE GRAPHICS AND AN AMUSING FILM CLIP, THE SITE DRAWS ATTENTION TO THE FACT THAT MANY OIL COMPANIES INVEST LARGE SUMS OF MONEY IN PAYING LOBBYISTS TO PERSUADE POLITICIANS TO SUPPORT THEIR ACTIVITIES.

**LEARN MORE/GET INVOLVED:**

www.polluterharmony.com www.polluterwatch.com
www.greenpeace.org

You may want to persuade people to take action on climate change whereas an advertising company may want to persuade people to buy a new fizzy drink, but the available methods of communicating – the medium – will be the same, from pamphlets and posters, to film clips and internet virals.

Advertising companies have millions of pounds and thousands of people working for them, while you are a small group of young people with no budget. But that does not mean that you cannot be successful in communicating your ideas. In fact, because you are young, digital natives – and therefore part of the biggest emerging market in the country – and because you are not selling something, you already have a tremendous advantage over the advertisers.

There are several ways of using 21st-century technology to help your campaigns with which you will already be familiar, and there's no point in the Toolkit trying to introduce you to a rapidly changing field, which you may already know well. However, it may be useful to consider a few areas.

> IF THE ADVERTISING WORLD WERE DEVOTED TO ADVOCATING FOR UNIVERSAL PEACE, RESPECT FOR THE EARTH'S FINITE RESOURCES AND PUTTING PEOPLE BEFORE PROFITS, THEN THE FUTURE MIGHT BE SO BRIGHT THAT YOU'D HAVE TO WEAR SHADES.

## Ⓐ CREATING A MEME THAT GOES VIRAL

**A MEME** IS A SHORT FILM CLIP – OFTEN ANIMATED – A PHRASE OR A STILL IMAGE THAT IS ABLE TO CAPTURE THE INTEREST OF THE USER IMMEDIATELY.

*Memes* are often funny, cute (many memes feature animals or children for this reason) or thought-provoking and often have the feeling of being an 'in joke'. The most important aspect of a meme is that it is very short, is understood instantly and you can share it with your friends in seconds, either through Bluetooth, text, social networking sites, e-mails, links embedded in a service like Twitter or other digital devices. They have to be something that people will want to talk about and this is how they can become an 'in joke'.

*Famous* internet memes include a cat playing a keyboard (nearly 6 million hits since 2009), a Canadian student pretending to use a *Star Wars* light sabre (over 900 million hits since 2002), a baby giggling (over 90 million views since 2006) and a squirrel popping up in front of a tourist holiday snap (over 82 million hits since 2009).

If a meme has immediate appeal and generates enough interest from users, it will spread very quickly. This process is called 'going viral' and it is why advertising companies have been so interested in the phenomenon.

**MEMES CAN ALSO BE A PHRASE OR A SIMPLE IMAGE THAT GENERATES INTEREST OR PROVOKES THOUGHT.**

For the purposes of active citizenship an important meme is a photograph of a polar bear on a small ice flow. Some media experts argue that this one simple image, which went viral, drew more people to think about climate change than all campaigns on the issue put together. In the same way, the phrase 'Frankenstein food' or 'Frankenfood' – which was introduced in 1992 to draw the public's attention to the arguments against the use of genetically modified (GM) foods – is seen by some media experts as having had a deeper impact on the public than all the campaigns against the use of GM crops that had been running at the time.

Memes that go viral are a technique in which advertising companies invest large sums of money. But memes are easy to create and your campaign has the advantage that it is not selling anything. Consider creating a meme with a message that backs up or advocates for your campaign for change. HOWEVER SERIOUS YOUR MESSAGE IS, THE MEME HAS TO BE SHORT, SIMPLE, FUNNY, CUTE OR THOUGHT-PROVOKING AND EASY TO SHARE. One of the best ways to judge a meme is to ask yourself: "Is this something that would be cool to send on to my friends?"

**A SUCCESSFUL MEME CAN REACH THE WORLD IN A MATTER OF HOURS.**

## ⬤ ACTIVITY IN GROUPS BE THE BARD

 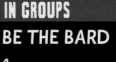 

*In* groups, you have **15 MINUTES** to **COMPOSE A 30-SECOND SONG** that encapsulates an idea for a campaign and could become a meme.

See if you can make it as catchy as possible. Try the Old Grey Whistle Test and see if it is so catchy that when you sing it to someone, they can whistle the main tune back to you.

Feed back your ideas to the class. You can have a class vote on which song is the most catchy and which one has the clearest campaign message.

# THE POWER OF THE IMAGE

**MANY** MEDIA ANALYSTS POINT OUT THAT IF WILLIAM WILBERFORCE AND THOMAS CLARKSON HAD BEEN IN POSSESSION OF MODERN TECHNOLOGY, THE FIGHT TO END SLAVERY MIGHT HAVE BEEN WON FAR MORE QUICKLY, AS PEOPLE WOULD THEN HAVE BEEN ABLE TO SEE IMAGES SHOWING HOW CRUELLY SLAVES WERE TREATED.

AN IMAGE THAT SUMS UP A STRUGGLE FOR NEW RIGHTS OR FREEDOMS CAN CONNECT WITH PEOPLE EMOTIONALLY AND INSPIRE THEM TO ACT. A PRIZE-WINNING PHOTOGRAPH – SHOWING A YOUNG GIRL SUFFERING FROM NAPALM BURNS AFTER HER VILLAGE HAD BEEN ATTACKED IN THE VIETNAM WAR – HAD A DEEP EMOTIONAL IMPACT ON ORDINARY AMERICANS. THE ANTI-WAR MOVEMENT IN THE US BECAME MUCH STRONGER AS A RESULT. SIMILARLY, IMAGES AND FILM CLIPS TAKEN BY SOLDIERS IN THE GULF MADE THEIR WAY INTO THE PUBLIC DOMAIN IN 2005 AND PROMPTED WIDESPREAD OUTRAGE AT THE WAY IRAQI PRISONERS WERE BEING MISTREATED. IF YOU CAN FIND AN IMAGE THAT HAS AN EMOTIONAL IMPACT CONNECTED TO YOUR CAMPAIGN AND PROVOKES THOUGHT THEN YOU WILL HAVE A SIGNIFICANT TOOL THAT MAY GAIN YOU SUPPORT.

## HOW DID THAT COME INTO MY HEAD?

**ADVERTISING** EMPLOYS SOME UNUSUAL METHODS TO COMMUNICATE THE IDEA OF A PRODUCT OR BRAND. OUT-OF-WORK ACTORS AND MODELS ARE OFTEN PAID BY ADVERTISING AGENCIES TO START UP CONVERSATIONS WITH STRANGERS AND DROP IN A RECOMMENDATION FOR A PARTICULAR PRODUCT. SOMETIMES THESE PEOPLE WORK IN PAIRS AND ARE GIVEN TICKETS TO FASHIONABLE SHOWS SO THAT THEY CAN SPEND THE INTERMISSION TALKING LOUDLY WITH EACH OTHER ABOUT A NEW PRODUCT. ONE AGENCY EVEN PAYS PEOPLE TO HAVE TATTOOS OF PRODUCTS AND BRANDS ON THEIR SKIN!

FOR YOUR CAMPAIGNS YOU COULD HAVE YOUR OWN IMAGES AND SLOGANS PRINTED ON TO T-SHIRTS AND MANY SCHOOLS HAVE THE FACILITIES TO DO THIS. THIS CAN BECOME PART OF A PROJECT THAT TIES IN WITH YOUR ART OR DESIGN AND TECHNOLOGY LESSONS. IF YOUR CAMPAIGN INCLUDES THE USE OF SPECIALLY DESIGNED T-SHIRTS, THIS NOT ONLY PROVIDES AN IDENTITY FOR YOUR GROUP, AND A WAY OF COMMUNICATING YOUR IDEAS TO THE PUBLIC, BUT ALSO PROVIDES A MORE ATTRACTIVE PHOTOGRAPH THAT WILL ENCOURAGE MEDIA COVERAGE.

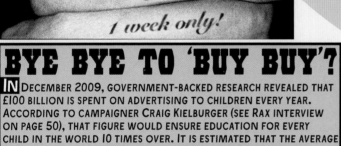

*2 for the price of 1 today at George's Café 1 week only!* (a)

TWO IMAGES THAT HAD A POWERFUL EFFECT ON THE WORLD (d)

TIANANMEN SQUARE PRO-DEMOCRACY PROTESTS 1989

ABU GHRAIB TORTURE AND PRISONER ABUSE 2004

# BYE BYE TO 'BUY BUY'?

**IN** DECEMBER 2009, GOVERNMENT-BACKED RESEARCH REVEALED THAT £100 BILLION IS SPENT ON ADVERTISING TO CHILDREN EVERY YEAR. ACCORDING TO CAMPAIGNER CRAIG KIELBURGER (SEE RAX INTERVIEW ON PAGE 50), THAT FIGURE WOULD ENSURE EDUCATION FOR EVERY CHILD IN THE WORLD 10 TIMES OVER. IT IS ESTIMATED THAT THE AVERAGE BRITISH CITIZEN IS EXPOSED TO OVER 500 ADVERTS EVERY DAY AND THAT WE SEE MORE ADS IN A YEAR THAN OUR GRANDPARENTS DID IN A LIFETIME. THERE ARE MANY CAMPAIGNS THAT QUESTION THE ETHICS AND MORALS BEHIND ADVERTISING AS WELL AS ITS PSYCHOLOGICAL EFFECTS. ONE REPORT – BY THE NEW ECONOMICS FOUNDATION – ARGUES THAT ADVERTISING DAMAGES OUR WELL-BEING AND LEADS US INTO DEBT. ANOTHER REPORT – FROM THE COMPASS THINK-TANK – ARGUES THAT ALL OUTDOOR ADVERTISING TARGETING CHILDREN UNDER 12 SHOULD BE BANNED. ON THE OTHER HAND, THE ADVERTISING ASSOCIATION ARGUES THAT THE INDUSTRY IS A POSITIVE ADDITION TO BRITISH CULTURE AND AN IMPORTANT PART OF THE ECONOMY.

500 ADVERTS A DAY! (b)

**LEARN MORE/GET INVOLVED:**
www.adcreep.co.uk www.neweconomics.org
www.dcsf.gov.uk/everychildmatters
www.adassoc.org.uk www.adbusters.org

# KNOW YOUR MEMES

**THERE** ARE SEVERAL SITES WHICH FOCUS ON THE PHENOMENON OF MEMES AND VIRALS. IT'S IMPORTANT TO REALIZE THAT ALTHOUGH MANY MEMES ARE JUST FOR FUN OR ARE JUST NOVEL WAYS OF ADVERTISING, THEY HAVE A SERIOUS SIDE TO THEM WHEN IT COMES TO CAMPAIGNING. MAJID TAVAKOLI IS AN IRANIAN STUDENT ACTIVIST WHO WAS ARRESTED BY THE AUTHORITIES AFTER GIVING A SPEECH IN TEHRAN IN DECEMBER 2009. CONTRARY TO THE EYE-WITNESS ACCOUNTS OF STUDENTS WHO WERE THERE FOR THE SPEECH, THE STATE MEDIA PUBLISHED PICTURES OF TAVAKOLI WEARING A HIJAB AND CLAIMED THAT HE HAD TRIED TO SLIP PAST THEM IN DISGUISE. IN REACTION, HUNDREDS OF MALE SYMPATHIZERS POSTED PICTURES OF THEMSELVES WEARING HIJABS TO SHOW THEIR SUPPORT FOR TAVAKOLI. THIS SERIES OF MEMES MEANT THAT THE WORLD'S ATTENTION WAS DRAWN TO THE INCIDENT.

**GOOD PLACES TO START TO LEARN MORE ABOUT MEMES AND VIRALS ARE:**

www.knowyourmeme.com
www.theviralfactory.com (c)

## B BLUETOOTH, SMS AND TWITTER

*As* well as allowing you to send on memes, these techno tools are an excellent way to update people about your campaign and campaign events. As suggested in *The Gift of the Gab*, it's important to spend time and care composing any messages that relate to your campaign – remember that these messages are representing you to the world. Messages should always be short and only used sparingly as you do not want to hassle people whose support you want to win and keep.

The last thing you want is to send out a mass text, only to realize you have left out a vital piece of information and will have to bother people with a follow-up message – so take your time!

If you want to include a link in your text or tweet but it has a long web address, you can use tinyurl.com or www.tiny.cc to shorten it.

### ACTIVITY — IN PAIRS
### ART ACTION

*In* pairs, you have **10 MINUTES** to **COME UP WITH A STORYBOARD FOR A VERY SIMPLE 30-SECOND FILM,** which could be easily made with no budget and which could become a meme that goes viral.

You may want to use ideas from the winning Be The Bard song in the last activity so that your clip goes with the song.

Feed back your ideas to the class.

### RECORD BOOK

*Report* on the class activities under the headings:
**WAYS TO PROJECT YOUR IDEA FOR CHANGE:**
**USING SONGWRITING SKILLS FOR A MEME CAMPAIGN THAT COULD GO VIRAL.**

**CREATING A STORYBOARD FOR A 30-SECOND FILM THAT COULD GO VIRAL.**

Notes on any class feedback sessions.

## C MAKING YOUR OWN WEBSITE

*Although* it is easy to set up a page on a social networking site to represent your campaign, there are many limitations to how you can manage those pages. Often, when a campaigning group has generated enough interest on a social networking site, they will go on to set up their own website. This allows them to manage the amount of traffic that may come from their supporters more easily. It also offers people the opportunity to contribute their ideas on a specialized wall or comments page. The website can update supporters on the key issues and events, and films, images and songs can be posted that will make people feel that they are part of something.

It is surprisingly easy to set up a website and many of you will already be experts at it. Here are some useful sites:

| | | |
|---|---|---|
| **CREATING A BLOG SITE** | www.wordpress.org | **TIPS 'n' HINTS** |
| **USING DIGITAL TECHNOLOGY FOR CAMPAIGNING** | www.tacticaltech.org www.digiactive.org www.informationactivism.org http://hub.witness.org www.meta-activism.org | |
| **STAYING UP TO DATE WITH THE LATEST DEVELOPMENTS** | www.netmag.co.uk www.techcrunch.com | |
| **OPEN SOURCE SOFTWARE** | http://en.flossmanuals.net | |

One of the most important aspects of a website is that it is unique and allows a lot of scope for creativity. If you have an advanced web designer in your campaigning group, they should be encouraged to use their skills to make your campaign website stand out.

**A BAD WEBSITE CAN END UP DAMAGING YOUR CAMPAIGN – BUT A GOOD ONE CAN MEAN THE DIFFERENCE BETWEEN MINOR SUCCESS AND GLOBAL CHANGE.**

## D A MEDIA SUITE IN YOUR HAND

*Handheld* digital devices such as 3G mobile phones allow you to browse, create, record, capture and share material easily. As time goes on, handheld digital devices are going to become more sophisticated. These are excellent tools to use in your campaigning, not only as ways to send on messages and memes but also to make and edit films, to record your own ideas for songs and to record interviews and events you have organized.

**MOBILE TECHNOLOGIES CAN BE THE EQUIVALENT OF HAVING AN ENTIRE TEAM OF MEDIA PROFESSIONALS AT YOUR DISPOSAL.**

# SERRASALMUS AND PYGOCENTRUS

**WHEN** YOU ARE USING TEXTING EITHER TO INFORM PEOPLE ABOUT YOUR CAMPAIGN OR TO UPDATE FOLLOWERS, IT'S IMPORTANT TO TAKE YOUR TIME AND USE THE RIGHT LANGUAGE FOR YOUR AUDIENCE. THAT'S AS LONG AS YOU AREN'T TRYING TO GET IN TO THE *GUINNESS WORLD RECORDS* AS THE WORLD'S FASTEST TEXTER. IN THAT CASE, YOU WILL HAVE TO STICK TO THE 160-CHARACTER MESSAGE THAT THEY HAVE DEVELOPED FOR WORLD RECORD CONTESTANTS: "THE RAZOR-TOOTHED PIRANHAS OF THE GENERA SERRASALMUS AND PYGOCENTRUS ARE THE MOST FEROCIOUS FRESHWATER FISH IN THE WORLD. IN REALITY THEY SELDOM ATTACK A HUMAN." IF YOU ARE INTERESTED IN HAVING A GO, BEAR IN MIND THAT TO BEAT THE WORLD RECORD YOU WOULD HAVE TO COMPLETE THIS IN LESS THAN 40 SECONDS, WITH NO MISTAKES!

# TIGWEB

**ONE** OF THE MOST IMPORTANT SITES FOR YOUTH CAMPAIGNING IS WWW.TIGWEB.ORG. IT IS EXCEPTIONALLY USEFUL FOR CONNECTING YOUNG CHANGE-MAKERS GLOBALLY AS WELL AS OFFERING ADVICE ABOUT UTILIZING 21ST-CENTURY TECHNOLOGY TO AID YOUR CAMPAIGNS.

*TAKING IT GLOBAL (TIG WEB) CONNECTS YOUNG ACTIVISTS FROM AROUND THE WORLD, ALLOWING THEM TO SHARE IDEAS AS WELL AS PARTICIPATE IN ONLINE TRAINING SESSIONS TO EQUIP YOUNG PEOPLE WITH THE SKILLS TO CAMPAIGN SUCCESSFULLY.*

SCOTT FORBES, FOUNDER OF GLOBAL FORUM 40 (SEE RAX INTERVIEW ON PAGE 195).

# MOBILE MOVIE

**THERE** ARE ALREADY SEVERAL FILM FESTIVALS AND COMPETITIONS CELEBRATING MOVIES MADE ON MOBILE PHONES. ALTHOUGH IT IS A NEW ART FORM AND MOBILES HAVE ONLY BEEN WITH US FOR A SHORT AMOUNT OF TIME, THERE ARE ALREADY THOUSANDS OF PEOPLE WHO HAVE STARTED TO MAKE MOBILE MOVIES. SOME OF THEM ARE FEATURE-LENGTH FILMS BUT MOST ARE SHORT FILMS OF BETWEEN 5 AND 10 MINUTES LONG.

**1** EXPERTS IN THE FIELD ADVISE THAT YOU DON'T SHOOT FURTHER THAN FIVE METRES AWAY FROM YOUR SUBJECT AS ANY FURTHER DISTANCE WILL GIVE A GRAINY EFFECT TO YOUR SHOT. KEEPING THE SUBJECT CLOSE TO THE CAMERA ALSO MEANS YOU WILL PICK UP SOUND MORE SUCCESSFULLY – MOBILE PHONE MICROPHONES ARE NOT EFFECTIVE AT TARGETING AND GENERALLY PICK UP ALL THE SOUND AROUND YOU.

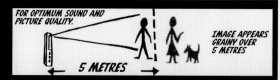

FOR OPTIMUM SOUND AND PICTURE QUALITY.

5 METRES

IMAGE APPEARS GRAINY OVER 5 METRES

**2** BECAUSE THE CAMERA IS SO LIGHT, YOU SHOULD NEVER USE THE ZOOM FACILITY ON THE CAMERA AND SHOULD INSTEAD WALK TOWARDS YOUR SUBJECT. IT'S ALSO IMPORTANT TO SHOOT IN GOOD LIGHT ALTHOUGH YOU CAN CARRY SOME BASIC LIGHTING EQUIPMENT WITH YOU TO HELP IN POOR LIGHT. AS WITH ALL TECHNOLOGIES, YOU NEED TO PRACTISE AND EXPERIMENT FOR A WHILE UNTIL YOU ARE READY TO START MAKING A USEFUL CAMPAIGN FILM.

**3** EXPERTS ALSO SUGGEST THAT YOU MAKE A VIRTUE OF SHOOTING WITH A MOBILE, WHICH ALLOWS YOU TO TAKE SHOTS FROM UNUSUAL ANGLES – EXPERIMENT WITH THIS FACILITY FIRST AND SEE WHAT WORKS.

**LEARN MORE/GET INVOLVED:**
www.mobifest.net www.dogmamobile.com
www.festivalpocketfilms.fr/english/

# TWITTER FEEDS

**MANY** CAMPAIGNING WEBSITES HAVE A TWITTER FEED, WHICH ALLOWS YOU TO KEEP UP TO DATE WITH ALL THE LATEST INFORMATION RELATED TO THE CAMPAIGN. THIS ENABLES USERS TO UPDATE OTHERS INSTANTLY AS WELL AS ENCOURAGING THE SENSE THAT EVERYONE IS PARTICIPATING TOGETHER IN THE CAMPAIGN. WITH LARGER ORGANIZATIONS THAT ENGAGE IN ACTIONS, THIS TOOL MAKES IT POSSIBLE FOR PEOPLE TO HAVE UP-TO-THE-MINUTE INFORMATION ABOUT HOW THE ACTION IS GOING.

STUDYING TWITTER ALSO ALLOWS YOU TO SEE THE KINDS OF ISSUES THAT ARE CURRENTLY INTERESTING PEOPLE. IT MAY BE INTERESTING FOR YOU TO STUDY SITES DEDICATED TO TRACKING THE TRENDS IN TWITTER.

**LEARN MORE/GET INVOLVED:**
www.tweetstats.com

# JONATHAN HARRIS

**IF** YOU ARE THINKING OF CREATING A CAMPAIGN WEBSITE, IT'S WORTH LOOKING AT THE WORK OF ONE OF THE WORLD'S LEADING WEB DESIGNERS, JONATHAN HARRIS. HARRIS REPRESENTS THE CUTTING EDGE OF WEB DESIGN AND ALL OF HIS SITES ARE UNIQUE, INTERACTIVE AND LET THE USER EXPLORE RATHER THAN FOLLOW CLUMSY SIGNPOSTS ABOUT WHERE TO GO AND WHAT TO DO. HIS ABILITY TO CREATE PROGRAMS THAT TRAWL THE WEB FOR RANDOM INFORMATION AND THEN PLACE THEM ON BEAUTIFULLY DESIGNED SITES – WHICH ARE UPDATED EVERY FIVE MINUTES – ALLOWS YOU TO FEEL THAT YOU ARE GETTING A SPECIAL INSIGHT INTO THE CYBER UNIVERSE AND MAKING CONNECTIONS THAT WOULD NOT ORDINARILY BE MADE. IF YOU ARE A KEEN SCIENCE OR IT STUDENT OR INTERESTED IN MODERN PHILOSOPHY AND THE POSSIBLE FUTURES FOR OUR SPECIES, THEN IT'S WORTH LOOKING AT HARRIS' SPUTNIK OBSERVATORY SITE: www.sptnk.org.

**LEARN MORE/GET INVOLVED:**
www.number27.org

# CHAPTER 6 *The* PROJECTOR ROOM

## Ⓔ A MEDIA SUITE IN YOUR SCHOOL

*Don't* forget that your school may well have a range of digital tools you can use, from IT rooms, cameras and microphones to a film editing suite and recording studio. The Drama Department may well support you in creating your own film clips.

### THE STAFF AT YOUR SCHOOL ARE EXPERTS IN THEIR FIELD AND WILL HELP YOU IF THEY BELIEVE YOU HAVE A GOOD CAUSE AND ARE PASSIONATE ABOUT IT.

## IN PAIRS
## HEADS TOGETHER

*In* groups, you have **FIVE MINUTES** to **LIST HOW EACH DEPARTMENT IN YOUR SCHOOL CAN HELP WITH AN ACTIVE CITIZENSHIP CAMPAIGN.**

Feed back your answers to the class.

## Ⓕ KEEPING UP TO DATE WITH EMERGING TECHNOLOGY

*Advertising* always focuses on new technologies, taking advantage of the appeal of the new to sell products. For this reason, new special-effects techniques for filmmaking and new technologies in general are often used in adverts first.

### A GOOD EXAMPLE

of this was the set of advertisements that appeared in the US version of a magazine called *Entertainment Weekly* in September 2009 where an entirely new medium was tried out on the public for the first time. New technological developments had enabled the advertising companies to embed a wafer-thin page in the magazine, which activated a film – with sound as well as moving images – when you turned the page. This technology is called 'video-in-print' and may well become a popular new medium for people to use around the world. *The Daily Prophet* from JK Rowling's Harry Potter series may become an everyday reality!

Although video-in-print technology is beyond the budget of a school citizenship project, it is worth bearing in mind how important it is to stay ahead of emerging technologies and, wherever possible, to use them to represent your campaigns. There is a great appeal in anything that arrives through a new medium. One example of an emerging technology that you may be able to use is 3D web design. This is becoming easier for people to use for little or no cost and it may be something that you could turn into an IT project that also covers your Citizenship Studies work.

Again, to keep ahead of emerging technologies, you are very likely to know of many sites, forums and media outlets yourselves so the Toolkit will only suggest a few to you. www.newscientist.com, www.netmag.co.uk and www.wired.com are useful sites to start you off.

### THE TECHNOLOGICAL REVOLUTION PROVIDES ACTIVE CITIZENS WITH MORE AND MORE WAYS TO SPREAD THE WORD, SO IT'S IMPORTANT TO STAY AHEAD OF THOSE CHANGES.

## Ⓖ BE THE MEDIA

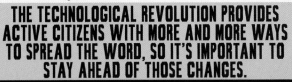

*Whether* you have your own digital tools or are able to use your school's equipment, it's important to arm yourself with this technology when you are engaged in your citizenship activities. It is no longer necessary for us to rely on news teams to cover news, for recording studios and music companies to provide us with music or for film companies to provide us with films. More and more, ordinary citizens are becoming the media themselves. This is one of the most important developments of the information revolution and an active citizen would do well to take advantage of it.

There are several examples of citizen journalists or video activists who have already had a major impact on world news. **SOME RECENT EXAMPLES INCLUDE:**

**PEOPLE IN BURMA WHO WERE ABLE TO SEND OUT FILM SHOWING THE VIOLENT SUPPRESSION OF PRO-DEMOCRACY DEMONSTRATIONS;**

**IRANIANS WHO SENT OUT FOOTAGE FILMED ON THEIR PHONES, 'TWEETS' ON TWITTER AND BLOG REPORTS COVERING THE CLAMPDOWN ON PRO-DEMOCRACY PROTESTS;**

**ORDINARY HAITIANS WHO SENT OUT THE FIRST FOOTAGE AND REPORTS ON THE AFTERMATH OF THE EARTHQUAKE THERE IN 2010.**

By being the media, you can cover your own events and campaigns in a way which can easily be uploaded to websites or blogs and even published in local or national newspapers.

### DON'T JUST CONSUME THE MEDIA, BE THE MEDIA!

# SPECIAL EFFECTS THAT HAVE FAILED

IN THE 20TH CENTURY, THERE WERE MANY NEW TECHNIQUES OF FILMMAKING THAT TOOK THE 'SPECIAL' OUT OF SPECIAL EFFECTS AND INSTEAD LEFT THE AUDIENCE LESS THAN IMPRESSED. SCRATCH-AND-SNIFF WAS ONE OF THESE IDEAS AND INVOLVED THE CINEMA AUDIENCE BEING GIVEN A NUMBERED CARD AS THEY ENTERED CINEMAS. DURING THE FILM, A NUMBER WOULD APPEAR AT CERTAIN MOMENTS AND THE AUDIENCE WAS REQUESTED TO SCRATCH THAT NUMBER ON THEIR CARD AND SNIFF! ALTHOUGH THE IDEA INTERESTED PEOPLE, IN PRACTICE IT WAS A TURN-OFF. OTHER IDEAS HAVE INCLUDED A SOUND SYSTEM CALLED SENSURROUND – USED FOR A FILM CALLED *EARTHQUAKE* – WHICH INVOLVED SPECIAL SPEAKERS BEING PUT UNDER PEOPLE'S CINEMA SEATS SO THAT THEY VIBRATED AS IF A REAL EARTHQUAKE WAS HAPPENING. PEOPLE COMPLAINED THAT IT DISTRACTED THEM FROM THE FILM AND THEY DIDN'T ENJOY IT BUT, WORSE STILL, SOME CINEMAS SUFFERED STRUCTURAL DAMAGE, AS DID THE BUILDINGS NEXT TO THEM! IN 2009, A NEW SYSTEM WAS DEVELOPED CALLED D-BOX MOTION CODE, WHICH MAKES YOUR CINEMA SEAT ACTUALLY SHAKE WHILE YOU WATCH THE MOVIE. ALTHOUGH IT IS NOT WIDESPREAD YET, ALREADY MANY FILM COMMENTATORS HAVE WARNED OF PEOPLE COMING OUT OF THE FILM COVERED IN FIZZY DRINKS, HOTDOGS AND, IN SOME EXTREME CASES, VOMIT!

SCRATCH AND SNIFF CARD
1 BODY ODOUR 3 RUBBISH DUMP
2 CAT PEE 4 CAR EXHAUST

## MOLDOVA NETWORKING

IN EARLY APRIL 2009, ACTIVISTS USED SOCIAL NETWORKING SITES SUCH AS FACEBOOK AND LIVE JOURNAL TO START A FLASHMOB-STYLE PROTEST IN MOLDOVA AFTER AN ELECTION WHICH THEY BELIEVED HAD BEEN MANIPULATED ILLEGALLY. ACCORDING TO WEB STATEMENTS BY NATALIA MORAR – A MOLDOVAN INVESTIGATIVE JOURNALIST – SIX PEOPLE SPENT 10 MINUTES PLANNING THE ACTION AND THEN A FEW HOURS USING THE WEB TO ORGANIZE IT. AS A RESULT, OVER 15,000 YOUNG PEOPLE TOOK PART IN THE PROTEST THE NEXT DAY.

CITIZEN JOURNALISTS ON SITES SUCH AS YOUTUBE AND TWITTER CONTINUALLY POSTED THE PROTEST EVENTS SO THAT THE REST OF THE WORLD COULD WITNESS WHAT WAS ACTUALLY HAPPENING. SOME PARTICIPANTS REPORTED THAT THE AUTHORITIES WERE TRYING TO BLOCK MOBILE SIGNALS SO AS TO STOP REPORTS GETTING OUT.

# TECHNOLOGY OF THE FUTURE

THE TECHNOLOGICAL REVOLUTION IS ADVANCING AT A REMARKABLY FAST PACE. NO SOONER HAS THE WORLD GOT USED TO ONE NEW FORM OF TECHNOLOGY THAN EVEN NEWER DEVELOPMENTS ARRIVE. FUTUROLOGISTS OR FUTURISTS ARE EXPERTS IN PREDICTING DEVELOPMENTS IN THE FUTURE. ONE OF THE MORE FAMOUS BRITISH FUTURISTS IS IAN PEARSON, WHO WORKS FOR BRITISH TELECOM AND HAS HELPED DEVELOP BT'S EXCELLENT TIMELINE FOR THE FUTURE. SOME OF THE BT TEAM'S PREDICTIONS FOR YOUR LIFETIME INCLUDE:

**2011-25:** A FORM OF ARTIFICIAL INTELLIGENCE (AI) PASSES A DEGREE; FULL VOICE INTERACTION WITH PC; ANDROIDS FORM 10% OF THE POPULATION; ELECTRONIC PETS OUTNUMBER ORGANIC PETS; GLOBAL VOTING ON SOME ISSUES; HOLOGRAPHIC TELEVISION; FIRST HUMAN MISSION TO MARS.

**2026-51:** ROBOTS SUPERIOR TO HUMANS; FULLY TELEPATHIC COMMUNICATION; BRAIN DOWNLOADS; HUMANOID ROBOTS BEAT ENGLAND FOOTBALL TEAM.

**2051 ONWARDS:** CONTACT WITH EXTRATERRESTRIAL LIFE; TIME TRAVEL INVENTED; PEOPLE BEGIN TO LIVE THEIR LIVES IN CYBERSPACE; FASTER-THAN-LIGHT TRAVEL.

OF COURSE, NOT ALL OF THESE PREDICTIONS WILL COME TRUE, BUT IT'S INTERESTING TO CONSIDER THAT EACH NEW INVENTION AND DISCOVERY THROW UP SERIOUS ETHICAL AND MORAL QUESTIONS.

SOURCE: www.btplc.com/innovation/news/timeline/

# SMELLOVISION

IN 1965, THE BBC PLAYED AN APRIL FOOL'S DAY JOKE ON THEIR VIEWERS WHEN THEY SHOWED AN INTERVIEW WITH A MAN WHO CLAIMED HE HAD INVENTED SOMETHING CALLED 'SMELLOVISION', WHICH HE CLAIMED ENABLED VIEWERS AT HOME TO SMELL WHAT WAS HAPPENING IN THE TELEVISION STUDIO. HE CHOPPED UP ONIONS AND GROUND COFFEE AND SOON THE BBC WAS BEING FLOODED WITH CALLS FROM VIEWERS SAYING THAT THEY HAD BEEN ABLE TO SMELL WHAT HE HAD BEEN DOING IN THEIR OWN HOMES!

IN 1957, THE BBC HELD WHAT IS BELIEVED TO BE THE FIRST EVER TELEVISION HOAX WHEN THEY AIRED A PROGRAMME – ON APRIL FOOL'S DAY – THAT PRETENDED TO BE A SERIOUS DOCUMENTARY SHOWING HOW SPAGHETTI GROWS ON BUSHES. THE *PANORAMA* SPECIAL SHOWED 'SPAGHETTI FARMERS' IN SWITZERLAND HARVESTING THE SPAGHETTI, ANXIOUS TO GET IT ALL IN BEFORE A FROST CAME AND RUINED THE CROP! THOUSANDS OF PEOPLE FELL FOR THIS HOAX.

AS WITH THE WORK OF CULTURAL JAMMERS SUCH AS THE YES MEN, THE SPACE HIJACKERS AND THE BARBIE LIBERATION ORGANIZATION, PLAYFUL HOAXES AND SPOOFS ARE ALSO EXCELLENT WAYS OF DRAWING PUBLIC ATTENTION TO A CAUSE OR CAMPAIGN.

THE SPAGHETTI HARVEST

TWO AERIALS MEET ON A ROOF – FALL IN LOVE – GET MARRIED. THE CEREMONY WAS RUBBISH BUT THE RECEPTION WAS BRILLIANT.

# 6 The PROJECTOR ROOM

## IN GROUPS
## ART ACTION

*In* groups, USING EITHER SCHOOL EQUIPMENT OR YOUR OWN MOBILE TECHNOLOGIES, HAVE A GO AT INTERVIEWING YOUR TEACHER OR EACH OTHER.

Experiment with your technique and be creative both as the filmmakers and as the people being interviewed (the interviewees). If you are being interviewed, you can use any of the 3.9.27s you have developed over the past lessons, talk about an issue or reflect upon some of the Citizenship Studies activities you have been involved in. Play back your films and see what works and what doesn't, not just in how a shot is taken but also in the way people present themselves.

Feed back your work to the class.

## RECORD BOOK

*Report* on the class activities under the headings:

MORE WAYS TO PROJECT YOUR IDEA FOR CHANGE:

WAYS IN WHICH DIFFERENT DEPARTMENTS AT SCHOOL CAN SUPPORT ACTIVE CITIZENSHIP PROJECTS.

EXPERIMENTING WITH USING SCHOOL EQUIPMENT OR OUR OWN MOBILE TECHNOLOGIES TO INTERVIEW AND BE INTERVIEWED.

Notes on any class feedback sessions.

## 3 How do I make a good campaign film?

*Not* only has citizen journalism and media activism flourished due to the development of cheap digital filmmaking equipment and simple editing programs, now anybody has the opportunity to make their own documentaries, too. In recent years, some documentaries made on a shoestring budget have gone on to be seen by millions of people.

### FOR EXAMPLE

*McLibel* (www.mclibel.com), directed by Franny Armstrong, was made for very little money but has been seen by 25 million people. (See Rax interview with Franny on page 158).

Documentaries are often a form of campaigning in which the filmmaker is trying to raise awareness about an issue. Although you will not have time to make a full-length documentary to support your campaigns, you may want to consider making a short film to advocate for your cause or to raise awareness about an issue. Your campaign film can be shown in school assemblies, posted on the web, added to your school intranet and shown at community events. It can be sent to people who are in a position of power too and can even be entered for documentary competitions.

The Toolkit has already pointed you towards websites where you can view documentaries and you may well have accessed some in order to support your critical thinking and enquiry. These are a good place to start as you seek ideas for your short documentary.

## HERE ARE SOME OTHER IDEAS TO HELP YOU WITH MAKING YOUR DOCUMENTARIES.

**A** *Make* sure that you have spent plenty of time experimenting with using your equipment and that you understand how to get the best shots possible. You also need to experiment with the post-production stage of your filming so that you understand how to edit, how to use sound and how to insert titles.

**B** *Keep* it simple. For the purposes of your citizenship project, it's wise to set out to make something that is manageable. It is easier to edit and complete to your satisfaction a documentary project that involves no more than 10 shots than to try editing a film with 100 shots.

**C** *Research* your subject in depth first. Make sure that your information is current and reliable and that you make it easily accessible to the viewers.

**D** *For* the purposes of a school film project which is not seeking to make money, it may be possible to access clips from professional films and include them in your documentary.

**E** *Wherever* possible, make the story personal, either by focusing on your personal experiences or on people who have been affected by the issue.

**F** *The* more people who talk about their first-hand experience to camera the better. Try to show both sides to a story in your documentary – if it seems biased, the viewers will not be convinced.

**G** *Instead* of using moving film, you can make a video that is a slide show of images with text superimposed or a narrator's voice laid over it. There are several sites which offer the opportunity to do this, as well as programs that may well exist within your school. One site that many people use is: www.animoto.com

CONTINUED

# MOCKUMENTARY

**ONE** OF THE ADVANTAGES OF SHOOTING SHORT FILMS ON CAMCORDERS OR MOBILE PHONES IS THAT IT'S EASY TO MAKE THE FILM LOOK LIKE IT IS A REAL DOCUMENTARY, COVERING REAL LIFE RATHER THAN SOMETHING STAGED. MOCKUMENTARIES ARE FILMS THAT ARE MADE TO LOOK LIKE THEY ARE REAL DOCUMENTARIES BUT ARE IN FACT STAGED. FAMOUS EXAMPLES ARE *SPINAL TAP* (WHICH FOLLOWS THE EXPLOITS OF AN IMAGINARY HEAVY METAL BAND), *THE BLAIR WITCH PROJECT* (WHICH APPEARS TO BE A NEWLY DISCOVERED FILM MADE BY TEENAGERS WHO ARE PICKED OFF ONE BY ONE BY A MURDEROUS WITCH) AND *PARANORMAL ACTIVITY* (WHICH SEEMS TO RECORD GHOSTLY HAPPENINGS IN A YOUNG COUPLE'S HOUSE).

OTHER VARIATIONS ON THIS IDEA INCLUDE DOCUMENTARIES WHERE THE PRESENTER PLAYS A CHARACTER AND SEEKS TO MAKE A FOOL OF THE PEOPLE FEATURED IN THE FILM. A RECENT EXAMPLE OF THIS IS THE WORK OF SACHA BARON COHEN, WHO HAS USED THE CHARACTERS OF ALI G, BORAT AND BRUNO TO MOCK INDIVIDUALS AND EVEN WHOLE NATIONS.

WITH A LITTLE IMAGINATION AND A LOT OF PREPARATION, IT'S POSSIBLE TO MAKE A MOCKUMENTARY THAT DRAWS ATTENTION TO YOUR CAUSE OR ISSUE. IF IT IS ENTERTAINING AND CAREFULLY MADE, THEN YOU MAY WIN AUDIENCES OVER AND RAISE AWARENESS ABOUT AN ISSUE WITHOUT THEIR FEELING THEY HAVE BEEN LECTURED.

**THE** QUICKEST-GROWING FILM INDUSTRY IN THE WORLD IS IN NIGERIA. 'NOLLYWOOD' MAKES NEARLY TWICE AS MANY FILMS AS HOLLYWOOD DOES IN A YEAR. IT IS VITAL THAT AFRICANS ARE ABLE TO TELL THEIR OWN STORIES ON SCREEN RATHER THAN SIMPLY CONSUMING STORIES FROM OTHER COUNTRIES AND CULTURES.

FILM IS AN EXCELLENT MEANS OF EXPRESSING CULTURAL IDENTITY. IF YOUR CITIZENSHIP PROJECT WERE DEDICATED TO RAISING AWARENESS ABOUT IDENTITY AND DIVERSITY IN THE UK, FOR EXAMPLE, YOUR GROUP MIGHT CONSIDER MAKING A FILM ON THE ISSUE.

> *FILM AND VIDEO PRODUCTION ARE SHINING EXAMPLES OF HOW CULTURAL INDUSTRIES, AS VEHICLES OF IDENTITY, VALUES AND MEANINGS, CAN OPEN THE DOOR TO DIALOGUE AND UNDERSTANDING BETWEEN PEOPLES.*
>
> KOICHIRO MATSUURA,
> UNESCO DIRECTOR GENERAL.

## LEARN MORE/GET INVOLVED:
www.nollywood.com

> *PRACTISING TALKING IN FRONT OF FRIENDS' CAMCORDERS HAS HELPED MANY ACTIVISTS TO GO IN FRONT OF MAINSTREAM TV CAMERAS. THIS HAS PRODUCED MORE COHERENT AND CONFIDENT SPEAKERS.*
>
> PAUL O'CONNOR,
> UNDERCURRENTS (SEE RAX INTERVIEW ON PAGE 162).

# LOGORAMA™

**A** SHORT ANIMATED FILM DRAWING ATTENTION TO THE WAY IN WHICH BRANDING LOGOS INUNDATE MODERN LIFE WON AN OSCAR IN 2010. *LOGORAMA* TAKES PLACE IN A WORLD THAT HAS ACTUALLY BECOME MADE OF LOGOS. ALL THE MAIN CHARACTERS ARE FROM BRAND LOGOS AND THE MAIN STORY FOLLOWS TWO MICHELIN MEN IN A POLICE CHASE FOLLOWING A CRAZED, GUN-TOTING RONALD McDONALD. THE FILM HAS A SURPRISING CLIMAX THAT DRAWS CONNECTIONS TO ANOTHER MAJOR CAMPAIGNING ISSUE. IT'S AN INTERESTING AND THOUGHT-PROVOKING SHORT MOVIE THAT RAISES MANY ISSUES FOR THE VIEWER IN AN ENTERTAINING AND NON-'PREACHY' WAY. *LOGORAMA* CAN BE FOUND ON THE WEB OR YOU CAN SEE THE TRAILER ON THE FILM'S OWN SITE.

## LEARN MORE/GET INVOLVED:
www.logorama-themovie.com

# KNOW YOUR STUFF

THE STORY OF STUFF WITH ANNIE LEONARD

**THIS** 20-MINUTE ANIMATED DOCUMENTARY WAS MADE IN 2007. BY 2009 IT HAD BEEN VIEWED BY OVER SEVEN MILLION PEOPLE IN MORE THAN 228 COUNTRIES. IT RAISES AWARENESS ABOUT CONSUMERISM AND DRAWS ATTENTION TO THE RARELY UNDERSTOOD BACKGROUND STORY OF HOW PRODUCTS ARRIVE ON SHOP SHELVES AND WHAT HAPPENS TO THEM ONCE THEY ARE DISPOSED OF.

THE FILM HAS CREATED PLENTY OF CONTROVERSY, WINNING GREAT PRAISE FROM SOME CRITICS AND CAMPAIGNING GROUPS WHEREAS OTHERS HAVE SEEN IT AS ANTI-CONSUMERIST AND EVEN ANTI-AMERICAN. ALTHOUGH SOME PEOPLE HAVE QUESTIONED THE ACCURACY OF SOME OF THE FILM'S STATISTICS, A SCRIPT CAN BE DOWNLOADED AND THIS GOES INTO DETAIL ABOUT THE RESEARCH BEHIND THE FILM. THIS IS A GREAT EXAMPLE OF HOW CRITICAL THINKERS – WHO WANT TO LOOK DEEPER INTO A SOURCE – CAN ACCESS THE MATERIAL THEY NEED TO DRAW THEIR OWN CONCLUSIONS.

## LEARN MORE/GET INVOLVED:
www.storyofstuff.com  www.storyofstuff.org/bottledwater  www.storyofstuff.com/capandtrade

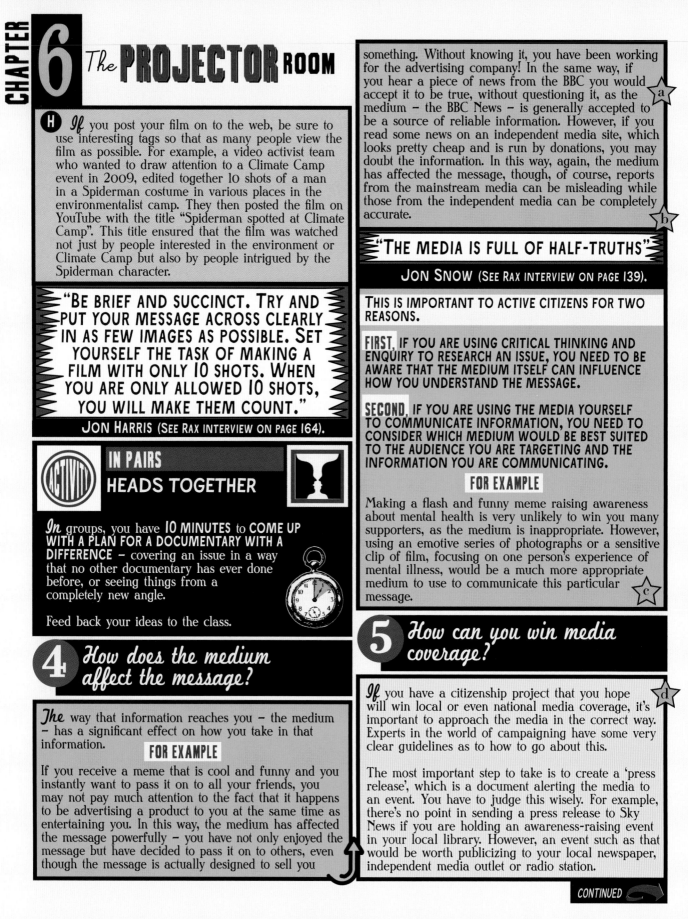

**H** *If* you post your film on to the web, be sure to use interesting tags so that as many people view the film as possible. For example, a video activist team who wanted to draw attention to a Climate Camp event in 2009, edited together 10 shots of a man in a Spiderman costume in various places in the environmentalist camp. They then posted the film on YouTube with the title "Spiderman spotted at Climate Camp". This title ensured that the film was watched not just by people interested in the environment or Climate Camp but also by people intrigued by the Spiderman character.

> "BE BRIEF AND SUCCINCT. TRY AND PUT YOUR MESSAGE ACROSS CLEARLY IN AS FEW IMAGES AS POSSIBLE. SET YOURSELF THE TASK OF MAKING A FILM WITH ONLY 10 SHOTS. WHEN YOU ARE ONLY ALLOWED 10 SHOTS, YOU WILL MAKE THEM COUNT."

JON HARRIS (SEE RAX INTERVIEW ON PAGE 164).

### ACTIVITY — IN PAIRS
### HEADS TOGETHER

*In* groups, you have **10 MINUTES** to **COME UP WITH A PLAN FOR A DOCUMENTARY WITH A DIFFERENCE** – covering an issue in a way that no other documentary has ever done before, or seeing things from a completely new angle.

Feed back your ideas to the class.

## 4 How does the medium affect the message?

*The* way that information reaches you – the medium – has a significant effect on how you take in that information.

### FOR EXAMPLE

If you receive a meme that is cool and funny and you instantly want to pass it on to all your friends, you may not pay much attention to the fact that it happens to be advertising a product to you at the same time as entertaining you. In this way, the medium has affected the message powerfully – you have not only enjoyed the message but have decided to pass it on to others, even though the message is actually designed to sell you something. Without knowing it, you have been working for the advertising company! In the same way, if you hear a piece of news from the BBC you would accept it to be true, without questioning it, as the medium – the BBC News – is generally accepted to be a source of reliable information. However, if you read some news on an independent media site, which looks pretty cheap and is run by donations, you may doubt the information. In this way, again, the medium has affected the message, though, of course, reports from the mainstream media can be misleading while those from the independent media can be completely accurate.

> "THE MEDIA IS FULL OF HALF-TRUTHS"

JON SNOW (SEE RAX INTERVIEW ON PAGE 139).

THIS IS IMPORTANT TO ACTIVE CITIZENS FOR TWO REASONS.

**FIRST,** IF YOU ARE USING CRITICAL THINKING AND ENQUIRY TO RESEARCH AN ISSUE, YOU NEED TO BE AWARE THAT THE MEDIUM ITSELF CAN INFLUENCE HOW YOU UNDERSTAND THE MESSAGE.

**SECOND,** IF YOU ARE USING THE MEDIA YOURSELF TO COMMUNICATE INFORMATION, YOU NEED TO CONSIDER WHICH MEDIUM WOULD BE BEST SUITED TO THE AUDIENCE YOU ARE TARGETING AND THE INFORMATION YOU ARE COMMUNICATING.

### FOR EXAMPLE

Making a flash and funny meme raising awareness about mental health is very unlikely to win you many supporters, as the medium is inappropriate. However, using an emotive series of photographs or a sensitive clip of film, focusing on one person's experience of mental illness, would be a much more appropriate medium to use to communicate this particular message.

## 5 How can you win media coverage?

*If* you have a citizenship project that you hope will win local or even national media coverage, it's important to approach the media in the correct way. Experts in the world of campaigning have some very clear guidelines as to how to go about this.

The most important step to take is to create a 'press release', which is a document alerting the media to an event. You have to judge this wisely. For example, there's no point in sending a press release to Sky News if you are holding an awareness-raising event in your local library. However, an event such as that would be worth publicizing to your local newspaper, independent media outlet or radio station.

CONTINUED ⟶

# MISLEADING MEDIUM

THE SKY IS NOT BLUE...
APPLES DO NOT GROW ON TREES...
KOALA BEARS ARE FROM VENUS...

BIG BUSINESS

TRUTH INC.

**A**S YOU HAVE ALREADY SEEN IN RELATION TO THE TOBACCO INDUSTRY IN 1954, INVENTING A SEEMINGLY RELIABLE MEDIUM – SUCH AS THE TOBACCO RESEARCH INDUSTRY COMMITTEE – CAN BE A WAY OF MANIPULATING PEOPLE INTO RECEIVING AN INCORRECT OR BIASED MESSAGE.

ONE INTERESTING MODERN-DAY EXAMPLE OF THIS IS THE WORK OF STEVEN MILLOY, A PRESENTER FOR FOX NEWS IN THE US. HE RUNS AN INFLUENTIAL WEBSITE – WWW.JUNKSCIENCE.COM – AS WELL AS BEING HEAD OF THE FREE ENTERPRISE ACTION FUND AND THE ADVANCEMENT OF SOUND SCIENCE CENTER. ALL THESE MEDIUMS ARE SEEMINGLY RELIABLE PLATFORMS WHERE YOU WOULD EXPECT TRUTH TO BE FOUND. AS A RESULT, WHEN MILLOY QUESTIONS THE SCIENCE BEHIND GLOBAL WARMING, THE DANGERS OF PASSIVE SMOKING, THE DANGERS OF THE USE OF THE CHEMICAL DDT AND THE DANGERS OF MAD COW DISEASE, MILLIONS PAY ATTENTION TO WHAT HE HAS TO SAY. HOWEVER, MANY CRITICS – INCLUDING THE BRITISH JOURNALIST GEORGE MONBIOT – HAVE SUGGESTED THAT MILLOY RECEIVES FUNDING FROM THE LEADING OIL COMPANY IN THE WORLD, EXXON, AS WELL AS SIGNIFICANT FUNDING FROM THE TOBACCO INDUSTRY. A LITTLE RESEARCH CAN LEAD YOU TO DOUBT WHAT THIS SEEMINGLY RELIABLE SOURCE HAS TO SAY. IS HE DEVOTED TO TRUTH OR IS HE DEVOTED TO THE AGENDAS OF HIS ALLEGED FUNDERS?

**LEARN MORE/GET INVOLVED:**
www.junkscience.com   www.monbiot.com

# CHALLENGE THE MEDIUM

**THE** PRACTICE OF MANIPULATING THE PUBLIC BY INFLUENCING THE MEDIUM BY WHICH THEY RECEIVE INFORMATION IS WIDESPREAD TODAY. SEEMINGLY RELIABLE MEDIUMS SUCH AS 'SOLID SCIENTIFIC RESEARCH', 'GOVERNMENT SOURCES', 'RESPECTED PUBLICATIONS', 'INTELLIGENCE REPORTS', 'NEWS REPORTS' AND 'RESPECTED WEBSITES' CAN ALL BE ABUSED BY PEOPLE SEEKING TO MISLEAD THE PUBLIC. AS *THE PROCESSING PLANT* SHOWED, ADVANCED CRITICAL THINKING CAN TAKE YOU CLOSER TO THE TRUTH OF AN ISSUE BUT ALWAYS BE AWARE OF THE FACT THAT THE MEDIUM ITSELF CAN OFTEN INFLUENCE THE MESSAGE.

# SEE ME

**A** THIRD OF ILLNESSES IN THE UK ARE CONNECTED TO MENTAL HEALTH. DESPITE THIS, MENTAL HEALTH IS AN ISSUE THAT IS OFTEN KEPT IN THE BACKGROUND OF EVERYDAY LIFE AND 9 OUT OF 10 PEOPLE WITH MENTAL ILLNESSES HAVE SAID THAT THEY EXPERIENCE STIGMATIZATION AND DISCRIMINATION.

IT IS NOT UNUSUAL FOR YOUNG PEOPLE TO EXPERIENCE SOME FORM OF MENTAL HEALTH PROBLEM – USUALLY TEMPORARY. HOWEVER, MANY YOUNG PEOPLE FEEL ISOLATED BY THIS EXPERIENCE AND UNABLE TO TALK ABOUT IT WITH ANYONE. IN FACT, BY TALKING ABOUT IT AND COMMUNICATING WITH FRIENDS, FAMILY OR PROFESSIONALS, THE NEGATIVE EFFECTS OF THE ILLNESS ARE GREATLY REDUCED.

THERE ARE SEVERAL ORGANIZATIONS THAT ADDRESS THIS ISSUE. THE YOUTH-LED BRITISH YOUTH COUNCIL HAS MADE THE MENTAL HEALTH OF YOUNG PEOPLE ONE OF ITS CENTRAL CAMPAIGNING ISSUES. IN SCOTLAND, THE SEE ME CAMPAIGN FOCUSES ON REAL STORIES OF PEOPLE WHO HAVE BEEN HELPED THROUGH MENTAL ILLNESS BY BEING ABLE TO TALK WITH FRIENDS AND FAMILY; SO TOO DO THE ORGANIZATIONS YOUTH HEALTH TALK AND YOUNG MINDS. PERSONAL STORIES LIKE THESE BREAK DOWN STIGMA, END THE FEELING OF ISOLATION AND MAKE THE ISSUE VERY REAL TO PEOPLE THINKING OF SUPPORTING A CAMPAIGN.

**LEARN MORE/GET INVOLVED:**
www.seemescotland.org.uk
www.youngminds.org.uk
www.youthhealthtalk.org
www.byc.org.uk

ISOLATION

YOU DON'T HAVE TO BE ALONE

*IT'S REALLY EASY TO GET LOCAL PRESS COVERAGE – YOU JUST NEED TO LET YOUR LOCAL MEDIA KNOW IN ADVANCE YOU'RE DOING SOMETHING, AND OFFER THEM A PHOTO OPPORTUNITY. WRITE A PRESS RELEASE BUT DON'T ASSUME ANYONE'S READ IT – JOURNALISTS ARE BOMBARDED BY THEM. SO SEND IT TO ALL YOUR LOCAL NEWSPAPER, TV AND RADIO NEWSDESKS (FIND THE E-MAIL ADDRESSES ONLINE) BUT ALWAYS FOLLOW UP WITH A PHONE CALL. THEN THEY'LL READ IT. TO GET NATIONAL MEDIA COVERAGE IS MUCH HARDER, BUT IF YOU'RE DOING SOMETHING ORIGINAL, OR ON AN ISSUE THAT'S CURRENTLY NEWSWORTHY, THEN YOU HAVE A SHOT. THE MOST IMPORTANT THING IS THE RING-ROUND. MY TOP TIP IS BE PERSISTENT!*

JESS WORTH (SEE RAX INTERVIEW ON PAGE 200).

# The PROJECTOR ROOM

## HERE ARE SOME USEFUL TIPS ON HOW TO ISSUE A PRESS RELEASE AND ATTRACT MEDIA COVERAGE:

### THE DOCUMENT
**TIPS 'n' HINTS**

*Journalists* are busy people, so a press release should do as much of their work for them as is possible. Your press release should be as close to the article they may write about you as possible. This means that you could start with a suggested headline for them –

#### FOR EXAMPLE

"School students speak out against closure of local hospital." You should then follow up with two or three paragraphs outlining the campaign, the background to the campaign, the event or action planned and the impact you seek to have. You should include contact details for your group or school at the top of the document and again at the bottom. Be very clear about the time and location of your planned event.

### TIMING
**TIPS 'n' HINTS**

*A* press release should be timed so that the staff at a local newspaper or radio station have enough time to be aware of the event but not so much warning that they will have forgotten about it by the time it is happening. It's a good idea to send a first press release 10 days before the event and a second press release two days before the event.

It's also worth considering holding an action or an event on a Sunday – there is little news that happens on a Sunday so you are more likely to gain media attention. Another idea to help you get the timing right is to study the media and see if there are any major stories that tie in with your campaign – journalists like to be able to make links with major stories that are already in the public's mind.

### CONTACT
**TIPS 'n' HINTS**

*If* possible, it's always best to phone the news organization to ensure that they have received your press release and to make personal contact – ideally, with the reporter who would be covering the story. If you can, it's worth finding out the name of the journalist most likely to be interested in your event and contacting them directly.

### THE HOOK
**TIPS 'n' HINTS**

*Stories* need to stick out and have a hook that allows the journalist to see how the story will be unique and therefore draw interest from their audience. The fact that you are a group of teenagers is itself a hook but it's worth seeing if you can add a further hook.

#### FOR EXAMPLE

If you are organizing a demonstration to advocate for taking action on climate change, this does not sound like anything particularly new or unique. However, journalists will sit up and take notice if your group has decided to make the demonstration a silent one, with all your mouths taped over to symbolize your feeling that the government is not listening to you.

### THE PICTURE
**TIPS 'n' HINTS**

*Newspapers* and magazines use photographs to make their stories more interesting and attractive. Think about what would look good in a newspaper. For example, imagine you are holding an event raising awareness about the working conditions for child labourers around the world, Even though you may all be devastatingly good-looking, a picture of a group of teenagers lined up outside a community hall where they are holding their event is not going to be very striking. However, if those students have turned up dressed in rags, with blackened, dirty faces and make-up that gives the appearance that they have been wounded or hurt – symbolizing the working conditions of child labourers – then that kind of picture is a gift to a local paper and may even assure you the front page.

### THE INTERVIEW
**TIPS 'n' HINTS**

*As* you will have learned through *The Processing Plant*, all media have their own element of bias, so you need to do everything that you can to be represented through the media exactly as you want. This is why the 3.9.27 technique has been so important to campaigners in the past. If you have a carefully prepared 3.9.27 statement, it is practically impossible for you to be quoted out of context or to be presented as meaning something else entirely.

Your group should designate a 'media officer' who will be responsible for meeting with the media and representing your group. That person should be the only person to give statements to the media and it's important that you stick to that rule. Even if you find a journalist being friendly to you and apparently having a nice chat, whatever you say can become the headline that represents your campaign – so be very careful.

Your media officer should always make sure that they have someone film or record them when they are being interviewed so that you have a record of what has been said.

**MAKE THE MEDIA WORK FOR YOU AND YOUR CAMPAIGN HAS A MUCH GREATER CHANCE OF SUCCESS.**

*Copy of the press release I sent to Mr Teds at The Cornington Post.*

Contact: Mark McCarthy
E-mail address: xxxx
School phone-number: xxxx
Teacher responsible for project: Ms Peacock, Head of Citizenship Studies.
Date and time of planned event: Midday, Sunday 16 August.
Venue of planned event: The Town Square.

Dear Mr Teds,

I am the media officer for a group of Year 10 students at St Aloysius Secondary School and we are engaged in a citizenship campaign to raise awareness about mental health issues amongst the young in the UK. This is part of our GCSE Citizenship Studies course. We have studied your reporting for *The Cornington Post,* covering local campaigning events and can see that you may be interested in the following event we have planned for midday, Sunday 16 August in the town square.

Possible headline:

'SCHOOL STUDENTS PUT MENTAL HEALTH CENTRE STAGE.'

Possible intro paragraph: "Five GCSE students from St Aloysius provided a spectacle that nobody could ignore in the Town Square today. Hundreds of shoppers drawn to the Sunday market were stopped in their tracks by an arresting spectacle. Five teenagers were dressed as prisoners, with blindfolds and earmuffs, walking in a line, each with a hand on the shoulder of the person in front, walking in a wide circle right in the centre of the Town Square. The crowds grew as more and more people wondered what was going on."

What we plan to do is to draw attention to the fact that one third of the UK population suffer mental health problems. Teenagers often fall between the cracks and receive no help. We believe the best solution is communication, not isolation or stigmatization. We have chosen to represent this feeling of isolation by acting blind and deaf, shut off from the world. This ties in with several stories in the national press at the moment.

Once we have gathered a large enough crowd, we will sing a short and upbeat rap about young people and mental health, gather signatures on a petition and hand out flyers with a link to our Facebook campaigning site.

We hope the photo opportunity will make for an arresting image in *The Cornington Post.*

Please do not hesitate to get in contact with me or with Ms Peacock and thank you for taking the time to read this.

Best wishes

*Mark McCarthy*

Mark McCarthy

Contact: Mark McCarthy
E-mail address: xxxx
School phone-number: xxxx
Teacher responsible for project: Ms Peacock, Head of Citizenship Studies.
Date and time of planned event: Midday, Sunday 16 August.
Venue of planned event: The Town Square.

**THINK ABOUT THE PHOTO. WHAT DOES YOUR ACTION LOOK LIKE? IF YOU MAKE IT LOOK EXCITING AND COLOURFUL, IT MIGHT GET IN THE PAPERS. BUT GETTING IN THE PAPERS ISN'T EVERYTHING. IT'S IMPORTANT TO DO ACTIONS THAT ARE GENUINELY TRYING TO CREATE CHANGE AND NOT JUST PHOTO STUNTS. IT DEPENDS ON THE CAMPAIGN AND WHO YOU ARE TRYING TO COMMUNICATE WITH. CRUCIALLY – WRITE A PRESS RELEASE.**

**ROBBIE GILLETT** (SEE RAX INTERVIEW ON PAGE 159).

# 6

## *The* PROJECTOR ROOM

 **ACTIVITY**

### IN PAIRS
### 3.9.27

*In* pairs, you have **10 MINUTES** to **WRITE A SPEECH THAT WOULD LEAVE A LASTING IMPRESSION ON THE PRIME MINISTER.** Imagine that you have the opportunity to have nine seconds with the Prime Minister. Take the opportunity to make three points, using 27 words, which get across how you feel the country should be improved.

Feed back your ideas to the class.

### RECORD BOOK

*Report* on the class activities under the headings:
**COMING UP WITH IDEAS FOR A UNIQUE DOCUMENTARY.**

**GIVING A 3.9.27 SPEECH TO THE PRIME MINISTER.**
Notes on any class feedback sessions.

## 6  *Rax Interview with Franny Armstrong*

**FRANNY ARMSTRONG IS A WELL-KNOWN DOCUMENTARY MAKER AND THE FOUNDER OF THE 10:10 CAMPAIGN. HER FIRST DOCUMENTARY – *MCLIBEL* – HAS BEEN VIEWED BY 25 MILLION PEOPLE WORLDWIDE AND HAS RECENTLY BEEN SELECTED BY THE BRITISH FILM INSTITUTE TO BE PART OF THEIR SERIES, *TEN DOCUMENTARIES WHICH CHANGED THE WORLD.* ARMSTRONG'S LATEST FILM – *THE AGE OF STUPID* – HAS WON INTERNATIONAL PRAISE AND IS STILL TOURING THE UK AND GLOBALLY. THE RAX TEAM CAUGHT UP WITH HER IN FEBRUARY 2010.**

## WHAT ISSUES DO YOU THINK ARE OF MOST CONCERN FOR YOUNG PEOPLE TO ADDRESS TODAY?

*If* we fail to stabilize global carbon emissions by 2015, we'll trigger unstoppable runaway climate change, which will, by the time we hit about six degrees towards the end of this century, wipe out most of life on Earth – including a good chunk of the human population. All other issues pale in comparison.

### THE GENERATIONS BEFORE US DIDN'T KNOW ABOUT CLIMATE CHANGE AND THOSE WHICH FOLLOW WILL BE POWERLESS TO STOP IT. SO IT IS DOWN TO US.

Other generations managed to solve the big problems of their time – whether ending slavery or overturning apartheid or what have you – and there is nothing intrinsically more stupid or useless about us. We have all the knowledge and technology we need to avert disaster – the only thing stopping us is ourselves. Our collective actions in the coming months and years will define our generation for all time. Are we going to be the Age of Stupid or shall we give saving ourselves a go?

## WHAT IS THE CAMPAIGN THAT YOU ARE PART OF NOW AND WHAT ISSUES ARE YOU ADDRESSING?

*10:10* aims to cut 10% of the UK's emissions in 2010 by asking individuals and businesses and schools and scout clubs and knitting circles to cut their own emissions and to then persuade everyone they know to do the same. And the good news is that cutting 10% is easy: driving a bit less, flying a bit less, sorting out your home insulation, changing your diet slightly, wasting less stuff, that kind of thing. Everyone who achieves it should be fitter, healthier, richer and have more friends at the end of the year. Plus they will have helped avert the greatest humanitarian disaster of all time. What's not to love?

In the six months since 10:10 launched on 1 September 2009, more than 55,000 people, 2,000 businesses

# The PROJECTOR ROOM

*Rax Interview with Robbie Gillett*

and 1,000 schools have signed up, including big names like Microsoft, Pret A Manger, Royal Mail, Adidas, Sony, Edinburgh University, Colin Firth, Lord Stern, Lord Puttnam, the Science Museum, all the Cabinet, all the Shadow Cabinet and the Prime Minister. Also, a third of all Britain's local councils have so far agreed to provide their services to 22 million people with 10% less energy this year.

## HOW HAVE YOU USED THE MEDIUM OF FILM TO REPRESENT YOUR CAMPAIGN FOR CHANGE AND WHAT ADVICE WOULD YOU GIVE YOUNG PEOPLE WANTING TO USE FILM TO HELP THEIR CAMPAIGNS FOR CHANGE?

**Someone** recently called independent cinema documentaries "the new rock'n'roll". Forget writing books, singing songs, taking photographs, or even building websites. If you have a burning idea that you want to communicate – uncensored, with the biggest possible emotional punch – to tens of millions of people, you have to make a doc.

When I started my first documentary – *McLibel* – back in 1995, I never for a moment thought it would have any effect on the immovable mountain that was McDonald's. But only 10 years later – thanks also to *Fast Food Nation, Jamie's School Dinners, Super Size Me* and all the rest – there had been a sea-change in public awareness about healthy eating, McDonald's profits had collapsed and advertising junk food to kids had been banned.

We managed 25 million viewers for *McLibel*, with just two of us and no budget whatsoever. This time, with *Age Of Stupid*, we have 1,000 times the resources, so surely we could manage 10 times the viewers? And if we do reach 250 million people, and the majority of them do agree with the film's key thesis – that unless we move very, very fast we will make the planet uninhabitable – then so what? What influence could 250 million angry, inspired, motivated citizens possibly have?

## WHAT KEY ADVICE WOULD YOU GIVE YOUNG PEOPLE WHO WANT TO SET UP THEIR OWN CAMPAIGNS AND MAKE A POSITIVE CHANGE TO THEIR WORLD?

**Listen** to everyone's advice, but don't let anyone tell you what to think. Get started straight away as there's not much time left. And always have an afternoon nap!

### LEARN MORE/GET INVOLVED:
www.mclibel.com
www.10l0uk.org
www.ageofstupid.net
www.spannerfilms.net

ROBBIE GILLETT (23) LIVES IN MANCHESTER. SINCE HE WAS A TEENAGER HE HAS BEEN INVOLVED IN CAMPAIGNS AROUND SWEATSHOP LABOUR, THE ARMS INDUSTRY, THE WAR IN IRAQ, FREE EDUCATION, COAL, AIRPORT EXPANSION AND CLIMATE JUSTICE. ALTHOUGH HE GOT IN TROUBLE FOR BUNKING OFF SCHOOL TO ATTEND A PROTEST AGAINST THE WAR IN IRAQ, HE HAS RECENTLY BEEN INVITED BACK TO HIS SCHOOL TO GIVE A TALK ABOUT CLIMATE CHANGE. HE LIKES SKATEBOARDING, FILM AND DUBSTEP. THE RAX TEAM CAUGHT UP WITH ROBBIE IN JANUARY 2010.

## WHAT ISSUES DO YOU THINK MOST CONCERN YOUNG PEOPLE TODAY?

**I** think the privatization of public space really affects young people. Our town centres are increasingly turned into places to shop and consume. And when you're young you don't have much money, so you're excluded. People get bored and excluded and when you're bored and excluded you do all sorts of stupid things.

## WHAT IS THE CAMPAIGN THAT YOU ARE INVOLVED IN AND WHAT IS IT AIMING TO ACHIEVE?

**I'm** currently looking at the role of aviation and airport expansion in causing climate change with a group called Plane Stupid. I got inspired after going to a protest site called the Camp for Climate Action in Yorkshire in August 2006. I learnt about the science and realized that if we didn't do something now, loads of people were going to die from dangerous weather systems like drought, floods and hurricanes as well as the resulting wars and conflicts. Climate change isn't just about the environment, it's about people and justice.

## WHAT TIPS WOULD YOU GIVE YOUNG PEOPLE ABOUT HOW TO BE A GOOD ADVOCATE FOR THEIR CAMPAIGN?

**Talk** to your friends. Ask them what they think about a subject. Listen to what they say and don't rant at them. Make your campaign fun – use music, cool artwork, fancy dress, theatre techniques if you like. Take action together because you'll be more effective. Be calm but passionate.

CONTINUED

# 6 The PROJECTOR ROOM

IF PEOPLE TELL YOU THAT YOU CAN'T CHANGE ANYTHING, POINT TO ALL THE EXAMPLES IN HISTORY WHERE PEOPLE HAVE CHANGED THINGS. POINT TO THE WORKERS' MOVEMENTS IN THE 19TH CENTURY THAT IMPROVED HOURS AND CONDITIONS IN FACTORIES AND ESTABLISHED THE RIGHT TO FORM A TRADE UNION. POINT TO THE SUFFRAGETTES THAT GOT THE VOTES FOR WOMEN, OR THE CIVIL RIGHTS MOVEMENT THAT GOT VOTES FOR AFRICAN-AMERICANS IN THE USA.

All these benefits are not given to us. We rise up and take them. It's important to remember that.

*WHAT KINDS OF ACTIONS HAVE YOU TAKEN PART IN AND WHY DID YOU THINK THEY WOULD BE EFFECTIVE?*

Plane Stupid is a direct action group. Direct action is when you directly intervene in a situation in order to create change, rather than asking someone else to do it for you. It's about taking responsibility for the world around you rather than deferring that responsibility to others like politicians or corporate businessmen. For example, if an airport wants to bulldoze my house

to build a new runway, I could write a letter to my MP and the airport and ask them not to do it. That's called lobbying and it might work, but it might not. But if I get together with my friends and form a human chain around the bulldozers and prevent them from knocking down my house, that's an example of direct action. It's Doing-it-Yourself.

Sometimes, it's good to use other methods for creating change, such as lobbying decision makers, protest marches, media stunts, petitions, political graffiti as well as direct action.

*WHAT KEY ADVICE WOULD YOU GIVE YOUNG PEOPLE WHO WANT TO SET UP THEIR OWN CAMPAIGNS?*

Set up a campaign that is relevant to you and that you can act upon in lots of different ways, with lots of different people. Sometimes, if you're tackling a big problem like aviation, it's good to find a bigger organization that is also working on the issue. That way, your smaller actions fit into a bigger picture. When you face a big problem by yourself, it can seem really scary and daunting. But when you take action collectively with others, you feel empowered and stronger together.

**LEARN MORE/GET INVOLVED:**
www.climatecamp.org.uk www.planestupid.org
www.stopmanchesterairport.blogspot.com
www.peopleandplanet.org

## 8 Rax Interview with Peter Tatchell

PETER TATCHELL IS A WELL-KNOWN HUMAN RIGHTS AND LGBT ACTIVIST. HE HAS RUN AS A CANDIDATE FOR THE LABOUR PARTY AND CURRENTLY IS AFFILIATED WITH THE GREEN PARTY. AMONGST MANY SPECTACULAR AND RISKY DIRECT ACTIONS, HE HAS TRIED TO MAKE A CITIZEN'S ARREST ON ZIMBABWE'S PRESIDENT MUGABE TWICE FOR HUMAN RIGHTS ABUSES AND TORTURE. THE RAX TEAM CAUGHT UP WITH PETER IN MARCH 2010.

# *The* PROJECTOR ROOM

### WHAT IS YOUR CAMPAIGN AIMING TO ACHIEVE?

*My* goal is a society without homophobic prejudice, discrimination and violence, where lesbian, gay, bisexual and transgender (LGBT) people have full acceptance and total equality. But a post-homophobic society is not enough. I want a new sexual democracy, which banishes erotic shame and anti-sex laws, and which no longer judges people by their sexual orientation. My vision is sexual freedom and human rights for everyone – where the labels queer, bisexual and straight become irrelevant because no one cares who sleeps with whom.

### WHAT CAMPAIGNING METHODS HAVE YOU USED?

*I* often work within the system, by writing letters to MPs and newspapers, lobbying government ministers, organizing petitions and doing phone, e-mail and fax blitzes. But when this doesn't work, I step outside the system and break the rules. My political inspirations are people like Mahatma Gandhi, Sylvia Pankhurst, Martin Luther King and, to some extent, Malcolm X. They used direct action and civil disobedience protests as a way of overturning injustice. I have adapted their methods and invented a few of my own, including: in 1994 outing 10 Church of England bishops who opposed gay equality; two attempted citizen's arrests of the Zimbabwean tyrant, President Robert Mugabe (1999 and 2001); interrupting the 1998 Easter Sunday sermon of the then Archbishop of Canterbury, Dr George Carey, over his support for homophobic discrimination; and in 1994 ambushing the motorcade of Prime Minister John Major in protest at his opposition to an equal age of consent for gay men (he supported 18, we wanted equality at 16).

### WHAT IMPACT HAS YOUR CAMPAIGNING HAD?

*In* the 1980s, Britain had more anti-gay laws than any other country. A combination of lobbying and protest changed all that. During the last decade, nearly all homophobic laws have been repealed – the biggest, fastest and most successful law reform campaign in British history. We've also changed the way institutions like the media, police and schools treat LGBT people. Public opinion has shifted too, with only one-third of the population still anti-gay. Millions more LGBT people have come out, creating queer visibility and thereby helping to undermine ignorance about same-sex relationships.

### WHAT WOULD BE YOUR KEY ADVICE FOR YOUNG PEOPLE SEEKING TO MAKE A CHANGE IN THEIR WORLD THROUGH CAMPAIGNING?

❶ FOLLOW YOUR CONSCIENCE.
❷ DO WHAT YOU BELIEVE TO BE RIGHT.
❸ DON'T FOLLOW THE MOB OR DO SOMETHING JUST BECAUSE IT'S POPULAR.
❹ THINK FOR YOURSELF. IF YOU WANT TO CHANGE SOMETHING, IDENTIFY WHAT NEEDS TO CHANGE AND WHY.
❺ DRAW UP A PLAN OF ACTION.
❻ FIND ALLIES.
❼ BE PATIENT AND DETERMINED. CHANGE OFTEN DOESN'T COME OVERNIGHT.
❽ ACT CONFIDENT. IT WILL INSPIRE OTHERS.
❾ BE IMAGINATIVE AND CREATIVE IN YOUR METHODS. DON'T PLAY SAFE. IT'S USUALLY BORING AND INEFFECTIVE.
❿ SHOW BOLDNESS AND TAKE A FEW RISKS. IF YOU ARE BEING STONEWALLED AND FOBBED OFF, GET A BIT RADICAL AND FEISTY.
⓫ BREAKING THE RULES AND SHAKING UP THE SYSTEM MAY BE NECESSARY TO SECURE SOCIAL CHANGE.

**IF YOU HAVE SETBACKS, DON'T BE DETERRED. TRY AGAIN. WHO DARES WINS. YOU CAN MAKE A DIFFERENCE.**

**LEARN MORE/GET INVOLVED**:
www.petertatchell.net www.outrage.org.uk
www.tatchellrightsfund.org

## 9 *Rax Interview with Emily Thornberry MP*

EMILY THORNBERRY HAS BEEN A LABOUR MEMBER OF PARLIAMENT FOR ISLINGTON SOUTH AND FINSBURY SINCE 2005. BEFORE ENTERING POLITICS, SHE WAS A BARRISTER SPECIALIZING IN HUMAN RIGHTS. THE RAX TEAM CAUGHT UP WITH EMILY IN FEBRUARY 2010.

CONTINUED ⟶

# The PROJECTOR ROOM

## WHAT ARE THE ISSUES THAT YOU THINK ARE MOST IMPORTANT FOR YOUNG PEOPLE TO ADDRESS TODAY?

*I* think the most important issues for young people differ a lot depending on their situation. If a young person is living in overcrowding at home, then getting better housing will be a big issue; if they're working part-time, then workers' rights will matter to them; if they're coming out at school, then bullying may be an issue.

Young people should address what's important to them – though there are also some issues which will affect all young people as they grow up. All young people have a stake in limiting and mitigating the effects of climate change, and making sure we have a fair economy where they can get a job and earn a decent wage.

## HOW CAN YOUTH ENGAGEMENT WITH POLITICS BE ENCOURAGED?

*I* think the expenses scandal did enormous damage to MPs' reputation. However, I hope that we have got rid of the MPs who have most seriously abused the system, and we can now start to rebuild trust.

I think getting young people engaged in politics is a two-way process. Politicians should spend time going to schools, inviting young people to Parliament, and getting themselves known. But young people should also realize that whatever the drawbacks, MPs and political parties are still the most effective way to get things changed.

## WHAT ARE YOUR VIEWS ON CAMPAIGN GROUPS THAT USE NON-VIOLENT DIRECT ACTION AS PART OF THEIR STRATEGY?

*I* greatly respect the courage of anyone who will put themselves on the frontline and use direct action to make their point. It can be a very effective part of a campaign strategy – and clever campaign groups will work out when it is most effective to use direct action, and when quiet negotiation behind the scenes is what's needed.

The suffragettes, who campaigned for women's rights to vote, used direct action. Suffragettes chained themselves to statues in the Houses of Parliament to make the point that they were, as women, being denied the right to vote. Direct action was a central part of their strategy and it was the right thing for them to do.

## WHAT WOULD YOUR KEY ADVICE BE FOR YOUNG PEOPLE TAKING INFORMED AND RESPONSIBLE ACTION?

*First,* find out more about party politics. Single-issue campaigns are very important, but political parties in government make the changes. Take a look at the parties of government and see which one you like. Neither Labour nor the Conservatives are perfect –

but they are each broad movements of people, and one of them will have their hands on the levers of power so you need to understand them.

*Second,* be prepared to compromise. No one wants to compromise, but sometimes we have to. You should never compromise your inner convictions and your driving principles – but in real life, when you're arguing with lots of different people and the world is a difficult place to get things done, you often have to compromise. It's infinitely better to compromise and get 70% of what you wanted, than to refuse to compromise and get nothing.

*Third,* have confidence in yourself. People are not necessarily more likely to be right just because they are older. They may have more experience, and it is often wise to learn from them, but believe in the value of your convictions about what you want to achieve.

**LEARN MORE/GET INVOLVED**:
www.labour.org.uk

## 10 Rax Interview with Undercurrents

PAUL O'CONNOR IS THE CO-FOUNDER OF UNDERCURRENTS, AN ORGANIZATION WHICH HAS BEEN A REGULAR SOURCE OF ALTERNATIVE FILM NEWS SINCE THE MID- NINETIES AS WELL AS PROVIDING PRACTICAL MEDIA SUPPORT AND TRAINING TO ACTIVIST GROUPS IN THE UK. UNDERCURRENTS HAVE BEEN ON THE CUTTING EDGE OF MEDIA ACTIVISM AND HAVE BEEN AN INSPIRATION TO PEOPLE WHO HAVE DECIDED TO 'BE THE MEDIA' WORLDWIDE. THEIR BOOK, *THE VIDEO ACTIVIST HANDBOOK*, IS RECOGNIZED AS ONE OF THE LEADING BOOKS ON THE SUBJECT. THE RAX TEAM CAUGHT UP WITH PAUL IN MARCH 2010.

## WHAT ISSUES DO YOU THINK ARE MOST IMPORTANT FOR YOUNG PEOPLE TO ADDRESS TODAY?

*Climate* change is the obvious answer, as this is going to have the most dramatic impacts on all our lives.

# The PROJECTOR ROOM

However, I think the corporate control of the internet is an issue which needs campaigning on. The net is the ideal method for coming together to solve the challenge of halting future climate chaos. Corporations meanwhile are relying upon bullying and harassment to stop people from illegal filesharing. The internet belongs to us all, so what message do we want to give back to the corporations?

## WHAT WAS THE MAIN MISSION OF UNDERCURRENTS?

**When** we launched Undercurrents in 1994, we wanted to create an outlet for stories of people taking inspiring actions to bring about positive change. We wanted to put camcorders into the hands of people who were on the frontline of environmental activism – to give the views which rarely, if ever, made it to the TV screens of the general public.

## IN THE EARLY DAYS OF VIDEO ACTIVISM AND 'BEING THE MEDIA' WHAT IMPACT DID THAT HAVE ON CAMPAIGNING?

**Video** activism as we know it began in the 1980s when the camcorder was introduced from Japan. Suddenly anyone could make a film, copy it and share it with friends, supporters and beyond. In the 1990s, as camcorders got smaller and less expensive, we trained activists to use video in various ways:

**1** **FOR PRODUCING SHORT VIDEOS TO INSPIRE OTHERS** to join a direct action campaign. These videos would use music and dramatic images to show the fun, the techniques, the issues and who else was involved.

**2** **FOR LEGAL SUPPORT.** Filming police actions on protests has proved vital in many cases, showing very different stories from police accounts in court. Camcorder footage has prevented many cases of injustice.

**3** **HELPING ACTIVISTS TO GO IN FRONT OF MAINSTREAM TV CAMERAS** by having them practise in front of friends' camcorders. This has produced more coherent and confident speakers.

**4** **FILMING THEIR OWN ACTIONS HAS ALLOWED ACTIVISTS TO SHARE THEIR TECHNIQUES WITH OTHER GROUPS ACROSS THE WORLD.** In Australia, campaigners sent videos to London of themselves blockading rainforest logging trucks by erecting bamboo tripods and sitting on top. In London, the videos were watched by anti-car campaigners Reclaim the Streets, who then used similar tripods made from scaffold poles to blockade motorways and city streets.

**5** **PROVIDING DIFFERENT ACCOUNTS FOR NEWS REPORTS.** Activists' footage has made stories possible. When the mainstream reporters won't arrive in time or refuse to trespass, it has been the activists' footage which has enabled the story to be told.

## CAN YOU GIVE A FEW EXAMPLES OF CAMPAIGNS THAT BENEFITED FROM YOUR INVOLVEMENT AND SAY HOW THIS IMPROVED THEIR SUCCESS?

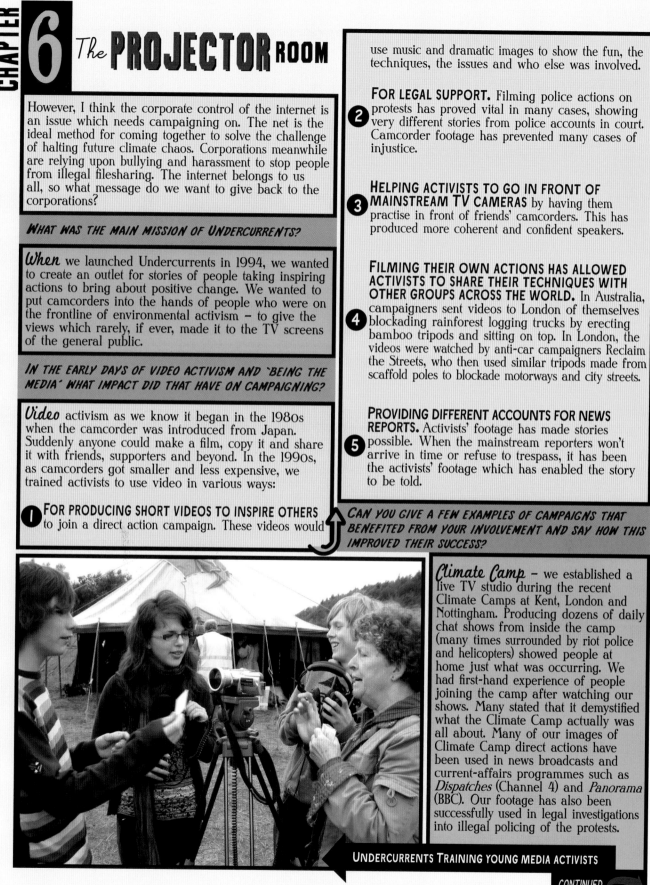

**Climate Camp** – we established a live TV studio during the recent Climate Camps at Kent, London and Nottingham. Producing dozens of daily chat shows from inside the camp (many times surrounded by riot police and helicopters) showed people at home just what was occurring. We had first-hand experience of people joining the camp after watching our shows. Many stated that it demystified what the Climate Camp actually was all about. Many of our images of Climate Camp direct actions have been used in news broadcasts and current-affairs programmes such as *Dispatches* (Channel 4) and *Panorama* (BBC). Our footage has also been successfully used in legal investigations into illegal policing of the protests.

UNDERCURRENTS TRAINING YOUNG MEDIA ACTIVISTS

CONTINUED

# The PROJECTOR ROOM

**HOW DOES 21ST-CENTURY TECHNOLOGY IMPACT ON CAMPAIGNING TODAY?**

The internet and digital media such as camcorders and cameras have given us all the opportunity to tell and share our own stories like never before in history. However, the skills to portray a campaign are still areas which need work if we expect to reach a wide audience.

**WHAT TIPS CAN YOU GIVE YOUNG PEOPLE WHO WANT TO BE THE MEDIA TODAY?**

YOUNG PEOPLE HAVE BEEN DEMONIZED BY POLITICIANS AND THE MEDIA FOR YEARS. SO TURN OFF YOUR TV SETS, BEG, BUY OR BORROW A CAMCORDER AND MAKE A FILM ABOUT HOW YOU SEE THE WORLD. CONTACT A LOCAL CAMPAIGN WHICH INTERESTS YOU AND HELP THEM OUT BY MAKING A FILM ABOUT THEIR CONCERNS.

**WHAT KEY THREE PIECES OF ADVICE WOULD YOU GIVE TO YOUNG PEOPLE TODAY WHO WANT TO CAMPAIGN FOR CHANGE?**

**1** Work out what you want to achieve and when. We have all set out to change the world overnight but become overwhelmed. By choosing and writing down your targets, you will get a better sense of achievement. Build upon them.

**2** The key issue for individuals who want to change the world is to realize that the problem is not different political parties. It is the structure of governance – not who is governing – that matters most. Focus on changing the rules. Be bold and seek truth. Be humble, but also confident in what you know and don't lose your curiosity in trying to figure things out. And, based on your search for truth and discovery of truth, speak that truth loudly and clearly to power if given that chance.

**3** DON'T TRY TO DO IT ALONE. SEARCH FOR OTHER ACTIVISTS IN YOUR LOCAL AREA. USE THE NET, READ LOCAL NEWSPAPERS FOR STORIES OF PEOPLE TAKING ACTION AND GO AND MEET THEM – VOLUNTEER WITH LOCAL NATURE OR SOCIAL ACTION GROUPS. GET ACTIVE WITHIN YOUR OWN COMMUNITY. IT WILL CHANGE YOUR LIFE.

## LEARN MORE/GET INVOLVED:

www.undercurrents.org   www.azclimatechange.com
www.azbushcraft.com     www.bike2Oz.com
www.onthepush.org       www.livinginthefuture.org
www.thesolcinema.org    www.rts.gn.apc.org
www.kinokast.net

**11** Rax Interview with Jon Harris

JON HARRIS IS ONE OF THE LEADING FILM EDITORS IN THE UK. HE HAS WORKED ON A LONG LIST OF FILMS INCLUDING *KICK-ASS*, *SNATCH*, *LAYER CAKE*, *DESCENT* AND *127 HOURS* AS WELL AS DIRECTING *THE DESCENT II*. THE RAX TEAM CAUGHT UP WITH JON EARLY IN 2010.

**WHAT ISSUES DO YOU THINK ARE MOST IMPORTANT FOR YOUNG PEOPLE TO ADDRESS TODAY?**

A sense of society. If we are civil and helpful to people they are likely to be civil and helpful back.

**DO YOU THINK THAT FILMMAKING CAN BE A TOOL FOR CREATING CHANGE?**

Yes, if it is used responsibly. Also, with the internet it can reach a lot of people very quickly.

**WHAT EDITING TIPS CAN YOU GIVE YOUNG PEOPLE?**

Be brief and succinct. Try and put your message across clearly in as few images as possible. Set yourself the task of making a film with only 10 shots. When you are only allowed 10 shots, you will make them count.

## The PROJECTOR ROOM

### 12 Rax Interview with Thom Yorke

THOM YORKE IS THE LEAD SINGER IN RADIOHEAD, ONE OF THE MOST SUCCESSFUL ROCK BANDS IN THE WORLD. THE RAX TEAM CAUGHT UP WITH THOM IN FEBRUARY 2010.

**WHAT KINDS OF ISSUES DO YOU THINK ARE MOST IMPORTANT FOR YOUNG PEOPLE TO ADDRESS TODAY?**

*Oh,* I really don't feel qualified to answer that...

*I'd* like to think they are extremely concerned about climate change.

*I'd* like to think they are concerned about the demise of a political establishment that does not represent them and is concerned with itself only.

*I'd* like to think they are bothered by the influence of large corporates over political decisions and the constant PR b\*\*\*\*\*\*t they throw out.

*I'd* like to think they are concerned about inheriting an economic system that is being propped up like the Leaning Tower of Pisa.

*I'd* like to think they view this generation's inability to bring about the necessary changes with complete contempt.

*I'd* like to think they don't really believe Facebook and Twitter are better than sitting in a forest at dusk listening to the sounds.

**HOW DO YOU GO ABOUT GATHERING STATISTICS AND INFORMING YOURSELF ABOUT THE ISSUES THAT MOST CONCERN YOU, AND WHAT ADVICE WOULD YOU GIVE TO YOUNG PEOPLE PURSUING THEIR OWN FORMS OF CRITICAL THINKING AND ENQUIRY?**

*Statistics* can be used and abused. I have been in debates where the climate change deniers just reel out statistics that you have never heard and have no time to check, thus derailing any constructive debate. How useful! Statistics are the favourite weapon of choice by PR firms and newspapers. Climate change is a particularly hectic one cuz there is so much technical science and it is such an emotive subject with people desperate to be told it ain't true.

**WHAT TIPS WOULD YOU GIVE YOUNG ADVOCATES ABOUT HOW TO USE LANGUAGE BEST TO REPRESENT THEIR CAMPAIGNS?**

*Try* to retain a sense of humour.

*Try* to retain a belief in the common sense of others and try to respect their views at least enough to find the holes in them.

*Don't* become the upper-middle-class English wind-farm woman who believes god is on her side and uses fear, anger, indignation, prejudice and ignorance.

*Remember* it is the job of MPs to listen to you. They don't have a choice.

*Oh,* and get some natty artwork.

**WHAT TIPS CAN YOU GIVE YOUNG PEOPLE WHO WANT TO WRITE LYRICS THAT WILL MAKE A DIFFERENCE TO THEIR WORLD?**

*That* there is nothing more dry and boring in art than politics. It has to be fermented and distilled. It has to be personal. It has to be light of touch. It is much more about how you do stuff, your state of mind and less about the words on the page.

**WHAT ADVICE WOULD YOU GIVE YOUNG MUSIC MAKERS WHO WANT TO MAKE A DIFFERENCE WITH THEIR TALENT?**

*This* is one for Ed in Radiohead... it is his obsession. When we discuss it, he says it's simply a matter of time – months rather than years – before the music business establishment completely folds. He is involved in trying to build a world where artists would finally get paid. But we are up against the self-protecting interests of that industry. They are currently trying to lobby to take all the cash themselves whilst claiming to protect the interests of their artists. Oh yeah? When the corporate industry dies it will be no great loss to the world. So, I guess I would say, don't tie yourself to the sinking ship because, believe me, it's sinking.

CONTINUED

**WHAT KINDS OF INFORMED AND RESPONSIBLE ACTIONS DO YOU THINK WOULD BE MOST EFFECTIVE FOR YOUNG PEOPLE TO CREATE OR TAKE PART IN?**

**Well,** violence is always a drag. You will always get monkeys at big protests who are angry or just looking for a fight. But it plays into the hands of those against you. And nowadays police tactics don't exactly help. Events that have wit. That take the piss. That expose and ridicule... without anger and with little judgment. And you are far more likely to get favourable press from that. Face to face contact. That sense of a common thing between people when they get together.

**WHAT KIND OF OBSTACLES DO YOU THINK YOUNG PEOPLE SEEKING A CHANGE MAY COME UP AGAINST AND HOW DO YOU THINK THEY CAN OVERCOME THEM?**

**People** find it harder and harder as they get further sucked into their lives to see how things could be different. It requires energy. It also requires you to imagine it for them. Nothing can be done if it has not first been imagined. And it's the job of others to make that hard. Lobbyists installed at Portcullis House and Westminster, for example.
Also we have been brought up – since Thatcher, I think – to believe our communal voice is dead politically. That we are atomized, selfish animals. The biggest obstacle to change is always the conditioned belief that we are on our own – fearful, powerless, like some Kafkaesque nightmare. Very convenient if you run Tesco or BP, right??

**IN WHAT WAYS IS 21ST-CENTURY TECHNOLOGY MAKING A DIFFERENCE TO A YOUNG PERSON'S WORLD AND HOW DO YOU THINK IT CAN BE USED TO BRING ABOUT CHANGE?**

**It** offers the opportunity to share information and circumvent traditional media, but I think that the cloud of information and semi-relations with others over the net can be an illusion, or rather a dangerous distraction. It is not so good for the mind to be constantly elsewhere – or to believe that by posting stuff on the internet that in itself will change anything. I wonder how much of this technology is a total waste of time and energy? That we fill it up because it is there? And that in turn it further feeds our sense of isolation and belief that we can change nothing. To stand with others on a march through a city about something you really care about is more likely to have a profound effect on how you see the world.

> PEOPLE FIND IT HARDER AND HARDER AS THEY GET FURTHER SUCKED INTO THEIR LIVES TO SEE HOW THINGS COULD BE DIFFERENT. IT REQUIRES ENERGY. IT ALSO REQUIRES YOU TO IMAGINE IT FOR THEM. NOTHING CAN BE DONE IF IT HAS NOT FIRST BEEN IMAGINED.

**WHAT'S YOUR MAIN ADVICE TO YOUNG PEOPLE TODAY WHO WANT TO MAKE A DIFFERENCE TO THEIR WORLD?**

**Do** it now while you're young, while it is clear in your mind, while the energy is there ready to be used – before you become enmeshed in the web of responsibilities and the complications of life that creep up on you unawares. For example, it is much easier to risk arrest if you do not have kids!! Haha!

**LEARN MORE/GET INVOLVED:**
www.radiohead.com/deadairspace

## 13 Rax Interview with Denzil Armour-Brown

DENZIL HAS BEEN INVOLVED IN ACTIVISM THROUGHOUT HIS LIFE, HAVING TAKEN INSPIRATION FROM HIS MOTHER LINDA, WHO TOOK HIM ON CND MARCHES AND ACTIONS WHEN HE WAS A BOY. HE LEARNED FROM HIS MOTHER THE SENSE THAT CAMPAIGNING AGAINST INJUSTICE IS PART OF AN INDIVIDUAL'S DUTY TO SOCIETY. HE WAS PARTICULARLY INVOLVED IN THE SUCCESSFUL ANTI-GM CAMPAIGNS IN THE 1990S. THE RAX TEAM CAUGHT UP WITH DENZIL IN MARCH 2010.

**WHAT CAMPAIGN WERE YOU INVOLVED IN AND WHAT WERE YOU AIMING TO ACHIEVE?**

**I** was involved in GM campaigning around 1998 -2000 (the movement against the genetic modification of our food). I felt that biotech companies were taking dangerous, possibly irreversible, risks with our health, and the planet's health, by releasing genetically modified organisms into the environment through politically sanctioned crop trials. At the same time I didn't believe that multinational biotech corporations were really doing it for the 'greater good' of the world as they purported to do, but that they were producing GM crops with the aim of tightening their grip on our food supply for their financial gain. Why produce a terminator gene in a plant seed that causes second-generation seeds to be sterile?

## WHAT CAMPAIGNING METHODS DID YOU USE?

*I* went on marches, demonstrations, and attended anti-GM campaign meetings at crop trial sites in the UK. Direct action resulted in the destruction of fields of GM crops by activists pulling modified plants up with their roots. I contributed money to various anti-GM campaign groups. I designed, produced, and sold anti-GM T-shirts with the slogans: 'SAY gmNO – Russian Roulette with our Health.' I distributed them widely and donated the money made through sales to the cause.

## WHAT IMPACT HAS YOUR CAMPAIGNING HAD?

*I* believe that, at the time, the above actions helped bring and keep the issues of genetic modification in the public arena/consciousness and contributed to the government deciding to abandon further GM crop trials (temporarily it now seems!). It was a very happy and fulfilling time for me to feel that I was actually 'doing something' instead of feeling impotent and frustrated as I watched negative events unfolding in front of my eyes.

GENETIC ENGINEERING • RUSSIAN ROULETTE WITH OUR HEALTH!

# Stop the Crop
## National Rally & GM site visit
### Watlington, Oxfordshire
### May 18th July • 2pm

Farm near Watlington (12 miles south of Oxford) is growing Genetically Modified (GM) oilseed rape, covering an area of aprox 24 football pitches.

Come along to celebrate GM campaign successes to date and to demonstrate that opposition is not going to go away! Bring banners, music, family and friends. With speakers and music. All Welcome.

...port and meeting ...Genetic Engineering ...rk

## WHAT WOULD BE YOUR KEY ADVICE FOR CAMPAIGNERS?

**1** *Only* campaign for issues that you really 'BELIEVE' in.

**2** *Regularly* question authority and 'conventional wisdom' – research it and make up your own mind.

**3** *While* campaigning, push the boundaries of the status quo with your belief and determination but without violence to others.

**LEARN MORE/GET INVOLVED**:
www.gmfreeze.org www.greenpeace.org.uk/gm
www.geneticsaction.org.uk www.genewatch.org

# *The* PROJECTOR ROOM

## 14 *Rax Interview with Bob Crow*

BOB CROW IS A TRADE UNION LEADER, THE GENERAL SECRETARY OF THE NATIONAL UNION OF RAIL, MARITIME AND TRANSPORT WORKERS (RMT) AND A MEMBER OF THE GENERAL COUNCIL OF THE TRADES UNION CONGRESS (TUC). THE RAX TEAM CAUGHT UP WITH BOB IN FEBRUARY 2010.

**WHAT ARE THE MAIN ISSUES THAT YOU THINK YOUNG PEOPLE SHOULD BE MOST CONCERNED ABOUT TODAY?**

*The* economic crisis which gripped Britain and the rest of the world from 2008 has led to an uncertain future for us all, but particularly young people as they prepare for their working lives in the midst of a deep recession. Ordinary people are paying the price for the reckless folly of the bankers and the politicians who egged the financial class on with the mantra that greed is good. Unemployment, particularly youth unemployment, is rocketing and the government is cutting health, education and other vital public services while wasting billions on nuclear weapons and pursuing criminal foreign wars. Meanwhile the fascist British National Party is exploiting the crisis to pursue its divisive, bigoted agenda with lies about foreigners being to blame.

**HOW DO YOU THINK YOUNG PEOPLE CAN BE BEST ENGAGED IN THE POLITICAL PROCESS?**

*When* the veteran campaigning MP Tony Benn retired from Parliament he joked that it was to "spend more time involved in politics". His point was that politics is not just confined to Parliament or about voting in an election every five years. Democracy is not a spectator sport. There are countless campaigns for peace, anti-racism and the environment for people to get involved with – and of course trade unions, which fight to win a fair deal for workers both in the workplace and through political lobbying. Most of these organizations have their own youth section to help introduce young people to campaigning and ensure that their voice is heard.

**HOW DOES THE WORK OF THE RMT CONNECT TO THE LIVES OF YOUNG PEOPLE?**

*RMT* has thousands of members between the ages of 16 and 25. These are young workers who have joined the union because they know that it will fight to defend their interests in the workplace in the face of employers

who continually try to drive down pay and conditions in order to cut costs and boost profits for shareholders. The union negotiates on behalf of its members with employers and is not afraid of using its most powerful weapon – the strike – if it believes they are being treated unfairly. RMT wants the lower rate of the national minimum wage for workers aged 16-21 to be abolished, believing that they should receive the full amount paid to other adults. The union is also affiliated to Youth Fight for Jobs (www.youthfightforjobs.com) – which campaigns for measures to combat unemployment among young people.

**LEARN MORE/GET INVOLVED:**
www.youthfightforjobs.com

## 15 *Rax Interview with Sir Hugh Orde*

SIR HUGH JOINED THE LONDON METROPOLITAN POLICE IN 1977. AFTER A LONG AND SUCCESSFUL CAREER, HE WAS APPOINTED PRESIDENT OF THE ASSOCIATION OF CHIEF POLICE OFFICERS (ACPO) IN 2009. THE RAX TEAM CAUGHT UP WITH SIR HUGH IN MARCH 2010.

**WHAT ARE THE ISSUES THAT YOU BELIEVE ARE MOST IMPORTANT FOR YOUNG PEOPLE TO ADDRESS?**

*We* have seen huge changes in society in recent years, many of them based around our world 'getting smaller' as people, money and information all travel around across international borders in a way never seen before. Those changes create new challenges. One thing vital to the police service is to find ways to preserve a sense of local community so that people can feel safe and secure where they live.

# CHAPTER 6 — The PROJECTOR ROOM

## HOW CAN YOUNG PEOPLE MAKE A POSITIVE CONNECTION WITH THE UK POLICE FORCE?

*Young* people today are often given a bad reputation, but the reality is that just 6% are serious or persistent offenders. Neighbourhood policing teams have gone a long way to building connections with young people, alongside work with schools. But the first interaction the police have with a young person will still often be after they have committed a crime, when we need to try and avoid them getting into trouble in the first place. Young people should not feel intimidated standing up for what they believe in.

## WHAT ARE YOUR VIEWS ON CAMPAIGN GROUPS THAT USE NON-VIOLENT DIRECT ACTION?

*Balancing* the rights of protesters with those of others to go about their business unaffected can place the police in a difficult position, where it has to strike a balance between upholding the law and acting proportionately. But exercising the right to protest is a fundamental part of our society and one the police service should always protect. The protest at the G20 in London in 2009 – where the world's leaders met to discuss global issues – has led to a reappraisal of policing which is welcome. By and large, though, many thousands of protests take place daily in our country without incident.

## WHAT ARE THE MAIN PRIORITIES FOR POLICING PROTESTS?

*The* job of the police is to keep the peace. Good communication makes that task much easier and has to be a priority – where the police can talk to those protesting and know what to expect, then it is far easier to police in a fair and proportionate way. Ultimately we want to protect the public from harm while allowing maximum freedom to all.

## FROM A POLICE OFFICER'S POINT OF VIEW, WHAT IS THE POLICING OF PROTESTS LIKE?

*At* the extreme end, it can be difficult. Police officers are first and foremost human beings, but no matter what provocation offered their standards of behaviour must be beyond reproach. Those officers who cross the line must be dealt with, but the majority, who don't, deserve our support. And we have to remember that the extreme end is not the norm: each year many thousands of people choose to protest and the overwhelming majority is peaceful and lawful.

## WHAT WOULD BE YOUR THREE TOP TIPS TO YOUNG ACTIVE CITIZENS SEEKING TO TAKE INFORMED AND RESPONSIBLE ACTION?

*My* first would be not to underestimate your influence: when it comes to stopping youth crime, for instance, we know that young people listen to their peers more than anyone else.

*Second,* on community issues particularly I would encourage young people to talk to the police: we want to hear from you and very often in fact we can only tackle issues together with you.

*Finally,* go for it! The kind of society I want to live in is where people speak out for what they believe in and take a stand against crime and anti-social behaviour.

### LEARN MORE/GET INVOLVED:
www.npiadocuments.co.uk/volunteeringguidance.pdf

## 16 Rax Interview with Lord Phillips, President of the Supreme Court of the UK

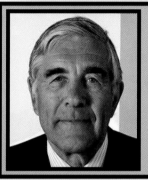

LORD PHILLIPS WAS APPOINTED AS A HIGH COURT JUDGE IN 1987. IN 2009 HE WAS APPOINTED AS THE FIRST PRESIDENT OF THE SUPREME COURT OF THE UK. THE RAX TEAM CAUGHT UP WITH LORD PHILLIPS IN JANUARY 2010.

## WHAT ISSUES DO YOU THINK ARE MOST IMPORTANT FOR YOUNG PEOPLE TO ADDRESS?

*Global* warming.

## WHAT CAMPAIGNS DID YOU TAKE PART IN AS A YOUNG MAN AND WHAT IMPACT DID THEY HAVE?

*When* I was at university I campaigned against the UK having atomic weapons. The government was not persuaded and we did not overcome this.

## HOW CAN YOUNG PEOPLE MAKE POSITIVE CONNECTIONS WITH GOVERNMENT?

*They* must take an interest in current affairs and in what the politicians are doing on their behalf and make their opinions known to those politicians.

## WHY IS THERE AN ELEMENT OF EPHEBIPHOBIA IN MAINSTREAM MEDIA AND HOW CAN IT BE AVOIDED?

*This* is because some elements of the media constantly publicize youth crime. To combat this, young people should behave with consideration for others, and try to help other young people to keep out of trouble, and the press should give young people credit when credit is due.

## RESEARCH SHOWS THAT PEOPLE LAUGH LESS THAN THEY DID IN THE 1950S, WHY DO YOU THINK THIS IS?

*Because* we spend less time talking to each other face to face.

# SECOND Campaign NATIONAL ACTION

## 1 What is the second campaign?

*You* have now reached the stage where you can engage in your second active citizenship campaign. This campaign is optional, depending on whether you are taking a GCSE in Citizenship Studies and what examination board you are using. It's for you and your teacher to decide. There will be a final major campaign opportunity at the end of *Tools For Change*.

Remember to use the ideas in *The Mirror* that show you how to record, evaluate and assess the whole campaign process. Use the checklist under the title: "How do I keep a record of my campaigns?"

IF YOU ARE TAKING THE GCSE, YOU WILL ALSO NEED TO MAKE SURE THAT YOUR CAMPAIGN IS CLEARLY CONNECTED TO THE CONTENT PART OF YOUR CITIZENSHIP STUDIES COURSE (DEMOCRACY AND JUSTICE, RIGHTS AND RESPONSIBILITIES OR IDENTITIES AND DIVERSITY). YOU MAY BE ASKED TO CHOOSE YOUR ISSUE FROM A LIST BUT YOU WILL STILL HAVE PLENTY OF FREEDOM IN TAKING IT FROM THERE. ON ALL MATTERS CONNECTED TO YOUR GCSE, TAKE YOUR TEACHER'S ADVICE.

## YOUR IDEAS FOR CHANGE ARE VITAL TO THE COUNTRY, SO GO NATIONAL!

## 2 What kind of actions should you take?

YOUR SECOND CITIZENSHIP ACTION NEEDS TO ADDRESS A NATIONAL ISSUE USING THE SKILLS YOU HAVE LEARNED SO FAR – CRITICAL THINKING AND ENQUIRY, ADVOCACY AND REPRESENTATION AND TAKING INFORMED AND RESPONSIBLE ACTION. THERE ARE SEVERAL KINDS OF ACTIONS YOU CAN TAKE AND THE FOLLOWING ARE JUST A FEW IDEAS. YOU SHOULD USE MORE THAN ONE OF THEM FOR YOUR CAMPAIGN.

## SCHOOL

### FOR EXAMPLE:

- LAUNCHING AN AWARENESS-RAISING CAMPAIGN IN SCHOOL ABOUT A NATIONAL ISSUE.
- GIVING A YEAR SEVEN, EIGHT, NINE, TEN OR WHOLE-SCHOOL ASSEMBLY ABOUT YOUR OWN NATIONAL CAMPAIGN OR AN EXISTING ONE.
- MAKING AND SHOWING YOUR OWN CAMPAIGN FILM ABOUT A NATIONAL ISSUE SO THAT THE WHOLE SCHOOL CAN HAVE ACCESS TO IT.
- CREATING A CAMPAIGNING MEME THAT DRAWS ATTENTION TO A NATIONAL ISSUE AND MAY GO VIRAL THROUGH THE STUDENTS IN YOUR SCHOOL.
- ORGANIZING A CAMPAIGN FOR CHANGE RELATED TO A NATIONAL ISSUE THROUGH YOUR SCHOOL COUNCIL.
- SETTING UP AN EVENT TO CELEBRATE A PARTICULAR NATIONAL CULTURE IN YOUR SCHOOL.
- CO-ORDINATING A LOCAL SCHOOL NETWORK TO ENCOURAGE OTHER SCHOOLS TO ADDRESS A PARTICULAR NATIONAL ISSUE.
- ORGANIZING A SCHOOL CONCERT WHERE YOU CAN PLAY SOME OF YOUR OWN MUSIC CREATED TO ADVOCATE FOR A NATIONAL ISSUE.
- HOLDING A SCHOOL DEBATE CONNECTED TO A NATIONAL ISSUE.
- HOLDING A CREATIVE CAMPAIGN ACTION IN YOUR SCHOOL ADDRESSING A NATIONAL ISSUE.

CONTINUED

# THE LOCAL COMMUNITY

## FOR EXAMPLE:

- Holding a debate or series of meetings in the community to raise awareness or promote taking action over a national issue.
- Creating a performance or production open to the community to raise awareness or promote action over a national issue.
- Organizing a local demonstration, protest or creative action connected to a national issue.
- Utilizing the local media to raise awareness or promote taking action over a national issue.
- Holding an event to promote national support and cohesion for different racial, religious, gender or sexuality groups.
- Volunteering to work with a recognized national organization that promotes active citizenship.
- Creating an event that allows for a variety of voices and cultural opinions to be shared within one group.
- Making links with a national union to support a campaign or create your own.
- Contacting your local MP about a national issue.
- Contacting people in authority or in a position to make change related to a national issue.

# BEING THE MEDIA

## FOR EXAMPLE:

- Creating a website or blog that raises awareness about an issue or provides ways for people to take action.
- Taking part in online discussion forums and comments pages where you make your opinions known on a national issue.
- Contributing to independent or mainstream news sources, giving your opinion on a national issue.
- Creating a campaigning meme addressing a national issue that could go viral.
- Making a campaigning film dealing with a national issue.
- Staging a media-friendly event raising awareness about a national issue.
- Creating a pamphlet that raises awareness about a national issue or promotes taking action.
- Joining national campaigns and contributing to them through online campaigning.
- Taking part in radio phone-ins where a national issue is being discussed.

These lists have shown some examples of actions you could take. But it is up to you to decide what to do. If you have an idea for a campaign that's not on the above list but is connected to a national issue, then go for it!

## 3 What kinds of issues should you address?

You may already have found issues that you care about. They may be ideas that have been sparked off by the Toolkit or you may have always had an idea for change burning inside you. The only restriction is that the issue you choose must be connected to an issue that affects the nation. Once you find something that you are passionate about, you're on the right path!

## FIND YOUR PASSION AND YOU'VE FOUND THE ROAD TO CAMPAIGN SUCCESS!

# TOOLS for CHANGE

## 1 Why is this chapter important?

*The* *Projector Room* gave you plenty of ideas about how to use technology and the media to help you project your campaign to a wider audience. *Tools For Change* introduces you to a variety of skills that use creativity, imagination and humour to win support for your campaign.

**CREATIVE AND HUMOROUS CAMPAIGNING ACTIONS ARE OFTEN THE ONES THAT HAVE THE MOST IMPACT.**

### THIS CHAPTER WILL HELP ENSURE THAT:

YOU ARE AWARE OF HOW YOUR ACTIVE CITIZENSHIP CAMPAIGNS TIE IN WITH ALL OF YOUR SUBJECTS IN SCHOOL.

YOU HAVE CONSIDERED METHODS OF CAMPAIGNING THAT WILL ENGAGE THE PUBLIC IN CREATIVE WAYS. **a**

YOU KNOW THAT HUMOUR CAN BE A POWERFUL TOOL FOR CHANGE. **b**

YOU UNDERSTAND WHAT CULTURE JAMMING IS AND HOW IT CAN BE USED TO DRAW ATTENTION TO A CAMPAIGN.

YOU WILL HAVE ADDED THE USE OF COSTUME TO YOUR COLLECTION OF CAMPAIGNING TOOLS. **c**

YOU UNDERSTAND HOW THE UNDERGROUND MUSIC SCENE CAN BE AN AVENUE FOR YOUR CAMPAIGNING.

**IN OTHER WORDS, YOU WILL USE ADVANCED MEDIA AND CAMPAIGNING SKILLS TO A VERY HIGH LEVEL IN ORDER TO CREATE A WINNING CAMPAIGN THAT WILL REACH THE MAXIMUM NUMBER OF PEOPLE.**

*This* is the last chapter in the Toolkit and supplies you with the final set of techniques you will need in any campaign for change. For that reason, the chapter is called *Tools for Change*.

**THE ONLY TOOLS THAT CAN'T BE PROVIDED ARE YOUR IMAGINATION, CREATIVITY AND PASSION. THAT'S UP TO YOU.**

## 2 How does active citizenship tie in with my other school subjects?

*The* Citizenship Studies course has been designed so that it is easy to have your work spread over into other subjects. You have already seen how your Art, IT, English, History, Music, Media Studies and Drama lessons can add to your citizenship work. It is important to consider how your other subjects can also tie in with your citizenship work.

### FOR EXAMPLE

**TECHNOLOGY** can help you design and make objects that will aid your campaign, such as placards, T-shirts and sets for a piece of drama. It can also help you consider the importance of sustainability within design and production. **d**

**LANGUAGE STUDIES** are important to help you ensure that people whose first language is not English can understand your campaigns.

**RELIGIOUS STUDIES** enables you to make sure that your campaign is inclusive of all the diverse cultures in the UK.

**MATHEMATICS** plays a big part in your ability to assess statistics, create and record useful surveys and represent the impact of your campaign through accurate bar charts and graphs.

CONTINUED

As part of our active citizenship project, we decided to design and make 50 T-shirts that raise awareness about the campaign to support the 283,500 refused asylum seekers who live in destitution in the UK. We had found out about the campaign through Amnesty International, who are part of the coalition to raise awareness of the issue.

Cassady, Jamie, Amy and myself all have the same Technology teacher – Mr Walmsley – so we asked him if we could tie in this project with our GCSE projects. It was easy! He actually reckoned that this would make for a better project than the ones we had originally been planning as it ties in with Citizenship Studies and allows for evidence of the fact that we are using our own creative skills to produce a product that actually sells. We had to make a 'point of sales' stand as well for our Technology GCSE project but, instead of it being for an imaginary product that will never end up in shops anyway, it turned out to be really useful for us to sell the T-shirts in school. This made us feel that we weren't making something for no reason other than to get a good grade in GCSE Technology.

The Technology department has a Heat Press, which Mr Walmsley let us use to make the T-shirts. On Tuesday after school, we made 50 T-shirts that used the campaign slogan: 'Still Human Still Here'. We also added the website for the campaign: www.stillhumanstillhere.wordpress.com They looked great!

The next week, we were allowed to sell the T-shirts in school, using our point of sales stands. With the money, we paid back the cost of materials and sent the rest to the campaign organization. We took pictures of the project and these pictures can be used for our Citizenship Studies and our Technology GCSEs.

# HEADS OF THE HEADS ★c

**IN** 2005, THE LEADERS OF EIGHT OF THE MOST POWERFUL COUNTRIES IN THE WORLD CAME TO GLENEAGLES IN SCOTLAND TO DISCUSS GLOBAL ISSUES; THIS GROUP WAS CALLED THE G8. THERE WERE TWO WEEKS OF ACTIONS, PROTESTS AND MASS DEMONSTRATIONS CALLING ON THEM TO ADDRESS ISSUES SUCH AS GLOBAL POVERTY, THE ABUSE OF THE WORLD'S RESOURCES, CLIMATE JUSTICE AND ENDING WAR. AT THE HEAD OF THE MAKE POVERTY HISTORY MARCH WERE EIGHT PEOPLE WEARING MASKS THAT REPRESENTED THE EIGHT LEADERS.

THIS USE OF COSTUME DRAWS ATTENTION AND ENCOURAGES PEOPLE TO CONSIDER THE IMPORTANCE OF THE ISSUE BEING HIGHLIGHTED – IN THIS CASE THE FACT THAT EIGHT MEN HAD THE POWER TO MAKE DECISIONS THAT COULD DETERMINE THE WELL-BEING OF BILLIONS OF PEOPLE ACROSS THE WORLD.

# ONE MAN PROTEST ★a

**WHEN** NEWS OF THE INHUMANE TREATMENT OF PRISONERS IN THE ABU GHRAIB DETENTION CENTRE IN IRAQ REACHED THE UK, ONE MAN CHOSE TO MAKE HIS OWN CREATIVE PROTEST BY RE-ENACTING THE ICONIC PICTURE THAT HAD COME TO SYMBOLIZE THE HUMAN RIGHTS ABUSE.

# BILL HICKS ★b

**BILL** HICKS WAS A LEGENDARY AMERICAN COMEDIAN AND SOCIAL CRITIC. ALTHOUGH HE DIED AT 32, HE HAD AN ENORMOUS IMPACT ON THE WORLD OF COMEDY AND GENERATED CONTROVERSY MANY TIMES. HE IS A GOOD EXAMPLE OF SOMEONE WHO USED COMEDY TO QUESTION THE ESTABLISHED WAY OF SEEING THE WORLD AND TO CRITICIZE AUTHORITY. COMEDY IS A POWERFUL VEHICLE AND IS AS MUCH A FORM OF PHILOSOPHY AS IT IS A REASON FOR LAUGHTER. HICKS USED TO FINISH HIS SHOWS BY SAYING THAT LIFE IS LIKE A FAIRGROUND RIDE:

*... IT'S JUST A RIDE, AND WE CAN CHANGE IT ANY TIME WE WANT. IT'S ONLY A CHOICE. NO EFFORT, NO WORK, NO JOB, NO SAVINGS OF MONEY. JUST A SIMPLE CHOICE, RIGHT NOW, BETWEEN FEAR AND LOVE. THE EYES OF FEAR WANT YOU TO PUT BIGGER LOCKS ON YOUR DOORS, BUY GUNS, CLOSE YOURSELF OFF. THE EYES OF LOVE INSTEAD SEE ALL OF US AS ONE. HERE'S WHAT WE CAN DO TO CHANGE THE WORLD, RIGHT NOW, TO A BETTER RIDE. TAKE ALL THAT MONEY WE SPEND ON WEAPONS AND DEFENCES EACH YEAR AND INSTEAD SPEND IT FEEDING AND CLOTHING AND EDUCATING THE POOR OF THE WORLD, WHICH IT WOULD PAY FOR MANY TIMES OVER, NOT ONE HUMAN BEING EXCLUDED, AND WE COULD EXPLORE SPACE, TOGETHER, BOTH INNER AND OUTER, FOREVER, IN PEACE.*

**BILL HICKS 1961-94**

**P.E** allows you to focus on issues related to health and the physical body as well as considering sports-based events to draw attention to and support for your campaigns.

**SCIENCE** is central to your ability to assess statistics and research as well as keeping you abreast of new developments and what ethical and moral questions they may raise.

**GEOGRAPHY** enables you to conduct research related to specific countries as well as assessing issues related to the environment and sustainability.

**Many** schools create citizenship campaigns that become a whole-school project, with all the different subjects fulfilling a different aspect of the same campaign.

**WHOLE-SCHOOL PROJECTS ARE A POWERFUL WAY OF CREATING A CAMPAIGN THAT HAS MAXIMUM IMPACT ON THE SCHOOL COMMUNITY AND THE LOCAL COMMUNITY. THEY CAN ALSO HAVE CONSIDERABLE IMPACT ON A NATIONAL AND LOCAL SCALE TOO.**

## 3 What kinds of creative campaign techniques are there?

**Although** using 21st-century technology has an impact, nothing has more of an impact than people actually going out and doing something that is memorable, that captures the imagination and makes you think again about what is really happening in your world. Very often, the most successful campaigns have used innovation and creativity to make them stand out and have a positive impact on their world.

**IF THERE WERE JUST ONE TIP THAT THE TOOLKIT COULD GIVE YOU, IT WOULD BE THIS: BE AS CREATIVE AND IMAGINATIVE AS POSSIBLE IN YOUR CAMPAIGNING.**

Always devote a lot of time in your planning to thinking about how you can make your campaign stand out. This will become one of the most enjoyable parts of your campaign, not only because being creative is fun but also because – as you will see – humour is one of the best tools for bringing about change.

You will have looked at a great many different ways of creative campaigning through this Toolkit and you will also have discovered many of your own through your research and self-directed learning. Below are just a few ideas to help inspire you to take things further.

---

### IN PAIRS
### ALIEN'S EYES

**You** have to **MAKE A REPORT TO THE LEADER OF YOUR PLANET ABOUT THE PHENOMENON OF MARCHES AND DEMONSTRATIONS ON PLANET EARTH.** You need to say what they are, why people take part in them, what they look like, what kinds of things happen during them and the kind of impact that they can have.

You have **FIVE MINUTES** to complete this report in groups.

Feed back your ideas to the class.

## UNUSUAL EVENTS THAT CAPTURE THE IMAGINATION

**From** dropping leaflets from an air balloon to posting themselves to the Prime Minister, the Suffragettes brought a great deal of creativity to the process of campaigning. Over the years, campaigners have come up with many other ways to use creativity to draw attention to their cause.

**FOR EXAMPLE**

In the early 1990s, a campaign group called the Barbie Liberation Organization (BLO) came up with an ingenious and media-friendly way to raise awareness about the damage caused to children by the kind of stereotyping encouraged by popular toys. This was because the new 'Talking Barbie Doll' said things like "Math is hard" and "I love shopping" as well as being skinny with flowing long blonde hair in the style of a model. The BLO managed to get hold of hundreds of talking Barbie Dolls and talking GI Joes/Action Men. They switched the voice boxes in the toys and then placed them back into toyshops nationwide, with a small message inside explaining their campaign and telling children to contact their local television stations.

Children bought the toys and were surprised to hear their Barbie dolls barking out lines in a deep voice like "Vengeance is mine!" and "Eat lead Cobra!" and their Action Men figures saying things like "Let's plan our dream wedding!" and "Will we ever have enough clothes?" in a high-pitched female voice. This ended up as an interesting and amusing story, perfect for the end slot on TV news. This led to the BLO's campaign statement being read out, explaining how Barbie and Action Man dolls reinforce stereotypes that are not always healthy for young children.

CONTINUED

**a** SAS IS CONSTANTLY TRYING TO MAKE OUR MESSAGE INTERESTING AND ENGAGING AND USE HUMOUR WELL... SUPPORTERS AND THE PRESS WILL GET BORED OF THE SAME ACTION TIME AND AGAIN, SO TO GET OUR MESSAGE ACROSS EFFECTIVELY WE NEED TO CONSTANTLY IMPROVE AND EVOLVE OUR CAMPAIGNS.

SURFERS AGAINST SEWAGE (SEE RAX INTERVIEW ON PAGE 198).

# THE AIRPLOT PLOT

**THE** CAMPAIGNING GROUP GREENPEACE CONSISTENTLY COMES UP WITH CREATIVE ACTIONS THAT CAPTURE THE IMAGINATION. IN 2009, GREENPEACE BOUGHT A PLOT OF LAND THAT WAS TO BE PART OF A THIRD RUNWAY FOR HEATHROW AIRPORT AND THEN INVITED THE PUBLIC TO SIGN UP TO BECOME OWNERS OF A SMALL PLOT OF THAT LAND. BY 2010, THERE WERE NEARLY 100,000 'OWNERS' – INCLUDING SOME CELEBRITIES, WHO HELPED MAKE THE ACTION MORE MEDIA-FRIENDLY. THE ORGANIZATION BELIEVED THAT BY DOING THIS, THEY WOULD MAKE IT MORE DIFFICULT FOR THE AIRPORT EXPANSION PLANS TO GO AHEAD.

GREENPEACE BELIEVES THAT A THIRD RUNWAY WOULD MAKE IT IMPOSSIBLE FOR THE GOVERNMENT TO MEET ITS TARGETS FOR REDUCING CARBON EMISSIONS. PEOPLE SUPPORTING THE AIRPORT'S EXPANSION ARGUE THAT A THIRD RUNWAY WOULD PRODUCE MORE JOBS, BOOST THE ECONOMY AND MAKE THE UK MORE ACCESSIBLE FOR PEOPLE VISITING. SOME ALSO ARGUE THAT HUMAN ACTIVITY IS NOT RESPONSIBLE FOR CLIMATE CHANGE.

## LEARN MORE/GET INVOLVED:

www.airplot.org.uk www.greenpeace.org.uk
www.futureheathrow.com

# B.L.O

**c**

**THE** BLO BECAME A LEGENDARY PIECE OF CULTURE JAMMING.

EAT LEAD COBRA!

LET'S PLAN OUR DREAM WEDDING!

IN APRIL 2010, THE PLANS FOR A THIRD RUNWAY AT HEATHROW AIRPORT WERE CANCELLED.

## CULTURE JAMMING AND SPOOFS

CULTURE JAMMING IS AN ACTIVIST TECHNIQUE WHICH INVOLVES CAMPAIGNERS SUBVERTING OR DISRUPTING MAINSTREAM CULTURAL ORGANIZATIONS OR MAINSTREAM ADVERTISING TO DRAW ATTENTION TO AN ISSUE.

### FOR EXAMPLE

*Every* year, around Christmas, anti-consumerist activists hold carol-singing concerts in major shopping centres where they sing traditional carols that have had their words changed to suit the campaign. For example, they sing, to the tune of 'Jingle Bells': "Profits here, profits there, profits everywhere. Christmas time is funny, we smell money in the air." This draws attention to their idea that consumerism is a negative phenomenon in modern human society which brings no long-term pleasure and has the side-effects of debt and environmental damage. All this is achieved in a non-violent, non-confrontational way, which usually brings a smile to the bemused shoppers who come across the carol-singing teams.

### FOR EXAMPLE

*Another* effective, creative method of campaigning has emerged over the past 20 years whereby activists who want to draw attention to the questionable ethical and moral practices of certain companies have bought a share in the company. If you become a shareholder, it gives you the right to attend the annual shareholders' meetings. Campaigners are then able to stand up at the meetings and make statements drawing the attention of other shareholders to the company's ethically and morally questionable practices. Very often, companies that use unethical practices spend huge amounts of money on advertising to give the impression that they are good, kind and caring. For the price of one share, it is possible to draw attention to the other side of a company that will never be shown in its advertising and this can lead to changes in policy.

> "EVENTS THAT HAVE WIT... THAT EXPOSE AND RIDICULE. WITHOUT ANGER AND WITH LITTLE JUDGMENT. YOU ARE FAR MORE LIKELY TO GET FAVOURABLE PRESS FROM THAT."
>
> THOM YORKE (SEE RAX INTERVIEW ON PAGE 165).

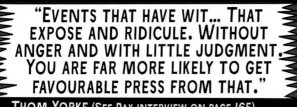

### IN GROUPS
## HEADS TOGETHER

*In* groups, you have FIVE MINUTES to COME UP WITH A CREATIVE AND IMAGINATIVE WAY TO GET YOUR POINT ACROSS ON ANY ISSUE THAT YOUR GROUP CHOOSES.

Feed back your ideas to the class.

### FOR EXAMPLE

*A* recent example has been the work of a team known as the Yes Men, which specializes in posing as important members of corporations or governments. One of the Yes Men famously posed as a spokesperson from a corporation called Dow Chemicals. The company had taken over Union Carbide, owner of a factory in Bhopal, India, where a poisonous gas leak in 1984 killed over 8,000 people. Despite this disaster, the company had only offered small amounts of compensation to the people who had lost family members or had become so ill that they needed medical care for the rest of their lives.

In 2004, Jude Finisterra appeared on the BBC News, claiming to be from Dow Chemicals. Finisterra stated that the company had finally accepted full responsibility and wanted to do something to repair the awful damage they had caused. He said they had decided to offer significant compensation to the people of Bhopal to the tune of $12 billion. The story went global for the next two hours before a shocked Dow Chemicals pointed out that Finisterra was not from their company and they had never heard of him before.

The Yes Men's culture jamming had managed to draw attention to an injustice and to encourage debate about the way the people of Bhopal had been mistreated. Although the people of Bhopal were at first saddened to hear that the 'promise' of fair compensation had been false, it is widely believed that they were grateful that interest in their plight had been reignited and that Dow Chemicals had been seriously embarrassed. The Yes Men have made several culture jams of this nature and clips of their films can be easily found on the web.

*Creating spoofs* is another popular form of culture jamming. This involves using a recognized form of media and subverting it to send out an unexpected message.

### FOR EXAMPLE

The global justice movement in the 1990s made many spoof newspapers which at first glance looked like a famous paper until you looked more closely. The *Evening Standard* was one target – a paper looking very much like the famous London news publication was given out free to commuters as they returned home from work. It was only when the commuter sat down on their train that they realized the paper was actually called *The Evading Standards* and all the stories were encouraging people to question the financial systems and corporate values that drove the global economy.

CONTINUED ➜

# THE YES MEN

ANDY BICHLBAUM AND MIKE BONANNO AKA THE YES MEN.

**BY** USING SATIRE, HUMOUR AND CULTURE JAMMING, THE YES MEN HAVE BEEN ABLE TO DRAW PUBLIC ATTENTION TO SERIOUS CONCERNS ABOUT THE ETHICAL BACKGROUND TO BUSINESS AND GOVERNMENT POLICIES ON THE ENVIRONMENT. THERE HAVE BEEN SEVERAL MEDIA STUNTS OR CULTURE JAMS THAT HAVE BEEN PULLED OFF BY THE YES MEN. HERE ARE A FEW EXAMPLES:

LIVE
BBC WORLD
**BHOPAL LEGACY**
"Dow accepts full responsibility"
bbcnews.com
BUSINESS 2-WEEK LOW WITH BRENT CRUDE SLIPPING BELOW $40

YES MAN ANDY BICHLBAUM AS JUDE FINESTERRA, PRETENDING TO BE A REPRESENTATIVE FROM DOW CHEMICALS, LIVE ON TV.

ANDY WITH GILDA

**IN** 2005, THE YES MEN TURNED UP AT AN INTERNATIONAL BANKERS' CONFERENCE POSING AS CORPORATE REPRESENTATIVES AND SUGGESTED A COMPUTER PROGRAM THAT PUTS A PRECISE FINANCIAL VALUE ON HUMAN LIFE. IT WOULD CALCULATE HOW MANY INNOCENT PEOPLE COULD DIE BEFORE IT REDUCED COMPANY PROFITS. 'GILDA' THE GOLDEN SKELETON REPRESENTED THIS IDEA OF ACCEPTABLE RISK. SOME PEOPLE AT THE CONFERENCE APPLAUDED THE PLAN BEFORE THEY REALIZED THAT THEY WERE BEING FOOLED.

## RECLAIM THE NEWS
**A** SELECTION OF SPOOF NEWSPAPERS.
LEARN MORE/GET INVOLVED:
www.rts.gn.apc.org

**IN** 2002, THE YES MEN POSED AS EXPERTS FROM THE WORLD TRADE ORGANIZATION (WTO) AT A STUDENT CONFERENCE IN PLATTSBURGH.

THEY BEGAN THE CONFERENCE BY HANDING OUT FREE HAMBURGERS.

EVERYBODY BEGAN TO TUCK INTO THEIR BURGERS WHILE THE YES MEN DESCRIBED THEIR LATEST SOLUTION TO HUNGER IN THE GLOBAL SOUTH...

IT WAS ONLY AFTER A WHILE THAT THIS SOLUTION BECAME CLEAR... A NEW PROCESS THAT ALLOWED BURGERS TO BE MADE FROM RECYCLED HUMAN FAECES!

LEARN MORE/GET INVOLVED:
www.theyesmen.org

SPECIAL EDITION
**Evading Standards**
LONDON, FRIDAY 18 JUNE 1999    FREE
FREE trip to Cologne for G8 Summit celebrations. see page 19
WAR STARS Clinton and Albright's dark secret
INTERFERENCE FM - TUNE IN TO THE SOUND OF THE STREETS  ON 107.4 FM

**GLOBAL MARKET**

**FINANCIAL CRIMES**

**World Bank**

**THE Spun**
Friday, November 9, 2001    free
**Win** a year's free NHS plc healthcare! see page 14 for further details
IT'S DAY 60 OF OUR WAR - MORE ALL-ACTION COVERAGE INSIDE!
PHWAR!
SHOP 'TIL

# CHAPTER 7

# TOOLS for CHANGE

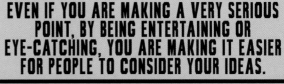

**EVEN IF YOU ARE MAKING A VERY SERIOUS POINT, BY BEING ENTERTAINING OR EYE-CATCHING, YOU ARE MAKING IT EASIER FOR PEOPLE TO CONSIDER YOUR IDEAS.**

**SPENDING TIME ON FINDING CREATIVE WAYS TO GET YOUR POINT ACROSS WILL BENEFIT YOUR CAMPAIGN ENORMOUSLY BY MAKING IT STAND OUT AS COMPELLING AND MEMORABLE.**

 **IN PAIRS**
## ART ACTION

*In* pairs, you have **FIVE MINUTES** to use any of the art action skills to come up with a way to **SUBVERT A FAMOUS IMAGE FROM THE WORLD OF ADVERTISING SO THAT IT IS MAKING A SERIOUS POINT ABOUT AN ISSUE THAT CONCERNS YOU BOTH.**

Feed back your ideas to the class.

### RECORD BOOK

*Report* on the class activities under the headings:

**CREATIVE CAMPAIGNS:**

**DESCRIBING WHAT DEMONSTRATIONS AND PROTESTS ARE USUALLY LIKE.**

**COMING UP WITH CREATIVE WAYS TO CAMPAIGN. USING ART ACTION SKILLS TO SUBVERT AN ADVERT TO MAKE A SERIOUS POINT.**

Notes on any class feedback sessions.

## COSTUME

*Costumes* are an excellent way to draw attention to your campaign, to create a more media-friendly photograph and to emphasize the aspect of fun and non-violence in the action you are taking.

### FOR EXAMPLE

There are countless examples of campaign groups that have used costumes to get across their point, from the Fathers 4 Justice campaign whose activists always dressed as superheroes to the Clown Army who would dress as clowns in army fatigues. Dressing up in costumes can make the difference between getting on the front page or ending up as a small article at the back of the paper.

 **IN GROUPS**
## NEWSPAPER GAME

*In* groups, you have **FIVE MINUTES** to **GO THROUGH NEWSPAPERS, MAGAZINES AND ONLINE NEWS SOURCES TO FIND AS MANY EXAMPLES AS YOU CAN OF CAMPAIGNERS USING COSTUMES TO GIVE THEIR ACTIONS GREATER IMPACT.**

The winning group will be the one that has found the most examples, which are verified by the rest of the class.

Feed back your answers to the class.

## USING HUMOUR

*You* are beginning to grasp the idea that campaigning can be great fun. It does not necessarily have to involve holding a meeting in a community hall or marching from A to B but can instead be something more inventive and, in fact, often benefits from fun and creativity.

### FOR EXAMPLE

The Clown Army were a successful activist group which used clowning and humour as their secret weapon. Started in the UK around 2005, their campaigning techniques have been adopted by groups across the world. When a demonstration or protest is becoming tense and it looks like conflict can arise, there is nothing more sure to calm the atmosphere down than for 20 people dressed as clowns to come running in and start dusting everyone with large, colourful feather dusters or trying to kiss and hug everyone, police officers and protesters alike. The Clown Army succeeded in drawing attention to many different issues while at the same time making members of the public and the police force laugh hysterically or stop still in wonder and amazement.

*CONTINUED*

178

HOW WOULD YOU LIKE YOUR MUMMY TO LOSE HER HOME. NO THIRD RUNWAY

# DRESS FOR CHANGE ☆a

**WHETHER** YOUR ISSUE IS LOCAL, NATIONAL OR GLOBAL, DRESSING UP HELPS YOU MAKE YOUR POINT, GIVES YOU A BETTER CHANCE OF BEING COVERED IN THE PAPERS AND IS FUN.

# UNDRESS FOR CHANGE

**SOME** ACTIVISTS, ON THE OTHER HAND, PREFER TO UNDRESS. NUDE PROTESTING IS A CAMPAIGNING TECHNIQUE THAT HAS OFTEN SUCCEEDED IN GAINING MEDIA ATTENTION AND THE INTEREST OF THE PUBLIC.

Climate Lies Uncovered SOUTHSIDE

# THE CLOWN ARMY

**THESE** CLIMATE CAMPAIGNERS CHOSE TO MAKE A NUDE PROTEST TO DRAW ATTENTION TO A PUBLIC RELATIONS (PR) COMPANY THAT IS PAID TO CREATE A 'GREEN' IMAGE FOR AN ENERGY COMPANY THAT BURNS FOSSIL FUEL. THIS PROCESS OF USING THE MEDIA TO CREATE A 'GREEN' IMAGE IS CALLED 'GREENWASHING'.

THE CEO OF THE PR COMPANY CALLED THIS ACTION A "CHEAP STUNT" AND STATED THAT HIS COMPANY WELCOMES DIALOGUE WITH CAMPAIGNING GROUPS AND NGOS. HE POINTED TO THE WORK OF THE FOSSIL FUEL COMPANY IN SEEKING SUSTAINABLE AND NON-POLLUTING SOURCES OF ENERGY.

LEARN MORE/GET INVOLVED:

www.climatecamp.org.uk ☆c

**BY** DRESSING UP LIKE COMIC MILITARY FIGURES AND ACTING LIKE CLOWNS, THIS ACTIVIST ORGANIZATION HAD A GREAT DEAL OF SUCCESS IN CALMING POTENTIALLY TENSE SITUATIONS AS WELL AS BRINGING A SMILE TO THE FACES OF POLICE AND PUBLIC ALIKE.

# TOOLS for CHANGE

*The* activist comedian Mark Thomas is famous for using humour to communicate serious issues. He has made several television series and documentary films, has written six books and constantly tours the UK with his comedy shows. His activist 'stunts' include helping a team of teenagers set up their own arms trading company to show how the arms trading laws are full of loopholes. He has also chased millionaires and demanded to see their furniture to draw attention to the fact that they were evading paying tax by claiming that their art and furniture was open to the public. He visited the Coca-Cola museum in the US, where he politely requested to see the full history of how Coca-Cola was connected to the Nazis in the Second World War. Film clips of Thomas' work can be found easily on the web and all details of his latest campaigns are at www.markthomasinfo.com.

"HUMOUR PLAYS A MASSIVE PART IN WHAT WE DO... IT HELPS US BRIDGE THE GAP BETWEEN US AND THE PEOPLE WE WANT TO TALK TO... IT'S MORE ENJOYABLE TO CAMPAIGN WITH A SMILE THAN WITH A SNARL!"

SPACE HIJACKERS (SEE RAX INTERVIEW ON PAGE 192).

## IN PAIRS/GROUPS
### BE THE BARD

*In* pairs or groups, you have **10 MINUTES** to **SUBVERT A WELL-KNOWN SONG OR ADVERTISING JINGLE** by creating your own humorous lyrics that fit with the tune but make a point about an issue you care about.

Feed back or perform your ideas to the class.

## CAMPAIGNS THAT BECOME SYMBOLIC

*Many* campaigns address such a wide-ranging issue – like achieving global justice, addressing climate change and stopping the abuse of the world's resources – that campaigners often choose to find one action that is symbolic of their wider cause.

*An* early example that you already know about is Gandhi's Salt Tax march, which identified one law that was symbolic of India's oppression by the ruling British government.

Climate Camp is a campaigning organization that focuses on fighting for climate justice. Since 2006, the group has chosen a symbolic site at least once a year where they hold a week-long activist camp. The activists then stage non-violent direct actions to draw public attention to the damage caused by the particular symbolic site as well as to the wider issues of pollution and the abuse of the earth's finite resources.

Climate Camp events in the past have focused on coal-fired power stations such as Drax and Kingsnorth, BP's headquarters, Shell Oil's headquarters, the main offices for advertising companies involved in creating positive and 'green' images for fossil fuel companies, Heathrow airport and the centre for carbon trading in London. The campaigning methods and strategies of Climate Camp are well worth looking at in more detail for an Active Citizen concerned with issues connected to climate change or if you are simply interested in how a successful national campaign group is run:

www.climatecamp.org.uk
(See Rax interview with Robbie Gillett on page 159)

An alternative and fast-growing youth-led campaign group that addresses issues connected to climate change is the UK Youth Climate Coalition:
www.ukycc.org (See Rax interview on page 104).

If you are tackling a wider, global issue, it's often possible to find an aspect of that issue represented in symbolic form in your local community.

You may be addressing the issue of human rights abuse and your research has shown that in your community there are the offices of a company that profits from trading with Burma, where full democratic rights are denied and torture and human rights abuse is common. By creating a campaign to put pressure on that company to cease trading with Burma on humanitarian grounds, you are addressing the global issue by acting locally. This technique is summed up by the well-known campaigning phrase, 'Think global, act local.'

**FIND A SYMBOL OF YOUR ISSUE AND ACT UPON IT.**

## IN GROUPS/WHOLE CLASS
### FIGHT YOUR CORNER

MOTION: THIS HOUSE BELIEVES THAT IT IS BETTER TO SET UP A CAMPAIGNING FACEBOOK PAGE THAN IT IS TO STAGE A CREATIVE ACTION.

# SUPPORT OUR SOLDIERS

**THE** CAMPAIGNS AGAINST THE WARS IN IRAQ AND AFGHANISTAN OFTEN MAKE THE POINT THAT THEY ARE NOT AGAINST THE TROOPS STATIONED IN THE CONFLICT ZONES BUT AGAINST THE LEADERS WHO HAVE MADE THE DECISION TO SEND THEM THERE. THERE HAVE BEEN SOME SOLDIERS AND EX-MILITARY FIGURES AS WELL AS FAMILIES OF SERVICE PERSONNEL WHO HAVE JOINED THE ANTI-WAR CAMPAIGNS. THEY HAVE GONE TO GREAT LENGTHS TO STRESS THAT IT IS VITAL THAT PEOPLE DON'T FORGET THE HARSH AND DANGEROUS CONDITIONS THAT SOLDIERS HAVE TO ENDURE WHILE AT WAR.

**LEARN MORE/GET INVOLVED:**
www.supportoursoldiers.co.uk
www.helpforheroes.org.uk www.mfaw.net

# SYMBOLIC ACTIONS

# WORLD'S SMALLEST ACTIVISTS!

**IN** AUGUST 2008, AS PART OF A PROTEST AGAINST KINGSNORTH COAL-FIRED POWER STATION, ENVIRONMENTAL ACTIVISTS CREATED A HUMOROUS AND MEDIA-FRIENDLY WAY OF GETTING THEIR POINT ACROSS. THEY WENT TO THE LEGOLAND THEME PARK IN WINDSOR, WHERE THERE WAS A LEGO MODEL OF THE POWER STATION AND PUT LEGO ACTIVISTS ON IT, CLIMBING UP THE FUNNEL OF THE SCALE MODEL AND RELEASING A MINI BANNER DOWN THE SIDE THAT READ 'STOP CLIMATE CHANGE'. THEY EVEN INCLUDED LEGO POLICE AND A LEGO POLICE HELICOPTER!

**WHILE** SOME ACTIONS DRAW ATTENTION TO A LARGER CAMPAIGN FOR CHANGE BY CHOOSING SYMBOLIC TARGETS, OTHERS ARE IN THEMSELVES LADEN WITH MEANING. IN 2008, IRAQI TELEVISION JOURNALIST MUNTADAR AL-ZAIDI THREW A SHOE AT THEN US PRESIDENT GEORGE BUSH. THIS WAS A SYMBOLIC ACT, SHOWING CONTEMPT FOR THE WAY BUSH HAD TREATED THE IRAQI PEOPLE. IN ARAB CULTURE, SHOWING YOUR FOOT TO (OR THROWING YOUR SHOE AT) SOMEONE IS CONSIDERED TO BE A SERIOUS INSULT.

THERE HAVE BEEN SEVERAL ANTI-WAR PROTESTS THROUGHOUT THE WORLD SINCE THE INVASION OF IRAQ AND AFGHANISTAN. ACTIVISTS SOMETIMES THROW PILES OF CHILDREN'S SHOES OUTSIDE THE OFFICES OF WORLD LEADERS TO SYMBOLIZE THE HUNDREDS OF THOUSANDS OF CHILDREN WHO HAVE DIED IN THE CONFLICTS.

**LEARN MORE/GET INVOLVED:** www.stopwar.org.uk

This Valentines day

Send The Sri Ram Sena
a Pink Chaddi.

*Because chaddis are Forever*

# PINK UNDERPANTS CAUSE A STIR

**THE** PINK CHADDI CAMPAIGN WAS BASED IN BANGALORE, INDIA AND USED A SOCIAL NETWORKING SITE TO RAISE AWARENESS ABOUT AN INCREASE IN VIOLENCE AGAINST WOMEN CAUSED BY THE OPINIONS OF A POLITICAL ORGANIZATION, WHICH ADVOCATED VIOLENCE AGAINST WOMEN WHO ACT INDEPENDENTLY. VERY QUICKLY, THE SITE HAD OVER 45,000 MEMBERS.

THE WOMEN DECIDED THAT THERE WOULD BE A BETTER CHANCE OF MEDIA COVERAGE IF THEY CAME UP WITH A CREATIVE AND HUMOROUS STRATEGY. THAT'S WHERE THE 'PINK UNDERPANTS' CAME IN. ON VALENTINE'S DAY 2009, OVER 5,000 PAIRS OF HUGE PINK UNDERPANTS WERE SENT TO THE GOVERNMENT FIGURES BELIEVED TO BE RESPONSIBLE FOR ENCOURAGING THE VIOLENCE.

THE CAMPAIGN WAS EXTREMELY SUCCESSFUL IN GENERATING NATIONAL COVERAGE. THE GROUP STATED THAT THERE WERE 10 TV NEWS VANS PARKED OUTSIDE THEIR BANGALORE CAMPAIGN OFFICES AND MEDIA ANALYSTS ESTIMATED THAT OVER A MILLION PEOPLE HAD VISITED THE CAMPAIGNING WEBSITE ON FACEBOOK. THE POLITICAL FIGURES WERE GREATLY EMBARRASSED AND BECAME A JOKE TO MUCH OF THE NATION. THE WOMEN'S COLLECTIVE HAD SUCCEEDED IN SHAMING THESE MEN INTO ACTING TO CURB THE VIOLENCE THEY HAD SEEMED TO CONDONE. **LEARN MORE/GET INVOLVED:**
www.thepinkchaddicampaign.blogspot.com

# 7 TOOLS *for* CHANGE

## RECORD BOOK

*Report* on the class activities under the headings:

### MORE CREATIVE CAMPAIGNS:

USING NEWS SOURCES TO FIND EXAMPLES OF CAMPAIGNERS WEARING COSTUME TO GET THEIR POINT ACROSS.

USING LYRICAL SKILLS TO SUBVERT A FAMOUS SONG TO MAKE A POINT.

DEBATING WHETHER SETTING UP A FACEBOOK PAGE HAS AS MUCH IMPACT AS A CREATIVE CAMPAIGN ACTION.

Notes on any class feedback sessions.

## 4. *How can you use the underground music scene to help your campaign?*

*The* underground or emerging music scene is not the same as the music scene represented by the pop charts. Underground music has always reflected changes in thinking about the world and has been at the heart of many social and cultural revolutions through history. It has always come from young people being creative and breaking new artistic ground, reacting to the world around them in a way that rarely coincides with the wishes of the music industry itself.

Musical acts like The Beatles, The Rolling Stones, Joan Baez and Bob Dylan became a focal point for the shifts in thinking that occurred in the 1960s. They were often seen as the voices of a generation. The UK reggae scene of the 1970s became a significant platform for black identity, as there were so few positive examples of black people in the media at the time. In the late 1970s, punk rock became the focal point of new ways of regarding what it meant to be young and British, questioning how authority should be regarded and spearheading a grassroots movement that fought against racism. The emergence of rap in the 1980s and 1990s signalled another new direction for youth music and was initially a reaction to inequalities, injustice and racism.

The underground music scene is often a reliable barometer by which to judge the feelings and aspirations of youth. It's important to distinguish this from the established music scene as dictated by the music industry, as this often marks the end of authenticity, with the original ideals and aspirations submerged under the prime motivation of making money.

Simply by virtue of the fact that you are young, you have a laminated VIP pass to the heart of the current underground music scene. This is something that you can use for your campaigns. The lyrics and ideals reflected in the pop charts may be utterly misleading and even advocate bland and mediocre ideas about life but the underground music scene will always contain passion, genuine empathy and the germs of ideas that can indicate how young people seek to change their world.

### FOR EXAMPLE

*You* may want to create campaigning songs, organize events that use the scene to project your campaign ideas for change or even interview prominent figures from the scene – through their MySpace site for example – who can speak about their ideals or the issues that their music highlights.

If you are addressing issues connected to race and identity in the UK, tapping into the music scene that is specific to a culture allows you to examine and understand that culture as well as celebrate it and bring it to a wider audience through its music.

The technological revolution has also marked a transformation in the way music is created. There is no longer the need to engage with the music industry for your music to be made, marketed and distributed. You can do it all yourself.

The Toolkit recommends that you use the current music scene as part of your active citizenship campaign but not as the campaign itself.

## THERE ARE NO CONTROLS ON YOUR ABILITY TO MAKE MUSIC AND GET IT HEARD; THE ONLY LIMIT IS YOUR OWN IMAGINATION AND PASSION.

# P.O.V

*In* groups of six, **ROLL THE DIE TO FIND YOUR CHARACTERS.**
Take **10 MINUTES** to **USE THE INTERNET TO RESEARCH YOUR ROLE**
(the names of the organizations have been made up).

*You* then have at least **20 MINUTES FOR THE MAIN ACTIVITY.**
Remember that all people have to remain in role throughout and
everyone has to have the chance to be heard.

## SITUATION:

A LOCAL COMMUNITY HALL IN A SMALL TOWN IN THE UK WHERE A MEETING
HAS BEEN CALLED TO DISCUSS A PROTEST PLANNED IN A MONTH'S TIME.
ENVIRONMENTAL ACTIVISTS WANT TO MARCH TO A COAL-FIRED POWER STATION –
OWNED BY POWERAGE INTERNATIONAL – ON THE EDGE OF THE TOWN AND HOLD A
PROTEST. THE PROTESTERS HAVE SAID THAT SOME OF THEM ARE PLANNING TO USE
DIRECT ACTION IN ORDER TO CLOSE THE STATION DOWN FOR A DAY. THE POWER
STATION SUPPLIES POWER TO TWO MILLION HOMES IN THE AREA BUT HAS RESERVES
THAT WOULD MEAN THOSE HOMES WOULD NOT BE IMMEDIATELY AFFECTED.
IT EMITS 20,000 TONS OF $CO_2$ EVERY DAY. YOU ARE DECIDING IF THE PROTEST
SHOULD BE ALLOWED OUTSIDE THE POWER STATION ITSELF.

## CHARACTERS: *The six characters to choose from are as follows...*

CONTINUED

**①** You are furious that the protesters want to close the power station down, think they are a dangerous lot and wish they'd have a rally in the town centre instead.

# MARY KELLY
## LOCAL MOTHER AND EMPLOYEE

**②** You think the protesters shouldn't be allowed anywhere near the power station.

# STEFAN KAYE
## PUBLIC RELATIONS OFFICER

# ① MARY KELLY
## LOCAL MOTHER AND POWER PLANT EMPLOYEE

### YOUR KEY POINTS TO MAKE ARE:

**1.** You agree that people should have the right to protest but not outside the power station and near your home. You think they should make their protest in the town centre.

**2.** You are furious that some protesters say that they will use direct action to close the station down as this will be a danger not only to them but to everyone living locally.

**3.** Powerage International pay you well, are very supportive to the community and even built a playground for the local children. You also know that they have a very green image and seem to do lots to help the global environment as well as your community.

**4.** You're not worried about what damage the station may be causing to the environment; you think it's more important that people's homes are supplied with power and that your job remains safe.

**5.** You believe that protesters who use direct action are dangerous and may harm you or your children.

### YOUR KEY SENTENCE:
"The protesters just want to cause trouble – they should stay away from the power station."

# ② STEFAN KAYE
## PUBLIC RELATIONS FOR POWERAGE INTERNATIONAL

### YOUR KEY POINTS TO MAKE ARE:

**1.** You think that the protesters are stupid even to consider going anywhere near the power station – it's dangerous and they may electrocute themselves.

**2.** If the protest is allowed to go ahead, it will cost Powerage International a fortune to bring in extra security staff.

**3.** You are aware that burning coal pollutes the atmosphere but your station is the cleanest coal-fired power station in the UK and Powerage International invest thousands in researching new green technologies because they care about the future as much as anyone else.

**4.** You point out that there are some scientists who claim that global warming is not real and, if it is, that humans do not cause it. If there is still doubt about it, then why should protesters be allowed to cause so much trouble when there's no definite proof that they are right?

**5.** It's more important that two million homes don't have their energy supply threatened and that the people who work in the station aren't put in any danger. Protesters have to grasp the reality that there are no real alternatives to fossil fuels to keep people living in the way they have become accustomed to.

### YOUR KEY SENTENCE:
"Powerage International has a duty to keep Britain's lights on."

**3** You believe the protest must go ahead at the power station, as it is symbolic of the industries that are the biggest polluters.

# KHADIJA BEGUM
## SCIENCE STUDENT AND ACTIVIST

**4** You support people's right to protest but are concerned about the safety of the public and feel it would be better if the activists had a rally in the town centre.

# PAUL POTTS
## POLICE OFFICER

---

**3** # KHADIJA BEGUM
## SCIENCE STUDENT AND ACTIVIST

### YOUR KEY POINTS TO MAKE ARE:

**1.** You are a student studying climate science and know that climate change is real, is human-made, and is the biggest threat humanity has ever known. You think that even if some people still doubt global warming, nobody can doubt that it's not good for our earth continually to spew filth into its atmosphere, poisoning the oceans and land with toxic chemicals.

**2.** The protest must be held at the power station, which is symbolic of everything that the climate justice movement is trying to change through protest and direct action.

**3.** The idea of any fossil-fuel-burning power station being considered clean is a joke.

**4.** You have been a climate activist for six years and have never once met an activist who is violent, dangerous or would threaten people in any way.

**5.** You are prepared for direct action and will do what it takes to close the power station down, thereby making the point that something radical has to be done to change the way in which we co-exist with the planet.

### YOUR KEY SENTENCE:

"Taking non-violent direct action is the only way for the public and the government to wake up to the seriousness of climate change."

---

**4** # PAUL POTTS
## POLICE OFFICER

### YOUR KEY POINTS TO MAKE ARE:

**1.** You believe strongly in people having the right to protest and sympathize with the activists as well as admire them for their determination. But you also have an obligation to ensure the safety of the public and of your officers.

**2.** You understand that, for the activists, global warming and industrial pollution seems a grave problem but so is the danger of a few protesters turning violent, doing something stupid and people ending up getting hurt.

**3.** Anyone who breaks the law will be arrested; any damage to property or any violence will result in serious charges and the possibility of a prison sentence.

**4.** You would rather the protesters held a rally in the nearby town as it would be safer and they would still have made their point. You can assure the protesters that they will be able to have all the main roads in the centre closed for the day so that their rally can go ahead safely there.

**5.** If the protest outside the power station goes ahead, it will cost the taxpayer millions to have enough police in place to control the protest and make sure everyone stays safe.

### YOUR KEY SENTENCE:

"You have the right to protest but I have a duty to protect, and it would be better for everyone if you had a rally in the town centre."

**5** Your mother was a suffragette, you have been an activist all your life, and fighting the pollution of the earth is the most important cause you have ever fought for.

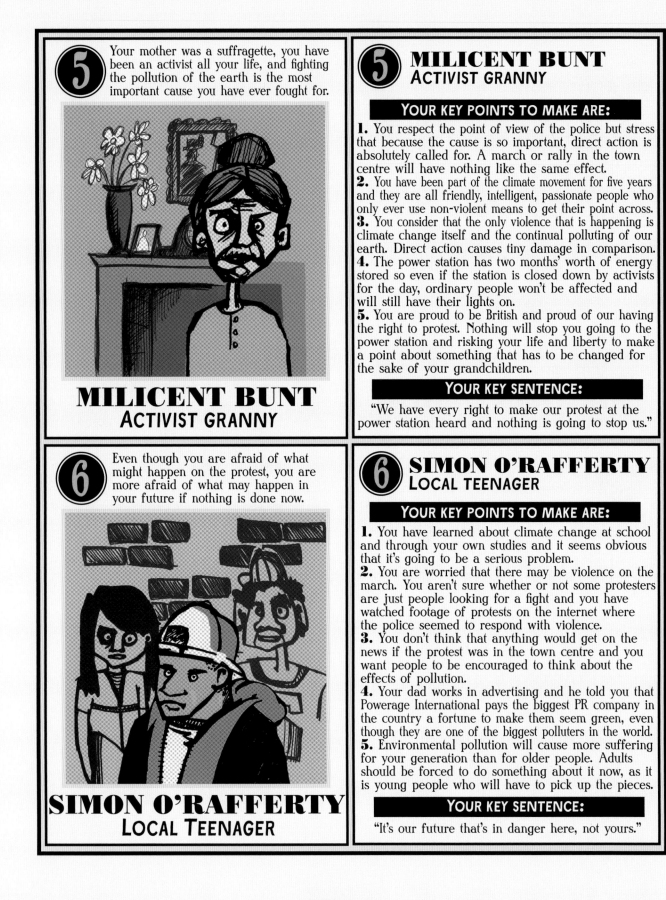

# MILICENT BUNT
## ACTIVIST GRANNY

---

**5** # MILICENT BUNT
## ACTIVIST GRANNY

### YOUR KEY POINTS TO MAKE ARE:

**1.** You respect the point of view of the police but stress that because the cause is so important, direct action is absolutely called for. A march or rally in the town centre will have nothing like the same effect.
**2.** You have been part of the climate movement for five years and they are all friendly, intelligent, passionate people who only ever use non-violent means to get their point across.
**3.** You consider that the only violence that is happening is climate change itself and the continual polluting of our earth. Direct action causes tiny damage in comparison.
**4.** The power station has two months' worth of energy stored so even if the station is closed down by activists for the day, ordinary people won't be affected and will still have their lights on.
**5.** You are proud to be British and proud of our having the right to protest. Nothing will stop you going to the power station and risking your life and liberty to make a point about something that has to be changed for the sake of your grandchildren.

### YOUR KEY SENTENCE:

"We have every right to make our protest at the power station heard and nothing is going to stop us."

---

**6** Even though you are afraid of what might happen on the protest, you are more afraid of what may happen in your future if nothing is done now.

# SIMON O'RAFFERTY
## LOCAL TEENAGER

---

**6** # SIMON O'RAFFERTY
## LOCAL TEENAGER

### YOUR KEY POINTS TO MAKE ARE:

**1.** You have learned about climate change at school and through your own studies and it seems obvious that it's going to be a serious problem.
**2.** You are worried that there may be violence on the march. You aren't sure whether or not some protesters are just people looking for a fight and you have watched footage of protests on the internet where the police seemed to respond with violence.
**3.** You don't think that anything would get on the news if the protest was in the town centre and you want people to be encouraged to think about the effects of pollution.
**4.** Your dad works in advertising and he told you that Powerage International pays the biggest PR company in the country a fortune to make them seem green, even though they are one of the biggest polluters in the world.
**5.** Environmental pollution will cause more suffering for your generation than for older people. Adults should be forced to do something about it now, as it is young people who will have to pick up the pieces.

### YOUR KEY SENTENCE:

"It's our future that's in danger here, not yours."

HERE ARE SOME EXAMPLES FROM THE RECORD BOOKS OF TWO YEAR 10 STUDENTS FROM A SCHOOL IN DEVON, CERYS AND BETH. THEY HOSTED A WORKSHOP IN THEIR SCHOOL AND THEN WENT ON TO USE A VERY CREATIVE CAMPAIGNING IDEA TO GET ON TO THE FRONT PAGE OF THEIR LOCAL PAPER. THIS HELPED THEM RAISE AWARENESS ABOUT THE NATIONAL 10:10 CAMPAIGN TO ENCOURAGE PEOPLE AND BUSINESSES TO PLEDGE TO CUT THEIR ENERGY USE BY 10% IN A YEAR. THIS WAS A NATIONAL CAMPAIGN PROJECT THAT FORMED PART OF CERYS' AND BETH'S CITIZENSHIP STUDIES COURSE.

## EXTRACT FROM BETH'S RECORD BOOK

15 February 2010

# HOLDING A WORKSHOP IN THE SCHOOL

_What a relief! The workshop went really well!_

Cerys and I had contacted 10:10 three weeks ago and they agreed to send two people to give us a workshop, Simon and Angela from ActionAid. ActionAid advocate for schools and their students to sign up to 10:10 and help provide them with the information to meet the target. They were amazing and really good at getting across some pretty complicated stuff in an easy way. Cerys was in charge of filming everything, making sure that they had the equipment they needed, as well as giving out the evaluation forms. That all went really well. I was in charge of booking the drama studio, looking after Simon and Angela and making sure the actual event went okay. There were three Year 10 classes there as well as our headteacher, Ms Evans, the head of Year 10, Mr Cotterill, and Mrs Scholtz, our Citizenship Studies teacher. Mrs Scholtz said it was the best workshop she'd ever seen and that it was well organized. She's going to write our witness statement. I also made a proper health and safety risk assessment, which meant that Simon and Angela had to show the audience where the fire exits were and what to do if there is an emergency.

Cerys and I had written out an evaluation form for all the students and separate ones for Simon and Angela from Action Aid and for the teachers. Everyone filled them in and we can show how everyone thought the workshops had gone, what impact it had, as well as ideas about how it could be better.

We took Simon and Angela into the staff room afterwards and made them tea and gave them some snacks that Cerys' mum had made. They were so enthusiastic about our project and really lovely. I thought people who do campaigns would be really serious but they were really, really funny. I said that to Angela and she said that campaigners were actually the happiest people she has ever known because they all know that they are actually doing something positive.

# FEEDBACK, EVALUATION FORMS, ACTION PLAN

We went through the evaluation forms with them. It was a really good response and the forms were anonymous so people could have said anything they wanted but everyone was really positive. There were some good ideas about how it could be better too, like one student saying that they should use more clips of students in schools doing 10:10 projects. Simon and Angela agreed and said that they were going to be adding two films soon to their workshops, one about a school

P.T.O ➜

that has built a polytunnel so that students can grow their own vegetables and one where a primary school is now using a walking bus, which is when students all walk together to school instead of taking a car or bus. They did point out that there are so many easy things to do, just by making sure that there is a team that checks that everything is turned off at the end of school will make a big difference, turning the school heating off at Friday lunchtime will cut 10% of energy consumption and some schools have even converted their school bus to run on chip fat!

Later, we had a meeting with Ms Evans so that we could evaluate the impact that the workshop had on her, as she is one of the key people who are in a position of power and able to make the change we want to see. She said that the workshop was excellent and invited us to talk at the next parents' and governors' meeting in March so that we can advocate for the school signing up to the 10:10 pledge!

That gives us three weeks to research the way the school uses energy and work out exactly how we can cut our school's carbon footprint. Simon and Angela had given out really easy-to-use instructions and ideas about how to do this and what kinds of things can be done to cut energy use and reduce our carbon footprint. It's all on their website so we will definitely be using that. It sounded like Ms Evans was keen to get the school to make the 10:10 pledge!

Meeting with Cerys tomorrow and we will make an action plan of all the things we have to do.

## USEFUL WEBSITES

Simon and Angela from ActionAid gave us a load of websites about people who will help the school make the energy reductions so I will look at them tonight! One of them is:

WWW.PFR.CO.UK , WHICH IS THE PARTNERSHIPS FOR RENEWABLES SITE, and they may actually give funding to help the school make the change. Another is:

WWW.ENERGYDISPLAYMETER.CO.UK WHO WILL INSTALL A FREE ENERGY DISPLAY METER, WHICH MAKES IT REALLY EASY TO MONITOR ENERGY USE AND SEE WHERE IT CAN BE CUT.

WE CAN ALSO CHECK THE MAIN 10:10 SITE FOR SCHOOLS _ WWW.1010SCHOOLS.NING.COM which has everything on it in one place.

Simon and Angela also gave me the ACTIONAID WEBSITE ADDRESS _ WWW.ACTIONAID.ORG.UK which has a really excellent schools section, including their work on 10:10, as well as covering all the other work that ActionAid does. They also gave us their e-mail addresses so that we can stay in touch about the project.

25 February 2010

## USING A CREATIVE TYPE OF CAMPAIGNING TO ENCOURAGE PEOPLE TO RECYCLE AND TO SIGN UP TO 10:10.

This afternoon, Beth and I had our photographs taken and were interviewed by the Tapelington Gazette! They said we might even get on the front page! The whole day was brilliant!

## LEAD-UP TO OUR ACTION:

After the workshop on 10:10 given by Simon and Angela from ActionAid, we wanted to come up with a really different idea for advocating for people to sign up to 10:10. We wanted to raise awareness about waste and to do something that would get us into the local papers. We started talking about recycling and how we could do something about that. It was my grandma who then said we should knit something — but then she's mad for knitting anyway, does it all the time. So, at first, we just thought she was being funny, because how could knitting have anything to do with recycling?

It was only later, when we were wondering if we could do anything about the amount of plastic bags that are wasted all the time that I suddenly thought of what Grandma had said. Why don't we collect hundreds of plastic bags that are being thrown away and then knit them together into really strong and attractive shopping bags so that people wouldn't throw them away?

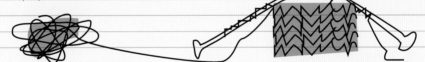

For the past week, we have been collecting hundreds of bags, brought in by all the students in our Citizenship Studies class as well as loads of other students and even some teachers. Mrs Scholtz went crazy and started getting loads off all her friends too. And every evening, Beth and I have been knitting them into carrier bags. We looked it up on the internet and it was amazing: not only do people already do this but there's advice about how to do it with instructions and everything. They actually look really cool. Grandma got really excited too and wanted to help. She showed us a better way of making them easily and they still look really cool. I've never seen Grandma get so excited. She said that what we were doing was brilliant and she wanted to help us because it's about our future.

We contacted the local paper a few times. We sent a press release to a journalist called Adrian Broad because we found out that he had covered a campaign to save Keeler Primary School last year and thought he'd be the best one to target. He was great and said he was really interested, liked the idea and wanted to see if he could cover our day of action.

## OUR DAY OF ACTION:

Today, we went to the local shop at the end of our road and set up with a big banner showing the 10:10 logo and loads of leaflets to give out as well as 43 of our knitted bags that we had made over the past week. We'd put a 10:10 leaflet in each of the bags. We went with my mum and some friends.

**P.T.O**

It was amazing! Everybody was really interested in what we had done and wanted one of the bags. People kept wanting to give us money for them and we were saying that all we wanted was for them to read the leaflet and use the bag we were giving them from now on instead of just using bags once and throwing them away. One really cool-looking girl came back with her friends so that they could all have a bag too. They said they were the coolest bags and could be really fashionable. We just said that all we want them to do is to look at the 10:10 leaflet and think about signing up. They said they definitely would.

Adrian Broad turned up with a photographer. He said we had been really smart choosing a Sunday as the photographer was really good and because of that he was always busy every other day of the week. Adrian was really impressed by the bags and the way they had been made and thought it was an idea that people would be really interested in reading about and reckoned that we may even get on the front page! When he asked me the first questions, I used the 3.9.27 statements that we had worked out and after that we just told him about the school and our Citizenship Studies course as well as how we had come up with the idea. He was really nice and said he'd never met young people who knew how to work with the media.
It was such a great day! Beth and I cannot believe how well it all went! Hope we get on the front page!

WE GOT ON THE FRONT PAGE!

# Gazette

## COMMUNITY FOR 80 YEARS

*...on Gazette series*

**PRICE 50p**

...re amazing homes ...n Tapelington's ...property guide...

## WIN FAMILY TICKETS TO SEE THE CIRCUS!

# Local Students Show us the Future

TWO TEENAGE girls brought a glimpse of the future to the streets of Tapelington yesterday when they set up outside Standish Stores to promote the national 10:10 campaign. Cerys Preen and Beth Geese *(pictured left)* both 15, from Bansmere School, came up with a novel way to get people thinking about recycling.

As part of their GCSE Citizenship Studies project, the two impressive young campaigners used hundreds of used plastic bags to create highly attractive and very fashionable reusable shopping bags. This was done through a knitting technique that they developed with Beth's grandmother. These bags were given out to shoppers along with leaflets promoting the 10:10 campaign, persuading people to cut their energy use by 10% in a year.

Beth and Cerys were excellent ambassadors for their campaign, showing a good knowledge of the issue of climate change and the importance cutting your carbon footprint. But what impressed us the most was their understanding of the media. I had been informed about the event through a professional press release sent from their school two weeks before. If these young girls are the future, it looks bright!

## 5 Rax Interview with Ben Stewart

BEN STEWART IS HEAD OF MEDIA AT GREENPEACE UK AND ONE OF THEIR MAIN ACTIVISTS, KEEPING THE ENVIRONMENTAL AGENDA IN THE HEADLINES IN BRITAIN. IN 2009, HE AND FIVE OTHERS CLIMBED THE SMOKESTACK OF KINGSNORTH POWER STATION – EUROPE'S LARGEST COAL-BURNING POWER STATION – TO DRAW ATTENTION TO THE ISSUE OF FOSSIL FUELS CAUSING ENVIRONMENTAL DAMAGE. THE RAX TEAM CAUGHT UP WITH HIM IN FEBRUARY 2010.

### WHAT ISSUES DO YOU THINK ARE MOST IMPORTANT FOR YOUNG PEOPLE TO ADDRESS TODAY?

*I* don't think it's up to me to tell people what they should care about – people know that themselves. The most important thing is to not be ignorant. Read, investigate, research your world and come to your own conclusions. Then, if you want to do something about it, start campaigning. For me it's climate change, and to be honest I think other people should be involved as well because (I think) it's so important for our futures. But if you think something else is more important, that's fine (though I think you're probably wrong!)

### WHAT TIPS WOULD YOU GIVE YOUNG CAMPAIGNERS IN THE STAGE OF "CRITICAL THINKING AND ENQUIRY"?

*Read,* read and read some more. Find a newspaper you like and read it every day, and focus especially on the opinion articles. Work out if you agree with the writers, and if you don't, why not. How would you argue back at them? Are their facts straight? Remember, it's very easy to write stuff that's both persuasive and wrong. Propaganda has always been with us. If you make sure you know enough to tell what's accurate from what's not, and you feel enough in your heart to know the difference between right and wrong, then you are a potent weapon for change in society. You are someone who can make the world a better place.

### WHAT CAMPAIGN ACTIONS HAVE YOU BEEN INVOLVED IN AND WHY DID YOU CHOOSE TO TAKE THOSE ACTIONS?

*I* have been involved for nine years in campaigning on climate change. I have taken non-violent direct action, breaking into polluting power stations and climbing the smokestacks then hanging off them. On one occasion I was part of a team of people who climbed the chimney at Kingsnorth power station and shut it down for a day, stopping 20,000 tonnes of $CO_2$ entering the atmosphere. We were put on trial but we argued in front of the jury that we were justified doing what we did because the harm we did to the power station was hugely outweighed by the harm the power station does to the planet. The jury agreed, and in a groundbreaking verdict we were acquitted.

PREPARING TO ABSEIL OFF THE TOP OF KINGSNORTH POWER STATION.

NO NEW COAL

CONTINUED

# 7 TOOLS *for* CHANGE

GRREENPEACE IN ACTION, CUTTING A WHALE FREE.

WORLD'S DIRTIEST OIL. STOP THE TAR SANDS

DRAWING WORLD ATTENTION TO THE TAR SANDS OIL EXTRACTION PROJECT IN CANADA.

**LEARN MORE/GET INVOLVED:** www.greenpeace.org.uk

## *WHAT KINDS OF IMPACT HAVE GREENPEACE CAMPAIGNS MADE?*

*Over* the years Greenpeace has had a huge impact. We were responsible for the ban on commercial whaling, we helped push the world to agree a treaty that closed the hole in the ozone layer, and now we're fighting for action on climate change and trying to protect the rainforests. We're having a big effect, but right now it's not enough, we need to achieve a lot more.

## *WHAT KEY ADVICE WOULD YOU GIVE YOUNG PEOPLE WHO WANT TO SET UP THEIR OWN CAMPAIGNS?*

*Work* out who you need to get to change their behaviour, ask yourself what you can do to make them change, then do it. That's actually a lot more difficult to work out than most people think, but if you do the research first then you save yourself a lot of time and effort and increase your chances of winning.

THERE HAVE BEEN TWO RAINBOW WARRIOR SHIPS SINCE 1978. THEY ARE USED TO SUPPORT GREENPEACE'S PROTEST ACTIONS ACROSS THE GLOBE. RAINBOW WARRIOR III WILL BE LAUNCHED IN 2011.

## 6 *Rax Interview with The Space Hijackers*

THE SPACE HIJACKERS ARE A GROUP OF CREATIVE ACTIVISTS WHO CHALLENGE THE WAY THAT PUBLIC SPACE IS OFTEN TAKEN OVER FOR CORPORATE USE WITHOUT ANY PROVISION FOR ORDINARY CITIZENS. THEY HAVE HIT THE HEADLINES ON SEVERAL OCCASIONS FOR THEIR HIGHLY IMAGINATIVE AND MEDIA-FRIENDLY ACTIONS WHICH HAVE ALWAYS HAD HUMOUR AT THEIR HEART. THE RAX TEAM CAUGHT UP WITH THEM IN MARCH 2010.

## *WHAT ISSUES DO YOU THINK ARE MOST IMPORTANT FOR YOUNG PEOPLE TO ADDRESS TODAY?*

*The* world is rapidly changing; public space is being sold off by government to private developers in the name of regeneration at an amazing rate. Any actual public space is being replaced with corporately owned space with rules over your conduct on it. No protesting is allowed, no socializing – basically, unless you're shopping or working, you're not welcome. Advances in technology are snapped up and put to use monitoring

GREENPEACE

THE SPACE HIJACKERS

our every move to ensure we play by the company rules, increasing our paranoia and destroying our trust in each other. At the same time, these corporations and especially banks are benefiting from huge public pay-outs with no strings attached, and the debt is being passed on to future generations. Quite simply we're accelerating towards a brick wall. The government and corporations are gambling on our futures and young people are going to have to pick up the pieces.

### WHAT KINDS OF ISSUES DOES YOUR ORGANIZATION FOCUS ON?

As a group we focus on the places we live in; our projects' themes come from events or situations that we find ourselves in. We try to actively take part in our city, and change the world in which we live. Living in London, the majority of our projects recently have focused around consumerism, corporate greed, public space, surveillance and the government's repression of dissent.

### WHAT KIND OF CAMPAIGNING TECHNIQUES DO YOU USE AND COULD YOU TELL US WHY YOU HAVE DECIDED TO USE THESE STRATEGIES?

The Space Hijackers was born out of a frustration with police-sanctioned A-to-B marches, which are wholeheartedly ignored by the powers that be, and seen as a way of letting a frustrated public let off a little

steam. Through our actions we aim to engage with the people actually affected by an issue, while using humour and spoof as a way of breaking down social barriers. We've turned up en masse in Harrods in t-shirts saying "EVERYTHING IN STORE HALF PRICE TODAY"... We've slipped secret messages into the loo roll in Parliament for MPs to find... We've even rolled up to riots in a tank dressed up as some kind of Mad Max-style Authoritarian Security Force (that one got us in a bit of trouble).

'EVERYTHING HALF PRICE TODAY' ACTION

CONTINUED

# TOOLS *for* CHANGE

THE HONOUR OF OUR LEADERS HAS BEEN CHALLENGED!
WHICH OF THEM HAVE THE MORAL FIBRE TO WALK TO THE CREASE AND DEFEND IT?

## MAYDAY CRICKET MATCH
### 2PM MAY 1ST - PARLIAMENT SQUARE

## THE SPACE HIJACKERS
FIRST 11
-VS-
## THE MEMBERS OF PARLIAMENT
FIRST 11

DRESS IN YOUR SUNDAY BEST OR CRICKET WHITES
JOIN US FOR THE MATCH OF THE CENTURY

---

**COULD YOU TELL US ABOUT SOME OF YOUR CAMPAIGN ACTIONS, WHAT HAPPENED AND WHAT RESULTS DID YOU ACHIEVE?**

*Our* actions have ranged from very subtle little changes to huge great media spectacles. Every two years, the UK government helps sponsor DSEi, the world's largest arms fair, in the Docklands in London. Generally they try to keep the whole thing under cover and hide the fact that the world's dictators are coming to London for a jolly with rocket manufacturers. In 2007 we decided to try and burst their bubble and get the whole thing all over the papers, so we announced we would be auctioning off a tank to protesters outside the fair. What followed was an insane week of us being chased around by police, holding press conferences, hiding decoy vehicles in gangster lock-ups and eventually rolling up to the front doors of the fair in a huge UN tank. The action got all over the papers with the headline "Anti-Arms Protesters Make Fools of the Police" and suddenly there was a lot more coverage of the semi-secret fair.

Other more subtle actions have involved replacing public benches, after councils removed them in an attempt to move on homeless people, and even turning up in private/public squares with huge lists of rules for people to obey.

**HOW IMPORTANT IS HUMOUR TO YOUR CAMPAIGNING ACTIONS AND WHAT KIND OF PLACE DOES IT HAVE IN MODERN CAMPAIGNING STRATEGIES?**

*Humour* plays a massive part in what we do. Not only does it help us bridge the gap between us and the people we want to talk to, but it also makes the police look very stupid if they try to get aggressive with us. It's more enjoyable to campaign with a smile than with a snarl, and it's great fun parodying large companies and getting to say out loud all the things they really think behind the greenwash and marketing.

**HOW IMPORTANT IS 21ST-CENTURY TECHNOLOGY TO YOUR CAMPAIGNING?**

*Very.* All of our actions are planned through online bulletin boards that we host. We used Twitter to relay news to the press while being escorted around by police in a tank. Photoshop and HTML skills have enabled us to successfully spoof and ridicule the large companies we've campaigned against. Our Circle Line Parties were huge purely because of our email lists and social networking. Finally, we've now started working on all manner of CCTV hacking and digital advertising override systems.

**WHAT WOULD BE YOUR TOP THREE TIPS TO YOUNG PEOPLE WANTING TO FORM THEIR OWN CAMPAIGN FOR CHANGE?**

1. *Certainly* don't take yourselves too seriously – no one wants to be lectured to by some know-it-all.

2. *Enjoy* yourselves – activists tend to end up with some sort of Catholic-style guilt trip trying to 'out-good' each other.

3. *As* the famous anarchist Emma Goldman said: "If I can't dance, it's not my revolution."

ARMOURED VEHICLE, ARMED WITH COMEDY, READY FOR ACTION!

**LEARN MORE/GET INVOLVED:** www.spacehijackers.co.uk

# 7 TOOLS *for* CHANGE

## 7 Rax Interview with Scott Forbes

SCOTT FORBES (20) STARTED AN INTERNSHIP WITH THE BRITISH YOUTH COUNCIL (BYC) AT THE AGE OF 17, BEGAN WORKING WITH THE BRITISH COUNCIL'S GLOBAL CHANGEMAKERS PROGRAMME AT THE AGE OF 19 AND CURRENTLY RUNS HIS OWN GLOBAL CAMPAIGN, GLOBAL FORUM 40. THE RAX TEAM CAUGHT UP WITH SCOTT IN JANUARY 2010.

### WHAT ISSUES DO YOU THINK ARE MOST IMPORTANT FOR YOUNG PEOPLE TO ADDRESS?

*There* are so many issues that blight our world today that it is hard to answer this question, but I'll name just a few issues both on a national and international scale. Young people are probably most concerned about the future of our environment – whether governments will step up to the mark to secure a fair and binding deal, which they so clearly failed to in Copenhagen. This is, however, not the only concern. Young people are worried about their future and what it holds, with the current recession leaving young people both vulnerable and unemployed. The latest statistics show that we are becoming a depressed generation in response to these problems, amongst many other factors.

### WHAT IS YOUR CAMPAIGN AIMING TO ACHIEVE?

*Global* Forum 40 is a new unique initiative led by young people for young people, where we share the values and desires to equip the younger generation with the information, knowledge, resources and skills on issues like HIV/AIDS. We aim to create a self-sustaining model of peer-facilitated learning; creating the opportunity for young people to become key actors on this major social issue around the world. Acting as a bridge between local traditions and communities and new ideas and practices, young people become leaders in society, empowered by our scheme to create real, tangible and lasting social change in the field of HIV/AIDS.

This is a global problem and isn't just restricted to certain regions and countries of the world. The grim reality is that young people are at the centre point of this issue and are being hit hardest. We at GF40 recognize this and we believe now is the time to act and to tackle HIV/AIDS effectively so as to save future generations. We need to develop a sex education that works, one that develops young people's skills so that they can make informed choices about their sexual behaviour, and feel confident and competent about the decisions and choices they make.

### IN WHAT WAYS IS 21ST-CENTURY TECHNOLOGY IMPORTANT FOR CAMPAIGNING AND HOW DOES YOUR CAMPAIGN USE IT?

*21st-century* technology is having a major impact on campaigning; the new media are proving to be very useful tools for activists/advocates around the world. We use both Twitter and Facebook, which allow us to get our message across to just over 2,500 people – and the number is growing on a daily basis. Twitter also proves to be a very useful tool in lobbying MPs and various other politicians around the world, saving time and energy instead of having to send a swarm of e-mails, as the response is more than likely guaranteed on the same day in a matter of minutes.

We also have an account on Taking IT Global, an amazing online network of organizations and just over 356,000 youth activists around the world. It provides a platform for exchanging ideas as well as seeking out new opportunities or potential funding – it really is a network worth belonging to and any young campaigner should consider registering: www.tigweb.org

SCOTT MEETING LORD KINNOCK, PRESIDENT CALDERON OF MEXICO AND GORDON BROWN DURING THE LONDON SUMMIT IN 2009

### WHAT CAMPAIGNING METHODS HAVE YOU USED?

*I've* taken part in many actions as an activist over the years, from demonstrations through Central London such as the 'End Child Poverty' rally to the 'Put People First' march during the G20, both of which were highly successful and had thousands of people joining the marches. This is a great way of sending a clear, strong message to the government, that we as a collective society demand a stronger commitment and change in various policies. It's also a good way to get your cause out through the media.

CONTINUED

Both of the marches that I attended had national coverage, they both even made the front pages of various established newspapers, like *The Guardian.* This is effective as decision-makers and politicians read these papers and get to know the issue first hand.

Another action, which can be just as effective, is simply lobbying your MPs. I remember spending an entire three days at Portcullis House in Westminster meeting with various MPs from different parties, to try and gain support for the British Youth Council's campaigns, which proved to be very useful. It allows you to speak face to face and present your case, plus engage in a light-hearted debate to try to convince the MP. At least you know where that person stands when you leave!

## WHAT KEY ADVICE WOULD YOU GIVE YOUNG PEOPLE WHO WANT TO SET UP THEIR OWN CAMPAIGNS?

*It's* fundamentally important you get to know the cause you're fighting for, carry out research, consult with experts, know the market in the area of the campaign you're working on and be different. Don't be afraid to challenge people, but at the same time learn to take criticism with a pinch of salt, as not everybody will agree with what you're doing and you're bound to face opposition. But ultimately never give up. As Gandhi once said: "If I have the belief I can do it, I shall surely acquire the capacity to do it even if I may not have it at the beginning."

### LEARN MORE/GET INVOLVED:

www.globalforum40.com www.global-changemakers.net
www.tigweb.org www.byc.org.uk www.do-it.org.uk
www.volunteering.org.uk

## 8  *Rax Interview with Jonathan Mazower*

JONATHAN MAZOWER IS THE MEDIA DIRECTOR OF SURVIVAL INTERNATIONAL, A GLOBAL ORGANIZATION THAT WAS STARTED IN 1969 AFTER AN ARTICLE IN *THE SUNDAY TIMES* RAISED AWARENESS ABOUT THE MASSACRES OF AND LAND GRABS FROM THE AMAZONIAN INDIANS. TODAY, THEY DEFEND THE RIGHTS OF INDIGENOUS PEOPLES WORLDWIDE. THE RAX TEAM CAUGHT UP WITH JOHNNY IN MARCH 2010.

## WHAT ISSUES DO YOU THINK ARE MOST IMPORTANT FOR YOUNG PEOPLE TO ADDRESS TODAY?

*I'd* say the biggest issue is the same as it's always been – the fact that a few people in the world have a lot, and most people have very little. It's all too easy for us to lose sight of how lucky we are – even those of us in the West who don't consider ourselves rich!

## WHAT KIND OF WORK DOES SURVIVAL INTERNATIONAL DO?

*We* campaign for tribal peoples' rights around the world – especially those who are more isolated, like Amazon Indians or Kalahari Bushmen. These people usually get ignored by politicians, who often want things on top of or underneath their land, like timber, coal, diamonds or oil. What makes it even worse is that tribal people usually live very healthy and happy lives – if only they'd be left alone. Actually, they're generally much better off than most poor people in the 'Third World', who usually live in slums and can't earn enough money to feed themselves.

## WHAT KIND OF CAMPAIGNING ACTIONS AND EVENTS HAVE YOU TAKEN PART IN?

*We've* climbed Nelson's Column to hang a banner from the top about Canadian Indians (I didn't climb it myself!); we've done loads of demos and vigils; we replaced a giant poster of a supermodel on the front of De Beers' new diamond shop with a poster of a Bushman woman with the slogan "The Bushmen aren't forever" (De Beers was looking for diamonds on the Bushmen's land); and we've brought many tribal people to Europe so that they can actually speak for themselves to the world's press.

**HAS THERE BEEN ONE MOMENT WHICH HAS STAYED WITH YOU WHERE YOU REALIZED THE IMPACT THAT YOUR CAMPAIGNING HAS HAD?**

*Probably* a recent demo we did outside the Paraguayan embassy in London, to draw attention to the invasion of uncontacted Indians' territory in Paraguay by cattle ranchers. Turned out it was the Ambassador's first day in the job, and he was a bit startled to find a large demo outside his front door when he turned up! He invited us in, listened to us outline the issue, which he hadn't been aware of, and has promised to take action.

CAROLINE LUCAS MP IS THE LEADER OF THE GREEN PARTY. SHE WAS FIRST ELECTED TO THE EUROPEAN PARLIAMENT AS ONE OF THE GREEN PARTY'S FIRST MEPS IN 1999 AND BECAME THE FIRST GREEN PARTY MP IN MAY 2010. THE RAX TEAM CAUGHT UP WITH CAROLINE IN MARCH 2010.

**WHAT ISSUES DO YOU THINK ARE OF MOST CONCERN FOR YOUNG ACTIVE CITIZENS IN THE UK TO ADDRESS?**

*Young* people have shown themselves to be very in tune with concerns about the environment and climate change – and have been at the forefront of demanding action from politicians via non-violent direct action and online campaigns. What's more, having grown up in an era characterised by the 'War on Terror', many have been vocal opponents of war and rightly challenged the morality of our foreign policy, particularly the war in Iraq.

Many of the young people I speak to are also concerned about child poverty, inequality and the availability of opportunities for the future. It's clear to them that our economic system has failed to lift those at the very bottom, and has allowed for the creation of an underclass marred by underachievement, low aspirations and low levels of personal wellbeing. They fear for a future in which secure employment seems far from guaranteed. Discrimination is a key factor here too; young people want to know that they will not be treated differently by others in society because of their race, ethnicity, gender or sexuality.

I think crime is also as much a concern for younger people as for older members of society; we all want to feel safer on the streets. Many youngsters believe that we live in a violent culture and indeed, although there has always been violence in human life, technological advances mean our society is now saturated by images of it.

**WHAT KEY ADVICE WOULD YOU GIVE YOUNG PEOPLE WHO WANT TO SET UP THEIR OWN CAMPAIGNS?**

*That* nothing worth fighting for has ever been achieved without a fight! Young people have always been the drivers of change – if we just accept the world as it is, for most people, that means continuing to have pretty miserable lives.

**LEARN MORE/GET INVOLVED:**
www.survivalinternational.org

**YOUNG PEOPLE HAVE SHOWN THEMSELVES TO BE VERY IN TUNE WITH CONCERNS ABOUT THE ENVIRONMENT AND CLIMATE CHANGE – AND HAVE BEEN AT THE FOREFRONT OF DEMANDING ACTION FROM POLITICIANS VIA NON-VIOLENT DIRECT ACTION AND ONLINE CAMPAIGNS.**

CONTINUED ⟫

# CHAPTER 7 TOOLS *for* CHANGE

*WHAT WOULD BE YOUR ADVICE TO YOUNG ACTIVE CITIZENS WHO WANT TO BRING ABOUT A CHANGE TO THEIR WORLDS THROUGH TAKING INFORMED AND RESPONSIBLE ACTION?*

*The* most important advice would be to believe that you can make a difference – because you can! Think about what really matters to you in your life and what you think could be done to improve the world you live in. You can then begin to actively engage in the political process by joining a political party, like the Greens, or an organization which campaigns on the issues that mean most to you. In fact, even just talking regularly with your friends and family about your views on key issues is a good way of getting the ball rolling.

Also, if you are to be taken seriously, it's really important for young people to fight the stereotypes that are often levelled against them – particularly by the tabloid press.

**WHEN YOU COME UP AGAINST UNFAIR LABELS, LET PEOPLE KNOW THAT THEY HAVE MADE THE WRONG JUDGMENT AND SHOW THAT YOU DESERVE TO BE LISTENED TO.**

You can make yourself heard by joining an organized demonstration, writing to your MP or MEP, contributing articles or letters to your local paper or to school, college or university publications, making art inspired by your beliefs, or by taking non-violent direct action.

*YOUNG PEOPLE OFTEN FEEL DISTRUSTFUL OF POLITICIANS. HOW CAN THIS PERCEPTION BE READDRESSED?*

*It's* true that our system of government is in crisis. It has lost the confidence of many people, and alienated swathes of potential voters. Spin and sleaze dominate national politics – and archaic elements like the House of Lords remain. What's more, we have an unfair electoral system and are one of the only countries in the world not to have a written constitution. Power and influence have been taken from cash-starved local councils, and decisions are taken far away from the communities which are most affected by them. This system certainly does not seem capable of facing up to the long-term decisions needed to create a more sustainable and just society.

To change the negative perception of politics, we must change the system itself. The Green Party wants to do this – by modernizing and decentralizing it, and by making it fairer, more open and more accountable. Decisions must be taken at the most appropriate level to ensure proper accountability to those people affected by them. This means more local and regional decision-making and greater public participation at all levels –

essentially, a more equal distribution of power across the country. Our elections should be run by a system of proportional representation, which would be much fairer, and ensure that people don't feel their vote is "wasted" in safe constituencies. We should also put pressure on the government to lower the voting age to 16 years. It seems very unfair that even though many young people now study politics and democracy at school before the age of 16, they have to wait until they are 18 to vote.

Finally, we must remind people why it is important to have a government at all – by fighting against the conservative 'small government' mentality and highlighting the benefits of good governance, especially for the weakest members of our society. The media has a key role to play in this. Above all, politicians must make it clear that they are listening carefully to young people and acting on their concerns to produce tangible improvements in their lives.

**LEARN MORE/GET INVOLVED:**
www.greenparty.org.uk

## 10 Rax Interview with Surfers Against Sewage

SURFERS AGAINST SEWAGE (SAS) ARE A CAMPAIGNING ORGANIZATION THAT HAS FOCUSED ON KEEPING UK BEACHES AND WATERS CLEAN. THIS MEANS THAT THEY ALSO COVER WIDER ENVIRONMENTAL ISSUES. THE RAX TEAM CAUGHT UP WITH THEM IN FEBRUARY 2010.

*WHAT IS YOUR CAMPAIGN AIMING TO ACHIEVE?*

*Surfers* Against Sewage (SAS) protects surfers, waveriders, waves and beaches from a myriad of environmental abuse. Historically, the sea has been used as a dumping ground with polluters repeatedly signing up to the "out of sight, out of mind" mantra. We are challenging governments and industry to change this tide of abuse enforced on our seas. We are surfers and waveriders wanting a clean and safe playground to do what we love most of all, surf.

198

# TOOLS *for* CHANGE

## WHAT CAMPAIGNING METHODS HAVE YOU USED?

*SAS* is constantly trying to make our message interesting and engaging and use humour well. Environmental NGOs (Non-Governmental Organizations/ campaigning groups) are often accused (and rightly so) of being preachy and this can turn people off. SAS strive to be interesting by utilizing a variety of campaigning techniques, from naked actions on the beach to crashing posh environmental media awards and shaming the sponsors (who were polluters in an SAS campaign).

Supporters and the press will get bored of the same action time and again so to get our message across effectively we need to constantly improve and evolve our campaigns. We make the campaigns accessible, employing a variety of platforms to highlight the problems and promote the sustainable, achievable solutions.

## WHAT IMPACT HAS YOUR CAMPAIGNING HAD?

**1** *SAS's* campaigns have changed industrial practices and influenced UK and EU legislations. As a small organization we've taken on some huge campaigns and because, as surfers ourselves, we are extremely passionate about clean seas, we're able to punch above our weight and secure tangible improvements for the UK's seas.

**2** *Improvements* in water quality and public information in the revised EU Bathing Water Directive (2006).

**3** *SAS* & the British Plastic Federation unveiling the Operation Clean Sweep aimed at reducing plastic lost down storm drains after SAS highlighted the problems with plastic pellets on our beaches.

**4** *The* inclusion of recreational water users in the Scottish Marine Bill's Regional Planning Partnerships will mean that surfers have a say about what happens to the coast and offshore environments at the appropriate level and on the highest platform.

## WHAT KEY ADVICE WOULD YOU GIVE YOUNG PEOPLE WHO WANT TO SET UP THEIR OWN CAMPAIGNS?

*The* most important advice for a campaigner is to be persistent! Rarely are campaigns easily won and the opposing side will often rely on you giving up. Second, be thorough and ensure you are confident of your campaign goals before putting them out into the world. Once you have the message spot on, communicate it effectively. A good campaign gets the message across to the right people, at the right time, in the right format. Last, make sure you are in the right place at the right time, and when the opportunity arises, jump at it: be confident, clear and on message.

**LEARN MORE/GET INVOLVED:**
www.sas.org.uk

## 11 Rax Interview with Jess Worth

JESS WORTH STARTED HER CAMPAIGNING CAREER AS AN INTERN AT THE CAMPAIGNING ORGANIZATION, PEOPLE AND PLANET. SHE IS NOW A CO-EDITOR AT NEW INTERNATIONALIST AND ONE OF THE KEY FIGURES IN THE CAMPAIGN AGAINST THE TAR SANDS INDUSTRIAL DEVELOPMENT IN CANADA. THE RAX TEAM CAUGHT UP WITH JESS IN JANUARY 2010.

### WHAT ISSUES DO YOU THINK MOST CONCERN YOUNG PEOPLE TODAY?

Climate change is terrifying because it's being caused by the emission of greenhouse gases today, but its worst effects will be felt in the future. One of the greatest injustices in the world is that the rich white men (and the odd woman) running our corporations and governments who are contributing to the problem now probably won't be around to suffer the consequences – but young people will. I think that's why young people 'get' the urgency of acting now on climate change in a way that so many of the generation in power just don't seem able – or willing – to grasp.

### WHAT IS THE CAMPAIGN THAT YOU ARE INVOLVED IN AND WHAT IS IT AIMING TO ACHIEVE?

I'm involved in a campaign to shut down the tar sands in Canada. A lot of people in the UK haven't heard of the tar sands – they're a new source of oil that companies have turned to now that traditional oil wells are starting to run dry. Oil from tar sands is even worse for the environment than conventional oil – it is more polluting to extract, producing 3-5 times more greenhouse gases that cause climate change, and destroying the local environment on an almost unimaginable scale.

It's already the biggest industrial project in the world, and they're only just getting started. The area targeted for destruction is the size of England and Wales. It is home to many indigenous communities who are finding that the animals and fish in their traditional territories that they depend on for food are being poisoned by toxins, or scared away by the scale of development. Some indigenous communities that live downstream from big tar sands mines are suffering – and dying – from abnormally high levels of cancer and other illnesses. There is evidence that this is being caused by toxins in their water and air from the tar sands.

### WHAT KIND OF CAMPAIGNING ACTIONS AND EVENTS HAVE YOU TAKEN PART IN?

Our campaign has revolved around a series of trips by indigenous representatives from tar-sands-affected communities to the UK, with the aim of putting the issue on the agenda over here. We did this by organizing speaker tours around the country, got them slots at high-profile events, used their presence to get a meeting in Parliament and the support of the Liberal Democrats, worked with them on several protests, and got masses of media coverage here and in Canada. Everyone they have come into contact with has been totally blown away by what they are hearing and the campaign has grown like wildfire. After a while we started to see local groups spring up, people

# TOOLS *for* CHANGE

organizing their own protests and putting pressure on the various companies involved, with the Canadian media faithfully reporting our every move. In six months, Tar Sands had shot to the top of many environmentalists' agendas, several NGOs started to take it on as an issue, Canada was generally known to be one of the world's top climate criminals, and BP and Shell were both forced to start playing down their tar sands involvement in public. So far so good!

## WHAT KEY ADVICE WOULD YOU GIVE YOUNG PEOPLE WHO WANT TO SET UP THEIR OWN CAMPAIGNS?

*I* think a lot of young people don't realize how powerful they are. I worked for the student campaigning network People & Planet as a campaigner for six years. Over that time we – amongst many other things – got Pepsi to pull out of Burma, got Fairtrade products into a load of schools and universities, persuaded the university pension fund to go ethical, managed to scupper a dodgy international investment agreement, and

forced an arms company to pull out of its graduate recruitment tour. I know that clever, strategic campaigning by young people can change things because I've seen it happen. So my advice would be "just do it!"

**LEARN MORE/GET INVOLVED:**
www.no-tar-sands.org www.peopleandplanet.org

## 12 *Rax Interview with Tamsin Omond*

AS WELL AS BEING A WELL-KNOWN CLIMATE ACTIVIST, TAMSIN OMOND RAN AS AN INDEPENDENT PARLIAMENTARY CANDIDATE IN THE 2010 GENERAL ELECTION, LEADING HER OWN PARTY, THE COMMONS. THE RAX CAUGHT UP WITH TAMSIN IN MARCH 2010.

## HOW ARE YOU TAKING PART IN THE GENERAL ELECTION OF 2010?

*I'm* campaigning to be the Member of Parliament of Hampstead and Kilburn. I'm leading a new political party called The Commons. We're offering something completely new, returning a meaningful democracy to the community. Leading up to the election we're organizing a series of events and discussions around key areas that affect the local community. Instead of telling people what I think they want to hear, I'm going to be out on the streets talking about what really matters

to them and finding out what would make people tick come Election Day.

## WHAT CAMPAIGNING TECHNIQUES HAVE YOU USED TO MAKE YOUR CAMPAIGN STAND OUT?

*Each* week I'll be out in the community discussing local issues with community leaders and members of the public, leading up to an open-invitation Saturday event. Locals can also look out for 'Text to vote' numbers on posters and leaflets asking key questions around each issue. Meanwhile The Commons will be gathering information online using social networks to launch polling and discussions.

## HOW IS DIGITAL TECHNOLOGY IMPORTANT TO YOUR POLITICAL CAMPAIGNING AND HOW DO YOU THINK IT CAN AFFECT THE FUTURE OF DEMOCRATIC ENGAGEMENT?

*Digital* technology is different because the audience can interact with it – voters don't just want to be told what's important, they want to be able to shape and affect it. Social media is all about conversation and it has to be a two-way exchange. Too often politicians try to use social media to push their own agendas instead of really listening.

## WHAT DO YOU THINK IT TAKES TO HAVE YOUNG PEOPLE IN THE UK BECOME MORE ENGAGED IN POLITICS AND HOW IS YOUR CAMPAIGN SEEKING TO ACHIEVE THIS?

*Young* people have grown up in a world of relentless branding and spin, and they can see straight through

CONTINUED ⟶

it. Above all, what young people want is an honest message about how the world they live in has come about (rather than just saying "we're good and the other guys are s\*\*t") and an honest approach to the future – that nobody has all the answers and that we're going to have to work together to find solutions.

### IN WHAT WAYS DO YOU THINK THE THREE MAIN PARTIES ARE FAILING TO MEET THE NEEDS OF THE YOUNGER GENERATION?

*Right* now politics simply isn't engaging the younger generation. Around 60% of people under 30 don't vote. Politics is too top down, too boring (even politicians seem bored by it most of the time). Parliamentary politics has nothing to do with what goes on in the real world – most politicians don't speak like people outside or look like the people outside, they think £65,000 a year is low pay and they don't seem to realize how irrelevant they are to everyone else.

### WHAT WOULD YOUR THREE TOP TIPS BE TO YOUNG PEOPLE WHO WANT TO BECOME MORE INVOLVED IN POLITICS?

*Start* with your peers – no one else is managing to engage them so you've got a clear playing field. Don't accept their terms – yes, politics is about compromise, but not their compromises! If you don't like the system do your own thing instead. Don't lose hope – there are huge challenges ahead but together we have the power to turn things around.

**LEARN MORE/GET INVOLVED:**
www.tothecommons.com

## 13 Rax Interview with Des Kay

DES KAY IS PART OF THE UK WING OF THE GLOBAL CRITICAL MASS MOVEMENT. IN 325 CITIES AROUND THE WORLD, CYCLISTS MEET ONCE A MONTH TO RIDE TOGETHER. THESE GATHERINGS CAN RANGE FROM A DOZEN CYCLISTS TO 85,000. CRITICAL MASS' GENERAL INTENTION IS TO ADVOCATE FOR CYCLING, CYCLING SAFETY AND MAKING CITIES MORE BIKE-FRIENDLY. THE RAX TEAM CAUGHT UP WITH DES IN MARCH 2010.

### WHAT IS YOUR CAMPAIGN AIMING TO ACHIEVE?

*Critical* Mass doesn't have a specific aim. It is considered a fortunate coincidence that a few hundred cyclists choose to meet together once a month in hundreds of cities and towns around the world to ride around – each rider having their own reason for doing so. There are those that celebrate cycling, others that enjoy the social aspect, whilst some see it as a platform for promoting a radical reassessment of transport policy.

### WHAT CAMPAIGNING METHODS HAVE YOU USED?

*When* the police informed us that our rides were illegal, we contested it in court, with the assistance of Friends of the Earth. After a lengthy process where we had to take the case to the highest court – the House of Lords – we won the right of unobstructed riding through a unanimous verdict.

### WHAT IMPACT HAS YOUR CAMPAIGNING HAD?

*We* have enjoyed mostly favourable publicity about the rides from press and television features. When we ride through the streets together, pedestrians generally show much support and I would hope it encourages some to join us and subsequently take up cycling as a transport option.

### WHAT WOULD BE YOUR KEY ADVICE FOR YOUNG PEOPLE SEEKING TO MAKE A CHANGE IN THEIR WORLD THROUGH CAMPAIGNING?

*Find* an unusual way to show you care; something that is fun and has a message that doesn't overwhelm the spectator. Remember you want them to be on your side. So if you attract their attention in a nice way you are far more likely to win their support. Entertain them into submission!

**LEARN MORE/GET INVOLVED:**
www.urban75.com/Action/critical

# THIRD Campaign GLOBAL ACTION

## 1 What is the third campaign?

**You** have now reached the stage where you can engage in your third and final active citizenship campaign, which needs to address a global issue.

**THE TOOLKIT HAS TRIED TO SHOW HOW ACTIVE YOUNG CITIZENS THROUGHOUT HISTORY AS WELL AS TODAY CAN CHANGE THEIR WORLD AND SHAPE A BETTER FUTURE FOR ALL BY ENGAGING WITH GOVERNMENT, CAMPAIGNING, JOINING GRASSROOTS MOVEMENTS AND ACTING UPON THEIR INFORMED CONVICTIONS. THERE IS NOTHING TO STOP YOU MAKING HISTORY YOURSELVES BY USING THESE SKILLS THROUGHOUT YOUR LIFE.**

## THESE TOOLS ARE FOR LIFE, NOT JUST FOR SCHOOL.

**You** now have all the skills you need to create a major campaign. This should be the most ambitious campaign you have attempted so far.

You already know that you must check with your teacher to make sure the campaign fits in with your GCSE and you understand how to keep a record of everything. The only aspect that is different in the third campaign is that it has to address a global issue, rather than a local or national one.

## 2 What kind of actions should you take?

**You** should already be familiar with the kinds of actions that you can take and will have tried out a number of them. This chapter has introduced you to a new set of tools. Use them with creativity and imagination to come up with unique ways of winning attention and support for your campaign.

## 3 What kinds of issues should you address?

**Global** issues can cover many different areas. It's important to remember that whatever global issue you choose to focus on, there may be local ways of acting upon the issue. For example, if you are addressing pollution, there may be businesses in your area that contribute to pollution or there may be local examples of renewable energy that you could highlight in your campaign.

## 4 What's the process?

**The** process is no different than in your previous campaigns – except for the fact that you need to address a global issue. However, as this is your last, major campaign, it's important that you use many different techniques and approaches as part of your overall campaign strategy.

## IF THE TOOLKIT HAS INSPIRED YOU, THIS MAY WELL BE THE LAST CAMPAIGN YOU TAKE PART IN AS A SCHOOL STUDENT BUT IT WILL NOT BE THE LAST CAMPAIGN OF YOUR LIFE!

**A**

**Act of Parliament** – An Act of Parliament creates a new law or changes an existing law.

**Activism** – Any form of action to bring about social, political, economic or environmental change. This can range from non-violent direct action to sending letters to Members of Parliament.

**Advocacy** – Speaking up for or arguing in favour of something, such as a cause, idea or policy.

**Analysis** – Detailed examination of something.

**Anthropogenic Global Warming (AGW)** – The belief that global warming is caused by human activity.

**Assumption** – A belief that something is true, although there is no proof.

**Atheist** – Someone who believes that there is no God.

**B**

**Ballot** – The system of voting, usually in secret.

**Bias** – Being unfairly prejudiced for or against one group of people, or one side in an argument.

**Boycott** – To make a protest by refusing to buy a product or take part in something.

**C**

**Campaign** – A series of planned activities that are intended to achieve a particular political, social or commercial aim.

**Capitalism** – An economic system in which a country's businesses and industry are controlled and run for profit by private owners rather than by the government.

**Civil disobedience** – Refusal by a large group of people to obey particular laws or pay taxes, usually as a form of peaceful political protest.

**Controversial** – Something that causes strong disagreement.

**Corporation** – A group of people legally authorized to act as an individual, usually a large business.

**Critical mass** – When a high enough level is reached for change to happen.

**Critical thinking** – Identifying and evaluating evidence to guide decision-making. A critical thinker uses broad in-depth analysis of evidence to make decisions and communicate his/her beliefs clearly and accurately.

**Culture jamming** – Any of various methods of changing mass media (especially advertisements) to convey a different message.

**D**

**Debate** – A formal discussion of an issue at a meeting of people or in a parliament. In a debate two or more speakers express opposing views and then there is often a vote on the issue.

**Democracy** – A system of government in which all the people of a country can vote to elect their representatives.

**Demonstration** – A public meeting or march at which people show that they are protesting against or supporting somebody or something.

**Digital native** – A person who has grown up with technologies such as computers, the internet and mobile phones.

**Direct action** – The use of strikes, sit-ins and other forms of protest instead of discussion in order to bring about change.

**Discrimination** – Treating somebody or a particular group in society less fairly than others.

**Dissent** – Having or expressing opinions that are different from those that are officially accepted.

**E**

**Egalitarian** – The belief that everyone is equal and should have the same rights and opportunities.

**Eloquent** – Able to use language and express opinions well, especially when speaking in public.

**Enquiry (Inquiry)** – Asking for or seeking out information. An official investigation.

**Ephebiphobia** – The fear or hatred of teenagers.

**Ethical** – Being connected to moral principles.

**F**

**Fanzine** – A magazine – usually homemade – dedicated to fans or followers of an idea, team or performer.

**G**

**Grassroots movement** – A group of ordinary people, united by the same wish for change.

**Green Paper** – A report or proposal laid out by the government which is the first step towards making a law.

**Greenwash** – The practice of making an unproven or misleading claim about the environmental benefits of a product, service, technology or company practice.

**H**

**Homophobia** – The fear or hatred of homosexuals.
**Human rights** – Provisions or freedoms to which a person is fundamentally entitled.

**I**

**Independent media (also known as 'alternative media' or 'free press')** – Sources of media that are not owned by big corporations.
**Indigenous** – Original inhabitants of a country or region.

**J/K**

**Junta** – A military group holding power over a country.

**L**

**Legislation** – Laws, or the process of making laws.
**LGBT** – Lesbian, gay, bisexual and transsexual.
**Lobbying** – Attempting to influence law-makers, politicians or decision-makers.

**M**

**Monopoly** – Having exclusive control over something (usually a segment of the market).
**Motion** – Movement, or a statement to be discussed and voted on in a debate.

**N**

**Non-Governmental Organization (NGO)** – An organization that is independent of the government.
**Non-violent** – A form of protest that does not use violence.
**NVDA** – Non-violent direct action.

**O**

**Orator** – Someone who speaks in public.

**P/Q**

**Pamphlet** – A small publication, usually with a paper cover.
**Pressure group** – A group of people who put pressure on law-makers, government or decision-makers in order to promote their own ideas or welfare.

**Protest** – A public way of people expressing their feelings or ideas, usually against something.

**R**

**Rally** – People united together, usually in public, under one cause or idea.
**Representation** – Standing in place of something or someone, to represent that person or idea.
**Republic** – A form of government where people or their representatives hold power, as opposed to a king or queen.

**S**

**Secret ballot** – Voting in secret.
**Self-directed learning** – Where students guide their own learning rather than being led by a teacher.
**Slogan** – A memorable phrase used in advertising or campaigning.
**Socialism** – An economic system where the means of production, distribution and exchange are owned by the community collectively.
**Soundbite** – A short, distinctive sentence or phrase – usually extracted from a longer speech – that is easily used on radio or television.
**Spin (in the media sense)** – To turn around the true meaning of something to make it seem like it means something else.
**Spoof** – A good-humoured deception or prank.
**Stigmatize** – To mark out someone or something as being bad.
**Subvert** – To undermine or ruin something.
**Sweatshop** – A workshop where employees work long hours for little money under harsh conditions.

**T**

**Transnational** – Across many countries and nations. In business, this represents a corporation that extends its business into many different countries.
**Transparent** – When something can be seen through completely and nothing is hidden.

**U/V/W**

**Vested interests** – Having a strong interest in something that is usually connected to personal (or corporate) gain.
**White Paper** – An official government proposal which sets out the government's policy on something – the second step towards making something law, after a Green Paper.
**Whitewash** – Deceptive statements or actions that cover up mistakes, lies, defects or failings.

## A

ActionAid 187, 188, 189
active citizenship
    definitions of 8
    qualities required for 10
advertising
    campaigns 69
    to children 147
    industry 146-7
    standards 25
    techniques 31
advocacy and representation 7, 38, 53, 106-33
Afghanistan 181
*Age of Stupid* 158, 159
Airplot 175
airport expansion 159, 160, 175
alien perspectives *see* games and activities: alien's eyes
American War of Independence 32
Amnesty International 127
Angelou, Maya 109
animal rights 69, 97-101
apartheid 40, 41, 52, 107
Argentina 27
Armour-Brown, Denzil 166-7
arms control 33
arms fairs 194
Armstrong, Franny 152, 158-91
Armstrong, Lance 43
artwork *see* games and activities: art action
Atkinson, Adrian 65
Aung San Suu Kyi 41
*Autogeddon* 21

## B

Babbs, David 103-4
Babyshambles 19
Bailey, David 69
Bangladesh 57, 122
banks, ethical 128
bar charts 59
Barbie Liberation Organization 174, 175
Bardy, Sophie 59, 109, 119, 138-9
Barlow, John Perry 77
Bastille, storming of 33
Battlefront 63
The Beatles 42
bees 69
Beethoven, Ludwig van 107
Bell, Debra 65
Beneson, Peter 127
Benn, Tony 168
Berners-Lee, Sir Tim 11
Bhopal disaster 176
*The Big Issue* 65
Bird, John 65
*Black Like Me* 63
Blarney Stone 107
blindness 23
    *see also* games and activities: blindfold game
Bluetooth 148
Bolivia 35, 48, 49
books
    influence of 30
    research using 78, 79
brain, human 11
Brand, Russell 11
Brazil 15
British Film Institute 81
British Library 55
British Youth Council (BYC) 55, 195, 196
broadcasting 40, 41, 42, 49, 63, 81
Brooke, Heather 55
Brown, Isla 136-7
bullying 107
Burma 150, 180, 201
Buy Nothing Day 47

## C

Campaign for Nuclear Disarmament (CND) 17

campaigning 13
    current issues 26, 27
    starting points 28, 62-4
campaigns, your 12
    first (local) 140-3
    second (national) 170-1
    third (global) 203
Canada 93, 200-1
cancer awareness 43
cannabis addiction 65
Carey, George 161
cars
    animatronics 21
    environmental damage by 21
*Cathy Come Home* 42, 43, 108
celebrity campaigners 42, 43
censuses 27
Chartist Movement 36
Chavez, Hugo 109
chewing gum 27, 78
Chilcot Inquiry 48, 103
children
    advertising aimed at 147
    child labour 50, 53, 122-4
    mortality 46
    rights 36, 40, 50, 53, 94-5
Children's Peace Prize 65
China 36, 52, 75, 147
Churchill, Sir Winston 11
citizen media 150
civil disobedience 40, 41, 53, 161
civil rights 27, 42, 43, 63
Clarkson, Thomas 34, 108, 147
Climate Camp 121, 154, 163, 179, 180
climate change 17, 44, 48, 49, 75, 86, 93, 104-5, 146, 158, 159, 162-3, 165, 169, 191
Climate Rush 39
clothing and textiles industry 57, 122-4
Clown Army 178, 179
coal-fired power stations 181, 183-6, 191
coffee industry 59
collation skills 54, 58, 60
coltan 45
The Commons 201
Communism 36
community events organising 138-9
compassion 102, 103
connectivity
    of campaigns 52, 118-19
    with other school subjects 172-4
consumerism 47, 153, 176
consumers
    power 59
    protection for 44
Controlled Assessment Tasks (CATs) 10, 54, 60
Cooper, Tommy 9
Co-operative Bank 129
corporal punishment 37
*The Corporation* 47
corporations
    challenges to 29, 46, 59, 176-7
    greenwash 86, 179
    unethical practices 53
costumes, use of 173, 178-9
creativity in campaigning 121, 172-82
Critical Mass movement 202
Cromwell, David 102
cross-curricular projects 12
Crow, Bob 168
Crusades 30
culture jamming 17, 176-7
currencies, local 29
cycling 202

## D

Dalai Lama 41
Darwin, Charles 107
De Beers 196
De Bono, Edward 23

debating *see* games and activities: fight your corner
democracy 30, 49
Democracy Now! 80, 81
Democratic Republic of Congo 45, 65
demonstrations
    silent 156
    street 27
Denmark 48, 49, 75, 86
deportation 65
development partnerships 46
diamonds
    conflict diamonds 77
    mining for 196
Dickens, Charles 37, 108
Diggers and Levellers 33
digital natives 11, 45
direct action 27, 38, 39, 159, 161, 162, 166-7, 191
discrimination 25
    gender 44, 45
    racial 44
    religious 29
dogs
    fighting 69
    fouling 63
Dow Chemicals 176
Drake, Dr Frank 21

## E

Edison, Thomas 29
education 44, 46, 53, 49
    right to 94-5
    women 119
    *see also* laptops, provision of and school closures
Edwards, David 102
Egypt 145
Einstein, Albert 41
electoral reform 32, 36, 198
Electronic Frontier Foundation 77
electronic messages, first 11
employment rights 48, 168
Enfield, Harry 11
Engels, Friedrich 36
English Civil War 32
environmental sustainability 46
ephebiphobia 15, 73
Epictetus 31
e-protest 37
equality 32
Esquivel, Adolfo Pérez 41
ethics
    banks 128
    corporations 53
    behind products 53
    in science 45
Ethiopia 59
European Union 46
evaluation and assessment 54, 58
evidence-gathering *see* collation skills
evolution, theory of 107
experts, involvement of 92-4, 101, 104

## F

fair trade 201
Farrow, Alex 104-5
Fathers 4 Justice 178
film-making 152-4, 158-9, 164
films 27, 47, 94-5
    documentaries 80, 81
    mobile movies 149
    mockumentaries 153
flash mobs 121
flower industry 52, 53
Forbes, Scott 13, 109, 129, 131, 149, 195-6
France 32, 33, 44, 48, 49
Free the Children campaign 50, 53
freedom of information 46, 55
freedom of speech 25, 50

French Resistance 49
French Revolution 32, 33
Friends of the Earth 202
fun campaigns 120-1
    *see also* humorous campaigns
fur trade 69

## G

games and activities
    alien's eyes 20, 21, 84, 173
    art action 16-17, 24, 30, 57, 60, 62, 108, 132, 148, 152, 178
    be the bard 18, 78, 132, 146, 180
    blindfold game 22
    fight your corner 16-18, 38, 44, 56, 120, 180
    heads together 22, 36, 56, 60, 64, 70, 76, 80, 82, 90, 94, 95, 96, 108, 118, 126, 150, 154, 176
    mystery activity 20, 22, 23, 30, 88, 108
    newspaper game 14-15, 26, 58, 62, 78, 114, 178
    P.O.V (points of view) 18-21, 96-9, 183-6
    3.9.27 activity 16-17, 50, 112, 116, 122-4, 130, 156, 190
Gandhi, Mahatma 40, 41, 52, 57, 108, 161, 180, 196
Gandhi International Peace Award 102
gender equality 28, 29, 44, 45, 46
Gentle, Maxine 125
Gillett, Robbie 63, 71, 115, 145, 157, 159-60
global campaigns 203
Global Forum 40 129, 131, 195-6
global justice movement 46, 47
Global Witness 45
GM campaigns 146, 166-7
Goodman, Amy 81
Gouges, Olympe de 33
government processes 26
    campaigns within 34, 38
gravity, theory of 23
Greece, ancient 21, 30, 31
Green Party 197, 198
Greenpeace 114, 115, 175, 191-2
greenwash 86, 179
Grey Panthers 117
Griffin, John Howard 63
group activities *see* games and activities: heads together

## H

Haiti 150
Hall, Suzanne David 49
happiness 91, 169
Harris, Jon 154, 164
Harris, Jonathan 149
Haw, Brian 131
Hayes, Charles D. 55
health and safety 24, 25, 44
Help the Aged 21
Hicks, Bill 173
Higgins, Polly 35
high-frequency sound 117
history of campaigning 24-53
Hitler, Adolf 31, 40, 57
HIV/AIDS 46, 65, 129, 195
Holliday, Billie 27
homelessness 42, 43, 65
homophobia 42, 43, 160-1
Hopkins, Ellie 104-5
Hubbard, Elbert 11
Hughes, Chris 85
Hughes, Simon 137-8
Hugo, Victor 29
human rights 24, 27, 42, 127, 160, 161, 173
humorous campaigns 145, 151, 172-4, 176-80, 194, 198-9
hunger 46

**I**

ideas, power of 29, 109
images
  manipulation 145
  power of 147
immigration 40, 46
inclusivity 25, 116
independent media 80-2
India 40, 41, 53, 119, 127, 176, 180
indigenous peoples 93, 196-7
Industrial Revolution 32, 33
Indymedia 82, 83, 101
information
  bias 86, 87
  reliability 57, 84, 101, 155
injustice 28
Instigate Debate 65
internet
  controls 75
  inaccuracies 75
  manipulation of 77
  negative aspects 57
  research 74-6
  security 76, 78
  spam 85
  see also social networking and websites
interviews
  media 16
  RAX 10, 12, 50-2, 100-5, 134-9,
    158-69, 191-202
Iraq 131, 147, 150, 173, 181
Iraq War (2003) 46, 47, 48

**J**

Jarrow March 121
Johnson, Nkosi 65
journalism
  badly-researched 75
  citizen 83, 84
  investigative 83
Junk Science 155

**K**

Kay, Alan 9
Kay, Des 201
Kenya 52
Kerala, India 119
Kielburger, Craig 50-3, 63,
  92, 94, 118, 147
King, Martin Luther 41, 42, 43,
  52, 108, 109, 161
Klein, Naomi 47
knife crimes 115
Kuwait 39
Kyoto Protocol 44

**L**

language, use of 112, 125
laptops, provision of 113
law-making 15, 28
learning by experience 15
Legoland 181
Leonardo da Vinci 31
lesbian, gay, bisexual and transgender
  (LGBT) campaigns 42, 43, 160-1
letter-writing 124-6
libraries 78, 79
lobbying 161, 196
local campaigns 139-43
Logorama 153
logos 63
London Gazette 15
Love Music Hate Racism 19
Lucas, Caroline 197-8
Lumley, Joanna 43
Luther, Martin 30

**M**

magazines 78, 79
Magna Carta 30
Major, John 161
Make Poverty History 109, 173
Malcolm X 161
Mandela, Nelson 40, 41, 107, 109
manifestos 128-9
manipulation of opinions
  by corporations 87
  on the internet 77

Margo, Julia 43
marine pollution 198-9
Martinon, Mandarine 49
Marx, Karl 36
maternal health 46, 119
Matsuura, Koichiro 153
Matters, Muriel 38, 108
Mazower, Jonathan 196-7
McDonalds 29
McLibel (film) 152, 158, 159
Mead, Margaret 13
Media Lens 102-3
medicines, access to 53
Members of Parliament (MPs) 36, 48,
  105, 115, 137, 161
  candidates 201
  expenses scandals 55
  letters from 59
  lobbying 196
  writing to 27, 78, 124
Members of the European Parliament
  (MEPs) 197
memes 146
Menon, YK Krishna 109
mental health issues 154, 155, 157
Mercer, Patrick 105
Mericourt, Theroigne de 33
Miah, Nelu 59, 113, 119, 134-5
micro-blogging 84
microfinance 53
Millennium Development Goals 46, 94
Milloy, Steven 155
mistakes, learning from 11
mobile phones 44, 45
  movies 149
  novels 113
  texting 149
mockumentaries 153
Moldova 151
monarchy, restrictions on 30, 32
Monbiot, George 155
money 28, 29
Morar, Natalia 151
The Mosquito 117
motivation for action 52
Ms Dynamite 19, 91, 107, 133, 135-6
Mubarak, Hosni 145
Mugabe, Robert 161
music
  campaign 121
  DIY 19
  underground 182
  see also song lyrics
music industry 165

**N**

nanotechnology 45
national campaigns 170-1
Nazism 40
Ndume, Baruani 65
needs and wants 50
New Internationalist 79, 200
New Scientist 45
New Zealand 38, 39
news media, independent 80-2
newspapers 15, 78, 79
  campaigns by 83
  spoofs of 176-7
  stereotyping in 15
  see also games and activities:
    newspaper game and press
    releases
Newton, Isaac 23
Nicaragua 127
Nigeria 153
No Logo 47
Nobel Prizes 41
Nollywood 153
non-violence 40, 41, 53, 109, 138,
  139, 162, 191
nude protests 179

**O**

Obama, Barack 85
O'Connor, Paul 153, 162-4
oil industry 145
  see also tar sands campaign
older people
  attitudes to 21

campaigns by 117
Oliver Twist 37
Omond, Tamsin 39, 71, 201-2
oratory 42, 109
Orde, Sir Hugh 168-9
The Origin of Species 107
Osborne, Adam 11
outcomes of action 118
Oxfam 59

**P**

Paine, Thomas 27
Palestine 30
pamphlets 27, 29, 33
Pankhurst, Christabel 38
Pankhurst, Emmeline 38, 108
Pankhurst, Sylvia 161
Paraguay 197
patience in campaigning 109, 130
pay
  equal 44, 45
  fair 57, 119, 122
People & Planet 200, 201
people power 103
People's Declaration 35
persistence in campaigning 155, 199
personal computers 44
personal stories 114
petitions 27
Phillips, Lord 115, 169
philosophy 31
pigeons, carrier 125
Pink Chaddi campaign 181
plagiarism 111
Plane Stupid 159, 160
Planet Earth Trust 35
planetary rights 35, 48
planets supporting life 21
Plato 15, 31
points of view 112
  see also games and activities: P.O.V
policing protests 163, 169
postcard campaigns 127
poster campaigns 29
poverty 43, 46, 52, 109, 173
preparation for learning 12
press releases 154-7
prisoners of conscience 127
privacy, invasion of 113
Pro Test 100
progress, reflection on 11
propaganda 30, 31
public space, privatization of 192, 194
Pycroft, Laurie 63, 94, 100-1

**R**

rabbits 69
racism 19, 40, 63
Radiohead 165
Rainbow Warrior (ship) 192
rape 127
Reclaim the Streets 163
record books 10, 54, 56
  exercises for 58, 60, 64, 68, 70,
    73, 76, 80, 84, 90, 95, 100,
    108, 116, 120, 130, 132, 148,
    152, 158, 178, 182
  extracts from 57, 59, 61, 72-3,
    88-90, 94-5, 122-4, 157,
    173, 187-90
recycling 189-90
religions
  ancient 29
  challenges to 29, 30
  similarity of ideas 31
Renaissance 30, 31
renewable energy 117
republicanism 32
research 54, 70-99
Reverend Billy and the Church of Life
  after Shopping 47
rights and responsibilities 50
Roddick Gordon 65
role-playing 21
  see also games and activities: P.O.V
Russian Revolution 36

**S**

Salt March 41, 53, 180
Santayana, George 25
Satyagraha 40, 41, 53
school closures 136-7
school media suites 150
science and ethics 45
self-directed learning 54, 56
Sen, Binayak 127
sexual rights 42, 43, 160-1
Shakespeare, William 19
shareholder activism 176
Sheeburger, Kirsty 75
Shelter 43
Sherine, Ariane 29
slavery
  abolition of 17, 34
  modern-day 88-91
slogans 33, 41, 128, 130-1
smellovision 151
Smith, Samantha 125
smoking and lung cancer 87
SMS 148
Snow, Jon 139, 154
snowball fights 121
social networking 84-5, 148, 149, 151
soldiers, support for 181
solutions, providing 116-17
song lyrics 27, 107, 130, 132-3, 136, 165
  see also games and activities: be the
    bard
soundbites see games and activities:
  3.9.27 activity
South Africa 40, 41, 52, 65, 107, 125
South Korea 45
Space Hijackers 180, 192-4
speech-making see oratory
spoofs 151, 176-7
Stapleton, Howard 117
star system 10, 11
Starbucks 59
statistics 93, 165
stereotypes, challenging 174, 175, 198
Stevens, James 71, 101
Stewart, Ben 13, 191-2
The Story of Stuff 153
street slang 47
Stryder, Tinchy 19
student protests 44
suffrage
  men 36
  over-16s 55, 60, 113, 198
  women 38, 39, 162
Surfers Against Sewage 175, 198-9
Survival International 196-7
Switzerland 39
symbolic campaigns 180, 181
symbols, campaign 17

**T**

Takakoli, Majid 147
tar sands campaign 93, 200-1
Tatchell, Peter 160-1
technologies, 21st century 144-52, 165,
  194, 195
techquake 43
teenagers
  fear of 15, 73
  rights 117
  violence by 72-3
10:10 campaign 158-9, 187-90
testimonials 61
texting 149
Theatre of the Oppressed 15
thinking
  critical 7, 62-4, 66-8
  lateral 23
38 Degrees 15, 37, 78, 103-4
Thomas, Mark 180
Thornberry, Emily 161-2
Tiananmen Square 52, 147
tigweb (TakingITGlobal) 149, 195
tobacco industry 87
trade descriptions 24, 25
trade unions 119, 168
trafficking, human see slavery
Trees have Rights Campaign 35
triangulating the truth 88
t-shirt design 173

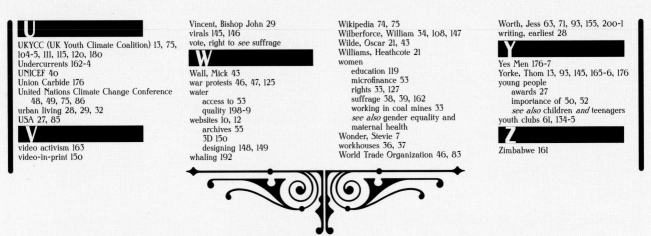

**U**

UKYCC (UK Youth Climate Coalition) 13, 75, 104-5, 111, 115, 120, 180
Undercurrents 162-4
UNICEF 40
Union Carbide 176
United Nations Climate Change Conference 48, 49, 75, 86
urban living 28, 29, 32
USA 27, 85

**V**

video activism 163
video-in-print 150

Vincent, Bishop John 29
virals 145, 146
vote, right to *see* suffrage

**W**

Wall, Mick 43
war protests 46, 47, 125
water
    access to 53
    quality 198-9
websites 10, 12
    archives 55
    3D 150
    designing 148, 149
whaling 192

Wikipedia 74, 75
Wilberforce, William 34, 108, 147
Wilde, Oscar 21, 43
Williams, Heathcote 21
women
    education 119
    microfinance 53
    rights 33, 127
    suffrage 38, 39, 162
    working in coal mines 33
    *see also* gender equality and maternal health
Wonder, Stevie 7
workhouses 36, 37
World Trade Organization 46, 83

Worth, Jess 63, 71, 93, 155, 200-1
writing, earliest 28

**Y**

Yes Men 176-7
Yorke, Thom 13, 93, 145, 165-6, 176
young people
    awards 27
    importance of 50, 52
    *see also* children *and* teenagers
youth clubs 61, 134-5

**Z**

Zimbabwe 161

The publisher would like to thank the following for permission to reproduce copyright images in this book:

p13 [Ben Stewart] Greenpeace; p17 [Barack Obama] Aslund/Greenpeace, [Joe Chemo] Adbusters; p29 [The Venus of Lespugue] replica sculpted by Joanna Peacock; p39 [All photos] Climate Rush; p49 [Copenhagen] Noel Douglas; p52 [Craig Kielburger] Emily McDowell/Element Films; p55 [BYC] Scott Forbes; p65 [Baruani Ndume] UNHCR/R Beusker; p100 [Pro-Test] Ian Robertson, [Headshot of Laurie] Kieran McCarthy; p104 [All photos]UKYCC; p105 [Ed Miliband & campaigners] UKYCC; p107 [Blarney Stone] Courtesy of Blarney Castle; p115 Greenpeace International; p119 [RMT] Andrew Wiard; [Gardening Club] Islington Council; p121 [All photos] Mike Langridge; p127 [All photos] Amnesty International; p129 [All images] Co-operative Bank; p135 [Ms Dynamite] David Lau; p137 [School] Phil Rider/Lighthouse Images; p139 [Jon Snow] Suzanne Martin; p162-4 undercurrents.org; p168 [Bob Crow] RMT; [Parliament Square] Andrew Wiard; p173 [One Man Protest] Jamie Lowe, [Heads Of The Heads] Iain Marshall; p175 [Alistair McGowan] Jiri Rezac/Greenpeace, [Heathrow] Greenpeace; p177 [Yes Men] Yes Men; p179 [Undress For Change] Amy Scaife, [The Clown Army] Iain Marshall; p181 [World's Smallest Activists] Legoactivist; p190 [Local Students] Vikram Dhillon; p191-2 [All photos] Greenpeace; p193-4 [All photos] The Space Hijackers; p195 [Both photos] Scott Forbes; p196 [Jonathan Mazower] Lewis Davids/Survival International, [Botswana] Survival International; p197 [Trafalgar Square] Survival International; 199 [Both photos] Surfers Against Sewage; p200 [Tar Sands BP] Mike Langridge; p201 [Tar Sands] Greenpeace.

Every effort has been made to trace all copyright holders, but if any have been inadvertently overlooked the Publishers will be pleased to hear from them.

Every effort has been made to ensure that website addresses are correct at time of going to press, New Internationalist cannot be held responsible for the content of any website mentioned in this book.

## About the New Internationalist

The New Internationalist is an independent not-for-profit publishing co-operative. Our mission is to report on issues of world poverty and inequality; to focus attention on the unjust relationship between the powerful and the powerless worldwide; to debate and campaign for the radical changes necessary if the needs of all are to be met.

### Books, diaries & calendars

We publish informative current affairs books, such as the No-Nonsense Guides and the World Changing titles, complemented by world food, fiction, photography and alternative gift books, as well as calendars and diaries, maps and posters.

### Magazine

The New Internationalist magazine tackles subjects of global significance, exploring each issue in a concise way which is easy to understand. Feature articles are packed full of photos, charts and graphs and each issue also contains reviews, country profiles, interviews and news.

### Mail Order

We operate mail order businesses in the UK, North America, Australia and New Zealand/Aotearoa, for our supporters and other clients. Besides our branded publications and products, we specialise in sourcing and marketing useful, fair trade, eco-friendly, organic and educational gift items.

**www.newint.org**